# INVITATION

# Effective Speech Communication

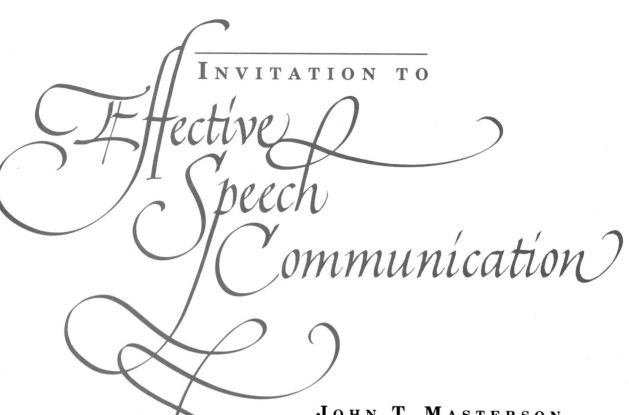

# INVITATION TO
# Effective Speech Communication

**JOHN T. MASTERSON**
UNIVERSITY OF MIAMI

**STEVEN A. BEEBE**
SOUTHWEST TEXAS STATE UNIVERSITY

**NORMAN H. WATSON**
UNIVERSITY OF SOUTH DAKOTA

**SCOTT, FORESMAN AND COMPANY**
GLENVIEW, ILLINOIS    BOSTON    LONDON

An Instructor's Manual is available. It may be obtained through a local Scott, Foresman Representative or by writing to Speech Editor, College Division, Scott, Foresman and Company, 1900 E. Lake Avenue, Glenview, IL 60025.

Credit lines for the photos, illustrations, and other copyrighted materials appearing in this work are placed in the Acknowledgments section on page 385 of this book. The Acknowledgments section is to be considered an extension of the copyright page.

**Library of Congress Cataloging-in-Publication Data**

```
Masterson, John T., 1946-
    An invitation to effective speech communication / John T.
Masterson, Steven A. Beebe, Norman H. Watson.
        p.    cm.
    Includes index.
    Bibliography: p.
    ISBN 0-673-18565-6 (pbk.) : $16.95
    1. Oral communication.   I. Beebe, Steven A., 1950-   .
II. Watson, Norman H.   III. Title.
P95.M35   1989
001.51--dc19                                              88-23570
                                                              CIP
```

    2   3   4   5   6-KPF-93   92   91   90   89

# Preface

*Invitation to Effective Speech Communication* encourages students to improve their understanding of and skill at human communication in interpersonal, group, and public speaking situations. It is designed to serve as the primary text for an introductory course in speech communication.

## GOAL

Speech communication is, at one and the same time, among the oldest and the newest of academic disciplines. Consequently, scholarship in the field is characterized by enormous volume and wide diversity in philosophical assumptions, theoretical approach, research methods, and focus of study. The dilemma in an introductory survey course is how to avoid overwhelming students and yet expose them to the broad scope of ideas in the discipline. Our solution, in drawing on the vast research base in speech communication, was to pursue one overriding goal: to help students improve their communication effectiveness. We want them to emerge from an introductory speech communication course as better communicators in interpersonal situations, in groups, and when standing before an audience to deliver a speech.

## EDUCATIONAL ASSUMPTIONS

We believe that an introductory college textbook should be comprehensive in scope, based on sound theory and research, and user friendly. With these ideas in mind, we have tried to interpret and make accessible to students what is known about speech communication in a variety of contexts. Because we are writing for beginning students, our chapters proceed in a careful and logical way, using examples to clarify and study aids to reinforce.

To ensure comprehension and mastery, we have used a *tell, show, and do* approach to skill development. First, we *tell* students key communication principles that help them understand how to improve their skills. Second, we present examples and illustrations that *show* students how to improve their effectiveness. Finally, at the end of each chapter, we provide activities and exercises that require students to *do* the new skill. We tell them, show them, and encourage them to do the things that will make them more effective communicators.

## SPECIAL FEATURES

We have incorporated many pedagogical elements that will ease students' progress through the material in each chapter and promote maximum retention. Specifically:

- Chapter-opening learning objectives direct students' attention to the particular information they will be expected to master.
- Explanations of principles and skills build systematically and are supported by concrete, everyday examples, making even the more challenging material easy to understand.
- Key terms are highlighted in boldface and clearly and concisely defined when they first appear. Key terms and their definitions are then grouped alphabetically both in end-of-chapter lists that support spot reviews and in an end-of-book glossary that facilitates ongoing reference.
- Running summary statements, set in the margins, call attention to key thoughts as they are introduced.
- Review boxes summarize the contents of entire sections and present noteworthy principles and practical suggestions in straightforward, memory-jogging formats.
- Thorough end-of-chapter summaries, based on the chapter-opening objectives, tie chapter contents together and provide one more opportunity for review.
- End-of-chapter discussion questions encourage students to think critically, while suggested activities help them polish practical skills.
- Lists of suggested readings broaden students' perspectives by proposing other resources for further study.

## ORGANIZATION

*Invitation to Effective Speech Communication* is organized into three main parts. Part 1, Foundations of Effective Speech Communication, presents the basic principles and skills that will be expanded on and applied to specific communication situations throughout the text. Part 2, Effective Interpersonal and Small Group Communication, focuses on helping students develop one-on-one relationships, improve listening and responding skills, enhance interviewing skills, and work with others in small groups. Part 3, Effective Public Communication, takes a step-by-step approach that will help beginning speakers confidently prepare and present a speech. Special attention is given to informative speeches, persuasive speeches, and speeches using visual aids.

We have designed this book to follow a logical progression of ideas from basic principles of communication through interpersonal, small group, and public communication. We recognize, however, that there are as many approaches to teaching as there are teachers, and so we have written each chapter as a complete, self-contained topic. Chapters may thus be resequenced in any order to suit the individual needs and preferences of each instructor.

## THE INSTRUCTOR'S MANUAL

A comprehensive instructor's manual is available from the publisher. It is written as a supplement to enhance your use of the text, whether you are an inexperienced teaching assistant, a beginning instructor, or a seasoned veteran. The manual includes three sections that cover the following information:

**Part 1**     **Approaches for varying course emphases**

       Hybrid approach vs. interpersonal emphasis vs. public speaking emphasis

       Cognitive emphasis vs. skills emphasis

       Sample syllabus

       Sample course schedules

       Guidelines for classroom activities

       Guidelines for evaluated assignments

**Part 2**     **Chapter-by-chapter information**

       Chapter outlines

       Suggested classroom discussion questions

       Suggested classroom activites and exercises

       Suggested assignments and evaluation forms

**Part 3**     **Test Bank**

       A four-part category system for test items

       Prepquizzes with multiple-choice items

       Test items—multiple-choice items, short-answer items, and essay questions

## ACKNOWLEDGMENTS

We are grateful to all who have helped bring this book into being. First, we thank our students, who provided the inspiration for the project. In our combined 50 years of university teaching we have been enriched and educated by our students, who have given us invaluable feedback about our teaching role.

Our editors at Scott, Foresman—Barbara Muller, Cynthia Fostle, and Carol Karton—have provided not only their editorial expertise, but just the right kinds of motivation to keep three different authors in three different cities on the same track.

We also wish to thank the following reviewers for their insightful and useful comments. They have helped make this a better book:

Martha Cooper, Northern Illinois University

Roy H. Eno, Jr., University of Texas at San Antonio

Suzanne P. Fitch, Southwest Texas State University

Diana K. Ivy, Southwest Texas State University

Lawrence W. Hugenberg, Youngstown State University

Richard G. Rea, University of Arkansas

Janet L. Sprague-Williams, Waubonsee Community College

Barbara Strain, San Antonio College

Beth M. Waggenspack, Virginia Polytechnic Institute and State University

Finally, we gratefully acknowledge our families for their encouragement and support. Nancy Masterson, Susan Beebe, and Shirley Watson have lent us their ears when we needed to test ideas. They have given us their editing and proofreading skills. And, most importantly, they provided us with emotional support during the long, time-consuming process of working on this project. We owe them much.

**John Masterson**
**Steve Beebe**
**Norm Watson**

# Table of Contents

**PART**

**1**

# FOUNDATIONS OF EFFECTIVE SPEECH COMMUNICATION

1

# 1 Introduction to Speech Communication

*After studying this chapter, you should be able to:*

▶ Define *speech communication.*

▶ List three criteria of effective communication.

▶ Discuss three principles of speech communication.

▶ Define the seven basic components of the communication process.

▶ Identify four levels of speech communication and explain the distinctions among them.

▶ Summarize the differences between mass communication and speech communication.

This is a book about you, the reader. It is about your thoughts, your feelings, and your relationships with others. It is about your ability to speak—to utter sentences to yourself and others—and the consequences for you and them when you do so.

Perhaps the most obvious and elusive fact of human existence is that you spend a large portion of each day communicating—talking, listening, reading, and writing. Your ability to communicate seems to be what most sets you apart from the other animals. It's what makes you human.

This book will help you increase your awareness and appreciation of the functions of communication in your life and will help you improve your skills as a communicator. It begins by defining *speech communication* and examining it as a subject of academic study.

## WHAT IS SPEECH COMMUNICATION?

Scholarship in the field of speech communication is enormously diverse—in philosophical assumptions, theoretical approach, research methodology, and focus of study. Within the diversity, however, resides a common concern with the spoken word as it functions in your daily lives. According to the Association for Communication Administration:

> *The core concepts explored within a study of communication include the creation, transmission, and analysis of differing types of messages as well as message impact. Students investigate communication processes as they occur within and among individuals, groups, organizations, and societies. They explore interpersonal and nonverbal communication, rhetorical and dramatic criticism, argumentation and persuasion, the oral performance of literature, broadcast messages, production and programming, advertising management, public relations campaigns, news reporting, and other aspects of communication.*[1]

*Speech communication is a broad field of study with a common focus on the spoken word.*

This description suggests the broad range of interests held by speech communication scholars and students. The spoken word occurs in a variety of settings and contexts, from poetry readings and public speeches to informal conversations and business meetings. Such diversity calls for a variety of approaches to the subject. While a structured, scientific approach may be appropriate for measuring the dynamics of a group or the attitude change caused by a presidential address, a more aesthetic approach is demanded by the oral interpretation of a Shakespearean sonnet. These diverse interests and methodologies are brought together in a single academic discipline through a common focus on the spoken word.

Speech communication is concerned with both *description* and *prescription*. Through research, scientists attempt to describe speech communication as it functions in a variety of settings. This research allows the development of principles that can be applied to real situations, such as public speeches and group discussions, so that, with practice, people can improve their communicative skills. This marriage of theory and research to skill development is one of the exceptional features of the study of speech communication.

For the remainder of this book we will define **speech communication** as *a human process through which people make sense out of the world and share that sense with others.* This definition alludes to the pervasive nature of the discipline. As we shall see in Chapters 2 and 3, speech communication helps to organize experience while shaping perceptions of the environment. It is also through the use of language that meanings are shared. Thus, speech communication serves as the foundation for all human relationships.

This textbook focuses on the application of speech communication theory and research to several contexts: communication within the self, interpersonal communication, small group communication, interviewing, and public speech communication. Its goal is to increase your skill as a communicator.

## The Goal: More Effective Communication

Effective communication is not simply the ability to be an engaging conversationalist or to charm an audience from behind a lectern. These skills are only part of the whole picture. Effective communication requires a high level of awareness as well as the ability to analyze, speak, and listen. Furthermore, communication that is effective in one context may not be effective in another. Indeed, it is difficult to identify even one specific behavior that is effective in all communication situations. Nevertheless, certain guidelines for effective communication apply, in varying degrees, to most situations.

## What Is Effective Communication?

There are three questions whose answers measure communication effectiveness. First, to what extent does the message received equal the message that was sent? That is, to what extent is the message understood? Second, does the communication achieve the effect intended by the communicator? And third, is the communication ethical?

**Effective communication is understood.** The more you study communication, the more complex you will find it. The potential for misunderstanding is always present and is heightened whenever the communicators differ in culture, status, language, experience, and education. By identifying the sources of misunderstanding, you can develop the skills to minimize them.

**Effective communication achieves the intended effect.** When you communicate, you usually do so with intent; that is, you communicate in order to accomplish certain objectives or goals. Some of the goals of communication are to inform, to persuade, to entertain, to solve problems, and to build or maintain trust and intimacy in interpersonal relationships. Different goals require different communication strategies. When you increase your ability to recognize the intent behind your actions, you can develop the communication skills that you need to accomplish your objectives.

**Effective communication is ethical.** Communication is a skill that can be used and abused. Truly effective communication not only achieves a speaker's objectives, but simultaneously allows others to maintain or increase their feelings of self-worth. It does not restrict their freedom of choice.

*Effective communication should be understood, achieve the intended effect, and be ethical.*

## PRINCIPLES OF SPEECH COMMUNICATION

So far we've talked generally about effectiveness in human communication and we've introduced a definition. Now let's get more specific and discuss some principles of speech communication—statements we can make that are so widely accepted that they are indisputable.

### Communication: A Process

Twenty-five hundred years ago, the Greek philosopher Heraclitus observed that a person can never step in the same river twice. From moment to moment, the person is different and so is the river. Like Heraclitus' river, communication is an ongoing process that reflects dynamic interrelationships among many simultaneously occurring variables. For example, have you ever tried to take back something you've said? Even as you did so, you probably realized the futility of your actions. The damage was done.

*Speech communication is never static; it is an ongoing process.*

Communication is *irreversible*. A human mind is like a tape recorder that can't be shut off. The "tapes" it makes cannot be erased. The only way it can store new information is to make new tapes. Consider the effect of the prosecuting attorney's words in the following situation:

| | |
|---|---|
| *Prosecuting Attorney:* | Ladies and gentlemen of the jury, my plea to you to find the defendant guilty as charged would not be as fervent were it not for the fact that he went free last year after being indicted on not one, not two, but *fifteen* counts of rape. . . . |
| *Defense Attorney (leaping up):* | Your Honor, I object!! The defendant's prior record is inadmissible in this court! |
| *Judge:* | Objection sustained. The jury is instructed to disregard the previous comment. |

In this case, the prosecuting attorney knew exactly what she was doing. She knew that her statements about the defendant were inadmissible and that the defense attorney would object. She also knew that the communication would be irreversible—that the jury would be unable to disregard her statements even though instructed by the court to do so.

Likewise, communication is *unrepeatable*. Its events are never repeated in exactly the same form. The communicators and the context are never static; they are always changing. Think, for example, of that "perfect evening" with a special someone. Though you may retrace your steps—go to the same restaurant, sit at the same table, order from the same waiter—you cannot duplicate the experience.

## Communication's Content and Relationship Aspects

Every communication has both a content aspect and a relationship aspect.[2] The **content aspect** is the verbal message. The **relationship aspect** provides either verbal ("I'm just kidding") or nonverbal (tone of voice, facial expression) information about the way the content aspect should be received. It is thus **metacommunication**—communication about communication. For example, the radio announcement, "This is only a test. For the next sixty seconds, . . ." tells how to understand what follows. It is communication about communication, or *metacommunication*.

When friends get together, they give each other verbal messages (the content aspect) and verbal or nonverbal information about the way the message should be received (the relationship aspect).

Often nonverbal behavior provides metacommunication about verbal messages. The words "I'm really glad to see you" will carry different meanings if accompanied by a limp handshake and a diverted gaze than if accompanied by a warm hug and a kiss. The content aspect of the communication is reported in the words "I'm really glad to see you," while the relationship aspect—how those words are to be received—is indicated through tone of voice, eye contact, movement, and touch.

*The ability to communicate effectively depends directly on the ability to metacommunicate appropriately.* Context, clothing, voice, energy level, eye contact, touching, body position, and movement are just a few of the factors that influence the way messages are understood.

*Nonverbal behavior can reinforce or contradict what you say.*

## Communication's Complexity

Clearly, if you are going to understand the factors that contribute to effective communication, you need to look at a great deal more than who says what to whom. The relationship aspect of communication is particularly complicated. Take, for example, a conversation you have with a friend over a cup of coffee in the cafeteria of the student union. Obviously, age, sex, ethnic or cultural differences, and all the factors mentioned in the previous section will influence the dialogue. But consider this—in your conversation there are, in a way, not two but six persons:

1. who you think you are;
2. who you think your friend is;
3. who you think your friend thinks you are;
4. who your friend thinks she is;
5. who your friend thinks you are; and
6. who your friend thinks you think she is.

Similarities among these "entities" increase the potential for understanding, but discrepancies—say, between who you think you are and who she thinks you are—can be a grave source of misunderstanding.

## COMPONENTS OF THE COMMUNICATION PROCESS

Analysis of any process involves breaking down that process into its basic components and examining the relationships between and among them. So it is with the process of speech communication. Keep in mind though, that the components of speech communication are never isolated from one another; they are interdependent parts of the whole system. The seven basic elements of the communication process are a source, a message, a channel, a receiver, noise, feedback, and context.

### A Source

*Some elements of communication are always present in all contexts.*

Communication involves information. The point at which information originates is the **source.** Loosely speaking, a source can be anywhere in the environment—a pet, a beautiful sunrise, your stomach, or anything that serves as a stimulus to your senses. Usually, though, a source is a human being who encodes a message. **Encoding** is the process through which messages are cast into a system of signals. If you wish to inform your friend that you are hungry, you must take that idea and put it in the form of words or gestures that will be recognizable to him or her. You may point to your stomach or your open mouth, or you may simply say "I'm hungry." Either way you have encoded your message.

### A Message

Messages are the products of encoding. They are the results of attempts by the source of a communication to put ideas or information in a form that can be understood. Within the context of speech communication, a **message** is defined as any signal or stimulus to which a receiver assigns meaning. Therefore, there are many kinds of messages. Messages may be encoded verbally ("I love you") or nonverbally (a long gaze, a warm smile, and a soft stroke on the cheek), intentionally (you meant to send it) or accidentally (you didn't intend to send it, at least not consciously—for example, a blush). Words, gestures, behaviors, clothing, tone of voice, even arriving late for a date— all are messages when they are interpreted by a receiver of communication.

### A Channel

You communicate through many channels. A **channel** is a pathway through which message-signals pass between a source and a receiver. Telephone lines and radio waves are examples of channels that are used for long-distance communication. Your senses serve as communication channels for face-to-face communication. Sight, sound, touch, and even taste and smell act as pathways for messages.

Different channels, however, lend themselves to different kinds of messages. For example, a gentle touch, a soft gaze, and the fragrance of cologne are particularly well adapted to messages of romantic love. The same channels are ill-equipped for giving directions to your home, however; written instructions and a map are more effective. By multiplying the number of channels, the message gets more emphasis. A hug added to a greeting gives added weight to the greeting; a visual aid to support a speech adds emphasis to the speech.

### A Receiver

A **receiver** is any individual or group toward whom communications are intentionally or unintentionally directed. Thus a receiver may be an audience for a public speech, a reader of a newspaper, a friend you have lunch with, or you yourself when you're listening to your friends. The characteristics of a receiver are essentially those of a source. In human communication, a receiver is usually the person for whom the message is intended; but, whereas the source encodes the message, the receiver decodes it. **Decoding** is the interpretive process of assigning meaning to a message. Therefore meaning is something that occurs within *people,* not within messages. A person reading a letter, for example, assigns meaning to the words on the page; the words do not themselves contain meaning. This is why misunderstandings often arise—different people assign different meanings to the same messages. You'll explore this further in Chapter 3.

## Noise

*In communication theory, noise is much more than sound.*

Usually you associate noise with sound. In communication theory, though, **noise** is anything that interferes with the clear reception of a message. Therefore, noise can be visual, oral, or internal. A baby's crying during a speech will interfere with the message and is, therefore, a source of noise. More subtle, but equally disruptive, is a room that is too crowded or too warm. Distracting mannerisms or inappropriate clothing can interfere with communication, and a receiver's preconceptions about a speaker or a topic can interfere significantly with the speaker's ability to get his or her message through.

## Feedback

Effective communication is virtually impossible without feedback. **Feedback** is a receiver's response to a message that enables a sender to gauge whether he or she has been understood. A receiver, in effect, feeds a message back to a sender by responding to the communication. Feedback either reinforces or corrects—that is, it may be positive or negative. Positive feedback (an affirmative nod of the head or a comment such as "I understand") lets a sender know that a message has been understood and that the sender may proceed. Negative feedback (a frown and a negative shake of the head or a comment such as "What on earth are you talking about?") tells a sender a message needs revision and to try again.

## Context

*Context affects meaning.*

In order to be fully understood, speech communication must be viewed within the context in which it occurs. **Context** is the entire communication environment. The same behavior may be interpreted very differently as the context, or environment, changes. For instance, there has been a change in the *historical context* of spreading the index and middle fingers and raising them overhead. Earlier this gesture meant "V for victory"; in the 1960s it meant "Peace." Similarly, the word *gay* has undergone a shift in meaning over the past several years.

*Cultural context* is another important consideration in understanding speech communication. Different cultures have different norms for communicative behavior. What is appropriate in one culture may be inappropriate in another. For example, an American considers it polite to admire and comment on a piece of art in someone's home; in many Arab countries, to do so would prove embarrassing. The host would be obliged to give the piece of art to the guest. There are many such cultural differences—norms about who speaks first, how far apart peo-

**Figure 1-1**
The Basic Components of Communication

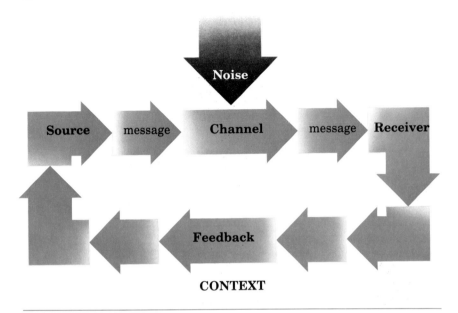

ple stand during conversation, how much eye contact people maintain, and how important promptness is. These are important variables when communication is between two people of different cultural backgrounds.

*Physical context* is another important variable; some environments are conducive to conversation while others are not. You know from your own experience that a conversation begun in a hallway changes dramatically, or stops altogether, when the people step into an elevator. Conversation stops in a room that is beautiful to look at, but too formal for comfort. Everything from color and decor to the placement of furniture affects a person's ability to communicate effectively. We will explore the effects of physical context more fully in Chapter 4.

The components of communication are summarized in Figure 1-1. Remember that none of these components is isolated from any of the others. Rather, they are interdependent. As we progress, we will add components that must be considered within specific contexts, but the components shown in Figure 1-1 can always be identified in *all* communication systems. As such, they provide a foundation for the understanding of human communication. The important thing to remember is that communication is never static. It is a flowing interrelationship of simultaneously occurring variables.

# THE LEVELS OF SPEECH COMMUNICATION

The levels of speech communication are based on the interaction of different classes of senders, receivers, and contexts with the
basic processes and components that have been described. The levels
of speech communication are (1) intrapersonal, (2) interpersonal,
(3) small group, and (4) public. While these levels are interconnected,
each one has unique features that warrant separate discussion. One
feature common to all four levels, yet different in each, is *intentionality*.
As you read about each level, note the steady progression of the degree
to which speech communication is a planned, purposeful event.

## The Intrapersonal Level

**Intrapersonal communication** is speech communication within
an individual. On this level, the sender and the receiver are the same
person. In one sense, then, intrapersonal communication is a person
talking to him- or herself—mentally debating the pros and cons of
sleeping an extra hour and skipping that early morning class, or
approaching a lectern, looking out over the audience, and thinking, "I
hope no one notices that my knees are shaking. . . ."

Intrapersonal communication is more, however. The way you communicate within yourself constitutes much of your uniqueness as an
individual human being. You process the information you receive
through your senses in different ways, according to your language,
beliefs, and experiences. Even speakers of the same language may
attribute different meanings to the same words. As a result, you bring
a unique system of interpretation to each communicative event. The
process through which you interpret communicative stimuli, either
from within or outside, takes place on the intrapersonal level. This
process will be discussed in greater detail in Chapters 2 and 3.

At the intrapersonal level you are often conscious of no particular
intentionality behind your actions. Thoughts seem to come to you ran-
domly. There are times when you may intend to solve a particular
problem or plan a particular activity, but you do not, even then, plan
your messages with a particular effect in mind. As you move up through
the other levels of speech communication, however, intentionality
comes increasingly to the fore.

*No two people communicate within themselves in quite the same way.*

## The Interpersonal Level

What does it mean to say that you are getting to know another
person? What is it about that person that you are learning? The recognition of a face and a name come quickly, but what is beyond that?

**Interpersonal communication** is face-to-face interaction between two persons with the potential for immediate feedback. It is a process of discovering the uniqueness of another person; it is learning what sets that individual apart from all other individuals. Getting to know someone makes that person more predictable—there is a growing sureness that, under certain conditions, the person will respond in a certain way.

As we noted in our discussion of intrapersonal communication, the uniqueness of each individual (other than the obvious physical differences) resides in his or her particular way of interpreting and representing the world to him- or herself. Interpersonal communication, then, forms a link between two unique inner worlds.

If interpersonal communication is aimed at discovering and responding to the uniqueness of another, it requires an increase of intentionality. When you converse, you formulate and adapt your messages to suit each individual you talk to and the level of each relationship. Whether you are simply passing the time of day, solving a problem, having an argument, or negotiating a contract, you actively choose those messages that are most likely to achieve the desired effect, according to your predictions of the other person's behavior. You may feel that you are simply "being yourself" in your communication with all the people you know, and in a way you are; but think about your two closest friends. Do you communicate about the same things in the same way with both of them? We will explore interpersonal communication further in Chapter 5.

*Interpersonal communication is based on intrapersonal communication.*

## The Group Level

When from three to about fifteen or twenty persons meet and, by exchanging views, attempt to accomplish some mutually agreed upon task or goal, speech communication is occurring at the **group level.** Whether for entertainment (a sailing club), information sharing (a study or computer users' group), planning (a community action group), or problem solving and decision making (a corporate board of directors), all groups use speech communication in an attempt to reach some common goal. The interrelationships among group members (the nature of the receivers) and the reason for group interaction (intentionality) again distinguish group communication from the other levels.

If you have ever worked in a group, you already know some of the problems associated with reaching a collective decision. What you say has to satisfy not one, not two, not three, but *all* members of the group. Every member is a critical listener and a potential speaker. When communicating in a group, you need to base your message both on what you know about the uniqueness of the individuals in the group

*Group communication involves a common purpose or goal.*

and on what you know about their common interests; you must consider both their similarities and their differences.

Because of the complexity of producing a message for a group of unique individuals who share a common goal and who are all potential respondents to all messages, a speaker's degree of intentionality is greater than at the interpersonal level. Any communicator in a group—even a casual one—must take into account the unique characteristics of the individual group member(s) for whom the message is intended, as well as the feelings, interests, and goals of all other group members. When Frazer responds to José's idea, and Joan responds to Frazer's attitude toward José, and Thompson yells at Joan for picking on Frazer, the complexity of speech communication at the group level becomes evident. We will discuss the group level of speech communication further in Chapters 8 and 9.

## The Public Level

Communication that is generated by one individual and directed toward an audience is **public communication.** This textbook includes six chapters on public speaking. They are intended to enhance your knowledge and skills in preparing and delivering formal spoken messages to audiences. Once again, we see both similarities and differences between the public level and other levels of speech communication. At all four levels, senders encode messages with a particular receiver in mind, and both senders and receivers perceive, think, feel, and interpret. There are two essential differences, however, between public speech communication and the other three levels. They are defined by the nature of the receivers and the degree of intentionality.

*Public speaking focuses on the commonalities among audience members.*

In contrast to the interpersonal level, where a sender addresses a receiver in terms of that person's *uniqueness,* a speaker at the public level looks for *commonalities* among the many members of the audience. For a speaker attempting to analyze the audience, the goal is predictability, just as it is at the interpersonal level. To be effective, the speaker must have some idea about the way different formulations of the message might be received. While each member of an audience is a unique individual, research has shown that members of particular groups (based on age, sex, political affiliation, and educational level) share many characteristics. It is these shared characteristics that enable a speaker to predict an audience's probable response to a message. A speaker whose audience is made up of conservative Republicans (or liberal Democrats) will be able to predict the probable response to a message about gun control, abortion, or school prayer.

Public speech communication is, essentially, a highly structured form of talking to one another. The formal structure is what sets it

Public speaking is a formal way of speaking to each other. A speaker plans the message well in advance, thinking about ways the listeners are similar and about the ways to appeal to them.

apart from the other levels, giving it the highest level of intentionality. Messages are planned, often well in advance, before they are delivered. Audiences and situations are analyzed carefully. Speakers are highly conscious of the effects they intend and, as a result, their mode of delivery is thoroughly organized and often rehearsed.

## SPEECH COMMUNICATION IN SOCIETY

Speech communication sets humans apart from the other animals. Through speech communication, they build relationships, form groups, make decisions, become educated, and educate others. In a very real sense, the effectiveness of a society is a reflection of the effectiveness of the communication within that society.

## MASS COMMUNICATION IN SOCIETY

When communication passes through a medium such as television, radio, newspapers, billboards, or motion pictures, it is classified as **mass communication.** The medium in this form of communication—

## The Levels of Speech Communication

| | Receivers | Audience Analysis | Intentionality | Tone |
|---|---|---|---|---|
| **Intrapersonal Level** | Individual | Aimed at self | Low (generally) | Informal (generally) |
| **Interpersonal Level** | Pair—a communicator and one other person | Aimed at discovering and adapting to individual uniqueness | ↑ | ↑ |
| **Group Level** | Group of three to fifteen or twenty persons | Aimed at both individualities and comomonalities among receivers | | |
| **Public Level** | One person to many persons | Aimed at commonalities among receivers | ↓ High (generally) | ↓ Formal (generally) |

the newspaper, film, television, or radio—plays such a dominant role that mass communication is usually considered separately from the four levels of speech communication. The absence of immediate feedback to the communicator further separates mass communication from the various levels of speech communication.

Media technologies provide a communicator access to very large numbers of receivers, often simultaneously. The ongoing development of new communication technologies makes it increasingly important that you understand the processes of human communication. Already the rapid advances in communications technology have made a dramatic impact on the way you live. Human-to-human contact, not long ago limited to face-to-face interaction and letters that could take months to arrive in some locations, now is possible through a variety of means, nearly instantaneously, almost anywhere in the world. The world is getting smaller, rapidly.

The term *mass communication* is somewhat misleading. When the anchor person of the evening news comes on the air, he or she is not really addressing the masses. The receivers of the news are usually alone or with a small group, typically at home in their living rooms. *Individuals* make up the mass audience, and it is individuals who make decisions based on the communications they receive through the media.

Fundamentally, listening to and understanding the evening news

*Mass communication is mediated communication.*

is no different from any other instance of speech communication. It is still a process in which senders and receivers of messages are engaged in an interpretive, meaning-assigning process that is influenced by the nature of the participants and the context in which communication occurs. What is different is that messages generated by so few can be received by so many.

In the midst of an explosion in information and communication technology, you must understand the communication process better. As an effective communicator, you can influence the lives of millions of people. You cannot control a process you do not understand.

## SUMMARY

The understanding of basic concepts coupled with the development of skills in speech communication can help you to become a more effective communicator, and, therefore, a more effective human being. This chapter has introduced you to some fundamental principles that provide a foundation for the rest of the book. In this summary, and in all subsequent summaries, we will help you to review the chapter's highlights by matching them to the chapter's objectives.

▶**Define *speech communication*.**

Speech communication is the human process through which we make sense out of the world and share that sense with others.

▶**List three criteria of effective communication.**

To be effective, communication should (1) be understood, (2) achieve the intended effect, and (3) be ethical.

▶**Discuss three principles of speech communication.**

First, communication is an ongoing process that reflects dynamic interrelationships among many simultaneously occurring variables. This means that communication events can never be repeated in exactly the same form because the communicators and the context are always changing. In addition, because communication is a continuous process, it is irreversible—once something is said, it cannot be taken back.

Second, every communication has both a content aspect and a relationship aspect. The content aspect is the verbal message. The relationship aspect provides verbal or nonverbal information about the way the content aspect should be received and, thus, is metacommunicational.

Third, communication is complex. There are an enormous number of variables that affect communication at any given moment. The personalities of the communicators, the communication context, the complexities of language and meaning, and the communicators' goals and objectives are just a few of the factors that shape the outcomes of communication.

▶**Define the seven basic components of the communication process.**

The *source* is the point at which information originates. A *message* is the product of encoding; it is any signal or stimulus to which a receiver assigns meaning. The *channel* is a pathway through which message-signals pass between source and receiver. A *receiver* is any individual or group toward whom communication is intentionally or unintentionally directed. *Noise* is anything that interferes with the clear reception of a message. *Feedback* is a receiver's response to a message that enables a sender to gauge whether he or she has been understood. *Context* is the entire communication environment. Although it is possible to break the communication process down into these seven basic elements, it is important to keep in mind that one is never isolated from the others. All are interdependent parts of the entire system.

▶**Identify four levels of speech communication and explain the distinctions among them.**

The levels of speech communication are based on the interaction of different classes of senders, receivers, and contexts with the basic processes and components of communication. Four levels of speech communication can be distinguished: intrapersonal, interpersonal, group, and public. Each level involves increasing numbers of receivers and higher levels of intentionality. The intrapersonal level is communication with the self. The level of conscious intent is usually very low. Interpersonal communication is two-person communication aimed at discovering the uniqueness of the other person. Because communicators adapt their messages to suit an individual and a situation, the degree of intentionality is increased. At the group level, communicators exchange views as they attempt to achieve a common purpose or goal. Because of the complexity of producing a message for a group of unique individuals who are all potential respondents to all messages, there is more intentionality than at the interpersonal level. Finally, the public level is the most formal, structured, and consciously intentional level of communication. At this level communicators identify similarities among the individuals in the audience and adapt their messages to them.

►**Summarize the differences between mass communication and speech communication.**

While many of the same processes are fundamental to both speech communication and mass communication, the absence of face-to-face interaction, the lack of immediate feedback, and the focus on the effects of the medium itself set the study of mass communication apart somewhat from speech communication.

## KEY TERMS

**channel:**  a pathway through which message-signals pass between source and receiver.

**content aspect:**  the portion of communication that is the verbal message.

**context:**  the entire communication environment.

**decoding:**  the interpretive process of assigning meaning to messages.

**encoding:**  the process through which messages are cast into a system of signals.

**feedback:**  a receiver's response to a message that enables a sender to gauge whether he or she has been understood.

**group communication:**  interaction that occurs when from three to about fifteen or twenty persons meet, and, by exchanging views, attempt to accomplish some mutually agreed-upon task or goal.

**interpersonal communication:**  face-to-face interaction between two persons with the potential for immediate feedback.

**intrapersonal communication:**  speech communication within an individual.

**mass communication:**  communication that is mediated, through television, radio, newspapers, billboards, or motion pictures.

**message:**  the product of encoding; any signal or stimulus to which a receiver assigns meaning.

**metacommunication:**  communication about communication.

**noise:**  anything that interferes with the clear reception of a message.

**public communication:**  communication that is generated by one individual and directed toward an audience.

**receiver:**  any individual or group toward whom communications are intentionally or unintentionally directed.

**relationship aspect:**  verbal or nonverbal information about the way the content aspect of communication should be received.

**source:**  the point at which information originates.

**speech communication:**  a human process through which we make sense out of the world and share that sense with others.

## DISCUSSION QUESTIONS

1. We have described effective communication as communication that is understood, achieves a desired effect, and is ethical. Cite examples of communication that you would consider effective even though it does not meet one or all of these criteria. What different criteria would you use to judge effectiveness?

2. What are your attitudes toward different communication media? Which are you most likely to believe? Newspapers? Magazines? Radio? Television? Why do you feel this way? How do you compare information you receive through the media to that which comes to you by word-of-mouth?

3. Do dogs, cats, and dolphins communicate? If so, how is their communication different from human communication? How is it the same? Does the definition of speech communication presented in this chapter apply to communication among animals?

4. This chapter presented four levels of speech communication. Discuss your feelings about these different levels. At which level are you the most comfortable? At which level are you the most anxious? What characteristics of communication levels relate to these feelings?

## SUGGESTED ACTIVITIES

1. To see how the content and relationship aspects of communication work together, read the following statements aloud, showing as little emotion as possible:

   I love you.
   You're fired.
   I can't think of anything I'd rather do.
   When are you going to clean your room?

   Now experiment with facial expression and tone of voice as you say the statements again. How many different meanings can you suggest for each statement? How does metacommunication shape meaning?

2. As you observe the meeting of a small group, note examples of the seven components of communication. Your note-taking task will be greatly simplified if you divide a sheet of paper into

seven columns—one for each component. What do your observations tell you about the complexity of the communication process?

3. Make a list of your strengths as a communicator. Make a second list of your weaknesses. Can you identify barriers that prevent you from being a more effective communicator? What strategies can you identify for overcoming these barriers?

## SUGGESTED READINGS

DeFleur, M. and Ball-Rokeach, S. (1982). *Theories of Mass Communication,* 4th edition. (New York: Longman Press).

Rubin, R.B. and Rubin, A.M. (1986). *Communication Research: Strategies and Sources.* (Belmont, CA: Wadsworth).

Severin, W.J. and Tankard, J.W. (1988). *Communication Theories: Origins, Methods, Uses,* 2nd edition. (New York: Longman Press).

Trenholm, S. (1986). *Human Communication Theory.* (Englewood Cliffs, NJ: Prentice-Hall).

Watzlawick, T., Beavin Bavelas, J. and Jackson, D. (1967). *Pragmatics of Human Communication.* (New York: W.W. Norton).

# 2 Speech Communication and the Self

*After studying this chapter, you should be able to:*

▶ Define *self-reflexiveness* and its importance to human behavior.

▶ Explain the distinctions between *self* and *self-concept*.

▶ Describe yourself in terms of your material, social, and spiritual selves.

▶ Tell how interpersonal communication contributes to the development and maintenance of self-concept.

▶ Distinguish between *self-image* and *self-esteem*.

▶ Give examples of the ways in which self-concept can affectyour communication with others.

▶ Discuss the relationship of your changing roles to your self-concept.

Pause for a moment and answer this question: Who are you?

How did you answer? Did you begin with your name? Perhaps you answered with some of the roles you assume: student, friend, lover, son, or daughter. Maybe you thought about your childhood and your upbringing (I grew up in a family of four in Larchmont, New York). Is that who you are? Do adjectives describe the self? Are you sensitive, assertive, caring, fat, tall, short, attractive, interesting, depressed, boring, lazy, or intelligent? Are you and the words you use to describe yourself the same? Are you who you say you are? Or is there a "real you" beneath all of those descriptions?

## THE DEFINITION OF SELF-REFLEXIVENESS

The definition of self has perplexed philosophers, theologians, psychologists, and other thinkers throughout history. Is there one great Universal Self of which we are all a part? Are we islands of consciousness in a cosmic ocean of Mind? Is the self, as Karen Horney stated, "that central inner force, common to all human beings and yet unique in each, which is the deep source of growth?"[1] Perhaps the Buddhists are correct in their belief that the whole idea of self is an illusion.

Whatever the true nature of the self may be, you know that you are conscious of something that you refer to as *I* or *me*. When you say "I," you include your body as well as all of your past experiences, thoughts, feelings, and possessions—in short, everything about you as you view it from within yourself:

*I think of myself*
*I speak of myself*
*I am the thinker*
*I am the thought*
*I am the speaker*
*I am the speech*

You are connected with the world simply because you are a conscious, responding organism. Speech communication takes you a step further by linking you with the environment through conceptual awareness. Put another way, you are not only aware, but you are aware of your awareness; you are not only conscious, but conscious of your consciousness. This phenomenon, known as **self-reflexiveness,** is the unique ability to think about what you're doing as you do it and to think about what you're saying as you say it. You respond not only to the environment, but to yourself responding in that environment. For example, as you step up to the lectern, you may have a sudden, acute awareness of yourself and the situation. In your mind

*One of the features that makes us unique as humans is our self-reflexiveness.*

you may say, "Well, here I am and there they are. I sure am nervous. Hope it goes all right." Walking into a party where you know only the host, you may experience a heightened consciousness of your own appearance and actions. Such self-consciousness is exaggerated self-reflexiveness. You become much more aware of your own awareness.

You are almost always self-reflexive to some degree. You monitor your own behavior and make decisions based on self-observations. There is a kind of duality within the self. You are both *I* and *Me*, subject and object. You are a participant as well as an observer in your life. The subjective self—*I*—is the active agent who lives and loves, acts and feels. The objective self—*Me*—is the object of your reflections about your actions and feelings. Your evaluations of *Me* (self-as-object) determine, in part, the further actions of *I* (self-as-subject).

## SELF-CONCEPT

When you answer the question, "Who are you?" your response is a verbal representation of yourself. Taken together, *all of the things that you believe to be true about yourself, across time and across situations, constitute your self-concept.* **Self-concept** is a relatively consistent set of beliefs you have about yourself. Note how the following statements reflect the relatively stable nature of the self-concept:

*Who are you?*
   My name is Freddy.
*Who are you?*
   I'm a student, a friend, a lover.
*Who are you?*
   I'm a shy and sensitive person.
*Who are you?*
   I'm an intelligent person.
*Who are you?*
   I'm a person who avoids competition.
*Who are you?*
   I'm OK looking, but that's all.
*Who are you?*
   I seem boring because I'm shy, but I can be fun once you get
   to know me.
*Who are you?*
   I'm a good listener. I care about others.

As you shall see in this chapter, you develop your beliefs about yourself through communication with others. Your self-concept provides the basis for your further interactions with others at all levels

Who are you? Does the way you see yourself coincide with the way others see you?

of speech communication (interpersonal, small group, and public). In this way, communication gives rise to self-concept, and self-concept affects communication.

But who are you *really?* What do you mean when you want to "just be yourself"? You are not one self, but many. In different situations, contexts, and relationships, different components of your self-concept come to the forefront. Think about it: Does your mother see the same "you" that your professor sees? Do you feel like the same person in the classroom and on the athletic field? Do you feel the same when you're talking with your best friend as you do while the police officer is writing you a speeding ticket? The self-concept, as we shall see, has more than one component.

One of the earliest theorists to talk about the different facets of self-concept was the psychologist William James.[2] James described three components of the self: the material self, the social self, and the spiritual self.

*Self is an ambiguous word for a complex idea. For our purposes, self-concept is a more useful term.*

## The Material Self

The **material self** is a composite of all your physical elements— your body, your home, your possessions—that reflect who you are. Do you like your body? Are you too tall, short, fat, thin? Are you shaped like an hourglass? Are you broad at the shoulders and narrow at the hips? Are you pear-shaped? Do you wish that your body weight were distributed differently? Do you exercise regularly? Why or why not? Do you take good care of your body? Do you abuse it?

How do you dress? Do you have a closet full of the latest fashions? Do you wish you did? Are you glad you don't? Are nice clothes important to you, or are you proud not to be shackled to the changing tides of the fashion world? How do you like to appear to others? Preppy? Trendy? Laid back?

Where do you live? Does your home reflect your personality? Does it represent a life-style that fits you? Is it formal or informal? Is it a comfortable place to be?

*Your body, your clothes, even your furniture are all a part of who you are.*

Do you drive a car? What kind is it? Are you proud of your car? Are you ashamed to be seen in it? Does it matter to you? Perhaps you ride a motorcycle or a bicycle. Do you identify with these things? To what degree?

All of these things—your body, your clothes, your home, your car— are parts of your material self. They all reflect your self-concept because they represent choices you have made based upon who you think you are. While many of the items listed are "just things" and may not seem like a real part of you, they are all reflections of that part of you that assigns values to things—the material self.

## The Social Self

The **social self** is the self that interacts with others. William James suggested that you have as many social selves as there are people who recognize you. Think of any two people you know. Imagine yourself interacting with each of them. How much eye contact do you maintain? What is your posture like? How much distance is there between the two of you? How do you feel with each person? What do you talk about— school? your love life? politics? your innermost feelings?

*Your social self changes as you interact with different people.*

If you compared your interaction with your mother and your interaction with your professor, you probably found dramatic differences. Even if you chose two close friends, you probably discovered that your responses to each are slightly different; each relationship defines you slightly differently.

Ironically, with as many social selves as you have, it is through social interaction that your entire self-concept is built and maintained. You make your decisions about who you are based on your relationships with others. We shall explore this idea more fully later in the chapter.

## The Spiritual Self

Even without your material possessions and your relationships with others, you exist; you are conscious of your being. The **spiritual**

Review Box

## William James' Components of the Self

|  | **Definition** | **Examples** |
|---|---|---|
| **Material Self** | A composite of all the physical elements that reflect who you are | Body, clothes, home, car, possessions |
| **Social Self** | The self in interaction with others | Self-adjustments in response to different roles, friends, and statuses |
| **Spiritual Self** | Your process of introspection, as well as your moral and spiritual aspirations | Belief systems, religious experiences, consciousness, awareness |

**self** includes your process of introspection as well as your moral and spiritual aspirations. On one hand, it is your consciousness of being-in-the-universe; it is your essence, your awareness. As such, it is rather like the "true self" discussed at the beginning of this chapter. On the other hand, the spiritual self is an attempt to understand this inner essence, whether you call it consciousness, spirit, or soul. Your religious feelings and beliefs and your other attempts to understand or explain the meaning and purpose of your life on Earth compose the spiritual self.

It is interesting to observe how different aspects of the self vary in importance from person to person. For some, religious faith is the dominant force in their lives and is central in guiding their behavior and interactions with others. For others, the pursuit of material possessions is primary to their existence. For all, however, social interaction—communication with others—is the basis for the overall self-concept. Self-concept is built and maintained through speech communication.

## SPEECH COMMUNICATION AND SELF-CONCEPT

Self-concept is not simply something you *have,* but something you *do.* Indeed, the development of self-concept is a process in which you actively participate. You are born with no self-concept whatsoever. It is not until you begin to speak, at around the age of two, that you have any sense of self at all; this is the time it begins.

Think back. What are your earliest memories? What is the earliest age at which you actually recall being "you"? For you to recall past events, it is necessary for you to *displace*. **Displacement** is the mental ability to step outside of the present moment and think about the past, the future, or what's happening across town right now. This ability to displace is dependent on speech communication.

You do not carry around with you events from the past, but *symbols* of those events. A **symbol** is an arbitrary representation of a thing or idea that bears no resemblance to that which it represents. The most common examples of a symbol is a word. A word directs your attention to what it represents while having only an arbitrary relationship to the object. For example, there is nothing about the word *dog* that actually looks like, or even sounds like, the animal curled up by the fireplace; but the symbol is your only tool for conceptual thinking.

Self-awareness is linked to your ability to speak. Look around you. Try to imagine yourself without the ability to use words at all. All of the things you see—this book, your own hands, the curtains, the window—would be meaningless. The world would be a phantasmagoria of sight, sound, color, and sensation. You would be a point of awareness, perceiving all of these things, but you would not be aware that you were aware. You would seem to be at the center of a small world. Displacement would be impossible. Nothing would exist for you outside of the present moment.

We are asking you to imagine a return to infancy, to a prelinguistic state. It is a world you once inhabited, but in which you didn't remain. The people around you *talked*. They talked to you and near you. They talked about the things around you. Perhaps they said *bottle* and soon you learned to associate *bottle* with a warm, pleasurable, liquid. You probably didn't associate *bottle* with a class of containers that come in varying sizes and shapes, but you learned to use the sound "bottle" (or, more likely, "ba-ba") to get what you wanted. Before long, you learned that words could be put together to achieve a desired effect ("mama . . . ba-ba") and soon came the realization that words not only were a means to personal pleasure but were representative of objects! You heard your own words and realized that they came from somewhere. They came from you, and yet you could hear them. In that moment, when your power of words was turned back on yourself, your self-concept was born.

Self-concept arises from, is developed by, and is maintained through spoken symbolic interaction with other symbol-using humans. You learn to speak simply through exposure to speech communication. It is this ability to symbolize that enables you to see yourself as the object

*Self-concept is something you achieve through interaction with other people.*

## Communication and the Development of Self-Concept

of your thoughts. It allows you to ask the question, Who am I? The development of self-concept over the entire span of your lifetime is essentially a very lengthy response to this question.

## Self-Concept and Interpersonal Communication

Self-concept does not develop in a vacuum. Just as it is impossible to see your face without some reflective surface, it is impossible to view the self without using the reflected appraisals of others. You decide who you are by interpreting others' responses toward you.

*How other family members treat you when you're very young can have a profound effect on your self-concept.*

A small child stumbles in a grocery store, knocking down the toilet paper display, and her mother scolds, "What a naughty little girl! Look what you've done!" Her Aunt Bonnie calls her an adorable child. Her father hugs her warmly and kisses her goodnight. These are all messages from which the child builds her self-concept. Some messages will be taken more seriously than others. Messages from those to whom she is closest will be taken most seriously. Messages that are repeated continually are the strongest. Her self-concept will evolve through a selection process from the immense number of messages she receives about herself from others. This is the centrality of the social self: Who you are is defined and redefined through interaction with others.

## Self-Concept: An Ongoing Process

Every message you send forth says something about your self-concept. The way you sit, dress, act, speak—the things you choose to talk about and the people you choose to talk to—whether you are assertive, shy, or tender in your presentation are all reflections of your self-perceptions, which are based on all of your previous interactions. You continuously monitor the feedback you receive from others in interpersonal transactions and check it against your self-perceptions. If you find a discrepancy between the message you intended and the one received, you reformulate the message in an attempt to be understood.

*Everything you say and do is a reflection of your self-concept.*

Usually, you encode messages that are consistent with your self-concept. If you see yourself as assertive, for example, you will communicate in an assertive, forthright manner. The feedback you receive, then, will be not only about the specific content of your verbal message, but also about your assertiveness. Imagine the manner that Ralph would have used in order to produce the following reaction from Alice:

*Ralph:*    I love you, Alice.
*Alice:*    Don't be so pushy.

Alice's response provides Ralph with information about the way she perceives him. It is then up to Ralph to interpret this information and to choose how it will affect his behavior.

Speech communication is an interpretive process. In an interpersonal transaction people interpret others' interpretations of their interpretations of themselves. Alice's message, "Don't be so pushy," may be consistent or inconsistent with Ralph's self-concept. If he sees himself as aggressive, Alice's comment will reinforce his self-concept. If, however, her feedback is inconsistent with the way he sees himself, he will probably do one of two things: either he will adjust his behavior to bring Alice's impression of him more in line with his view of himself, or he will begin to adjust his self-concept to be more consistent with the feedback he's getting.

We can summarize this interpretive process as follows:

- You are linked with yourself symbolically through speech communication.
- You possess a symbolic representation of yourself that is based on all of your previous experiences and interactions—your self-concept.
- In an interpersonal transaction, you regulate your behavior according to the nature of your link with yourself (self-concept) and your link with the other person (how well you know that person, that person's role).
- The other person's responses to you (feedback) are compared with your responses to yourself. Others' responses will be either consistent or inconsistent with your self-concept.
- If the other person's responses are consistent with your self-concept, your self-concept has been reinforced. If the other person's responses are inconsistent with your self-concept, your self-concept has been called into question; the other person does not see you as you see yourself.
- When there is inconsistency between the way the other person sees you and your self-concept, you may either:
  —try to change the other person's perceptions of you to be more consistent with your self-concept, or
  —try to adjust your self-concept to be more consistent with the other person's feedback.

These two alternatives are stated very generally. Obviously there are many responses to feedback that don't reinforce your self-concept. Most of them fall into one category or the other, or combine the two.

Self-concept, then, is an ongoing process of adaptation. You adapt yourself to messages, and you adapt messages to yourself and others. You regulate your communicative behavior—intrapersonally and interpersonally—according to your interactions with others.

## Self-Concept: Consistency and Change

*Your self-concept can change to match the feedback you get from others.*

A person's self-concept may remain relatively stable over time because he or she tends to select only those messages that reinforce it and to ignore those that do not. We will discuss the process of selective perception more fully in Chapter 3, but for now consider this: *Most of us would rather be consistent than happy.* This may seem like a bold statement, but think about it for a moment. The self-concept is a very personal matter. To change a person's self-concept is to change that person's identity. It is to sacrifice what is familiar (and perceived as safe) and to move into the unknown (which can be threatening). To take on a new identity is to relinquish an older one. For a new self-concept to emerge, the old one must die. Such a "death" is threatening to most people, even those whose self-concepts are negative and uncomfortable. Therefore, people tend to pay close attention to messages that reaffirm who it is they believe themselves to be (positive *or* negative) and to disregard messages that do not support their self-concepts. You probably know someone who has such a low opinion of him- or herself that words of praise will "bounce off," but a sharp criticism will be met with a cynical smile, a shrug of the shoulders, and a comment such as "See? I told you so."

Self-concepts can and do change. On the negative side, a boy with a healthy opinion of himself in his early years may shift his self-concept when the other boys in the schoolyard discover that he is uncoordinated, that he consistently strikes out in baseball and can't control the

Self-concept arises from, is developed by, and is maintained through spoken symbolic interaction with other symbol-using humans. It does not develop in a vacuum. You decide who you are by interpreting others' responses toward you.

ball in any sport. Receiving persistent messages that he is unwanted on the team and that he "stinks at sports" can negatively affect his self-concept.

When a music teacher discovers that this boy has a real gift for tuba playing, and when people voice new approval and admiration, his self-concept may shift again toward the more positive side. In both cases, it is the persistency of the messages from others that can change his self-concept.

At times the boy's youthful self-concept will be positive and at other times negative. On the ball field, he probably feels insecure and somewhat worthless. In the music room, he is happy and confident. This leads us to two important components of self-concept: self-image and self-esteem.

### Self-Image and Self-Esteem

Take a moment and picture yourself in the following situations. Relax and allow yourself to feel the way you'd feel when:

delivering a public speech;

answering questions during a job interview;

attending a campus party;

having a conference with the dean;

taking an examination;

introducing yourself to a stranger;

participating in a group discussion;

losing an argument; or

playing basketball.

Are you a skilled athlete? Are you an accomplished musician? Are you a competent and capable student? What is your view of yourself as a communicator? Are you comfortable talking with strangers? Are you a good speaker? Are you a natural leader? Are you sociable or are you a loner? **Self-image** is your view of yourself in a particular situation. Thus, it changes from situation to situation. For example, the words you use to describe yourself as a student are probably very different from those you use for your image as a "party animal." You have many different self-images.

Whereas self-image is what you *think* about yourself in a particular situation, **self-esteem** is how you *feel* about that view of yourself. It is the degree to which you have a sense of self-worth—a subjective judgment about your self-concept and your various self-images. Self-esteem varies from person to person and from situation to situation. Some persons have generally high self-esteem; they tend to like them-

*Self-image and self-esteem can vary widely from situation to situation.*

selves. Others have generally low self-esteem; they tend to be highly critical of themselves. There are students who have high self-esteem in the classroom and the professor's office, but whose confidence evaporates on the athletic field. Self-image and self-esteem combine to have a powerful effect on the way you communicate, the message you give, and on the way others communicate back.

## THE EFFECTS OF SELF-CONCEPT ON YOUR COMMUNICATION

While your self-concept is clearly affected by others' communication with you, it also influences your communication with others. Your self-concept affects your communication in two ways: through *self-fulfilling prophecy* and *selection of messages*.

### Self-fulfilling Prophecy

One of the greatest obstacles to overcome in a public speaking class is students' perceptions about the public speaking situation. Many students communicate dynamically and enthusiastically outside the classroom, but turn glazed-eyed and dull when presenting a speech assignment. They picture themselves as poor public speakers. To be consistent with that self-image, they do not perform well. This is an example of a **self-fulfilling prophecy**—a prediction that comes true because people expect it to come true. The self-concept directs behavior in ways that are consistent with that self-concept.

People behave consistently with their beliefs about themselves. They then react to that behavior, and their feedback reinforces both the behavior and the self-image that generated it. Their beliefs about themselves literally become who they are. In a public speaking class, when students *act* like effective communicators, they receive feedback from the class and the professor that helps them improve their self-images and self-esteem. The feedback also helps them improve their performances as truly effective communicators.

### Selection of Messages

Self-concept is not something that happens to you; it is something you *do*. The way you participate in the shaping of your own self-concept is through *selection of messages*—both the messages you send and those you receive.

As a sender of messages, you select those messages that are consistent with your self-concept. *Intrapersonally* you engage in explaining

---

**Self-Image Versus Self-Esteem Versus Self-Concept**

| | Key Characteristics | Examples |
|---|---|---|
| **Self-Image** | Reflects your view of yourself in a particular situation<br>Varies from situation to situation | I am an outstanding math student.<br>I can beat anybody at tennis.<br>I'm awful at making small talk with strangers. |
| **Self-Esteem** | Reflects how you feel about your view of yourself<br>Exists at both general and specific levels<br>Varies from situation to situation | I'm self-conscious about my math ability because some people think that math whizzes are weird.<br>My tennis ability makes me unique and admirable.<br>I feel socially awkward because of my inability to make small talk. |
| **Self-Concept** | Reflects your view of yourself over time and across situations<br>An ongoing process but relatively stable | I'm an intelligent person.<br>I'm athletic.<br>I'm shy. |

and rationalizing your behavior to yourself so that it will make sense within the context of your self-concept. *Interpersonally,* and at the other levels of speech communication, you communicate according to your view of yourself. (This phenomenon has been discussed in several previous sections.)

You are also actively engaged in message selection as a *receiver* of messages. The selectivity you exhibit to maintain consistency in an interpersonal transaction has already been noted. On a broader level, the television shows you watch, the books you read, and the magazines you buy are all reflections of the message-selection process. For example, each generation has a tendency to claim a type of popular music as its own. Whether your tastes run toward Glen Miller; Crosby, Stills and Nash; Prince; or The Dead Milkmen depends, in part, on your self-concept as a member of your generation or of a subgroup within your generation.

## ROLES AND SELF-CONCEPT

*Role expectations can shape behavior, and behavior shapes self-concept.*

To a great extent, you are what you do. What you do is an expression of the way you see yourself, the way you define your *roles*.

A **role** is a set of expectations about the way to behave when you occupy a certain position. New roles that you take on—husband, wife, business person, graduate student—bring new expectations both from yourself and from others. You tend to conform your behavior to these expectations. Thus, if you believe that business persons are aggressive and you join the business world, you are likely to begin to behave more aggressively in order to conform to your own expectations of that role. When you behave more aggressively as a function of your new role, people will begin to respond to you as an "aggressive person." Their feedback then reinforces your new self-image. What began as role playing becomes a routine part of your self-concept.

Your self-concept is a function of your ability to use speech communication; it is your ability to symbolize—to interact with others, to reflect upon that interaction and yourself—that brings self-concept into being. Speech communication is an *interpretive* process; it is a process of making sense out of the world—including yourself.

### Self-Concept and Change

Self-awareness and an understanding of the contexts of communication can help you change your self-concept. Since the one common denominator in all the situations in which you find yourself is *you*, it is important that you become more than a participant in your own life. The following suggestions may help you become a participant-*observer*:

- Examine the situations in which you find yourself—the classroom, your part-time job, parties, and intimate relationships. What are your beliefs about yourself in each of these situations? How are these beliefs reflected in your behavior? Do you have beliefs and/or behaviors you'd like to change? Try to identify the alternatives that are available to you.
- Analyze the messages you send to others—through dress, behavior, punctuality (or its lack), speaking style, choice of topics, and choice of friends. How do these behaviors relate to your self-image? Are there any inconsistencies?
- In any and all of the things you do from day to day, ask yourself why you choose to do them.
- Examine your beliefs about yourself, both positive and negative (for example, "I'm a good student" or "I'm not a very good conversationalist"). Explore the origins of these beliefs.

The idea that self-concept can change and that you can choose your behaviors is powerful and liberating; but a word of caution is in order. Though change is possible, it is not easy. There are no shortcuts. Changing your self-concept is very hard work. Be patient, and keep at it.

## SUMMARY

This chapter has focused on the role of speech communication in the development and maintenance of the self-concept. Self-concept is not something static that you simply *have*—it is something you *do*, something you *achieve*. It is inextricably entwined with your communicative behavior. You behave according to your beliefs about yourself. Through your interpretations of others' responses to you, you develop and maintain your self-concept.

▶**Define self-reflexiveness and its importance to human behavior.**

*Self-reflexiveness* is your ability to think about your own behavior. Because you are self-reflexive, you can contemplate your behavior and plan your actions based on expected outcomes.

▶**Explain the distinctions between self and self-concept.**

*Self* is the core of consciousness referred to as *I* or *me*. It includes your body as well as all of your past experiences, thoughts, feelings, and possessions—everything about you as you view it from within yourself. In contrast, self-concept is a set of beliefs you have about yourself. *Self-concept* is shaped by your communication with others and guides your behavior. You behave in ways that are consistent with your self-concept.

▶**Describe yourself in terms of your material, social, and spiritual selves.**

William James identified three components of the self—the material, social, and spiritual selves. Your material self is a composite of all the physical elements that reflect who you are—your home, body, car, clothes, and possessions. Your social self is your self in interaction with others—the ways you adjust to different friends, roles, and statuses. The spiritual self includes your process of introspection, as well as your moral and spiritual aspirations, and your religious beliefs and experiences.

▶**Tell how interpersonal communication contributes to the development and maintenance of self-concept.**

You decide who you are by interpreting others' responses. You behave, others respond, and in their responses, you see yourself reflected.

By sorting through the many messages you receive about yourself, you form a conglomeration of self-perceptions that becomes your self-concept. The formation of self-concept is an ongoing process. You continuously monitor the feedback you receive from others and check it against your self-perceptions. If the feedback is inconsistent with your self-concept, you either adjust your behavior to bring the other person's impression in line with your own or you adjust your self-concept to reflect the feedback you've received.

▶**Distinguish between self-image and self-esteem.**

*Self-image* is the way you view yourself in a particular situation. Self-esteem is the way you feel about that view. Whereas self-concept is relatively stable over time and across situations, both self-image and self-esteem can vary widely from situation to situation.

▶**Give examples of the ways in which self-concept can affect your communication with others.**

Self-concept affects communication in two primary ways: through self-fulfilling prophecies and through selection of messages. Self-fulfilling prophecies refer to the tendency to behave in ways that are consistent with self-concepts. If you believe, for example, that you have a certain trait, you tend to behave as if it were so. Others reinforce this behavior, and it becomes true. Selection of messages is also based on the tendency toward consistency. The messages you select both as a sender and as a receiver reflect your self-concept. For example, if you see yourself as aggressive you will communicate aggressively.

▶**Discuss the relationship of your changing roles to your self-concept.**

Roles are sets of expectations about the way to behave when you occupy a certain position. When you perform new behaviors to conform to new role expectations, others respond to and reinforce those behaviors. Over time, the new behaviors become natural and you adjust your self-concept to include them.

## *KEY TERMS*

**displacement:**   the mental ability to step outside of the present moment.

**material self:**   a composite of all the physical elements that reflect who you are.

**role:**   a set of expectations about the way to behave when you occupy a certain position.

**self-concept:**   a relatively consistent set of beliefs you have about yourself.

**self-esteem:**   how you feel about your view of yourself.

**self-fulfilling prophecy:**   a prediction that comes true because you expect it to come true.

**self-image:**   your view of yourself in a particular situation.

**self-reflexiveness:**   your uniquely human ability to think about what you're doing as you do it and to think about what you're saying as you say it.

**social self:**   the self in interaction with others.

**spiritual self:**   your process of introspection as well as your moral and spiritual aspirations.

**symbol:**   an arbitrary representation of a thing or idea that bears no resemblance to that which it represents.

## DISCUSSION QUESTIONS

1.  Self-awareness is an important ingredient in effective communication. Discuss ways in which you feel self-awareness can be expanded and improved. What parts do others play in expanding your self-awareness?

2.  What messages received from others were instrumental in shaping your self-concept? Did you receive any conflicting messages? What are the common characteristics among those people who were most important in helping you to become who you are?

3.  Which of the three components of the self—material, social, or spiritual—is most important to you? Would your choice have been different five years ago? If so, why? How does your answer reflect past and future changes in your self-concept?

4.  Do you ever talk to yourself? Are thinking and speaking really different forms of the same thing? How are thinking or talking to yourself different from communicating with another person?

5.  Bonaro Overstreet once observed that "We are not only our brother's keeper; in countless large and small ways, we are our brother's maker." How does this quotation relate to the discussion of self-concept presented in this chapter?

---

## SUGGESTED ACTIVITIES

1. Make a list of various books and periodicals you read. What common elements do you find throughout this list? How do your choices of literature reflect your self-concept?

2. In this chapter we discussed the importance of role expectations to communicative behavior. Write five adjectives that you associate with each of the following roles. How do your role perceptions influence your behavior toward persons in those roles?
   Mother
   Clergyperson
   Police Officer
   Professor
   Friend

   Try the same exercise with roles of your choosing. Discuss the results.

---

## SUGGESTED READINGS

Hamachek, D. (1971). *Encounters with the Self.* (New York: Holt, Rinehart and Winston).

Jaynes, J. (1976). *The Origin of Consciousness in the Breakdown of the Bicameral Mind.* (Boston: Houghton Mifflin Company).

Kinch, J.W. (1972). "A formalized theory of the self-concept," in Manis, J. and Meltzer, B. (eds.) *Symbolic Interaction,* 2nd edition. (Boston: Allyn and Bacon).

Stewart, J. (1986). *Bridges not Walls,* 4th edition. (New York: Random House).

# Language and Perception

*After studying this chapter, you should be able to:*

▶ Define *perception*.

▶ Explain four components in the perception process.

▶ Differentiate among beliefs, attitudes, and values, and discuss their relationship to human perception.

▶ Describe how language is related to perception.

▶ Show how words have the power to create and affect attitudes and behaviors.

▶ Identify five word barriers that lead to inaccuracies in perception and communication.

▶ Suggest some ways of overcoming word barriers to effective communication.

What do you mean when you say that seeing is believing? Why is the testimony of an eyewitness so compelling? Why do witnesses of the same event often provide drastically different accounts of what they saw? Is beauty *really* in the eye of the beholder?

## SEEING IS BELIEVING . . . OR IS IT?

This chapter is about language and perception. Once you have read it, your answers to these questions may be very different from what they might be now. One conclusion you will probably reach is that it may be more accurate to say that *believing is seeing* than it is to say that *seeing is believing*.

The physiological processes through which you see, hear, feel, touch, and taste the world are very much like those of the other mammals. *Human* perception, however, has a whole different dimension that makes it infinitely more complex and fascinating than animal perception. That different dimension is human symbolic language—words.

> *I know*
> *You believe*
> *You understand*
> *What you think*
> *I said but,*
> *I am not sure you*
> *Realize that what*
> *You heard is not*
> *What I meant*

*Symbolic behavior is what sets you apart from the other animals.*

Words have the power to transform your experience and to make it something that is uniquely your own. *Seeing* is a physiological process shared by most of the vertebrates, but *believing* is a uniquely human, mental process that acts on what you see (or hear, or smell, or touch, or taste). Human perception is an interaction of seeing *and* believing.

### What Is Perception?

**Perception** is the process by which people select, organize, and interpret sensory stimulation into meaningful pictures of the world.[1] Before continuing, read this definition again slowly. Note that the process of perception consists of four main components: (1) sensory stimulation, (2) selection, (3) organization, and (4) interpretation.

## Sensory Stimulation

All perception begins with some kind of **sensory stimulation**—your nervous system's response to the environment. Your eyes, ears, nose, taste buds, or skin's touch receptors must be stimulated to begin the process. This sensory stimulation is continuous. At any given moment, an infinite number of stimuli bombard you—sights, sounds, smells, sensations, and tastes. Scientists say that if you were to become aware of all the stimuli assaulting you at any one time, you would immediately lapse into a state of seizure, caused by the overload to the nervous system. Therefore, just to function normally you screen out a majority of these unnecessary stimuli. This screening, or filtering, process takes place through both physiological and psychological selection.

## Physiological Selection

**Physiological selection** is the filtering of stimuli by the natural limitations of sensory organs. Thus, much of the screening process is involuntary. Your eyes can see only certain colors of the light spectrum. Your ears can hear only sounds within a range of frequencies from 20 to 20,000 cycles per second. The pressure sensors in your skin do not notice that the air is pressing on you with a force of 14 pounds per square inch.

Other animals, of course, have different sensory abilities. Eagles and hawks can see the movement of a field mouse from 2000 feet. Dogs can hear sounds that are far above a normal human's frequency range, and you should be grateful that you don't have a dog's sense of smell.

There are differences between individual humans as well. For example, one of your authors cannot hear high frequencies because of ear damage incurred while playing lead guitar in a rock band. Since turning 40 he also has trouble reading these words without his glasses!

## Psychological Selection

Because your physical limitations filter out the majority of the sensory stimulation around you, you might think that you would be aware of all the rest. Not so. By the time you get through with the mental process of **psychological selection**—a perceptual screening process based on beliefs and selective attention—you are actually aware of very little. Psychological selection takes different forms: foreground/background screening, expectation, selective exposure, and selective attention.

*You are capable of processing only a small portion of the information in the environment.*

**Figure 3-1**
Figure/Background Screening

**Foreground/background screening.** **The process of fore-
ground/background screening** is based on the relationships among
objects and sounds in the environment. If you are near a window, look
outside. Hold your hand between your eyes and the window, and shift
your gaze to your hand. Then switch your focus, again, outside the
window. Did you notice the perceptual shift as you moved your attention from outside, to your hand, and then back again? Now look at
Figure 3-1. What do you see? Some people see a vase while other people
see two faces in profile. If you look again, you should be able to see
both, but *not simultaneously*. One will always be in the foreground
while the other will be in the background.

This phenomenon is noticeable through the other senses as well.
As I am writing, I can shift my attention from the click of the keys on
the word processor to the water lapping on the lakeshore (I'm writing
in a cabin in the mountains), to the flute-like sound of a wood thrush,
to the hum of the refrigerator that just went on. With each shift, the
other sounds all fall into the background (but the wood thrush gets
my attention every time). Even my sense of taste is selective. A friend
of mine makes an exquisite lamb stew in which the taste of dill pre-
dominates, but the subtle undertones of other herbs and spices contribute to the total effect.

Selectivity is part physical and part environmental; the stimulus
that is most intense will get attention. Another part is psychological,
however. Whether you see the faces or the vase in Figure 3-1 depends
on a choice—a mental operation.

**Expectation.**   In perception, **expectation** is the tendency to see
what is anticipated. It serves as a kind of self-fulfilling prophecy. You
tend to select those stimuli that conform to your expectations and

**Figure 3-2**
Expectation

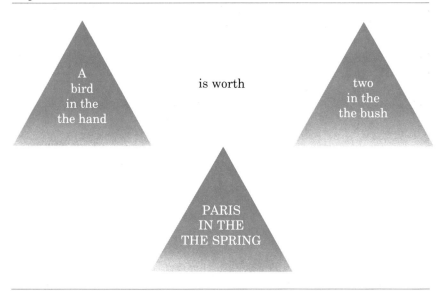

screen out those that do not. For example, if, before you examined Figure 3-1, you had been told to look at the two silhouettes, you would probably have seen the two faces first. If someone you trust tells you that the party Saturday night will be fantastic, the chances increase that you will experience it that way.

Look at Figure 3-2 and read the statements aloud.

If you read them as "A bird in the hand is worth two in the bush" and "Paris in the spring," you made three mistakes. Look again. Can you find where you went wrong? Because you thought that you recognized some very familiar phrases, you screened out the additional word *the* in each of the phrases. You saw what you *expected* to see rather than what was there.

*What you see is often what you expect to see.*

**Selective exposure.**   You have a tendency to open yourself to some experiences and not to others—a process called **selective exposure.** There are many stimuli that you will never perceive, simply because you do not choose to put yourself in a position to receive them. This is one of the effects of self-concept that was discussed in Chapter 2—the selection of messages. Depending on your beliefs about yourself, you will or will not go to a hockey game, read *Atlantic Monthly,* take a course in physics, or attend a lecture by a Marxist. You make these choices based on your beliefs, attitudes, and values, three topics we'll discuss later in this chapter.

**Figure 3-3**
Organization

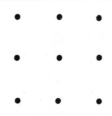

**Selective attention.**    The tendency to filter out unwanted or un-needed information is known as **selective attention.** Once you have been exposed to a set of stimuli—say, a course in mathematics—you attend to these stimuli selectively as well. According to one estimate, college students spend only 12 percent of their classroom time actively listening to lectures. The other 88 percent of the time, they select other stimuli for their attention, erotic thoughts being the most common.

Presented with the vast array of sensory stimulation in any situation, a person selects some at the expense of others. Do you ever tune out what another person is saying? Even though you appear to be listening attentively, you are vigorously pursuing other activities, such as listening to your own thoughts or the conversation in the next room where someone has just mentioned your name.

*Sometimes perceptual organization limits our problem-solving ability.*

## Organization

In perception, the mental arrangement of objects into a recogniz-able pattern is called **organization.** Look at Figure 3-3. See if you can connect the nine dots using no more than four straight lines.

Does it appear to be impossible? A solution is possible, but you'll have to change your perception habits. When you look at the nine dots, your mind probably organizes them into a square, although no square actually exists on the page. As long as you try to work within the limits of the square, you will fail to find a solution. The key lies in extending your lines beyond the imaginary limitations of the square, as shown at the end of the chapter summary (see page 62).

Perceptual stimuli can be organized by using language to join in-dividual clues into total concepts, even if there is very little sensory data. For example, the aroma of a sizzling charbroiled steak can be quickly organized into the image of a backyard barbecue. This tendency to experience the world according to organizational categories can be misleading, however. For example, look carefully at Figure 3-4. What do you see?

**Figure 3-4**
The Old Hag/Young Woman

The drawing can be seen as either an old hag or a young woman. If you look long enough, you will see first one, then the other.

In 1935 a psychologist named Robert W. Leeper conducted an extraordinary experiment using the drawing in Figure 3-4. Leeper had the picture redrawn so that one version emphasized the young woman and the other emphasized the old hag. He exposed his subjects to either one or the other of these redrawn figures. Then, at a later time, he showed them the original, ambiguous drawing. In *100 percent* of the cases, subjects were locked into the image to which they had first been exposed. That is, even when looking at the ambiguous sketch, those who had been shown the version emphasizing the young woman could see only the young woman, and those who had seen the version with the old hag could see only the old hag.[2] This research suggests that people actively process information to conform to preexisting categories.

The categories into which stimuli are organized are based on language, beliefs, culture, and experience. Based on these categories, people direct their attention toward certain features and away from others. This means that in their perceptions of other persons and events, they may be missing important aspects. If, for example, one of your friends tells you that a certain professor is a crashing bore, research suggests that you will be much more likely to see that professor as boring. This

## Psychological Selection

| | Definition | Example |
|---|---|---|
| **Foreground/ Background Screening** | A selection process based on the relationships among objects and sounds in the environment | When you look at your hand, all else within your sight becomes background |
| **Expectation** | Your tendency to see what you anticipate seeing | The way your own name seems to jump out of a list of names |
| **Selective Exposure** | Your tendency to open yourself to some experiences and not to others | If you see yourself as very cautious you will probably not try skydiving |
| **Selective Attention** | Your tendency to filter out unwanted or unneeded information | When you daydream during a classroom lecture |

is not fair either to the professor or to you. The probability that you will enjoy the course has been reduced because your perceptions have been distorted by your tendency to see new things in expected ways.

In your perceptions, you never see the whole picture; but the need for consistency, or to have things make sense, leads you to mentally fill in the gaps so that things look complete. This is the principle on which television game shows like "Wheel of Fortune" are based. Phrases and sentences are revealed one letter at a time until a contestant mentally fills in the blanks and recognizes the winning answer.

The tendency to perceive complete wholes, even when some of the parts are missing, is known as the **closure principle.** If you saw a square in Figure 3-3, you experienced that principle. Now look at Figure 3-5.

If you see a circle and a famous brand name, look again—neither is actually present. The items in Figure 3-5 bear a strong enough resemblance to the expected forms so you think that you see them. This example leads to the fourth and final component in the perceptual process.

**Figure 3-5**
Closure

## Interpretation

Because people's perceptions are so subjective, their interpretations of the same phenomenon are likely to vary. In fact, even if two persons were to select and organize the same stimuli in the same way, there is still a high probability that their perceptions would differ. **Interpretation** is the assigning of meaning—either denotative or connotative—to perceptions. **Denotative meaning** is the level of meaning upon which all members of a language group can agree. For example, if two people smell a steak sizzling on a backyard barbecue, they will both identify the smell as *steak* and associate backyard barbecue with the smell. If one of them is a vegetarian, however, the *interpretations* of that perception will differ dramatically. What is pleasurable to the steak lover is revolting to the vegetarian. Likewise, we may tune in the same TV news program and see the face of the same presidential candidate, but if one of us is a liberal and the other a conservative, our interpretations of the event are likely to disagree, and may cause conflict. This individual, unique level of meaning is called **connotative meaning.**

Two people can look at
the same object, but
because they stand in
two different places, they
perceive it differently.
Because they have
different perceptions,
they have different
interpretations.

*Some meanings
are unique to the
individual.*

The interpretation of perceptions is based on an intricate mix of language, culture, selective exposure and attention, individual life experiences, the organization of those experiences, and individual beliefs, attitudes, and values. Based on this, you can see how two persons witnessing the same event may have drastically different experiences of that event.

By now you probably agree that perception is a complex process. To be an effective communicator, you must never assume that your way of looking at something is the only way. To do so is to ignore the fact that what you perceive is only a small, subjective part of what is actually going on. Once you understand that you are an active agent in the perception process, you can choose to broaden your perspective, to take others' points of view, and to improve your understanding of yourself and others. Figure 3-6 gives a visual summary of the components of perception discussed in this section.

**Figure 3-6**
Selection and Organization

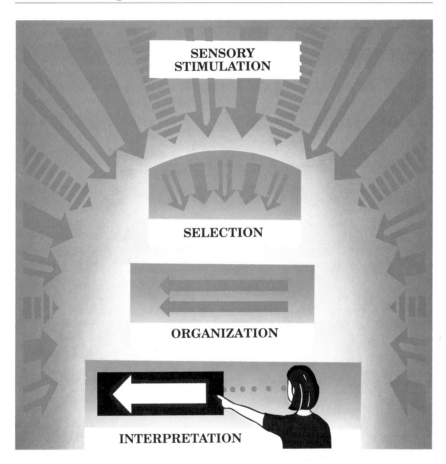

## BELIEFS, ATTITUDES, AND VALUES

Your beliefs, attitudes, and values are primary determinants of your perceptions and your behavior. Whatever you believe to be true is true *for you* simply because you believe it to be so. You act on the basis of your beliefs, attitudes, and values.

### Beliefs

A **belief** is a conviction that something is true. Whether a person believes in God, for example, will shape his or her experience about the death of a loved one. One person may see the loss as God's will, while another will see it as a tragic and senseless waste. Likewise, a belief about types of people—"nerds," for example—will affect a perception about individuals who fit that *stereotype*.

*Everyone relies on stereotypes, even if they are often inaccurate.*

A **stereotype** is a generalized grouping of people that overemphasizes presumed similarities and ignores individual differences. Everyone relies on stereotypes—of national or religious groups, of politicians, and of professors. The danger of stereotyping lies in the tendency to see a person in terms of a category rather than as a unique individual. The need for consistency drives people to look for those characteristics of an individual that conform to a stereotype. This can result in inaccurate perceptions, considerable unfairness, and miscommunication. A stereotype is a belief that can hinder the ability to perceive others accurately and to communicate with them appropriately.

## Attitudes

An **attitude** is a learned tendency to respond positively or negatively to a given stimulus. In some cases, attitudes are derived from experiences. Perhaps all it took was one taste for you to learn that you don't (or do) like anchovies on your pizza. Other attitudes are based on beliefs. Your political or religious beliefs, for example, often affect your attitudes toward those who hold different political or religious beliefs.

## Values

**Values** are judgments about the importance or worth of things. Your values reflect a hierarchy, or arrangement, of beliefs from most important to least important. When you have conflicting beliefs about a situation, your values help you decide how to behave. For example, the decision about going out with your friends or staying home and studying will be determined, in part, by your value system—by which activity is more important to you at the time.

Beliefs, attitudes, and values do not operate independently. They are interrelated and form a system that structures perceptions and determines behavior. Together, beliefs, attitudes, and values form a person's entire world view. Because they are interrelated, a change in one area may lead to changes throughout the system. For example, the stereotype (belief) you have of a particular group may be associated with a negative evaluation of that group (value), dislike (attitude), and avoidance (behavior). Yet when a member of that group becomes your best friend, your need for consistency among your beliefs, attitudes, values, and behaviors will require changes throughout.

*Review Box*

**Beliefs, Attitudes, and Values**

|  | *Definition* | *Example* |
|---|---|---|
| **Belief** | A conviction that something is true | To be successful you need a good education |
| **Attitude** | A learned tendency to respond positively or negatively to a given stimulus | I like going to school. |
| **Value** | A judgment about the importance or worth of something | An education is the most important gift that parents can give their children. |

Perception and language are integrally related. Without language, perception as we know it would not exist. Therefore it is important to look at the nature of language and how it can be used more accurately and effectively.

## THE POWER OF WORDS

Recall *speech communication* was defined earlier as a human process through which people make sense out of the world and share that sense with others. The basic tools used to do this are words. Thus it is important to realize just how powerful words are.

About forty-five years ago, Alfred Korzybski wrote a book called *Science and Sanity* in which he argued that the words people use (and misuse) have a strong effect on their behavior.[3] From Korzybski's writing grew the idea of **general semantics**—the study of the way language affects attitudes and behavior. A general semanticist believes that the inappropriate use of words creates serious problems as a result of the tremendous power that words have to affect attitudes and behavior.

The following discussion will be based primarily on the teachings of general semantics. First, it will examine how words can create and affect attitudes and behavior. Second, it will identify word barriers that hinder the communication process. And finally, there will be some suggestions for overcoming word barriers.

*Language is the primary tool of conceptual thought.*

In 1967, Joe McGinnis was hired to help elect Richard Nixon president of the United States. Based on his experiences, McGinnis wrote a book called *The Selling of the President 1968,* in which he described some of the behind-the-scenes problems with Nixon's quest for the presidency. In one passage McGinnis provided a good example of how words, or in this case, one word, could affect attitudes and behavior. He described a problem with one of Nixon's TV commercials that included a shot of a soldier wearing a helmet with the word *Love* written on it. Some of Nixon's advisers complained that the word had a very strong association with hippies and the antiwar movement—not the word a soldier should be wearing on his helmet—and wanted the picture taken out of the commercial. Others argued that only an extremely interesting young man would write *Love* on his helmet as he went into combat—a nice touch for the commercial. Then the group received a letter from the soldier's mother. "She told what a thrill it had been to see her son's picture in one of Mr. Nixon's commercials, and she asked if there were some way she might obtain a copy of the photograph. The letter was signed: Mrs. William Love."[4]

Words have the power to communicate beautiful images and great truths. Words can also create confusion and miscommunication. Specifically, words have the power both to create images and to affect attitudes and behavior.

### The Power to Create

*You think things into existence through language.*

To use language is to mentally call things into being. Words have the power to create the world. When something is given a name, it is created. For example, Sir Isaac Newton is credited with discovering gravity. Of course he did not really invent it: he named it; but he "created" the phenomenon known as *gravity* by giving it a name.

Words, then, help create the world by giving you the ability to call what you see and experience into existence. You probably don't remember when you were two years old and were learning to talk—to label your world. You were calling things into existence by giving names to people, objects, and places. Once your parents pointed to the TV screen and said, "This is Sesame Street," Big Bird, Grover, and the Cookie Monster came into existence for you. Since you had a word to describe him, you could call him into existence any time, just by saying, "Cookieeeeee."

### The Power to Affect Attitudes and Behavior

You're hungry. You have a couple of hours before your night class, so you decide to stop by a restaurant you've often passed but never tried. The hostess seats you and hands you a menu. You have your heart set on a thick, juicy steak, but, to your consternation, when you look at the menu, you see that the restaurant does not serve steak. Instead, it serves horse meat. You decide that you're not that hungry after all and you leave.

Why did you abruptly decide to leave the restaurant? Could it be because you saw the words *horse meat?* Would you have felt the same way if the menu listed steak and roast beef (cow meat) or pork chops (pig meat)?

In the late 1960s a sociology professor in Los Angeles decided to conduct an experiment to test the assumption that words have the power to affect behavior.[5] He selected two groups of students to participate in his research. In order to participate in the study, students had to have a car, have good driving records, and drive approximately the same distances each week. One group of students was told to drive normally and go about their business; the other group of students was given large orange and black bumper stickers with the words *Black Panthers*—the name of a radical political group—on them in large letters. This second group of students was also told to go about their business as they usually would.

It didn't take many days for a clear pattern to emerge. Those students who had "Black Panthers" bumper stickers were being issued traffic tickets at an alarming rate. At the end of the study, only seventeen days later, this group of fifteen students with good driving records had received thirty-three traffic citations! The obvious conclusion of the research was that words do affect behavior. The children's verse "Sticks and stones can break my bones, but names can never hurt me" was not supported by this study.

*The associations you have with certain words can dramatically affect your behavior.*

## WORD BARRIERS

Clearly, words have the power to create images and affect attitudes and behavior. It is precisely because of this power that words can become barriers to effective and accurate communication.

### Barrier 1: Bypassing

**Bypassing** occurs when the same word is interpreted to mean two different things. "Meet me at the circle drive after school," you tell your friend. After your classes you wait at the circle drive for your rendezvous. When thirty minutes pass without a sign of your friend, you leave, mumbling angrily to yourself. Where was your friend? She was dutifully waiting at the circle drive too—the circle drive on the north side of campus while you were waiting at the circle drive on the south side. Your meanings for the words *circle drive* bypassed each other.

One researcher estimated that the 500 most used words in the English language have more than 14,000 different dictionary definitions. The word *run*, for example, can have more than 800 different meanings! Given each individual's different perceptions and experiences, it should come as no surprise that bypassing is a common occurrence.

*Misunderstanding often occurs because people assign different meanings to the same word.*

## Barrier 2: Polarization

In the early movies about the Old West, you could always tell the "good guys" from the "bad guys" by the color of their hats; heroes wore white, villains black. Unfortunately, life is not that simple. **Polarization** occurs when something is described in terms of its extremes—good or bad, beautiful or ugly, hot or cold, positive or negative, black or white. There is no middle ground. The danger is that once something is pronounced good or bad, the midway position, where most realities lie, is ignored. Consequently, accurate perception and communication become increasingly difficult.

*It is inaccurate to see the world in black and white terms.*

## Barrier 3: Allness

In some ways, it would be very convenient to develop simple generalizations to describe the world. An *allness statement* is a simple, but untrue, generalization. You've probably heard such allness statements as "Women are smarter than men," "Men can run faster than women," and "Football players are stupid." An allness statement implies that everything is known about a subject and denies the variations that exist among individuals. These generalizations are convenient, but they simply aren't accurate. Nonetheless, as a result of language's power to create, when people use such sweeping generalizations, they begin to believe them. They judge, or prejudge, what they experience.

## Barrier 4: Static Evaluation

A **static evaluation** is a statement that fails to recognize change. Absence of change is a perceptual illusion. For example, since you started reading this chapter you have changed. You are older now. You may be more tired than when you began. Your hair has grown and so have your fingernails. Granted, you have not changed so much that you (or anyone else) would notice, but that's the point. Everything in the world is changing constantly, even though the changes may be gradual and hard to notice. The labels you use, however, do not always reflect or acknowledge that change. Once again, because you tend to

Can you tell who the good guy is in this picture? How do you know? Could it have anything to do with the color of the horse and the color of the hat?

believe what you say, the failure of your words to reflect change, or the possibility of change, can be a barrier to communication.

If you've ever used an old road map for a vacation trip, you know some of the problems it can cause. New highways are not shown, and old roads that are shown may be closed. Because you believe what you see on your map, you may waste time, get lost, or hit a dead end. Your map does not reflect the current reality. This situation is similar to what happens when words do not accurately reflect the changes that have occurred in people and the world. One common example of static evaluation as a barrier to communication is parents' tendency to see their sons and daughters as children, even after they have reached adulthood. The old language of the parent-child relationship is often difficult to shed. The tendency is to regress to conform to the old patterns ("Pick up your room; it's a mess." "Be home by midnight.") rather than to find new terms to describe an ever-changing, evolving relationship.

*Sometimes language doesn't keep pace with reality.*

## Barrier 5: Fact-Inference Confusion

What's a fact? Most people say that a *fact* is something that has been proven; or a *fact* is something that everyone agrees is true. Then the question arises, How has it been proven? At one time it was thought to be a "proven fact" that the world was flat. Did that make it a fact?

No, not necessarily. Perhaps a better, though not perfect, definition is that a *fact* is something you observe to be true. If you haven't observed it, you can't state with certainty that something is, or is not, a fact. You cannot say, for example, that the house on the hill is blue until you have walked all the way around it. The fact that the surfaces facing you are blue does not necessarily mean that the whole house is blue. Of course, as we stated earlier in the chapter, beliefs and perceptions play a large part in determining what you observe to be true. In a court of law, the judge and jury are interested primarily in facts in the form of eyewitness testimony.

While statements of fact can be made only after direct observation, inferences can be made before, during, or after an occurrence, and no observation is necessary. The key distinction is that a statement of inference can speculate about and interpret what a person *thinks* occurred. **Fact-inference confusion** occurs when a person responds to something as if it were something that person has observed, when, in reality, it is merely a conclusion the person has drawn.

Suppose you heard someone comment, "It's a fact that men are better than women at solving mathematical problems." If this statement were indeed a fact, it would mean that *all* men and women were tested and that the results indicated that men were superior to women in solving mathematical problems. The statement is, in reality, an inference. If the speaker is summarizing research that has attempted to investigate the issue, rather than saying, "It's a fact that . . . ," it would be more appropriate to say, "Some studies have found that . . . ." The second statement more accurately describes reality than does the claim that these differences are a "fact." Confusing fact for inference can lead to inaccuracy and misunderstanding.

## OVERCOMING WORD BARRIERS

Thus far we have focused on the problems words create. Meaning can *bypass* someone because that person is not sure what another person is referring to. *Polarization* can result from looking at the world in absolute terms—black or white, good or bad—and failing to consider the middle ground. *Allness* creates problems when the choice of language implies "all knowingness." *Static evaluations* can result in insensitivity to the ways in which the world is constantly changing. Finally, *fact-inference confusion* can arise when people mistake a conclusion for an observation. Because words have the power to create and the power to affect attitudes and behavior, word barriers will always exist. There are, however, ways to overcome these barriers. The following are some suggestions for coping with problems that occur when people use words inappropriately.

## Avoid Fixed Interpretations

In coping with word barriers, the challenge is to avoid responding to something as if it had a fixed meaning. Don't treat words as if they have only one interpretation. Before responding to what someone is saying, determine whether you are responding out of habit or have tried to understand what the person really means. Remember that polarization and allness stem from a failure to see the many perspectives in which anything may be viewed and the many shades of meaning that may result.

## Take Change into Account

Word barriers such as static evaluation occur when people fail to realize that the world is changing constantly. If they remind themselves that, as a result of change, a word or label may not always reflect a personal meaning for a concept, they can avoid many misunderstandings.

## Try to Clarify Fact-Inference Confusion

You often make the mistake of acting on information as if it were a fact rather than an inference. If you make the effort to determine whether you are responding to a fact or an inference, you will be in a better position to evaluate the conclusion you reach.

For example, imagine that you are a detective investigating two deaths. You are given the following information: (1) Tom and Mary are lying together on the floor; (2) Tom and Mary are dead; (3) they are surrounded by water and broken glass; (4) on the sofa near Tom and Mary is a cat with his back arched, apparently ready to defend himself. Given these sketchy details, do you, the detective assigned to the case, have any hypotheses about the cause of Tom's and Mary's deaths? Perhaps they slipped on the water, crashed into a table, broke a vase, and died (that would explain the water and the broken glass). Or maybe their attacker left the scene recently, and the cat is disturbed by the commotion? Clearly, several inferences can be made about the probable cause of death. Oh, yes, there is one detail we forgot to mention: Tom and Mary are fish. Does that help?

Perhaps you responded to the names Tom and Mary as if they were people, not fish. If so, you made an inference based on previous—although, obviously not applicable—experience.

People need to make inferences. Without them it would be difficult to make any decisions in life. The problem occurs when people respond to words and information as if they were facts, and not inferences. They then create communication problems that are difficult to correct.

*Awareness and avoidance of the ways to misuse language can improve communication.*

*Review Box*

## A Summary of Word Barriers and Their Solutions

| Barrier | Description | Solution |
|---|---|---|
| *Bypassing* | Interpretation of the same word to mean two different things | Use specific language; be aware of multiple interpretations of what you say; clarify. |
| *Polarization* | Description in terms of extremes—good or bad, black or white | Remember that few issues are simple questions of good or bad, right or wrong, positive or negative; most of reality is found on the middle ground. |
| *Allness Statements* | Simple but untrue generalizations | Don't overgeneralize; remember that all individuals are unique. |
| *Static Evaluation* | Statement that fails to recognize that everything is in process | Take change into account; remember that everything is always changing. |
| *Fact-Inference Confusion* | Mistaking a conclusion for an observation | Clarify and analyze; learn to recognize the difference between fact and inference and to communicate the difference clearly. |

## Realize That Meanings Are in People, Not in Words

This last suggestion summarizes the other three. Words don't have meanings; people assign words meanings. (If you can keep this in mind, you can save yourself several problems that result from word barriers.) Each individual assigns meaning to a word based on his or her culture, education, and experience. The person assigns meaning to a word or a phrase as that person tries to understand what another person is doing or saying. A message is never really *sent;* in reality it is *created* in the mind of the receiver. Meaning is *assigned,* not transported between speaker and listener. The meaning of the words is in a person, not in the words and phrases that person receives from others.

## SUMMARY

All human communication is based on perception. *Perception* is a complex process that is often the source of misunderstanding and conflict. This chapter discussed the process of perception, its relation to communication, and some suggestions for improving your perceptual and communication skills.

▶**Define** *perception.*

Perception is the process by which people select, organize, and interpret sensory stimulation into a meaningful picture of the world.

▶**Explain four components of the perception process.**

All perception begins with stimulation of the senses. From this sensory data certain stimuli are selected—physiologically and psychologically. Psychological selection includes the processes of foreground/background screening, expectation, selective exposure, and selective attention. The selected stimuli are then mentally organized, usually by using language to join individual clues into total concepts. The final step in the process is interpretation—the assigning of meaning to a stimulus. Meaning occurs at two levels—denotative and connotative. *Denotative meaning* is the level of meaning at which all members of a language group agree. *Connotative meaning* is the individual, unique level of meaning. Because people's perceptions are so subjective, their interpretations of the same phenomena are likely to vary.

▶**Differentiate among beliefs, attitudes, and values, and discuss their relationship to human perception.**

*Beliefs* are convictions that something is true. *Attitudes* are learned tendencies to respond positively or negatively to given stimuli. Values are judgments about the relative importance of things. Our beliefs, attitudes, and values form an interrelated system that structures our perceptions and determines our behavior. Because our beliefs, attitudes, and values form our entire world view, they direct our attention toward certain features of reality and away from others.

▶**Describe how language is related to perception.**

Words are the tools of thought. You can think conceptually only about those things for which you have words. You cannot call to mind a hippopotamus without the word *hippopotamus*. Thus, your perceptions are shaped and directed by your vocabulary.

▶**Show how words have the power to create and affect attitudes and behaviors.**

Insofar as words are the shapers of thought and behavior, they are the most powerful of creative tools. The words "We the people . . . " precede a document that has shaped the thinking and the history of our nation. The language you use to describe the world to your children will shape their beliefs, attitudes, and values. For example, calling a police officer "pig," "fuzz," or "flatfoot" can encourage a child to form negative attitudes toward these public servants. Through language you perpetuate prejudices, solve problems, wage war, and make peace.

▶**Identify five word barriers that lead to inaccuracies in perception and communication.**

Bypassing arises when the same word is used to mean two different things. Polarization occurs when something is described in terms of extremes, such as good or bad, beautiful or ugly, positive or negative. An Allness statement is a simple, but untrue, generalization, such as "Women are more sensitive than men." Static evaluation is a statement that fails to recognize everything is in process. Fact-inference confusion occurs when you respond to something as if it were observed when, in reality, it is merely a conclusion.

▶**Suggest some ways of overcoming word barriers to effective communication.**

The surest ways of overcoming word barriers are to (1) avoid fixed interpretations, (2) take change into account, (3) try to clarify fact-inference confusion, and (4) remember that meanings are in people, not in words.

Solution to puzzle in Figure 3-3:

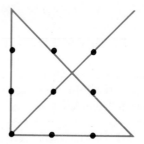

## KEY TERMS

**allness statement:**  a simple but untrue generalization.

**attitude:**  a learned tendency to respond positively or negatively to a given stimulus.

**belief:**  the conviction that something is true.

**bypassing:**  a barrier to communication that arises when the same word is interpreted to mean different things.

**closure principle:**  the tendency to perceive complete wholes, even when some of the parts are missing.

**connotative meaning:**  the individual, unique level of meaning.

**denotative meaning:**  the level of meaning at which all members of a language group agree.

**expectation:**  in perception, the tendency to see what is anticipated.

**fact-inference confusion:**  a barrier to communication that occurs by responding to something as if it were observed when, in reality, it was merely a conclusion.

**foreground/background screening:**  a selection process based on the relationships among objects and sounds in the environment.

**general semantics:**  the study of how language affects attitudes and behavior.

**interpretation:**  the assigning of meaning to perceptions.

**organization:**  the mental arrangement of objects into a recognizable pattern.

**perception:**  the process by which people select, organize, and interpret sensory stimulation into a meaningful picture of the world.

**physiological selection:**  the filtering of stimuli that stems from the natural limitations of the sensory organs.

**polarization:**  barrier to communication that occurs when something is described in terms of extremes, such as good or bad, beautiful or ugly, positive or negative.

**psychological selection:**  a perceptual screening process based on beliefs and selective attention.

**selective attention:**  the tendency to filter out unwanted or unneeded information.

**selective exposure:**  the tendency to be open to some experiences and not to others.

**sensory stimulation:**  the nervous system's response to the environment.

**static evaluation:**  a statement failing to recognize that everything is in process.

**stereotype:**  a generalized grouping of people that overemphasizes presumed similarities and ignores individual differences.

**value:**  a judgment about the relative importance of something.

## DISCUSSION QUESTIONS

1. In English the word *love* is used to mean many things. How many different meanings for *love* can you think of? In Thai there are 26 phrases that translate as *I love you*. How might speaking a different language affect your perceptions?

2. What were your expectations for the course you are taking now? How closely has the course conformed to those expectations? Can you see ways in which your expectations shaped your perceptions?

3. Discuss the characteristics you associate with the following stereotypes:
   football player
   born-again Christian
   Republican
   surfer
   politician
   professor
   musician
   beautician
   How reliable are these stereotypes in predicting behavior? Can you cite examples where one or more of these stereotypes has failed? What stereotypes describe YOU? Are they accurate? Have you ever been treated unfairly because of a stereotype?

## SUGGESTED ACTIVITIES

1. List three beliefs, three attitudes, and three values you have concerning a college education. What are the sources of these? How are they related to one another and to your behavior?

2. Write a brief essay describing perception and language usage as creative acts. Include personal experiences to illustrate differences in several individuals' perceiving and talking about the same event or object. What influences can you identify which may have contributed to these individual differences in perception and language usage? How might these differences be overcome?

3. *Bypassing* occurs when different meanings are assigned to the same words. Read aloud the following phrases:
   light house keeper
   verticle blind man
   eat here get gas

How many interpretations of these phrases can you identify? What are the differences?

**4.** Look at the following ink blot projective test pattern. What do you see? How many objects can you visualize from this pattern? What conclusions can you reach about the processes of selection, organization, and interpretation as you view the pattern?

## SUGGESTED READINGS

Ellis, A. and Beattie, G. (1986). *The Psychology of Language and Communication.* (New York: The Guilford Press).

Hastorf, A., Schneider, D. and Polefka, J. (1970). *Person Perception.* (Reading, MA: Addison-Wesley).

Lilly, J. (1972). *The Center of the Cyclone.* (New York: Julian Press).

Prideaux, Gary (1985). *Psycholinguistics: the Experimental Study of Language.* (New York: The Guilford Press).

Watzlawick, P. (1976). *How Real is Real?* (New York: Vintage Books).

# 4 Understanding Nonverbal Communication

*After studying this chapter, you should be able to:*

▶ Define *nonverbal communication.*

▶ Cite three important reasons for studying nonverbal communication.

▶ Identify eight sources of nonverbal communication and indicate the kinds of information each conveys.

▶ Specify six ways in which nonverbal communication functions with verbal communication to create meaning.

▶ Discuss the three dimensions that are commonly used to assign meaning to nonverbal behavior.

▶ Employ five key principles to improve your understanding of nonverbal messages.

Have you ever used your spare time at a shopping center or an airport to do some "people watching"? Whether you are only casually observing from a distance or are formally introduced, you make judgments about other people's status or personality from your observation of their appearances, the way they walk, or the sounds of their voices. Some researchers claim that in as little as three to five seconds after meeting someone for the first time, you begin to form an impression. Others claim that the first four minutes are critical to the impression-formation process. Of course, many of your first impressions of others may be wrong, but you make the inferences just the same.

First impressions are based not on detailed conversation, but on nonverbal communication. **Nonverbal communication** is communication behavior other than written or spoken language that creates meaning for someone. This includes body posture and movement, eye contact, facial expressions, vocal cues, use of personal space and territory, personal appearance, and the communication environment. This chapter will examine ways in which nonverbal communication influences your communication with others. Such information should help you to better monitor your own nonverbal cues and interpret the nonverbal behavior of others.

*Nonverbal communication is communication behavior other than written or spoken language that creates meaning for someone.*

## WHY LEARN ABOUT NONVERBAL COMMUNICATION?

When you read advice about the best way to prepare for a job interview, the importance of presenting a neat appearance is usually near the top of the list. Speaking loudly enough to be heard, maintaining good eye contact with the interviewer, and dressing on the conservative side are also typically mentioned. In interviewing, as in public speaking, your eye contact, posture, and vocal cues strongly influence the way your audience responds to you and your message.

If you were taking a tour of the offices of a large organization, even without being told, you could probably identify the individuals who had greater power and status in the company. Undoubtedly their offices would be larger than average, be more expensively decorated, have more windows, and be located in the corners of the work area with at least one, and possibly several, secretaries' desks situated in front.

As these examples show, nonverbal cues are extremely informative. Your employability, your success as speaker, and your skill in office politics all depend on your awareness of nonverbal cues. In fact, there are at least three reasons for studying nonverbal communication. First, nonverbal communication plays a key role in your overall communication with others. Second, nonverbal communication is the primary way in which you communicate your feelings and attitudes toward others. And third, nonverbal messages are usually more believable than verbal messages. Let's consider each of these reasons in greater detail.

### Nonverbal communication plays a key role in your overall communication with others.

It has been estimated that you rely on nonverbal cues for as much as 65 percent of your message's social meaning. This means that, in many situations, you spend more time communicating nonverbally than you do verbally. Most communication teachers agree with the statement, "You cannot *not* communicate."

Can you think of a time when you are not potentially communicating something to someone? Even when you are asleep, others make inferences about your need for rest. Your facial expression, appearance, clothing, and establishment or lack of eye contact all contribute to others' perceptions of you. Even when you do not intend to communicate, others will pick up and interpret nonverbal signals from you.

### Nonverbal communication is the primary way in which you communicate feelings and attitudes toward others.

You can often detect another person's feelings of frustration, anger, resentment, or anxiety before such feelings are verbalized. In many cases, if an employer is upset with something an employee has said or done, the employee knows he or she is in the doghouse before any words are spoken. This occurs because as little as 7 percent of the emotional impact of a message is communicated by the words.[1] About 38 percent of the emotional meaning is communicated by vocal expression and about 55 percent by facial expression. Therefore, approximately 93 percent of emotional meanings are communicated nonverbally. Even though some people question whether this formula can be applied to all communication settings, evidence suggests that nonverbal cues provide important information about interpersonal relationships and the communication of feelings and emotions.

### Nonverbal messages are usually more believable than verbal messages.

"Are you listening to me?" asks a mother as she tries to get her son's attention so that she can explain his household chores for the weekend.

"Yes, Mother," the son replies, his eyes intent on a "Star Trek" rerun. The mother is probably not convinced that her son is really tuning her in. The reason is that nonverbal cues are so important to the communication process that when the nonverbal behavior contradicts the words, listeners believe the nonverbal message.

Just how do nonverbal messages betray verbal messages? When attempting to deceive another, you may speak with a higher voice pitch, slower rate, and more pronunciation mistakes than normal. Your face, hands, and feet are also important sources of information when you are trying to hide the true meaning of the message you wish to communicate. Did you know that the pupils of your eyes dilate when you become emotionally aroused? Blushing, sweating, and changing breathing patterns also may betray your intended meaning.

## SOURCES OF NONVERBAL INFORMATION

You send and receive messages through movement, gestures, eye contact, voice, facial expressions, use of the space around you, touch, personal appearance, and even the appearance of your environment. Each of these is a source of nonverbal information—a specific form of nonverbal behavior that can be identified and studied in a systematic way. Based on these sources, you make assumptions about others and others make assumptions about you.

### Movement and Gestures

The phrase "body language" has been used as the title for books, speeches, and seminars. Perhaps you have seen the cover of Julius Fast's best-selling book, *Body Language*. It features a female model wearing a miniskirt, her legs crossed at the knee. She has a Mona Lisa smile and a cigarette dangling between two fingers of her right hand. The caption on the book cover reads, "Is she lonely? Is she a phony? Does her body say that she is a manipulator?" The implication is that these questions will be answered by "reading" the model's body language. Not so. Even though popular advice books and magazine articles suggest that you can "read someone like a book," the current state of nonverbal communication research does not permit you to make conclusive statements about people's personalities or likes and dislikes just by watching their movements and gestures.

While no clear dictionary of nonverbal communication exists, one team of researchers has developed a classification system to describe thousands of movements and gestures.[2] Depending on its use, a body movement or gesture may be classified as an emblem, an illustrator, an affect display, a regulator, or an adaptor.

**Emblems.**   An **emblem** is a movement that acts as a substitute for oral communication. A shrug of the shoulders to communicate, "I don't know," a thumb and index finger forming a circle to communicate that things are OK, or the wave of an arm to signal hello are examples of nonverbal emblems. By using an emblem you can communicate a clear message without saying a word.

**Illustrators.**   An **illustrator** is a nonverbal behavior used to add meaning to an accompanying verbal message. An illustrator may contradict, accent, complement, or regulate verbal statements. When your football team scores a touchdown and you stand up and clap your hands while yelling "Way to go," your standing and clapping are nonverbal illustrators that reinforce your verbal cheer.

**Affect displays.**   An **affect display** is a nonverbal cue that communicates emotions. Facial expressions and tone of voice play key roles in communicating how you feel about something. While your posture and gestures usually do not portray a specific emotion, they often provide cues about the intensity of your feelings. If you are sad, for example, your face expresses your unhappiness while your slumped shoulders and lowered head provide cues about the intensity of your grief.

**Regulators.**   A **regulator** is a nonverbal cue that helps control the flow of communication between you and other people. Eye contact with slightly raised eyebrows, an open mouth, and a raised index finger often signal your interest in someone's comment and a desire to say something yourself. A slight forward lean indicates a desire to be a part of a conversation.

**Adaptors.**   An **adaptor** is a nonverbal behavior that helps to satisfy a personal need and adapt to the immediate surroundings. You are usually not aware of your nonverbal adaptors. They include such behaviors as scratching, touching yourself, fanning yourself to keep cool, adjusting your glasses, and fixing your hair. When people become nervous and anxious, they often increase their number of adaptive behaviors.

These five ways of categorizing nonverbal communication can add interest to your "people watching" and vastly increase your understand-

You can probably tell a great deal about this event just by looking at the picture. The nonverbal communication is very clear.

ing of communication. By becoming aware of your own use of emblems, you can begin to recognize how unspoken cues affect your relationships with others. By keying in on nonverbal illustrators, you can see how nonverbal behaviors add further meaning to spoken messages. By observing affect displays, you can become more sensitive to the emotional climate of relationships. By noticing nonverbal regulators, you can become more aware of people who want to participate in a conversation. By tuning in to adaptors, you can gain clues about how anxious or irritated another person is becoming even though he or she may not verbalize such anxiety.

Body movement and gestures can often be indicators of other people's status, leadership, liking, affection, interest, and warmth. For example, interest or liking is often communicated by leaning toward someone rather than away. A person who smiles, makes eye contact, rarely fidgets, and avoids unnecessary hand movement will usually be seen as warm and friendly. In contrast, someone who avoids eye contact, rarely smiles, often fidgets, and orients his or her body away from another person is more likely to be seen as cold and aloof.

*Movement and gestures help in drawing conclusions about status, leadership, liking, affection, interest, and warmth.*

During a job interview or public speech, your nonverbal cues play a key role in determining your *credibility*—how knowledgeable, trustworthy, and dynamic you appear to be. If you are credible, you are believable. Try to avoid hand-to-face gestures, fidgeting, repeatedly tugging at your clothing, finger tapping, and gestures that seem tentative and weak. A rigid body position, crossed arms and legs, and arms and hands kept close to the body all tend to communicate that you are uncomfortable and tense. To communicate a more positive personal image, your posture and movements need to appear relaxed and spontaneous.

Rapport in a job interview can be established, in part, by leaning forward and smiling (when appropriate) as you begin to answer a question. When you are attempting to persuade someone, don't be surprised to find yourself using more gestures to emphasize key ideas, nodding your head more, and showing a more animated facial expression.[3]

No one can prescribe a precise set of movements and gestures that will get you the perfect job, make you a wonderful public speaker, and ensure that you win friends and influence people. You can monitor your posture and movements, however, so they do not distract from the message you want to communicate.

## Eye Contact

One of the most subtle yet important sources of nonverbal information is eye contact. Whether someone looks directly at you or avoids your gaze strongly affects the relationship you establish. Eye contact serves four key functions in your interactions with others.[4] First, it serves a **cognitive function** because it provides clues to a person's thought processes. For example, when your instructor asks you a question, you probably break eye contact as you try to think of an answer.

A second eye contact function is **monitoring**. You monitor others (look at them) when you are seeking feedback, when you want to know how they are responding to you. In public speaking you look at your audience to determine whether you still have their attention. If you are developing a creative excuse for being late for a date, you monitor your partner to see if your story is being accepted.

*Eye contact signals whether the communication channel is open or closed.*

A third function of eye contact is to **regulate** the back-and-forth flow of your communication with others and signal whether communication channels are open or closed. For example, when you want to get served at a restaurant, you try to get the waiter's attention through eye contact. In contrast, if you see someone coming down the sidewalk with whom you'd rather not talk, you will probably try to avoid making eye contact.

*Review Box*

## Body Movements and Gestures

| Category | Description | Example |
|---|---|---|
| Emblems | Movements and gestures that replace spoken messages | Making a circle out of your thumb and index finger to signal OK |
| Illustrators | Movements and gestures that add meaning to an accompanying verbal message | Describing how large an object is by holding your hand at your chest while saying, "It was this high." |
| Affect Displays | Expressions of feeling and emotion | Smiling, frowning |
| Regulators | Behaviors that control the flow of communication between people | Raising your hand in class when you want to be called upon |
| Adaptors | Movements that help you feel comfortable and adapt to your surroundings | Scratching, fanning yourself, adjusting your glasses |

Finally eye contact serves an **expressive** function. The area of your face around your eyes provides quite a bit of information about the emotions you are experiencing. Although the look in your eyes may not change, your eyelids and lower brow reveal significant information about your feelings.

Eye contact plays an important role in the way others perceive you. Researchers have found that you communicate a more positive impression if you look at others while you are talking to them. You should also look at others while they are talking to you to communicate your interest in their messages. Excessive blinking, shifty eyes, and looking down before answering a question all contribute to negative impressions.

## Vocal Cues

Voice plays a key role in communicating feelings. When you ask, "How was your biology class today?" and your friend responds by saying

"Oh, great" with a sigh of frustration, you probably get the message that the lecture was less than stimulating. As noted, as much as 38 percent of a message's emotional meaning is expressed through vocal cues.

*Vocal cues are conveyed by rate of speech and quality, volume, and pitch of voice.*

Vocal cues are conveyed by the speed with which you speak (rate); whether your voice is raspy, harsh, or rich in tone (quality); how loudly you speak (volume); and whether your voice is high or deep (pitch). Based on these factors, you often make inferences about a person's emotional state, personality, and physical appearance. While you can usually do a good job of determining how someone is feeling based on vocal cues, you are typically not very accurate in assessing a person's personality or physical characteristics on the same bases. Have you ever formed a mental picture of a blind date based on a telephone conversation, only to discover at your first meeting that your expectations were totally off-base? This occurs because you tend to stereotype others by sound of voice even though it frequently leads to inaccurate judgments.

A communicator's vocal cues frequently influence a listener's perception of his or her credibility, status, and power. Most TV news anchors' careers are based on their ability to project a credible image. To communicate a credible image, they usually speak with a conversational voice quality at a moderate rate with varied pitch. Individuals who use such a speaking style are viewed as more pleasant, likeable, and friendly than those with other speaking styles. Deliberately pausing before key points also makes speakers seem more competent and increases the likelihood that listeners will remember those points.

There are several vocal characteristics to avoid. Not clearly pronouncing your words is apt to undermine a listener's perception of your competence, as are nonfluencies such as "ah," incomplete words, and incomplete sentences. Even though well-timed pauses can have a positive impact on your communication, lengthy pauses may provoke questions about your competence and may make you seem indecisive. When you speak, breathe from your diaphragm; these are the muscles supporting your lungs. A flat or weak quality often stems from shallow breathing that lacks support from the diaphragm.

## Facial Expressions

As your sister opens the birthday present you've given her, you eagerly await her reaction. As the personnel counselor reads your résumé, you watch for clues to her thoughts. In both of these situations facial expressions provide key information about another person's feel-

| Review Box | |
|---|---|

**Functions of Eye Contact**

| | |
|---|---|
| Cognitive Function | Provides information about thinking and thought processes |
| Monitoring Function | Provides feedback about the way others are responding to us |
| Regulatory Function | Signals whether we want to talk to someone |
| Expressive Function | Provides information about feelings and attitudes |

ings and attitudes. In fact, the face is the most important single source of information about emotions. Consequently, it is usually the first place to look for another person's reaction. Although the face is capable of producing over 250,000 different expressions, the six primary emotions it displays are happiness, anger, surprise, sadness, disgust, and fear.

While the entire face must be observed to arrive at an accurate interpretation, certain areas are more important than others in communicating specific emotions.[5] Happiness, for example, is communicated in the area around the eyes and with a smile and raised cheeks. Disgust is displayed with a curled upper lip, wrinkled nose, lowered eyelids, and slightly lowered brow. The eyes are the most important area for communicating fear, although an open mouth is also an indicator. Anger is expressed with raised eyebrows, open eyes, and sometimes an open mouth. Sadness is displayed around the eyes and mouth. Armed with this information, you can enhance your skill in observing and identifying the emotional expressions of others. You can increase your ability to accurately assess and appropriately respond to the emotional climate of a relationship.

Body movement and posture add meaning to facial cues. While the face communicates a specific emotion, body posture and movement express the intensity or strength of that emotion. Someone who has just won a new car on a TV game show communicates happiness with a big smile and sparkling eyes; she demonstrates the intensity of her joy by jumping up and down, hugging the M. C., and waving her arms in delight.

*The six primary emotions communicated on the face are happiness, anger, surprise, sadness, disgust, and fear.*

**Figure 4-1**
Hall's Four Zones of Space

## Space and Territory

An individual's use of space provides important information about power, status, and intimacy. Edward Hall has developed a classification system that identifies four commonly used zones of space.[6] As shown in Figure 4-1, **intimate space** is the area within 0 to 1½ feet of an individual, where the most intimate personal communication, such as touching, hugging, and stroking occurs. You move closer to people you like and away from people you do not like. Unless you are in a situation of forced intimacy, such as in an elevator or a crowd of people, you permit only individuals with whom you are interpersonally close to come within this intimate zone of space.

The second zone, **personal space**, extends from 1½ feet to 4 feet from an individual. Conversation with family and friends, whether at home or at social gatherings, takes place in this zone. An individual who moves from a personal zone into a more intimate zone may make someone feel uncomfortable unless that person feels some interpersonal closeness with the other individual.

The third zone, **social space**, spans the distance from 4 to 12 feet. Most communication for business purposes takes place within this range. Such conversation is less personal and tends to relate to specific job-based tasks. The communication in this zone is more formal than it is in the two previous zones.

The fourth zone, **public space**, covers all territory more than 12 feet beyond an individual. In this zone the communication is even more formal and intentional, as when a public speaker addresses an audience or a teacher speaks to a class. Interpersonal communication is not likely to occur in this zone.

An individual's use of space depends on a variety of factors, such as (1) outgoingness of personality, (2) degree of liking or affection for other participants, (3) nature of the communication or task, (4) cultural background, (5) physical environment, and (6) status. For example, you stand closer to friends than you do to enemies, strangers, or individuals with high status. You also tend to stand closer to people in large rooms than you do in small rooms. Large people usually have more space around them; and most women can usually tolerate less space around them than can most men.

A fascinating place to observe how people use personal space is in a small group. The way in which people arrange themselves in such a situation can provide insights into leadership, status, and patterns of interaction.[7] For example, when group members are seated in a circle, they are more likely to talk to the person across from them than to the person on either side. This occurs because they have more eye contact with the person seated across from them. More dominant group members tend to select a seat at the head of a rectangular table or a seat that will maximize their opportunity to communicate with others. In addition, people who sit in the corner seats at a rectangular table generally contribute the least amount of information to a discussion. If you find yourself in a position to prepare the seating arrangement for a group discussion or conference, armed with this information, you should be able to make more informed choices about who should sit where and the probable effects of your decisions on communication.

Related to the use of space is your tendency to stake out and lay claim to the territory around you. You often do this to indicate that a specific area belongs to you. For example, if you are studying in the library and you need to leave your table to look up a reference, you

*The use of the space around a person communicates information about power, status, and intimacy.*

Even in a non-structured environment, people instinctively observe the zones of space. Notice how the audience members here have arranged themselves at an equal distance around the speaker

will probably spread out books or papers to communicate to others that the space is yours and that you intend to return. In some families everyone knows that no one sits in Dad's chair; like a reserved parking space, it is saved exclusively for him.

When your territory is threatened with invasion, you often try to defend it. While standing in a supermarket checkout line, you may put your hands on your hips to nonverbally signal others to keep their distance; or you may strategically position your shopping cart to mark your territory and protect it from line crashers.

## Environment

*The environment affects the way people respond to one another.*

The environment affects the way people interact. To examine this conclusion, two researchers "decorated" three rooms.[8] One room was refurbished to look ugly. It resembled a drab, cluttered janitor's storeroom and was described as "horrible" and "repulsive" by observers assigned to examine it. The second room was intended to look average. The third room was designed to be beautiful. It was adorned with carpeting, drapes, tasteful furniture, and stylish decorations. Individuals were then asked to sit in one of the three rooms and rate several pictures of people's faces. The results indicated that the environment had a significant effect on the way people rated the faces. Subjects in the beautiful room gave the pictures higher ratings than did subjects in the ugly room. In addition, subjects in the ugly room found the task more unpleasant and monotonous than did subjects in the beautiful room. Subjects assigned to the ugly room attempted to leave sooner than did subjects assigned to the beautiful room. The conclusion of the study has important implications for you: your environment may positively or negatively influence your response to others.

Color is one environmental factor that can affect your mood and even your ability to concentrate. One researcher concluded that the most pleasant colors, listed in order of preference, were blue, green, purple, red, and yellow.[9] The colors listed from most to least arousing were red, orange, yellow, violet, blue, and green. Isn't it interesting that the color schemes of most fast-food restaurants are designed to arouse you? McDonald's familiar red and yellow arch, Burger King's red and orange hamburger logo, and Wendy's red signs are all designed to encourage your appetite.

Lighting also affects behavior. Elegant restaurants with dim lighting create a mood of intimacy that encourages conversation. The bright lights of an office or classroom, on the other hand, arouse and stimulate thinking.

Room decor, color, lighting, and even music and temperature all influence communication with others; but there is no all-purpose environment. The ideal environment depends on the task that will be performed as well as on the needs and expectations of those present. The same environmental factors that encourage lively conversation and dancing at a New Year's Eve party cannot be expected to create a serene climate in which to study for final exams.

### Personal Appearance

One of the most important variables in nonverbal communication is personal appearance.[10] The way you look affects whether people choose to talk with you, whether you are hired during an employment interview, and how successful you are in persuading others to adopt your ideas. For example, females who are perceived as more attractive are more effective in persuading others than are females rated as less attractive. More attractive individuals of both genders are often perceived as having more credibility than less attractive ones. They are also judged to be happier, more popular, more sociable, and more successful than those who are rated as less attractive.

One of the factors that affects the way others perceive you is the shape of your body.[11] People with fat and round figures are seen as older, more old-fashioned, less good looking, more talkative, and more good-natured. People with athletic, muscular figures tend to be rated as better looking, taller, and more adventurous. And people with tall and thin bodies are perceived as more ambitious, more suspicious of others, more tense and nervous, more pessimistic, and quieter. Of course, impressions of others are based on more than just body shape; but the culture does, in fact, condition people to stereotype others in such ways.

*Clothes tell how people want to be treated.*

Clothing also influences how people are perceived. One interesting study found that a well-dressed man who violated a "Don't Walk" sign at a busy street corner was able to attract more followers than was a violator who was badly dressed.[12] Clothes are usually the first sign sent to others about the way people want to be treated. At a school where most students wear jeans and other casual clothes to class, a student who chooses to wear more formal attire signals, whether intentionally or not, that he or she is not just one of the gang. Some popular advice books prescribe certain clothes for people who want to be perceived as powerful. The power look for men consists of a dark suit, white or light-blue shirt, conservative tie (or a bold bright "power" tie), dark socks, and well-shined shoes. For women, a tailored dark suit with a light-colored blouse is supposed to project a more powerful image than a sweater and skirt. Although the popular slogan, "Clothes make the person" may be a good sales tool for a clothing retailer, we caution you against drawing long-lasting conclusions about others based *only* on the label on the back of their jeans or the insignia on the pocket of their shirts. Even though appearance has a profound impact on perceptions, like other hasty and narrow conclusions, judgments based solely on appearance can result in misperceptions.

## Touch

*Touch is one of the most powerful nonverbal cues to communicate intimacy and liking.*

While attending an orchestra concert you accidentally touch the arm of the stranger sitting next to you. Of course, you immediately apologize and then break eye contact with him or her. You react that way because touch is one of the most powerful and intimate sources of nonverbal information. Because it's so powerful, you feel the need to apologize to avoid appearing too aggressive or insensitive. Even unintentionally touching someone's toe with your foot when you sit down at a table can lead to an awkward apology.

A touch may prompt a hug or a slap. It is also the most basic and earliest form of communication people experience. Infants depend on the touch of their parents for comfort and security. In fact, studies suggest that touch is vital for normal development and that a lack of touching can result in numerous health problems. Those who advocate

---

## Sources of Nonverbal Information

| | |
|---|---|
| Movement and Gestures | Communicate information about status, leadership, liking, affection, interest, and warmth |
| Eye Contact | Serves cognitive, monitoring, regulatory, and expressive functions |
| Vocal Cues | Expresses personality and emotion through pitch, rate, quality, and volume of the voice |
| Facial Expression | Serves as primary source of information about feelings and attitudes |
| Space and Territory | Offers information about power, status, and intimacy through zones of intimate space, personal space, social space, and public space |
| Environment | Influences mood, concentration, and response to others through such factors as room decor, color, lighting, temperature, and sound |
| Personal Appearance | Influences others' perceptions and reactions through clothing, body shape, and attractiveness |
| Touch | Communicates intimacy and affection |

breast-feeding suggest that the bonding process of mother to child occurs more rapidly and is more intense than when mothers bottle-feed their children.[13]

There are predictable patterns in which you touch and are touched. You are more apt to touch someone when you give, rather than ask for, information, when you ask for a favor or give an order, when you try to persuade, when you are having an intimate conversation, and when you are excited.[14]

The amount of touch that you are comfortable with depends on the amount of touch you experience in your family. Some families touch one another frequently—hugs and kisses are generously exchanged among all members. In other families, touch is not so important. If you are from a family where touching is minimized and then you associate with a "touchy-feely" family, you may feel uncomfortable with the increased amount of touching that you see and that may be expected of you.

## FUNCTIONS OF NONVERBAL COMMUNICATION

Verbal and nonverbal communication work together to create meaning. To help you understand how these communication codes work together, consider six general functions of nonverbal communication: repeating, contradicting, substituting, complementing, accenting, and regulating.[15]

1. *Repeating.* Nonverbal communication may follow and silently reexpress a spoken message. When asked how to get to the personnel department, a security guard may say, "Just go up those stairs and to the right." If the job applicant still looks puzzled, the guard will probably just point to make it clear. The nonverbal message will simply repeat the verbal direction.
2. *Contradicting.* A nonverbal message may communicate just the opposite meaning of a verbal message. A professor who says, "Sure, I've got time to talk to you. What's on your mind?" while he is nervously looking at his watch, reaching for his pen, grabbing his attache case, and heading for the door illustrates contradictory verbal and nonverbal messages. As previously noted, when there is a contradiction between a verbal and a nonverbal message, people will believe the nonverbal one.
3. *Substituting.* Nonverbal emblems are used to substitute for verbal messages. When Mark, a usually cheerful father and husband, comes to the breakfast table with a stern facial expression and stares suspiciously at each family member, no one needs to be told that he is upset about something. No words are spoken, yet the message is communicated. Because nonverbal cues are often more subtle and ambiguous than actual words, people may rely on them to communicate negative messages.
4. *Complementing.* Nonverbal communication may add meaning to a verbal message. For example, if a secretary failed to complete an important project because he took too long a lunch break, he might use complementary nonverbal cues (illustrators) when apologizing to his boss. Through his reduced eye contact and contrite tone of voice, he would give additional information about the sincerity of his apology.
5. *Accenting.* Nonverbal communication may emphasize or accent a verbal message. By raising her voice and shaking her fist

---

**Review Box**

**The Functions of Nonverbal Communication**

**Repeating**—silently reexpressing a verbal message
**Contradicting**—communicating the opposite of a verbal message
**Substituting**—taking the place of a verbal message
**Complementing**—adding meaning to a verbal message
**Accenting**—emphasizing a verbal message
**Regulating**—controlling the back-and-forth flow of communication

---

during the climax of her speech, a public speaker may underscore her remarks. A person may often shake his or her head when saying no or nod his or her head when saying yes to accent rejection or affirmation.

6. *Regulating.* As we have noted, regulators help to control the flow of communication between people. In a formal situation, such as a large conference, an individual may nonverbally signal a desire to communicate by raising a hand. In a less formal situation, a person may make eye contact, lean forward, and raise his or her eyebrows to make a point.

## INTERPRETING NONVERBAL COMMUNICATION

Can you tell whether someone likes you even if he or she hasn't spoken to you? Can you spot a powerful person? Do you know whether someone is really following your conversation? When you observe others, you assign meaning to their nonverbal behavior along three dimensions: liking, power, and responsiveness.[16]

### Liking

When you are first introduced to someone, you usually decide quite quickly whether you find that person attractive, even though you may not be able to identify specific reasons for your reaction. The usual cause is the individual's display of **immediacy cues**—nonverbal behavior that communicates liking. According to the **immediacy principle**, you move toward persons and things you like, and avoid or move away from persons and things you dislike. Thus, such nonverbal cues as touch, forward lean, eye contact, and reduced space between people all may communicate **liking**. As a result, you tend to have more favorable impressions of people who sit comfortably close, establish eye contact, and orient their bodies toward you.

*Meaning is assigned to nonverbal behavior along three dimensions: (1) liking, (2) power, and (3) responsiveness.*

### Power

You also assess new acquaintances by the way they communicate status or **power**. A person of high status tends to have a more relaxed body posture when interacting with a person of lower status. While the personnel director may feel quite comfortable leaning back and relaxing in a chair, the job applicant (with considerably less status) is more likely to maintain a formal posture throughout the interview.

An individual's use of personal space provides another hint about status. High-status individuals generally maintain more personal distance from others, and they are usually the ones who determine the appropriate personal distance for a specific situation. The dean of a college probably has a larger desk than does a newly hired secretary. The larger desk not only signifies status, but also serves as a barrier that establishes the appropriate personal distance for visitors. When meeting with someone of equal status, the dean will, more than likely, come from behind the desk and converse at closer range.

### Responsiveness

Finally, people are gauged in terms of **responsiveness**—the way they are perceived to respond and whether they are perceived as active or passive, energetic or dull, fast or slow. The speed of a person's movement, the expression of emotion on the person's face, and the variation of the pitch, rate, volume, and quality of his or her voice all contribute to perceptions of that person as responsive or unresponsive, interested or uninterested. Some people just seem to be more responsive than others. Those who are perceived as more responsive usually lean forward, occasionally nod or shake their heads in reaction to a point, maintain an animated vocal quality, and express interest.

## IMPROVING YOUR UNDERSTANDING OF NONVERBAL MESSAGES

As we have already noted, you cannot really use nonverbal cues to "read a person like a book." Nonverbal communication is important in determining the way you respond to others and the way others respond to you; but great caution is necessary when trying to determine what a specific nonverbal cue means. Keep the following principles in mind when interpreting nonverbal cues.

### Context can affect how nonverbal cues are interpreted.

Do you remember your English teacher's warning not to take quoted material out of context because the meaning might get distorted? The

*Review Box*

## Dimensions of Nonverbal Meaning

| Dimension | Definition | Nonverbal Cues |
|---|---|---|
| Liking | Nonverbal behaviors that communicate interest and attraction | Eye contact, forward lean, touch, close personal space |
| Power | Nonverbal behaviors that communicate status and influence | Protected space, increased distance, relaxed posture, status clothing |
| Responsiveness | Nonverbal behaviors that communicate active interaction | Eye contact, varied vocal quality, animated facial expression, forward lean |

same principle holds true for nonverbal communication. Simply looking at someone's posture or facial expression without taking the context into consideration can result in a misinterpretation of the behavior. Because you see your professor wrinkle his forehead while he is reading your essay exam does not mean that your answer is wrong. He may think your answer is quite profound and may simply be considering its quality.

Nonverbal communication is more ambiguous than verbal communication, which increases the potential for misunderstanding. There is no comprehensive dictionary of nonverbal communication behavior. Therefore, you must be cautious not to overgeneralize or to think that you know what someone else is saying or feeling just by looking at his or her nonverbal cues.

*Beware of interpreting a nonverbal cue out of context.*

### What is appropriate in one culture may not be appropriate in another culture.

Each individual uses the nonverbal cues that are appropriate to his or her native culture. Acceptable movement, personal space, eye contact, facial expressions, and uses of time vary from culture to culture. For example, in many Asian cultures, children are taught not to make prolonged eye contact when addressing someone of higher status. Some people from Mediterranean cultures expect to transact business at very close personal range, whereas Americans tend to become uncomfortable if business acquaintances come closer than the social space zone (from 4 to 12 feet away).

Not only your culture, but each group to which you belong may have its own set of accepted nonverbal behaviors. Behavior that is acceptable in one group may not be appropriate in another. For example, in one class your instructor may expect you to raise your hand if you want to speak, while in another class the instructor may encourage you to speak without raising your hand. Learning the nonverbal norms of a group can help you better interpret the messages communicated.

**The longer you know someone, the more likely it becomes that you will be able to assess his or her nonverbal cues accurately.**

A wife may learn that when her husband comes home from work and turns on the television without offering a greeting, he has probably had a rough day. Children may also learn specific nonverbal cues that signal they can be rowdy because their parents are feeling tolerant or that they had better be on their best behavior because their parents are in no mood for foolishness. Family members are probably more accurate in judging the nonverbal communication of other family members than is someone from outside a family. When people have lived with one another for a considerable length of time, whether they are married, family members, or roommates, they learn unique cues that enable them to better interpret nonverbal behavior.

**When it comes to perceiving and interpreting nonverbal cues, some people are more sensitive than others.**

You probably know some people who just don't seem to take the hint to leave a party, get off the phone, or leave your room. They are not sensitive to the nonverbal cues of others. Nonverbal sensitivity seems to increase from about age five until the mid- to late twenties. Intelligence does not seem to strongly influence a person's ability to interpret nonverbal cues. On the other hand, gender may. One research team found that females are generally a bit more accurate than males in interpreting nonverbal cues.[17] To some extent, more outgoing, extroverted people are more sensitive than are introverted personality types. While we caution against overgeneralizing from these observations, they do support the notion that some people are better than others at receiving and interpreting nonverbal cues.

**The best way to ensure understanding is to ask others if your interpretation of their nonverbal behavior is accurate.**

*People judge others by their behavior, not by their intent.*

People are judged not by their intent but by their behavior. Therefore, it is crucial to check that your interpretation of their behavior coincides with their intent. An easy way to determine whether you are correctly interpreting someone's nonverbal behavior is simply to ask.

Imagine that you hand your semester grades to your father. He makes no comment but raises his eyebrows. You can't be sure how he is reacting to your average, but hard-earned, marks, so you ask, "Are you disappointed in my grades, Dad?" Asking for clarification of his nonverbal behavior can increase your skill in interpreting nonverbal cues. The feedback that others give you can help you evaluate your accuracy and teach you new interpretations.

*Asking for clarification of someone's nonverbal behavior can increase your skill in interpreting nonverbal cues.*

## SUMMARY

▶**Define nonverbal communication.**

Nonverbal communication is communication behavior, other than written or spoken language, that creates meaning for someone.

▶**Cite three important reasons for studying nonverbal communication.**

First, nonverbal communication plays a major role in the overall communication process. You cannot *not* communicate. Second, it is primarily through nonverbal means that you communicate feelings and attitudes toward others. Third, nonverbal messages are more believable than verbal messages; if there is a contradiction between verbal and nonverbal messages, people usually believe the nonverbal message.

▶**Identify eight sources of nonverbal communication and indicate the kinds of information each conveys.**

Movement and gestures may communicate information about status, leadership, liking, affection, interest, and warmth. Depending on the way it is used, a movement or gesture may be classified as an emblem, an illustrator, an affect display, a regulator, or an adaptor.

Eye contact strongly affects the way people are perceived and the relationships they establish. It serves cognitive, monitoring, regulatory, and expressive functions.

Vocal cues are conveyed by rate of speech and quality, volume and pitch of voice. Based on these factors, people often make inferences about another person's emotional state, personality, credibility, status, and power.

Facial expressions provide key information about a communicator's feelings and attitudes. Because the face is the most important single source of information about emotions, it is usually the first place to look for clues to the way someone is reacting. While the face communicates a specific emotion, the accompanying body posture and movement express the intensity of that emotion.

An individual's use of space and territory tells much about power, status, and intimacy. How a person uses space depends on outgoingness of personality, degree of liking for other participants, nature of the communication or task, cultural background, physical environment, and status. Hall identified four commonly used zones of space: intimate space, personal space, social space, and public space.

The environment, which includes such factors as room appearance, color, lighting, music, and temperature, strongly affects mood, ability to concentrate, and responses to others. The ideal environment depends on the task that will be performed as well as the needs and expectations of others.

Personal appearance, including attractiveness, body shape, and clothing, influences the way people perceive and react to one another. Clothes are frequently the first sign sent to others about the way people want to be treated.

Finally, touch is one of the most powerful and basic sources of nonverbal communication. Touch communicates liking, comfort, and intimacy.

▶**Specify six ways in which nonverbal communication functions with verbal communication to create meaning.**

The six functions of nonverbal communication are (1) repeating—that is, silently reexpressing a verbal message; (2) contradicting—communicating the opposite of a verbal message; (3) substituting—taking the place of a verbal message; (4) complementing—adding meaning to a verbal message; (5) accenting—emphasizing a verbal message; and (6) regulating—controlling the back-and-forth flow of communication.

▶**Discuss the three dimensions that are commonly used to assign meaning to nonverbal behavior.**

Nonverbal behavior is commonly interpreted along three dimensions: liking, power, and responsiveness. Liking is judged on the basis of immediacy cues—the amount of touch, forward lean, eye contact, and distance between the speakers. Power is assessed in terms of posture, use of space, and clothing. Responsiveness is gauged according to eye contact, vocal cues, facial expressions, forward lean, and speed of movement.

▶**Employ five key principles to improve your understanding of nonverbal messages.**

You can improve your understanding of nonverbal cues by remembering the following principles: (1) Context affects how nonverbal cues are interpreted; (2) what is meaningful or appropriate in one culture may not be appropriate in another culture; (3) the longer you know someone, the more likely it becomes that you will be able to accurately assess his or her nonverbal meaning; (4) when it comes to interpreting nonverbal cues, some people are more sensitive than others; (5) the best way to ensure understanding is to ask others if your interpretation of their nonverbal behavior is accurate.

## KEY TERMS

**Adaptor:**   A nonverbal behavior that helps to satisfy a personal need and to adapt to immediate surroundings.

**Affect display:**   A nonverbal cue that communicates emotions.

**Cognitive function:**   The function of eye contact that provides information about thought processes.

**Emblem:**   A nonverbal cue that acts as a substitute for oral communication.

**Expressive function:**   The function of eye contact that indicates feelings and emotions.

**Illustrator:**   A nonverbal behavior used to add meaning to an accompanying verbal message.

**Immediacy cues:**   Nonverbal cues that communicate liking or affection.

**Immediacy principle:**   The tendency to move closer to persons and things you like and to avoid or move away from persons and things you dislike.

**Intimate space:**   Zone of space within 0 to 1½ feet of an individual, where the most intimate personal communication occurs.

**Liking:**   Dimension of nonverbal meaning that communicates interest and attraction; conveyed through eye contact, touch, forward lean, and reduced space between people.

**Monitoring function:**   The function of eye contact that provides feedback about another person's response.

**Nonverbal communication:**   Communication behavior other than written or spoken language that creates meaning to someone.

**Personal space:**   Zone of space between 1½ and 4 feet from an individual, where most social conversations take place.

**Power:**   Dimension of nonverbal meaning that communicates status and influence; conveyed through protected space, increased distance, relaxed posture, and status clothing.

**Public space:**   All territory more than 12 feet beyond an individual, in which the most formal and intentional communication occurs.

**Regulator:**   A nonverbal cue that helps control the flow of communication between people.

**Regulatory function:** The function of eye contact that controls the back-and-forth flow of conversation and signals whether communication channels are open or closed.

**Responsiveness:** Dimension of nonverbal meaning that communicates active interaction; conveyed through eye contact, varied vocal quality, animated facial expression, and forward lean.

**Social space:** Zone of space spanning 4 to 12 feet from an individual, where most business communication takes place.

## DISCUSSION QUESTIONS

1. How will learning about nonverbal communication help you improve your relationships with others?

2. Is it really possible to "read" someone's nonverbal communication accurately?

3. How do you defend your personal space and personal territory?

4. What do the clothes you are wearing right now tell other people about the way you want to be treated?

5. What nonverbal cues do you use to communicate liking, power, and responsiveness?

6. What are some of the nonverbal behaviors that have a unique or special meaning to your family?

7. Identify some situations in which it would be appropriate and desirable to ask someone if your interpretation of their nonverbal behavior is correct.

## SUGGESTED ACTIVITIES

1. Read the following statements about nonverbal communication. Do you agree or disagree with each? After you have made an individual decision, compare your response with the response of others in your class. Discuss your reasons for either agreeing or disagreeing with each statement.

   _____ 1. Nonverbal communication is a more important part of the communication process than is verbal communication.

   _____ 2. Most people do a pretty good job of accurately interpreting others' nonverbal messages.

   _____ 3. Most people are good enough actors to hide their true feelings.

   _____ 4. Males are generally better than females at accurately interpreting body language.

_____ 5. Being sensitive to others' nonverbal behavior is a talent, rather than a skill that can be developed. Some people have it and some people don't.

_____ 6. Individuals usually communicate their importance, power, and status verbally rather than nonverbally.

2. Go on a nonverbal communication scavenger hunt. Find as many examples as you can of emblems, illustrators, affect displays, regulators, and adaptors, and write a brief description of each. How easy or difficult was it to identify and describe nonverbal communication using these five categories?

   Variation 1: Identify examples of nonverbal behavior that express immediacy, power, and responsiveness.

   Variation 2: Document examples of nonverbal behavior that repeat, contradict, substitute, complement, accent, and regulate verbal communication.

3. Watch a broadcast of the evening news. Analyze the anchor person's use of nonverbal communication. Note vocal cues, physical appearance, body movement and gestures, and facial expressions. How do the nonverbal cues affect your impression of the anchor person? What makes the person credible? Can you tell how the anchor person feels about an event from the way he or she reads the story? Take notes on your observations and compare them with those of other students in the class.

4. Spend thirty minutes "people watching" at a public place such as a shopping center, airport, or hotel lobby. Try to identify examples of the purposes of nonverbal communication: repeating, contradicting, substituting, complementing, accenting, and regulating.

## SUGGESTED READINGS

Leathers, D.G. (1986). *Successful Nonverbal Communication: Principles and Applications*. (New York: Macmillan Publishing Company).

Richmond, V.P., McCroskey, J.C., and Payne, S.K. (1987). *Nonverbal Behavior in Interpersonal Relations*. (Englewood Cliffs, New Jersey: Prentice-Hall).

Knapp, M.L. (1978). *Nonverbal Communication in Human Interaction*. (New York: Holt, Rinehart and Winston).

Malandro, L.A., and Barker, L. (1983). *Nonverbal Communication*. (Reading, Massachusetts: Addison-Wesley).

Hickson, M.L., and Stacks, D.W. (1985). *Nonverbal Communication: Studies and Applications*. (Dubuque, Iowa: Wm. C. Brown).

**PART**

2

# EFFECTIVE INTERPERSONAL AND SMALL GROUP COMMUNICATION

# 5 Speech Communication in Interpersonal Relationships

*After studying this chapter you should be able to:*

▶ Differentiate between the situational and developmental/relational perspectives on interpersonal communication.

▶ Explain two models of interpersonal communication.

▶ Discuss the relationship of self-concept to interpersonal communication.

▶ Describe four factors that contribute to interpersonal attraction.

▶ Outline the process through which self-disclosure builds trust and intimacy in interpersonal relationships.

▶ Trace the stages through which a relationship goes as it comes together and comes apart, and cite examples of communication at each stage.

▶ Explain how defensiveness interferes with interpersonal communication and discuss six categories of defensive and supportive communication.

This chapter is about the way you relate to others through communication. It is about the way you discover the uniqueness of another human being and the way you make yourself known to that person. It is about messages that bring people closer together and messages that push them apart.

The chapter is divided into four sections. The first presents some definitions and approaches that describe interpersonal communication as an area of academic study. The second section explains two models of the interpersonal communication process. The third section looks at the way interpersonal relationships develop through communication. The final section examines specific types of communication that can help or hinder the development of interpersonal relationships.

## WHAT IS INTERPERSONAL COMMUNICATION?

Interpersonal communication may be approached from two broad perspectives: the situational perspective and the developmental/relational perspective. Common to both is the definition of **interpersonal communication** as face-to-face interaction between two persons, with the potential for immediate feedback.

### The Situational Perspective

The **situational perspective** views interpersonal communication as a particular context or level in which human communication occurs. This approach was reflected in chapter 1 in the discussion of the intrapersonal, interpersonal, group, and public levels of speech communication. The situational perspective, then, focuses on those characteristics of interpersonal communication that set it apart from other levels of communication. Based on the definition of interpersonal communication, its three key characteristics are (1) face-to-face interaction, (2) the participation of two persons, and (3) the potential for immediate feedback.

Only transactions that occur in person can be classified as interpersonal communication. This rules out communication carried on through various media, such as letter writing and talking on the telephone, because the principles that apply to face-to-face situations may not hold true in less immediate situations. For example, the absence

*Interpersonal communication is the process through which relationships are built and maintained.*

*The situational perspective identifies features of interpersonal communication that set it apart from other levels of communication.*

of many nonverbal cues in telephone conversations and the considerable time delay involved in letter writing can alter the communication process.

1. *Interpersonal communication is between two persons.* Usually interpersonal communication is viewed as **dyadic**—that is, as occurring between *two persons* (a **dyad**). As discussed in chapter 1, interpersonal communication involves a higher level of intentionality, or purpose, than does the intrapersonal level, but it does not include the structured planning of messages found at the public level. The interpersonal level is spontaneous. This kind of communication can also be found in some small groups of individuals, so the term *interpersonal communication* is often extended to include such groups.

2. *Interpersonal communication has the potential for immediate feedback.* Because interpersonal communication occurs face-to-face and involves a small number of people, the potential for feedback is always present. Messages at this level may be adjusted continually to adapt to the other person.

Even with these criteria limiting what counts as interpersonal communication, this category still covers a wide range of interpersonal behaviors—from asking a store clerk for a package of gum to sharing the intimate details of your life with a close friend, lover, or spouse. To account for the differences along the entire spectrum of relationships, however, it has been argued that what is needed is another approach to interpersonal communication that considers the nature of relationships.

## The Developmental/Relational Perspective

*From the developmental/ relational perspective, interpersonal communication is a function of the familiarity between participants.*

The **developmental/relational perspective** views interpersonal communication as the result of a developmental, evolutionary process within a relationship.[1] Recall from chapter 1 the statement that communications with others have both content and relationship dimensions. The content dimension pertains to what is said, while the relationship dimension pertains to *how* it is said. Both what you say and how you say it affect and are affected by the nature of your relationship with another person. It is unlikely, for example, that you would share your pain over the death of your dog with a complete stranger or that you would give your boss a direct order. Thus, for interpersonal communication to be fully understood, it must be viewed in terms of the level of familiarity between the participants.

The speaker addressing a small group has the oppportunity to develop a relationship with his audience.

Interpersonal communication is aimed at increasing familiarity by discovering the uniqueness of another person. When you say that you are getting to know someone, it means that you are discovering what sets that person apart from all others. Someone you have learned to know well becomes relatively predictable. Your understanding of that person allows you to be quite certain about the way he or she will respond to variations in your behavior. This predictability is the basis for trust and increased intimacy, discussed later in this chapter.

## MODELS OF INTERPERSONAL COMMUNICATION

To increase your understanding of interpersonal communication, it is necessary for you to examine two models. The first takes a situational view of interpersonal communication. It is helpful in identifying the variables that are present whenever interpersonal communication occurs. The second model takes an approach that is more developmental. It relates well to your experience of interpersonal communication.

**Figure 5–1**
The DeVito Model

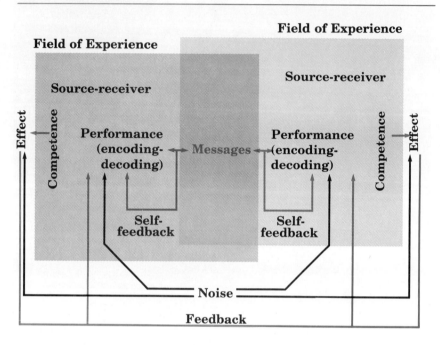

Source: From Joseph A. DeVito, *The Interpersonal Communication Book,* 4th edition.
Copyright © 1986 by Joseph A. DeVito. Reprinted by permission of Harper & Row, Publishers, Inc.

## The DeVito Model

The **DeVito Model**[2] is a descriptive model that identifies the principal components and processes of interpersonal communication. To orient yourself, look first at the center of the diagram in Figure 5-1. Note that DeVito's model includes many of the same communication components and processes discussed in chapter 1—source, receiver, encoding, decoding, messages, feedback, and noise. The model also introduces five new components—competence, performance, field of experience, effect, and communication context—that are important in understanding the interpersonal level of communication.

Competence. **Competence** refers to your knowledge of the rules in a communication setting. On one level, you have a certain degree of **linguistic competence**—a knowledge of the rules, vocabulary, and structures of language. On a second level, you have varying knowledge of social aspects of communication—that is, you know how to act in a variety of situations. For example, some messages, both verbal and nonverbal, that are acceptable on a construction site are inappropriate at a debutante ball. Your knowledge of social rules and your understanding of communication behavior as it relates to those rules is called **communication competence.**

**Performance.**  **Performance** is your actual behavior as you speak, listen, and adjust to a variety of situations and contexts. An excellent example of a competent communicator is Captain Kirk of the starship *Enterprise* in the television series "Star Trek."[3] Captain Kirk continually shows his knowledge (competence) by skillfully adapting his behavior (performance) to the situation. He has a vast communicative repertoire. He can be dominant or tender, authoritarian or democratic, formal or informal, aggressive or conciliatory—as the situation demands it.

*Both competence and performance are crucial aspects of effective interpersonal communication.*

**Field of experience.**  **Field of experience** is the sum total of all the facts and events you've ever observed. According to DeVito, the effectiveness of communication depends on the extent to which the participants share the same experiences. When participants do not share the same experiences, their communication is more likely to be ineffective. Thus, parents and children can be expected to have difficulty in communicating, because the children cannot share the parental experience and the parents have forgotten what it's like to be children. To communicate effectively with another person, people need to share not only a common language, but a similar frame of reference for that language. Your probably know from your own experience that it is easier to communicate with people who are like you—who share similar beliefs, attitudes, values, and experiences.

**Effect.**  Every communication act results in some effect, or consequence. Sometimes the effect is observable and sometimes it is not. The most common effect of interpersonal communication is its influence on further communication. Every communicative act defines and limits the possible responses to it. For example, when one person says, "Hi, how are you?" it is unlikely that another will respond, "My grandmother just had her house painted."

*All communication has an effect.*

Many effects of interpersonal communication are *intrapersonal.* The words and actions of others affect your feelings about yourself and thus shape and maintain your self-concept.

Of course, interpersonal communication can also have external effects. For example, you may use interpersonal communication to plan a date, buy a car, or persuade a professor to change a grade.

Context. **Context,** which is the situation in which communication occurs, has a powerful effect. Words and gestures may carry very different meanings depending on the circumstances in which they are used. For example, a professor repeatedly used the *A-OK* gesture (thumb and index finger touching, other fingers extended) to mean "good job" with a group of Bahamian students before learning that, in their culture, it is an obscene gesture. Also consider the radically different meanings of the phrase *three and two* on a baseball diamond or in an arithmetic lesson.

The DeVito Model offers us a visual image of a complex process. Surrounded by context and dependent on overlapping fields of experience, interpersonal communication takes place between persons whose performances depend on their abilities to successfully encode and decode messages to achieve the desired effect. Understanding this can help explain why communication sometimes breaks down and leads to misunderstanding. Effective interpersonal communication depends on the successful coordination of all of these elements.

*Context shapes communication.*

## The Baker Model

How comfortable would you be sitting with another person in absolute silence? Would your comfort (or discomfort) vary from person to person? Are there some people whose presence you could enjoy even without saying anything? A fairly good test of friendship is the ability to be with someone without feeling the need to speak. It seems to reflect high levels of comfort and acceptance.

Unlike most communication models, the **Baker Model** is based on *silence* being the aim of communication; people need to talk until there is no more to be said. The Baker Model is illustrated in Figure 5-2.

Reciprocal identification. **Reciprocal identification** is the degree of similarity and understanding between two (or more) persons. Once you truly get to know someone, that person becomes more predictable. You know without asking how the person responds to a situation. For example, I can sit silently on a mountainside in Montana with my wife as we watch the sun sink below the horizon and listen to a flock of pine siskens chirp their salute to another day completed. Neither of us needs to say, "Gee, honey, isn't it a nice sunset and aren't the mountains beautiful and isn't it nice that the birds are singing?" In fact, it would be an interruption of a very warm, beautiful, intimate moment. In such a situation, each of us knows how the other is feeling, and we enjoy a strong sense of togetherness and sharing in the beauty of the moment—with no words whatsoever passing between us. This is high reciprocal identification.

**Figure 5–2**
The Baker Model

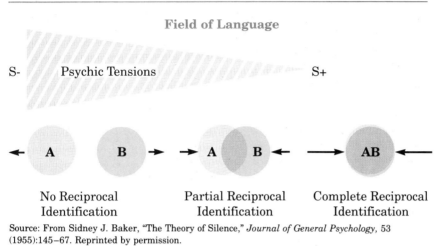

Source: From Sidney J. Baker, "The Theory of Silence," *Journal of General Psychology,* 53 (1955):145–67. Reprinted by permission.

Varying degrees of reciprocal identification are represented across the bottom of the model in Figure 5-2. At the left, person A and person B are in a situation where they have virtually nothing in common. Perhaps they are having a terrible misunderstanding and neither is able to see the other's point of view. Maybe the two persons are from vastly different backgrounds, perhaps even different cultures with different languages. As a result, there is little or nothing that they can say to one another.

In the center are two circles that overlap. The overlapping portion represents an area that is shared by persons A and B. It indicates that the two have some shared field of experience. To the extent of the overlap, each can identify with the other and reach understanding. Their common ground can be as basic as a common language and some shared thoughts within that language. If the two persons have an established relationship, they may have developed **empathy**—the ability to understand what the other is feeling and thinking.

The single circle at the right represents complete reciprocal identification. Here persons A and B are as one. They enjoy complete mutual understanding—a state rarely experienced, but certainly one to be desired.

**Psychic tension and silence.** At the center of the Baker model is an inclined plane labeled *Psychic Tensions.* **Psychic tension** is the discomfort you feel when there is misunderstanding or conflict. To the left is $S-$, to the right, $S+$. These $S$'s refer to silence. Thus, negative silence is on the left and positive silence is on the right. Putting these elements together with reciprocal identification, when there is little or no reciprocal identification, psychic tension tends to be high. You are uncomfortable with the situation and have nothing to say, so the silence is negative. In contrast, when there is total reciprocal identification, psychological discomfort is slight or nonexistent. Because you understand and feel understood by the other person, you feel quiet and content. The silence is positive.

*Positive silence reflects understanding.*

**Field of language.**   Language, expressed through speech communication, is the key to reciprocal identification. Because language enables you to step outside yourself, you can take the point of view of another person. Speech communication is the means through which understanding is achieved. When there is complete reciprocal identification, communication is unnecessary—positive silence. When there is complete misunderstanding, communication is (or seems to be) impossible—negative silence. Between these two poles of silence, there is a need for communication. There is enough reciprocal identification to make communication comfortable, but not enough to eliminate the need to find out more about the other person. Think about your own experiences. When you know someone only moderately well, you tend to be comfortable enough to carry on a conversation, but not comfortable enough to be silent together.

## DEVELOPING INTERPERSONAL RELATIONSHIPS

So far this chapter has examined some of the universals of interpersonal communication. This section will get more specific and look at the way interpersonal relationships develop through communication. Self-concept is the starting point for interpersonal communication, and it is the starting point for this discussion. Next the section will look at why you can be attracted to some people, but not to others. After examining self-disclosure as the key to intimacy in relationships, the section will conclude with a discussion of the stages that relationships pass through as they grow and develop.

### Self-Concept and Interpersonal Communication

As discussed in chapter 2, your self-concept develops and is maintained through interaction with others. This makes interpersonal communication potentially very risky. Each and every time you speak, you are putting your self-concept to a test. In response to your comments you may receive positive feedback that reaffirms your self-concept or negative feedback that calls it into question. That is why starting a conversation with an attractive stranger is so difficult for many people. The self-concept is on the line.

It has been noted that the three great existential questions are "Who am I?", "What am I doing here?", and "Who are all these other people?" The first two questions are rooted in self-concept and a system of beliefs, attitudes, and values. The third looks outward at the self in relation to others.

*You test your self-concept through interpersonal communication.*

## Interpersonal Attraction

**Interpersonal attraction** is the amount of liking one person feels toward another person. At a first meeting, you are attracted to some people and not to others. On the other hand, you may eventually be drawn to people whom you did not like at first, and you may lose interest in people whom you initially found attractive. Such rising and waning of interpersonal attraction is caused by many factors, including (1) physical attraction, (2) similarity, (3) complementarity, and (4) proximity, contact, and interaction.

**Physical attraction.**  Particularly in the initial stages of attraction, physical attractiveness plays an important role. Luckily, individual perceptions of attractiveness vary widely enough that virtually everyone appears attractive to someone. Attractiveness becomes much less important as you get to know a person. You probably have been attracted to some people because you thought they were handsome or beautiful, but after getting to know them, you like them for qualities other than their physical attributes. Likewise, you tend to overlook people's unattractive physical traits once you find other qualities about them that you like.

**Similarity.**  One of the strongest influences on interpersonal attraction is **similarity**—the degree to which two persons are alike. Remember your first day on campus and those feelings of newness, strangeness, and aloneness? You needed a friend, and you probably found one. Whom did you look for to be your friend? Did you seek out someone who seemed very different from you? Probably not. Based on the principle of similarity, you probably looked for someone to talk to who appeared to be in the same boat—another lonely freshman, perhaps someone who was dressed much like you.

Who are your closest friends? Do you share many of the same beliefs, attitudes, and values? Do you enjoy the same activities? More than likely, you do. One explanation for this phenomenon is that similar beliefs, attitudes, values, and experiences make it easier to understand one another—and we all like to feel as if we're understood. Therefore, we're attracted to people who resemble us.

**Complementarity.**  **Complementarity** is the degree to which two persons are compatibly different from each other. As you read the previous section on similarity, you may have been saying to yourself, "No, that's not the way it is at all. My best friend and I are about as similar as an orchid and a fire hydrant!" The old saying, "No generalization is true, including the present one," applies to the principle of similarity as well. That is, while it may be true that birds of a feather flock together, it is also true that opposites attract. Some interpersonal relationships are based primarily on similarity while others are based on complementarity. In fact, at times you may be attracted to others who exhibit qualities that you do not possess but that you admire.

*Proximity may reveal ways in which needs can be met.*

**Proximity, contact, and interaction.**  **Proximity, contact, and interaction** refer to the actual, physical availability of other people. You tend to be attracted to people who are physically close to you—people you live and work with, people you see and talk with often. If you know that you have to live or work closely with another person, you may tend to ignore or overlook his or her less desirable traits in order to minimize the potential for conflict and keep things running smoothly. Furthermore, proximity, contact, and interaction breed familiarity, and familiarity enhances interpersonal attraction.[4] As you interact with another person, you begin to get to know that person. In the process, you may uncover similarities, ways in which you complement one another, and ways in which you can satisfy one another's needs. It is not, then, the actual physical distance between people that influences attraction, but the interpersonal possibilities that arise as a result of proximity, contact, and interaction.

## The Role of Self-Disclosure

**Self-disclosure** is the sharing of information about yourself that would not otherwise be known. It means revealing your needs, your wants, your hurts, your dreams, your self-concept. Consider the following dialogue:

*He (contritely):*      Honey, I'm sorry. I didn't know it meant so much to you.

*She (emotionally):*      If you really loved me, you'd know what I need.

*Review Box*

## Factors in Interpersonal Attraction

| | *Definition* | *Notes/Comments* |
|---|---|---|
| *Physical Attraction* | Interpersonal attraction based on perceptions of physical beauty or handsomeness. | Especially important in the early stages of a relationship; less important after you get to know someone. |
| *Similarity* | The degree to which two persons are alike. | You tend to like people who resemble you in their thinking and experience; it's reinforcing and they are more likely than most to understand you. |
| *Complementarity* | The degree to which two persons are compatibly different from each other. | You tend to be attracted to persons who possess qualities that you admire but do not yourself possess. |
| *Proximity, Contact, and Interaction* | The actual, physical availability of other people. | Talking with others reveals their similar and complementary traits and, thus, their attractiveness to you. |

This exchange illustrates a common myth that many people hold about interpersonal relationships—that caring and affection bring knowledge. In reality, nobody can truly know another person unless that person chooses to reveal himself or herself. *Others cannot know who a person is and what that person wants unless the person tells them.*

Self-disclosure is a matter of *choice*. You can choose to allow others into your private world, or you can choose to exclude them. It is also very easy to talk for hours without engaging in authentic self-disclosure. For example, I could go to great lengths in telling you about what brought me to where I am today. I could tell you about my parents, my childhood, and my various interests, jobs, and skills. I could show you my résumé, which details my educational background, employment history, awards and honors, books, papers, and articles. At the end of all this you would know a great deal *about* me, but would you really know me? What I would have given you was *history*.[5] My history is something that you could have discovered from other sources. It deals with my *outer* life; but my *inner life* is my *story*—it is information that you will never find out unless I tell you. My story includes all my feelings about my family, my career, and my students, and the facts that I often cry in the movies and that sunrises give me feelings of hope and renewal. It is the sharing of *inner lives* that comprises authentic self-disclosure.

**The dyadic effect.**    Self-disclosure is the foundation of intimacy in interpersonal relationships. Through mutual self-disclosure, you reveal yourself to another person bit by bit. Without it you deal only with superficialities—roles, appearances, and stereotypes.

Self-disclosure does not happen all at once; it tends to come in small increments. Imagine yourself in David's situation in the following dialogue:

| | |
|---|---|
| *Sally:* | Hi, David. How's it going? |
| *David (dejected):* | I'm really bummed out. My cat died this morning. |

*Loving you and knowing you are different things.*

If Sally is a close friend, the news about the recent death of your cat is an appropriate response to her query. She will understand your sadness, because she knows you and understands the affection you felt for your pet. If, on the other hand, Sally is only a casual acquaintance, you probably will not reveal your feelings about your loss in the first place. If you do, it will probably make her uncomfortable, because self-disclosure tends to be *reciprocal* and *symmetrical*. Both partners tend to disclose at the same level of intimacy. If you disclose a lot of very personal information to someone who does not know you well, it will usually cause him or her psychological discomfort. Remember that interpersonal messages have both a content and a relationship dimension. High levels of disclosure imply a high level of trust, and it takes time for two persons to develop trust.

Self-disclosure is used to build interpersonal trust and intimacy; then trust and intimacy allow further disclosure. The **dyadic effect** occurs when disclosure by one person leads to disclosure by the other person. In a developing interpersonal relationship, the dyadic effect works something like this:

1. I disclose a small part of myself to you.
2. The relationship dimension of my message indicates that I trust you enough to tell you what I told you.

**Figure 5–3**
The Dyadic Effect of Self-Disclosure

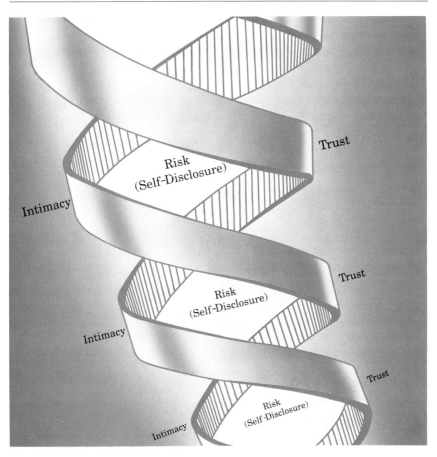

**3.** Because I trusted you, it is easier for you to trust me.
**4.** You disclose an equivalent part of yourself to me.
**5.** Now that we have both made a statement about the relationship, we trust each other. The presence of trust allows me to risk a little more and disclose more of myself to you.
**6.** This, in turn, makes it easier for you to disclose more of yourself, and the pattern repeats itself.

**Risk, trust, self-disclosure, and intimacy.**   Relationships develop through a spiraling process (see Figure 5-3). Self-disclosure is perceived as very risky by most people. To reveal who they really are makes them vulnerable. This is one of the greatest barriers to self-disclosure; but without risk, there can be no trust. Without trust, there

*Self-disclosure involves risk and trust.*

can be no intimacy; and without an intimate relationship with at least one other human being, people are alone.

**Self-disclosure and self-awareness.**   As indicated in Chapter 2, interpersonal communication plays a central role in the development of self-concept. One of the benefits of self-disclosure—and, ironically, one of the barriers as well—is increased self-knowledge.

In an interpersonal transaction you are communicating simultaneously with yourself and another person. Open, honest self-disclosure brings intrapersonal communication and interpersonal communication into a harmonious relationship. Putting your inner life into words to share with another externalizes your feelings. The other person then serves as a mirror to reflect back who you are by using feedback. If you truly self-disclose, the reflection you see is an accurate image of who you are.

The fact that self-disclosure brings self-knowledge actually may prevent you from self-disclosing. If you have a negative self-concept or low self-esteem, or if you believe that, beneath it all, you are not a very acceptable person, you are not likely to test your belief and find out for sure. Continuing the mirror analogy, if you don't want to see yourself, you'll avoid mirrors. Remember, though, that self-concepts can and do change; but they do not change in a vacuum. If you hesitate to disclose yourself because of a negative self-concept, perhaps you can find one person—a friend or counselor—whom you can trust enough to reveal your inner fears. You will, no doubt, find that you are not so unacceptable after all.

## Relational Stages and Interpersonal Communication

*Self-disclosure can lead to self-knowledge.*

Just as individuals pass through stages of development (infancy, childhood, adolescence), relationships pass through stages of interpersonal communication. One model of interactions that characterize various stages in the growth and decay of an interpersonal relationship is shown in Figure 5-4. According to this model, a relationship goes through two processes—coming together and coming apart—and each process has five stages. Within each stage, certain kinds of interpersonal communication are typical.

### The Process of Coming Together

Building a relationship through interpersonal communication happens incrementally, in step-by-step fashion. Often the following five steps can be observed.

**Figure 5–4**
A Model of Interaction Stages

| Process | Stage | Representative Dialog |
|---|---|---|
| **Coming Together** | Initiating | "Hi, how ya doin?"<br>"Fine. You?" |
| | Experimenting | "Oh, so you like to ski . . . so do I."<br>"You do?! Great. Where do you go?" |
| | Intensifying | "I . . . I think I love you."<br>"I love you too." |
| | Integrating | "I feel so much a part of you."<br>"Yeah, we are like one person. What happens to you happens to me." |
| | Bonding | "I want to be with you always."<br>"Let's get married." |
| **Coming Apart** | Differentiating | "I just don't like big social gatherings."<br>"Sometimes I don't understand you. This is one area where I'm certainly not like you at all." |
| | Circumscribing | "Did you have a good time on your trip?"<br>"What time will dinner be ready?" |
| | Stagnating | "What's there to talk about?"<br>"Right. I know what you're going to say and you know what I'm going to say." |
| | Avoiding | "I'm so busy, I just don't know when I'll be able to see you."<br>"If I'm not around when you try, you'll understand." |
| | Terminating | "I'm leaving you . . . and don't bother trying to contact me."<br>"Don't worry." |

Source: From Mark L. Knapp, *Interpersonal Communication and Human Relationships.* Boston: Allyn and Bacon, 1984, p. 33. Used by permission of the publisher.

**Initiating.** The purpose of messages in the initiating stage is to open channels of communication. A person is usually very cautious with a stranger or an attractive member of the opposite sex. The person tends to be hypersensitive to verbal and nonverbal cues, and choosing an opening line is often difficult. Once something is said, this stage passes very quickly, often in less than fifteen seconds.

*Relationships are built step by step.*

**Experimenting.**   At this stage each person tests the water, checking first impressions. They usually search for similarities: "Are you a student here?" "What's your major?" "Where are you from?" "Do you like to party?" In short, the experimenting stage is characterized by small talk. The importance of small talk should not be underestimated. Even though casual conversation involves little authentic self-disclosure and no real commitment to the other person, it provides the foundation on which deeper relationships can be formed.

**Intensifying.**   If the experimenting stage sparks an interest, the people become aware of one another and of the new relationship as well. They become less superficial in their conversation and begin to share more personal information. The resulting self-disclosure increases trust and intimacy. The talk tends to become more personal, and they begin to refer to "us" rather than "you and me." They also begin to express their feelings about the other person at this stage.

**Integrating.**   During the integrating stage of a relationship, the couple begins to think alike, act alike, and sometimes even look alike. They may have a tendency to say the same things at the same time. There is an emphasis on the similarities of the two friends and on anything that sets them apart from other people. This is a stage reached only by very close friends and/or lovers.

**Bonding.**   Bonding involves a public statement of a couple's commitment to each other. It is an institutionalization of a relationship and is included as a separate stage because of the powerful impact that a formal contract—whether it is going steady, getting engaged, getting married, or becoming blood brothers—can have. Such public commitments bring new role expectations that can literally change a relationship overnight.

## The Process of Coming Apart

Just as the stages of coming together build upon one another, the stages of relational deterioration proceed systematically. Again, five levels are observable.

**Differentiating.**   Unfortunately, not all interpersonal relationships continue happily forever. The decline of a relationship is also characterized by identifiable stages of interaction. The first of these is usually differentiating. Whereas similarity and connectedness were the hallmarks of the previous two stages, differences come into focus at

As children reach their teenage years, their relationships with their parents may move into the differentiating stage, marking a period of adjustment for the family.

this stage. The couple will talk about what sets them apart from each other rather than what holds them together. Most, if not all, love relationships reach this stage, but it does not *necessarily* mean the beginning of the end. Most couples who are in love and at the integrating and bonding stages have difficulty seeing each other as they really are. Their emotions prevent them from seeing that they are still unique human beings who have their natural differences. It is predictable then—and perhaps even desirable—that they will reach a stage where each will begin to recognize and reassert his or her individuality.

While in many cases the process of differentiating does foretell the end of the relationship, in others it marks a period of adjustment, a greater sense of reality, a truer acknowledgment of each other's personhood, and a renewed commitment to the relationship. Indeed, as a pair grow and change, their relationship may pass in and out of this stage repeatedly.

**Circumscribing.** By the circumscribing stage, the relationship has deteriorated so much that many topics have become too touchy or painful to discuss. The aim of communication is to control and limit discussion to safe areas and to avoid more volatile subjects. There is noticeable tension in the relationship and lapses of negative silence.

**Stagnating.** During this stage, each person believes that he or she knows what the other is thinking and feels that it is futile to try to break down the barriers to communication. The relationship is going nowhere, and there is virtually no discussion of the relationship itself. Communication is planned, hesitant, and awkward. Nonverbal messages are frequently negative. This stage is painful, of course; but some people prolong it, sometimes for years, because they believe that it is less painful than termination of the relationship.

**Avoiding.**   When this stage is reached, physical separation is the aim of communication. Communication may be blunt: "I don't want to see you any more." There may be tones of antagonism as a result of the pain at the imminent end of an intimate relationship. When physical separation is not possible, the pair tend to ignore each other—to say, in effect, "You don't exist for me anymore."

**Terminating.**   Terminating is the end of a relationship. It may come abruptly or gradually. Depending on the history of the relationship, the relative status of the people involved, their personalities, and a host of other variables, communication at this point can vary widely. It may be explosive or quiet, hostile or amicable. In any event, messages at the termination point are likely to convey a desire for distance, both physical and psychological.

As you can see, the stages of coming together are characterized by increasingly intimate communication, while the stages of coming apart are associated with a decrease in communication leading to eventual termination. The importance of effective communication in building and maintaining relationships is obvious.

## EFFECTIVE INTERPERSONAL COMMUNICATION

Sets of opposite behavior that are often seen at the interpersonal level are defensive and supportive communication. The negative element in each of these pairs is often at fault when attempts at communication seem to misfire. Consequently, consciously trying to be supportive and consciously avoiding defensiveness can dramatically improve your effectiveness as a communicator.

### Defensive and Supportive Communication[6]

Most of you know what defensiveness feels like. You feel as if you are under attack, as if you need to protect yourself. In fact, your self— your self-concept, your self-image, your self-esteem—is precisely what you are trying to protect when you feel defensive.

Arousing another person's defensiveness is the opposite of effective interpersonal communication. When someone becomes defensive, that person focuses on him- or herself and closes out the ideas and feelings of the other person.

## Avoiding Defensiveness

Messages and behavior that are likely to arouse defensiveness are classified as **defensive communication.** In contrast, messages and behavior that encourage openness are classified as **supportive communication.** Depending on a speaker's choice of words, the same message may either provoke defensiveness or express supportiveness. The following are some ways in which statements may be either defensive or supportive.

*Defensiveness stems from a need to protect the self-concept.*

### Evaluation versus description.

*"Look what you made me do!!!"*
*"C'mon, you moron, can't you do anything right?"*
*"Wow, is that ever a stupid idea!"*

Nobody enjoys being evaluated, criticized, and judged. It makes them feel defensive. In a nutshell, evaluation is "you" language. It directs itself to the *other* person's worth, ability, or idea. As a result, it can provoke much defensiveness. Description, on the other hand, is "I" language. It describes a speaker's thoughts and feelings about a person or idea. For example, you might say, "If I understand you correctly, I disagree." This form of response leads to greater interpersonal trust and facilitates further communication.

### Control versus problem orientation.   Communicative behavior that aims at controlling the behavior of others can produce much defensiveness. Methods of control are many and varied. For example, aggressive salespeople sometimes attempt to control their prospective customers by getting them to agree to a series of trivial questions as a lead-up to the final question of buying a product. Other people try to exercise control by strictly adhering to rules and invoking a higher authority ("How do you think the boss would feel about what is going on in this office?"). Implicit in attempts to control is the assumption that the controller is in a superior position to judge what is good for the controllee. When people become aware of this attitude, they usually become defensive.

A more effective approach is *problem orientation.* A problem-oriented speaker, rather than trying to get someone to do what he or

### Defensive and Supportive Communication

| | | |
|---|---|---|
| *Defensive Comment:* | Evaluation | "You language"; calls into question the worth of the person. |
| *Supportive Comment:* | Description | "I language"; describes your own feelings and ideas. |
| *Defensive Comment:* | Control | Aims at getting others to do what you want them to do. |
| *Supportive Comment:* | Problem-Orientation | Communication aimed at solving problems: "Let's find a solution that works for both of us." |
| *Defensive Comment:* | Strategy | Planned communication; working from a "script"— for example, saying something nice before criticizing someone; a "psychological sandwich." |
| *Supportive Comment:* | Spontaneity | Here-and-now orientation; being honest rather than planning how to manipulate. |

she wants, strives to find an alternative that is equally beneficial to *both* parties. Have you ever had the pleasure of working with a salesperson who you were convinced was working for your best interest, not just to make a sale? Such a person works toward solving problems, not controlling you. When others perceive that someone is genuinely striving for mutually satisfying solutions to problems, it can lead to more open communication, less defensiveness, and more effective solutions to interpersonal problems.

**Strategy versus spontaneity.**   Like controlling behavior, strategies suggest manipulation, because it implies preplanned communication. Such strategies range from "making a scene" and acting upset

| | | |
|---|---|---|
| *Defensive Comment:* | Neutrality | Emotional indifference; "You'll get over it." |
| *Supportive Comment:* | Empathy | Emotional involvement; nonverbal behavior is important. |
| *Defensive Comment:* | Superiority | Attitude that you're better than the other person; "I'm OK, you're not OK." |
| *Supportive Comment:* | Equality | Communication based on mutual respect; "I'm OK, you're OK." |
| *Defensive Comment:* | Certainty | Taking dogmatic, rigid positions; "Don't bother me with facts, my mind is made up." Usually more interested in winning an argument than in solving a problem. |
| *Supportive Comment:* | Provisionalism | Openness to receiving new information; showing some flexibility in the positions you take. |

to withholding information or acting "mysterious." When others detect that someone is acting a role rather than being open and honest, they can become defensive.

If others perceive someone as a person who acts *spontaneously*, however (that is, not from hidden motivations and agendas) and as a person who immediately and honestly responds to the present situation, they will feel more supported and more free in their own communication.

**Neutrality versus empathy.**   Almost any emotion another may feel toward someone is easier to deal with than neutrality or apathy. This is true because others' messages serve as feedback to self-concept—they tell a person who he or she is. Because neutrality is a lack of emotional involvement with another person, people who communicate neutrality are, in effect, telling the other person he or she isn't worth caring about. Even if someone is angry, at least he cares enough to feel some emotion.

In contrast, **empathy**—the verbal and nonverbal expression of involvement and concern for another person—is much more supportive. Empathy reflects genuine interest and caring, and an effort to understand. When other people listen carefully and respond appropriately, the implicit message is that someone is worthy of their time and effort, that they support that person.

### Superiority versus equality.

You probably know people who, after a test has been returned, always ask, "What'd ya get?" The real reason they ask this question is so they can show you their superior grade. Such behavior is obnoxious. It makes some people feel defensive when others flaunt their real or imagined superiority. In the same vein, some people begin their remarks with words such as *obviously* or point out their greater knowledge of the facts and broader experience. Such behavior is also usually met with defensiveness and resistance.

On the other hand, maybe you know someone—perhaps a favorite teacher—who makes you feel good about yourself by treating you with respect and talking with you like a friend or colleague. This teacher, treating you as a worthwhile human being despite differences in status, is exhibiting supportive communication. Secretaries who are treated with respect get much more work done and are much more satisfied with their jobs than those who are treated as inferior beings.

### Certainty versus provisionalism.

Do you know people who always have all the answers, whose ideas are truths to be defended, who make pronouncements rather than offer opinions, and who are intolerant of those with the wrong (that is, different) attitudes? These highly dogmatic people are well known for the defensiveness they can arouse in others. The usual response is to want to prove them wrong.

People are likely to be more effective if their opinions are held *provisionally*—that is, if they appear flexible and genuinely committed to solving problems. If they leave themselves open to new information and admit, from time to time, that they may be wrong about something, their communication with others will be much more productive.

The goal of interpersonal communication is the building and maintenance of satisfying interpersonal relationships. If you can learn to be confirming and supportive in your communication with others, and if you understand the need for self-disclosure, trust, and free and open dialogue, that goal will be better served.

## SUMMARY

The interpersonal relationship is the primary, and most important, human relationship. This chapter has explored interpersonal communication as it relates to the building and maintaining of interpersonal relationships.

▶ **Differentiate between the situational and developmental/ relational perspectives on interpersonal communication.**
The situational perspective views interpersonal communication as a particular context or level in which human communication occurs. According to this approach, the three key characteristics of interpersonal communication are (1) face-to-face interaction, (2) the participation of two persons, and (3) the potential for immediate feedback. The developmental/relational perspective views interpersonal communication as the result of a developmental, evolutionary process within a relationship. Both what you say and how you say it affect and are affected by the nature of a relationship with another person. Thus, for interpersonal communication to be fully understood, it must be viewed in terms of the level of familiarity between the participants.

▶ **Explain two models of interpersonal communication.**
The DeVito Model and the Baker Model offer two different perspectives on interpersonal communication. The DeVito Model is a descriptive model that identifies the principal components and processes of interpersonal communication. It is basically a situational approach contending that two persons' ability to communicate depends on shared experiences and the competent encoding and decoding of messages. At the heart of the Baker Model is silence. According to Baker, silence is the aim of communication. Language is used to increase reciprocal identification and reduce psychic tension. Negative silence occurs when reciprocal identification is low and psychic tension is high. In contrast, positive silence occurs when reciprocal identification is high and psychic tension is low. The better two people know each other, the more likely they will be comfortably silent in each other's presence.

▶ **Discuss the relationship of self-concept to interpersonal communication.**
Your self-concept develops, and is maintained, through interpersonal communication. Recall from Chapter 2 that self-concept results from internalizing the feedback you get from others. Self-concept then becomes the basis for your further communication with others. Each time you speak, you are putting your self-concept to a test. Positive feedback from others reaffirms your self-concept; negative feedback calls your self-concept into question.

▶**Describe four factors that contribute to interpersonal attraction.**

Interpersonal attraction is the amount of liking you feel toward another person. It is influenced by many factors, including personal attraction, similarity, complementarity, and proximity, contact, and interaction. Physical attraction is more important in the early stages of relationships than it is later on. Similarity is the degree to which two persons are alike. You are often attracted to people who resemble you, particularly in their beliefs, attitudes, and values. Complementarity is the degree to which two persons are compatibly different. Many times you are attracted to others who possess qualities that you lack but admire. Proximity, contact, and interaction refers to the actual physical availability of other people. It is a good predictor of attraction, probably because the availability of others reveals similarity, complementarity, and ways in which needs can be satisfied.

▶**Outline the process through which self-disclosure builds trust and intimacy in interpersonal relationships.**

Self-disclosure is the foundation of intimacy in interpersonal relationships. Through mutual self-disclosure, people reveal themselves to one another bit by bit. This process is called the dyadic effect. Through the dyadic effect, disclosure by one person makes it less risky for the other person to disclose at the same level of intimacy. When both persons have disclosed, there is increased trust, which allows for disclosure at a higher level of intimacy, and the process repeats itself. The continuing small increases in risk taking, trust, self-disclosure, and intimacy form a spiraling pattern through which relationships develop.

▶**Trace the stages through which a relationship goes as it comes together and comes apart, and cite examples of communication at each state.**

The processes of coming together and coming apart each contain five stages. The stages in coming together are (1) initiating (Hi, how ya doin?), (2) experimenting (Do you go to school here too? What's your major?), (3) intensifying (I really like you.), (4) integrating (Sometimes I feel like we're one person; what happens to you happens to me.), and (5) bonding (Let's get married.). The stages in coming apart are (1) differentiating (I just don't understand you sometimes.), (2) circumscribing (I don't want to talk about it.), (3) stagnating (Why bother? I know what you're going to say anyway.), (4) avoiding (I can't. I have to work.), and (5) terminating (And don't come back!!!).

➤ **Explain how defensiveness interferes with interpersonal communication and discuss six categories of defensive and supportive communication.**

When people become defensive, they focus on themselves and close out the ideas and feelings of other people—the opposite of effective interpersonal communication. Six sets of paired behaviors that provoke defensiveness or are supportive can be identified: evaluation versus description, control versus problem orientation, strategy versus spontaneity, neutrality versus empathy, certainty versus provisionalism, and superiority versus equality.

- Evaluation is "you language"; it calls into question the worth of the other person. Description is "I language"; it describes your own feelings and ideas rather than attacking the other person.
- Controlling communication aims at getting the other person to do what you want him or her to do. Problem-orientation is communication aimed at solving problems rather than controlling others.
- Strategy is planned or "scripted" communication such as that of the door-to-door salesperson. Spontaneous communication has a here-and-now orientation and is honest rather than manipulative.
- Neutrality is emotional indifference. Empathy is emotional involvement.
- Superiority is an attitude that you're better than the other person. Equality in communication is based on mutual respect.
- Certainty means taking dogmatic, rigid positions. Provisionalism is openness to receiving new information and showing flexibility in the positions you take.

---

## KEY TERMS

**Baker Model:**  a model of interpersonal communication that is based on silence as the aim of communication.

**communication competence:**  knowledge of social rules and understanding of communication as it relates to those rules.

**competence:**  your knowledge of the rules in a communication setting.

**complementarity:**  the degree to which two persons are compatibly different from each other.

**context:**  the situation in which communication occurs.

**defensive communication:**   messages and behavior that are likely to arouse defensiveness in another person.

**developmental/relational perspective:**   a view of interpersonal communication as the result of a developmental, evolutionary process within a relationship.

**DeVito Model:**   a descriptive model that identifies the principal components and processes of interpersonal communication.

**dyadic:**   occurring between two persons (a dyad).

**dyadic effect:**   mutual relationship-building process in which disclosure by one person leads to disclosure by another.

**effect:**   the consequence of communication.

**empathy:**   the ability to understand what another is thinking or feeling.

**field of experience:**   the sum total of all the facts and events you've ever observed.

**interpersonal attraction:**   the amount of liking you feel toward another person.

**interpersonal communication:**   face-to-face interaction between two persons, with the potential for immediate feedback.

**linguistic competence:**   knowledge of the rules, vocabulary, and structures of language.

**performance:**   your actual behavior as you speak, listen, and adjust to a variety of situations and contexts.

**proximity, contact, and interaction:**   the actual, physical availability of other people.

**psychic tension:**   the discomfort you feel when there is misunderstanding or conflict.

**reciprocal identification:**   the degree of similarity and understanding between two (or more) persons.

**self-disclosure:**   sharing information about yourself that would not otherwise be known.

**similarity:**   the degree to which two persons are alike.

**situational perspective:**   a view of interpersonal communication as a particular context or level in which human communication occurs.

**supportive communication:**   messages and behavior that encourage openness to others.

## DISCUSSION QUESTIONS

1.  Compare and contrast the situational and developmental/relational perspectives on interpersonal communication. Why is it useful to use more than one perspective when studying interpersonal communication?

2. What beliefs, feelings, and other information about yourself do you freely disclose to others? What parts of yourself do you keep hidden from others? What would be the consequences of revealing these hidden parts to your most intimate friends?

3. Think about a relationship in which you are now involved. Applying the classification of relational stages, how does your interaction with the other person reveal the nature of your relationship?

## *SUGGESTED ACTIVITIES*

1. List the names of ten people to whom you are attracted. Next to each name, identify the factor(s) or interpersonal attraction that you feel have the strongest influence. Are any patterns evident? Are you influenced by similarity? Complementarity? Is physical attractiveness especially important? Are these people with whom you have contact and interaction?

2. With a partner, take turns talking for a few minutes about each of the following topics:

   My childhood home

   Where I'd like to be in 10 years

   My idea of a perfect evening

   An embarrassing moment

   The relative of mine that I most admire

   Something that makes me sad

   My proudest moment

   My ideal job

   Discuss the results. Did you feel some resistance to disclosing yourself on any of these topics? What was the source of the resistance? How do you feel about your partner now? How is that different from when you began the exercise?

3. With a friend or classmate, find a topic about which you disagree and stage a conversation in which you attempt to use defensive behaviors exclusively. Note your feelings as you do this. Then repeat the conversation, covering as many of the same topics as possible, but this time be as supportive in your communication as possible. Again, note your feelings. What did you learn from this?

4. Imagine the most attractive person you could possibly meet. Close your eyes and really imagine what he or she would be like. Now create an even clearer picture of the person by filling in the following:

| | |
|---|---|
| Age | Favorite book |
| Sex | Favorite vacation |
| Height | Profession or professional goals |
| Weight | Physical attractiveness (1–10 scale) |
| Race | Athletic ability (1–10 scale) |
| Religion | Intelligence (1–10 scale) |
| Favorite music | Highest level of education completed |
| Favorite food | |
| Favorite pastime | Five adjectives that best describe this person |

Look over the results. What factors in interpersonal attraction appear? Which are the most important to you? Why? How does your fantasy person compare to the real people you listed in activity 1? What does this tell you?

---

## SUGGESTED READINGS

Jourard, S. (1964). *The Transparent Self.* (New York: D. Van Nostrand Co).

Miller, G. and Steinberg, M. (1975). *Between People: a New Analysis of Interpersonal Communication.* (Palo Alto, CA: Science Research Associates).

Powell, J. (1969). *Why Am I Afraid to Tell You Who I Am?* (Niles, IL: Argus Communications).

Trenholm, S. and Jensen, A. (1988). *Interpersonal Communication.* (Belmont, CA: Wadsworth Publishing Company).

# Listening and Responding to Others

*After studying this chapter, you should be able to:*

▶ Differentiate between listening and hearing, and describe the four stages of the listening process.

▶ Identify four goals of listening.

▶ Note six barricades to effective listening and tell how each can be overcome.

▶ Cite ten suggestions for improving your listening skill.

▶ Discuss why feedback is important and suggest four ways of enhancing your ability to give feedback.

▶ Explain how to improve your empathic listening skill.

Do you think most people are good listeners? Are *you* a good listener? Evidence suggests your listening skills can be improved. Forty-eight hours after listening to a ten-minute presentation, you probably can recall only about half of the information presented. Eventually, you retain less than 25 percent of what you hear. As one educator once noted, "We hear half of what is said to us, understand only half of that, believe only half of that, and remember only half of that."

## ARE YOU A GOOD LISTENER?

If you're typical you spend about 80 percent of your time on communication activities. Of that time, you spend about 14 percent writing, 17 percent reading, 16 percent speaking, and at least 53 percent listening.[1] These statistics suggest that listening is a very important skill, yet you probably have never had any formal listening training.

Although you spend the least amount of your communication time writing, you start learning how to write in preschool and continue to improve your writing skills through graduate school. You also start formal training in reading at an early age. Most elementary schools and many high schools and colleges have reading specialists. While fewer students receive formal training in speaking, they are far more likely to take a course in public speaking than a course in listening. In fact, many colleges and universities require students to develop oral communication skills. Yet, despite the amount of time spent listening to others, a relatively small number of universities offer a course in listening.

## WHAT IS LISTENING?

How many times have you asked someone, "Did you hear me?" Is that the question you really want to ask? Unless you think someone has a physiological hearing problem, you probably want to know whether he or she is *listening* to you, rather than simply *hearing* you. As George Burns said while portraying God in the movie "Oh God," "I can't help hearing, but I don't always listen."

**Hearing** is the physiological process of receiving sound waves through the mechanisms of the ear drum; the middle ear bones called the hammer, anvil, and stirrup; and, eventually, the auditory nerve. The vibrations that are carried through these organs are then turned into electrical energy and ultimately reach the brain, where they are decoded into a message. **Listening** includes not only hearing but also

*When you listen, you select, attend, understand, and remember.*

trying to make sense out of what is heard. Actually, listening includes four operations: selecting, attending, understanding, and remembering.

## Selecting

**Selecting** is the process of sorting through competing sounds and noise in the environment in order to focus on one sound. When you listen to a class lecture, there are a variety of competing sounds on which to focus. If you choose to focus on what your professor is saying, you have selected those stimuli from all the potential ones.

Stop reading for just a moment. What do you hear? What sounds surround you? Did you realize that someone was playing a stereo? Did you hear the sound of birds or rain or wind? Maybe you weren't really aware of the furnace, air conditioner, TV, voices, clock, a car, a plane, or a train. Sounds surround you. They are there to be heard if you select the ones you want to hear, the ones that are important to you.

## Attending

"Attention is a great deal like electricity: We don't know what it is, but we do know what it does and what conditions bring it about."[2] **Attending** is focusing on one sound; it is the sequel to selecting. You don't have to attend for a long period of time. You may zero in on it only for a fraction of a second, changing your focus of attention for a variety of reasons. However fleeting, you focus your attention so that you can listen instead of just hear. When you're hungry and looking for a place to eat, you would be more likely to attend to a radio commercial advertising a restaurant than to one promoting a tire store. What you attend to is based on your needs, preferences, and the intensity or novelty of the stimulus.

## Understanding

After you have selected and attended to a stimulus, you then attempt to understand it. **Understanding** is the process of assigning meaning to the stimuli to which you attend. Several theories attempt to describe how you assign meaning to what you see and hear, but as yet, there is no one commonly accepted explanation. We do know that you understand what you hear by relating it to something you have already seen or heard. If you have never had an algebra class, your instructor would probably not be very successful in trying to help you understand your calculus lessons. You would be able to hear what your

---

**The Listening Process**

| *Selecting* | *Attending* | *Understanding* | *Remembering* |
|---|---|---|---|
| Sorting through competing sounds in your environment | The sequel to selecting; focusing on a specific sound | Assigning meaning to what you hear | Recalling past events |

teacher said, but you probably would not understand it. You would have no experience or knowledge to help you assign meaning to what you hear.

### Remembering

**Remembering** is the process of recalling past events. Most listening experts believe that the best way to check whether listening has really occurred is to determine whether a person can remember what was heard. Some definitions of listening include the notion that you must actually respond to the information you hear. Remembering information is one way of responding. To prove that listening has taken place, the memory need not last a long time—a short time will suffice.

## THE GOALS OF LISTENING

*The goals of listening include enjoyment, evaluation, empathy, and gaining information.*

You spend the largest share of your communication time listening. The reason you spend so much time on this activity is that it serves so many purposes. There are at least four different goals of listening: (1) listening to enjoy, (2) listening to evaluate, (3) listening to empathize, and (4) listening to gain information.

### Listening to Enjoy

Did you listen to your stereo today? Did you recently attend a concert, watch a comedienne on TV, or go to a movie? In each of these situations your prime purpose was to listen because you wanted to be entertained. You were not necessarily concerned about learning or trying to be critical. You just wanted to enjoy yourself. You spend a

Friends may have different goals of listening at different times in their relationship. When listening to empathize, they may try to get away from distractions.

considerable portion of your time listening just because you want to hear good music, laugh, or hear a good story.

## Listening to Evaluate

When you listen to evaluate, you try to determine whether the information you hear is valid, reliable, believable, or useful. One problem you may have when you listen to evaluate is that you may become so preoccupied with your criticism that you often do not completely understand. When listening to a politician whose ideas are radically different from yours, you may miss the details of the message if you continually criticize the talk as it is occurring. Often the very process of evaluating and making judgments and decisions about information interferes with the capacity to understand and recall. To compensate for this tendency, it is important that you understand what a speaker is saying before you make a judgment about the value of his or her information.

## Listening to Empathize

Your best friend tells you that it's been one of those days. Everything just seemed to go wrong. His car didn't start. He overslept. And, worst of all, he found out he may lose his job. After a day like this, he just needs to talk to someone—someone who will listen. He doesn't need advice, just someone who will try to understand some of his troubles, for it seems that when someone understands, coping becomes a little easier. So you listen.

Listening to try to understand how someone else is feeling is called *empathic listening.* In effect, you act as a sounding board for the other person as that person discusses his or her situation. Empathic listening serves an important therapeutic function. Just having an empathic listener may help someone out. The empathic listener isn't there to judge or offer advice. He or she helps because the process of sharing and listening is a soothing one that can often restore a person's perspective on his or her problems. You will find out how to become a good empathic listener later in this chapter.

## Listening to Gain Information

Think about how much time you spend each week listening in order to learn something. How much time did you spend today listening to lectures and class discussions? Undoubtedly, you spend quite a bit of time listening to recall what a speaker has said, even taking a phone message or receiving instructions from your boss.

*Becoming a skilled note-taker will greatly enhance your ability to learn through listening.*

It is usually difficult to remember the details of a lengthy speech or discussion without taking notes. People who have mastered the art of listening for information have also usually perfected a note-taking system that works for them. When you need to listen for information, consider the following suggestions for improving your note-taking skill:

1. Come prepared to take notes, even if you're not sure you need to. Bring a pencil or pen and some paper.
2. If you do decide to take notes, choose the best approach for the occasion. Depending on the nature of the information and how you intend to use your notes, you may decide to outline the entire presentation, identify facts and principles, jot down key words, or just record main ideas. If the speaker is not following an outline pattern, it will be tricky to create an outline yourself. If you are going to take an objective examination over the material, maybe you just need to note facts (like names and dates) and basic principles. If you are going to prepare a report for someone else to read, noting key words may be sufficient to jog your memory. You may just want to write down main ideas to help you recall the key points of the speech.
3. Beware of taking too many notes. Determine how important the information is to you and why you should remember it. If you're going to report the essence of the presentation to someone else on the same day, you probably do not need to write it down because your memory will still be fresh. In addition, the less time you spend writing notes, the more time you have to concentrate on what is being said.

## LISTENING BARRICADES

A **listening barricade** is an obstacle that keeps you from listening well. It slows your progress, your efficiency, and your accuracy. The following are several common listening barricades; try to identify them so that when they arise you can eliminate them.

*Listening barricades interfere with the progress, efficiency, and accuracy of your listening.*

### Suffering from Information Overload

Have you ever noticed how most medical doctors' handwriting is illegible? One reason may be that, beginning in medical school and continuing throughout their careers, they must write so much so fast that they take shortcuts which result in sloppy, illegible handwriting. The same principle may apply to listening habits. If you spend a great deal of time listening to people speak, you may begin to tune them out. You become tired and want to take listening shortcuts.

It has been estimated that you are exposed to over a billion words a year! Because you spend so much of your time listening to others, you may begin to suffer from information overload. **Information overload** occurs when the accumulated quantity of words becomes so great that you experience listening fatigue.

What are some solutions to this problem? First of all, when you are speaking, be sensitive to the fact that your listener may be overloaded. If you suspect that your listener may have this problem, try to postpone your communication until he or she is rested. Don't assume that, just because you are ready to talk, the other person is ready to listen.

On the other hand, if someone wants to talk to you and you are feeling overloaded, you may have to recognize your fatigue and make a greater effort to focus on what he or she is saying. If you are really tired and you sense that the person has very important information to discuss, you may want to explain your situation and set aside some specific time later to respond to his or her needs.

### Deciding That the Topic Is Not Interesting to You

Most of you have been guilty of tuning a speaker out because you felt that the presentation was going to be boring or unimportant. While some listening situations may indeed be unexciting and worthless, you often miss out if you make negative judgments and close your mind too soon. Instead, in all fairness, you owe it to yourself and the speaker to keep an open mind.

The next time you're tempted to tune a speaker out, force yourself to pay attention. Really focus on what he or she is saying and try to identify at least one item that is worth remembering or applies to you. If you get actively involved, the time will pass faster and you may pick up some information that you may otherwise have missed.

## Becoming Wrapped Up in Personal Concerns

Although you may have been taught that it's impolite, most of you focus more on your own thoughts than on what someone else is saying. For example, how often have you been guilty of thinking about what you were going to say next, instead of focusing on a friend's immediate comments? Experts believe that you can really concentrate on only one thing at a time. Thus, if you are planning what you want to say or thinking about personal problems, you will not be able to give full attention to messages.

The solution? First, realize that this barricade exists. In most cases, you *will* be more interested in your own thoughts than in the thoughts of others. Second, try to turn off those internal distractions by concentrating on the other person's message. It will be difficult to block out your internal messages totally, but with sustained effort and self-motivation, you can make progress.

## Being Diverted by Outside Distractions

Have you ever noticed that it is difficult to concentrate on a friend's comments while the TV is on or when you're sitting in a noisy restaurant? Have you ever tried to concentrate on a lecture while two people behind you carried on their own conversation? No matter how interesting or important a message is to you, if you can't hear or if other messages are competing for your attention, your listening efficiency will decrease.

The best environment for listening is one that offers as few noises and distractions as possible. When you want to talk to someone, try to pick a quiet time and place. In the context of a family, for instance, it may be a challenge to find a quiet time to converse. With one family member going out to play ball, another going shopping, and a third coming home from a taxing day and wanting time to relax, it is difficult to find moments when all are available for conversation and willing to give their undivided attention.

Perhaps a good title for a book about listening skills would be *How to Turn Off the TV*. It is difficult to listen with the ever-present chatter of cartoons, situation comedies, news programs, and dramas in the background. Listening takes all the powers of concentration that you can muster.

## Differences Between Speech and Thought Rates

Dr. Ralph Nichols, a pioneer in listening research and training, has identified a barrier to effective listening related to the way you process the words you hear.[3] You usually speak at a rate of about 100 to 125 words a minute. You have the capacity to listen at a rate of up to 700 words a minute, and some suggest that you can listen as quickly as 1200 words a minute. What this means is that you have the ability to listen much faster than you normally need to. The resulting gap gives you time to daydream, permitting you to tune a speaker in and out and giving the illusion that you are concentrating more deeply than you actually are.

Fortunately, this phenomenon need not hinder your listening effectiveness. In fact, you can turn it to your advantage if you use the extra time to mentally summarize what a speaker is saying. Periodically reviewing a speaker's key ideas can significantly increase your effectiveness as a listener and help you retain additional information.

*The difference between a speaker's speech rate and the rate at which language is processed may lead to poor listening.*

## Criticizing the Way the Message Is Delivered

A person's appearance and speech characteristics can affect your ability to listen and comprehend the information he or she presents. Imagine that you and a friend have decided to attend a lecture about improving your business communication skills. The speaker is introduced and begins her remarks. The presentation, however, is not what you expected at all. She begins to read her speech from a manuscript. She makes virtually no eye contact with the audience. Her voice drones on in a monotone; and, to make matters worse, she has the annoying habit of constantly adjusting her glasses by wrinkling her nose. "I certainly expected a better presentation from an alleged expert on communication," you mumble. Your friend is aware of the distracting presentation style, but still tries to take notes on the speaker's main ideas. You, on the other hand, are irritated because you have wasted an evening on this boring presentation. "This is terrible," you whisper to your friend. "Yes," your friend replies, "but I'm picking up some good ideas for my term paper." You're puzzled by that remark, because you're finding it difficult to gain much of anything from the speech.

The problem, of course, is that you have let the speaker's delivery style affect your ability to listen. In fact, now that you are studying principles of communication, you may find this problem looms even larger, because you now pay more attention to nonverbal cues. Nonetheless, try not to let your increased awareness distract you from being a good listener. Try to focus on the message instead of on the speaker. Refuse to allow poorly executed presentations to rob you of your ability to comprehend their content.

| Review Box | |

## Listening Barricades

| *Problem* | *Solution* |
|---|---|
| Suffering from information overload | Concentrate harder on the message when you are tired or overwhelmed with details; identify the most important information. |
| Deciding the topic is not interesting | Listen for information that applies to you and your needs. |
| Becoming wrapped up in personal concerns | Turn off internal dialog with yourself by concentrating on the speaker's message rather than your self talk. |
| Being diverted by outside distractions | Actively try to optimize the listening environment by turning off the TV, moving to a quieter location, or moving closer to the speaker. |
| Differing in speech rate and thought rate | Mentally summarize the speaker's message while listening. |
| Criticizing the way a message is delivered | Focus on the message rather than the messenger. |

## SUGGESTIONS FOR IMPROVING YOUR LISTENING

Now that we have examined several common listening barriers and suggested some ways of overcoming them, let's look at some general strategies that can help you to improve your overall listening ability.[4] By listening well you can become a more valued friend. By listening well, you can also achieve more by retaining more information.

### Look for information you can use.

In every listening situation, ask yourself, "What's in this for me? "What can I use from this presentation? How can what this person is saying help me help others?" Try to relate the material you hear to yourself; that's how you will learn.

Of course, when you are listening empathically you should not try to apply the information to yourself. Focus instead on the other person and how to make the situation most useful to him or her.

### Listen for ideas, not just facts.

Facts are merely one type of information. In many cases, principles and main ideas will be more useful to you than individual facts (such as names, dates, and places). Most speakers try to make three to five main points. They then use facts, statistics, and specific examples to support those points. Therefore, to get the most out of a situation, try to listen for the main ideas instead of the specific facts, statistics, and examples. If you listen in this way, you should be able to concentrate for longer periods of time.

### Try not to be distracted by an emotion-arousing word or phrase.

Certain words or phrases can arouse emotions very quickly; and, of course, the same word may arouse different emotions in different people. You respond emotionally because of your cultural background, religious convictions, and political philosophy. Words that reflect negatively on your nationality, ethnic origin, or religion can trigger automatic emotional reactions. Cursing and obscene language may also reduce your listening efficiency.

As a listener, you must realize that you are going to hear words and phrases that will distract you from a speaker's message. The only solution is to try to keep your emotions under control. If you don't, be prepared to pay the consequences: reduced listening effectiveness.

### Adapt to the speaker.

A speaker's delivery and appearance may distract you from what he or she is trying to say. Clearly, not everyone to whom you must listen is an eloquent speaker or a fascinating conversationalist. To be a good listener, you must adjust to a speaker's idiosyncrasies, no matter how distracting they may be. If a speaker's appearance, gestures, voice, or posture divert your attention, try a bit harder to concentrate on the message rather than on the messenger.

### Adapt to the speaking situation.

Sometimes you will find that you need to adapt to an environment as well as to a speaker. If the room is too stuffy, you may need to open a window or ask that the air-conditioning system be adjusted. If you can't hear the speaker, move closer. If people are talking unnecessarily, politely ask them to be quiet. If a door needs closing, don't wait for someone else to do it. To be an effective listener do whatever is appropriate to ensure an environment that encourages comprehension.

| Review Box |
| --- |

## A Comparison of Good and Bad Listening Habits

| *Suggestion for Improving Listening Skill* | *The Bad Listener* | *The Good Listener* |
| --- | --- | --- |
| 1. Listen for information that you can use. | Tunes out dry subjects. | Looks for benefits and opportunities; asks "What's in it for me?" |
| 2. Listen for ideas, not just facts. | Listens for facts. | Listens for central themes. |
| 3. Don't be distracted by emotion-arousing words. | Is easily distracted by words and phrases. | Does not get hung up on words; stays on track. |
| 4. Adapt to the speaker's delivery style. | Tunes out if delivery is poor. | Judges content; skips over delivery errors. |
| 5. Adapt to the listening situation. | Distracted easily. | Fights or avoids distractions; knows how to concentrate. |

**Practice your listening skills.**

You learn how to write by writing, not just by studying the rules of grammar and spelling. Similarly, you learn about public speaking by giving speeches, not just by reading a book. In other words, you learn by doing.

Experts report that poor listeners are also inexperienced listeners. When they listen, it is usually to easy, entertaining information. Some critics of TV point to the situation comedies and superficial entertainment programs as culprits that promote poor listening. They claim we've become "Sesame Street" listeners because we expect to be entertained.

Good listening skills result from attention to more difficult material. Do you listen to news, documentaries, or interview programs like

| *Suggestion* | *The Bad Listener* | *The Good Listener* |
|---|---|---|
| 6. Practice your listening skills. | Avoids difficult listening situations. | Seeks opportunities to listen to difficult information. |
| 7. Decide what your listening objective is. | Doesn't have a listening goal in mind. | Decides whether to listen to enjoy, evaluate, empathize or gain information. |
| 8. Try to anticipate the speaker's next major idea. | Is not actively involved in what the speaker is saying. | Keeps one step ahead of the point a speaker is making. |
| 9. Identify the speaker's supporting material. | Does not pay attention to how the speaker is clarifying ideas. | Actively seeks to identify how a speaker is supporting major ideas. |
| 10. Mentally summarize key ideas. | Does not try to mentally restate what the speaker has been discussing. | Mentally summarizes a speaker's message at five-minute intervals. |

Source: Adapted from Lyman K. Steil, Larry L. Barker, and Kittie W. Watson, *Effective Listening: Key to Your Success (Reading, MA: Addison-Wesley Publishing Company. 1983): 72–73.*

"Face the Nation," "Meet the Press," and "Nightline"? Try listening to these or other more difficult material to stretch your skills.

## Decide what your listening objective is.

One of your first tasks should be to determine your reasons for listening. That is, are you listening to empathize, to evaluate, to enjoy, or to gain information? If you're having a conversation with a friend, you needn't try to remember everything your friend says; you should try to be a nonjudgmental sounding board. If you know that your objective is to evaluate, then you should make sure that you understand what your friend is saying before you begin your critique. If you are listening for enjoyment, you need not worry about taking notes or trying to identify the pattern of organization. When you listen for information, you need to focus on content instead of delivery and to identify the information that is most useful to you. If you don't know your listening objective, you can't choose an appropriate listening strategy.

### Try to anticipate a speaker's next main idea.

Trying to determine which point a speaker is going to make next can improve your listening ability for two reasons. First, it makes the speech-speed-versus-thought-speed problem less apparent, because you use your extra thought time to concentrate on the speaker, the message, and the objective of the presentation. This reduces the temptation to tune out the speaker. Second, trying to anticipate a speaker's next point can help your memory, because you, in essence, "hear" the point twice—once when you guess it and again when a speaker presents it. Even if you guess wrong, you can compare your anticipated point with the one the speaker actually makes to see why you misjudged. Such active participation can make the listening experience more interesting and increase your comprehension.

### Try to identify how a speaker supports the main ideas in the speech.

A public speaker who wants to inform will use facts, examples, statistics, and testimony to support the main points he or she develops. As you listen, try to determine how the speaker is doing this. Like anticipating a speaker's thoughts, analyzing evidence helps to lessen the speech-speed-versus-thought-speed problem. When you are listening to evaluate, it is vital to consider how a speaker documents his or her conclusions.

### Mentally summarize the key ideas.

Mentally summarizing a speaker's main ideas can significantly improve your retention of the information presented. Even when your listening objective is to empathize or to evaluate critically, mentally recapping the highlights can keep you alert and help you follow a speaker's train of thought. In a public speaking situation, a speaker should provide transitional phrases and internal summaries to help listeners follow along. Whether a speaker provides such guideposts or not, you, as a good listener, should be ready to provide them yourself. Concentrate on learning information while a speech is still in progress, rather than on waiting until later to study your notes.

## FEEDBACK: RESPONDING TO OTHERS

In simplest terms, **feedback** is a response given to another person about his or her behavior or communication. Feedback can be verbal and nonverbal, as well as intentional or unintentional. When your instructor returns a grade on a test or a paper, you are getting feedback about your comprehension of the course material. When you call in an order for a pizza and the order taker says, "Now let me see—you want a large pepperoni with extra cheese," you are receiving information about the success of your communication.

Feedback serves several purposes. First, it can tell a speaker how well his or her message has been understood. Second, it can indicate agreement or disagreement with the points a speaker has made. Finally, it can help a speaker to correct any statements that the audience finds vague or confusing. In essence, feedback tells a speaker how he or she is affecting others. It helps an individual keep the communication on target and thus better achieve a communication objective.

*A receiver's feedback enables a sender to gauge whether the sender has been understood.*

Earlier in the book we stressed that communication is an ongoing activity, a back-and-forth process. This reciprocal nature of communication illustrates the purpose of feedback. During a job interview, for example, an employer is interested in the responses to his or her questions. You, in turn, try to assess the impression you're making by watching whether the interviewer agrees with you, smiles or frowns, and generally seems interested in what you have to say. Both you and the interviewer are providing feedback to each other.

## SUGGESTIONS FOR IMPROVING FEEDBACK

Improving your skill in providing appropriate feedback can enhance your communication skill. It can help others avoid being misunderstood. The following specific suggestions should enhance your ability to provide useful feedback to others.

**Feedback should be well-timed.**

In general, feedback is most effective when given at the earliest opportunity. For example, when you are learning a new skill, such as driving a car, you will make better progress if the feedback from your teacher is immediate. If your teacher waits until after the lesson is over to tell you what you did wrong when you tried to parallel park, the information will not be as useful as it would have been while you were actually attempting the maneuver.

**Don't overwhelm a receiver with unnecessary detail.**

You have already read about the listening barricade of information overload. If too much detail is provided in one dose, a listener will have difficulty knowing exactly how he or she should respond. Feedback should be selective. Hit the high points.

**Be specific rather than general.**

A specific response is better than a vague reaction. Being told that you are "dominating" will probably not be as helpful as being told that "Just now, when we were deciding what to do, I felt that if I didn't agree with you, you would criticize and embarrass me in front of the rest of the group."

**Be descriptive rather than evaluative.**

"This is what I understand you to say" sounds better than "You're dead wrong." By avoiding evaluative language as much as possible, you reduce the need for an individual to react defensively. Of course, there are times when you will need to evaluate the appropriateness or inappropriateness of what you hear. In such cases, if you are not in agreement, say so tactfully and describe your reaction without passing judgment.

## EMPATHIC LISTENING: COMBINING THE BEST OF EFFECTIVE LISTENING AND FEEDBACK

The suggestions for improving your listening and feedback skills have primarily focused on increasing your accuracy in listening and responding to the content of a message. Besides just focusing on what is said, it is important to develop your skill in identifying how others are feeling.

*Empathy enables you to listen more accurately and respond more appropriately to other people.*

**Empathic listening** combines listening skills and feedback skills to enhance your sensitivity in responding to others. *To empathize is to attempt to feel how someone else is feeling.* It is trying to identify accurately both the feeling and the content of a message. In other words, *empathy* is attempting to walk in another person's shoes, trying to see and feel the world from another's perspective. As you become more skilled in empathizing, you will be able to listen more accurately and respond more appropriately to other people. To listen empathically involves a series of steps. You need to: (1) stop, (2) look, (3) listen, (4) question, (5) paraphrase content, and (6) paraphrase feelings.

To be a good empathetic listener, you must *stop* what you are doing, focusing on the thoughts of your partner, then *look* and *listen* for verbal and nonverbal cues that will help you understand what it's like to be in your partner's position.

## Step 1: Stop.

Before you can effectively tune in to what your partner is feeling, you need to *stop* what you are doing, eliminate as many distractions as you can, and focus on your partner's feelings instead of your own. Try a process called **decentering**—stepping away from your own thoughts and attempting to experience the thoughts of your partner.[5] To decenter effectively, avoid making judgments and evaluations. Note that decentering emphasizes thoughts rather than feelings. This is an important first step in turning off distractions, both intrapersonal and external, and concentrating on another person.

## Step 2: Look.

After setting aside your own thoughts and turning off outside distractions, you need to *look* for nonverbal clues that will help you identify how your partner is feeling. Remember that most of the communication of emotion comes from nonverbal cues. The face provides important information about the way a person is feeling, as do voice quality, pitch, rate, volume, and the use of silence. Don't forget that a person's body movement and posture help to communicate the intensity of his or her feelings.

## Step 3: Listen.

After stopping and looking for nonverbal cues, you need to listen to what another person is telling you. Even though your partner may not say exactly how he or she feels, you need to look for cues. Match verbal cues with nonverbal cues to decipher both the content and the emotion of the message. In addition, ask yourself, "How would I feel if I had the same experience?" A key to reaching accurate conclusions is to try to interpret the message according to the *sender's* code system rather than your own.

### Step 4: Ask questions.

As you listen for information and attempt to determine how another person is feeling, you may need to ask questions to help clarify your conclusions. Most of your questions will serve one of four purposes: (1) to obtain *additional information* ("How long have you been living in Grain Valley?"), (2) to find out how the person *feels* ("Are you troubled because you didn't get the raise you expected?"), (3) to ask for *clarification* of a word or phrase ("What do you mean when you say you thought you were on the flex-time schedule?"), and (4) to *verify* that you have reached an accurate conclusion about your partner's meaning or feeling ("Are you saying that you feel sad about not getting the promotion?").

Your ability to ask appropriate questions will show your supportiveness for your partner. Don't ask questions just for the sake of asking questions. Also, be sure to monitor the way in which you ask your questions. Your own verbal and nonverbal responses will contribute to the emotional climate of your conversation.

### Step 5: Paraphrase the content.

After you have listened and asked questions, to check if your interpretations are accurate, paraphrase the content you have heard. **Paraphrasing** is restating in your own words *what you think a person is saying*. Paraphrasing is different from repeating something perfectly without understanding what it means. Consider this example:

> *Bob:*    I think my job is too difficult for me. I'm not qualified to do it.
>
> *Jan:*    You think you lack the necessary skills to do your job.

Note that at this point Jan is dealing with only the content of Bob's message. Of course, the ultimate goal of empathic listening is to understand both the content and the feelings of the other person's message.

### Step 6: Paraphrase feelings.

Once you begin to understand the content of a message, you will be better prepared to paraphrase what you believe your partner is feeling. Jan may follow her paraphrase of the content of the message with a

> **Review Box**

**Improving Your Empathic Listening Skill**

| | |
|---|---|
| Stop | Eliminate as many distractions as possible and focus on your partner rather than yourself. |
| Look | Look for nonverbal cues, particularly in the area of the face. |
| Listen | Concentrate on what your partner is saying. |
| Ask Questions | Try to clarify your conclusions. |
| Paraphrase Message Content | Use your own words to summarize what you think the other person is saying. |
| Paraphrase Feelings | Summarize how you think the other person is feeling and ask if your understanding is accurate. |

question such as, "You are probably feeling pretty frustrated right now, aren't you?" Such a paraphrase will allow Bob either to agree with Jan's assessment or to clarify how he's feeling. For instance, he may respond: "No, I'm not frustrated. I'm just disappointed that the job is not working out."

Empathic listening, then, can help improve communication accuracy by clarifying both content and feelings. It can be particularly useful when someone needs a sounding board—when someone needs a listener to empathize, not to provide advice.

*Caution:* We are *not* suggesting that you go through each of these steps each time you try to communicate with someone. You may find these suggestions helpful, however, if you are having trouble understanding how someone else feels or if you are trying to resolve a conflict.

*When you paraphrase, you give someone a chance to correct your understanding of the message.*

## SUMMARY

 **Differentiate between hearing and listening, and describe the four stages of the listening process.**

*Hearing* is the physiological process of receiving sound waves through the ear. *Listening* includes hearing but adds the process of trying to make sense out of what is heard. Listening is actually made up of four operations: selecting, attending, understanding, and remembering. *Selecting* is the process of sorting through competing sounds in your environment in preparation for focusing on one sound. *Attending*, the sequel to selecting, is the process of focusing on one sound. *Understanding* is the process of assigning meaning to the stimuli to which we attended. *Remembering* is the process of recalling past events to verify that listening has occurred.

▶ **Identify four goals of listening.**

You listen for four principal reasons: to enjoy, to evaluate, to empathize, and to gain information. When you listen to enjoy, your purpose is to be entertained. When you listen to evaluate, you try to determine whether the information you hear is valid, reliable, believable, or useful. When you listen to empathize, you try to understand how someone else is feeling. When you listen to gain information, you hope to learn something useful. Developing strong note-taking skills can greatly enhance your ability to gain information through listening.

▶ **Note six barricades to effective listening and tell how each can be overcome.**

Because you spend so much of your time listening, the accumulated quantity of words may lead to listening fatigue. Such information overload can be overcome through sensitivity to your own and others' listening limitations and postponing serious discussion until all participants are feeling fresh.

Most of you have been guilty of tuning a speaker out because you've decided in advance that the presentation will be boring or unimportant. The solution is to force yourself to pay attention and try to find at least one piece of information that is worth remembering or personally applicable.

It is a common human failing to focus more on one's own thoughts than on what someone else is saying. Once you recognize this tendency in yourself, you can try to turn off internal distractions by concentrating on the other person's message.

Outside distractions, such as background noise or a stuffy room, are another barricade to effective listening. These can be avoided by choosing a quiet time and place for listening, or by altering the environment to make it more accommodating.

Because your rate of speech is much slower than your rate of listening, you have a tendency to tune a speaker in and out. You can turn this gap in speaking and listening rates to your advantage, however, by using the extra time to think about and summarize what a speaker is saying.

Finally, you may find that a speaker's appearance or speech characteristics are interfering with your ability to focus on the information he or she is presenting. To overcome this barricade to good listening, try to concentrate on the message instead of on the speaker.

▶ **Cite ten suggestions for improving your listening skill.**

The following general strategies can help you to improve your overall listening ability: (1) Be a selfish listener; look for information you can use. (2) Listen for main ideas rather than trying to remember every fact and detail. (3) Try to be conscious of the words or phrases that can emotionally distract you. (4) Adapt to the speaker; if the speaker has annoying mannerisms, try to ignore them and concentrate instead on the message. (5) Adapt to the speaking environment; open a window or close a door if the room temperature is making it difficult to concentrate. (6) Practice your listening skills by listening to more difficult material. (7) In each situation, decide what your listening objective is. Are you listening for information, to be entertained, to evaluate, or to empathize? (8) To stay actively involved and increase memory, try to anticipate the speaker's next point. (9) Attempt to identify how a speaker is supporting the main ideas in the speech. (10) Finally, to improve your recall of the information, mentally summarize key ideas every few minutes.

▶ **Discuss why feedback is important and suggest four ways of enhancing your ability to give feedback.**

Feedback is a response given to others about their behavior and communication. Through feedback, you tell a speaker how well you've understood his or her message, indicate your agreement or disagreement, and help the speaker to clarify any statements you may not have understood. As a result, the speaker can better assess the progress toward a communication objective.

To be optimally helpful, you should make sure that your feedback is (1) well timed, (2) well chosen, (3) specific rather than general, and (4) descriptive rather than evaluative.

▶ **Explain how to improve your empathic listening skill.**

First, *stop* what you are doing or thinking about and tune out distracting thoughts. Next, *look* at your partner and be sensitive to nonverbal cues. Then really try to *listen* to what the other person is saying. To see if you have understood what a person was saying, *ask clarifying questions*. Then *paraphrase the content* of the message; summarize your understanding in your own words. Finally, *paraphrase the feelings;* try to put into words how you think the other person is feeling.

## KEY TERMS

**Attending:**  the sequel to selecting; focusing on one sound.

**Decentering:**  stepping away from your own thoughts and attempting to experience the thoughts of another person.

**Empathic listening:**  a combination of listening skills and feedback skills that enhances the ability to identify and respond to the feelings of another person.

**Feedback:**  a receiver's response to a message that enables a sender to gauge whether he or she has been understood.

**Hearing:**  the physiological process of receiving sound waves through the ear and the auditory nerve.

**Information overload:**  a listening barricade that occurs when the accumulated quantity of words becomes so great that you suffer from listening fatigue.

**Listening:**  the process of making sense out of what you hear; includes the four stages of selecting, attending, understanding, and remembering.

**Listening barricade:**  an obstacle that keeps you from listening well.

**Paraphrasing:**  restating in your own words what you think another person has said.

**Remembering:**  the process of recalling past events.

**Selecting:**  the process of sorting through competing sounds in the environment in preparation for focusing on one sound.

**Understanding:**  the process of assigning meaning to the stimuli to which you attend.

## DISCUSSION QUESTIONS

1. What is the difference between listening and hearing?
2. Which of the listening barricades described in this chapter are the most problematic for you? What do you intend to do about them?
3. Besides the suggestions in the text, what other techniques do you use to adapt to the speaker and the environment when you listen?
4. What kinds of feedback have you received from others about your communication today?
5. Describe a situation in which someone gave you inappropriate feedback.
6. What are the characteristics of someone you know who is a good empathic listener?

## SUGGESTED ACTIVITIES

1. To gain a better perspective on listening habits, keep a journal in which you record your thoughts and objectives and the barriers you encounter in your listening experiences.[8] Your journal may include:

   a. goals for improving your listening skills

   b. daily entries that
      (1) identify the types of listening you engage in
      (2) describe each listening experience (situation, participants, etc.)
      (3) identify what you learn

   c. a one-day listening log that describes every listening experience you had that day

   d. a summary of how well you achieved the goals you established for yourself

2. Make a list of the emotion-arousing words that affect your listening ability. How can you try to overcome some of the listening problems these words create for you?

3. Try this exercise in a class where you are having listening problems. Make a special effort to concentrate on what is being said in this class. Keep a log of those instances in which you find it difficult to pay attention. Identify, for example, when you found yourself tuning a speaker out. What was the speaker saying? How was the delivery of the message? Try to determine why you are having difficulty concentrating on the message. Use the suggestions in this chapter for overcoming listening barriers to help you improve your listening skills.

## SUGGESTED READING

Steil, L.K., Barker, L.L., and Watson, K.W. (1983). *Effective Listening: Key to Your Success*. (Reading, Mass.: Addison-Wesley).

Wolff, F.I., Marsnik, N.C., Tacey, W.S., and Nichols, R.G. (1983). *Perceptive Listening*. (New York: Holt, Rinehart and Winston).

Wolvin, A.D. and Coakley, C.G. (1988). *Listening*. (Dubuque, Iowa: Wm. C. Brown).

Roach, C.A. and Wyatt, N.J. (1988). *Successful Listening*. (New York: Harper & Row).

Barker, L.L. (1971). *Listening Behavior*. (Englewood Cliffs, New Jersey: Prentice-Hall).

# 7  Interviewing

*After studying this chapter, you should be able to:*

▶ Define *interview.*

▶ Identify the main differences between an interview and other forms of interpersonal communication.

▶ List and briefly explain four basic types of interviews.

▶ Plan the four elements of an interview.

▶ Perform the role of an interviewer, using speech communication behaviors that fulfill the five responsibilities of an interviewer.

▶ Perform the role of an interviewee, using speech communication behaviors that fulfill the three responsibilities of an interviewee.

*"How'd the interview go? Did you get the information we need for our report?"*

*"Well, I got some information, but I'm not sure we can use any of it."*

*"What happened? I thought you said this guy was an expert!"*

*"He didn't answer any of the questions I asked. He talked about what it was like when he was in college and avoided most of the important questions. I guess I'm not the hotshot interviewer I thought I was."*

Many people think that the process of interviewing is simple. Whether it's a job interview, a counseling session, or a sales pitch by an encyclopedia salesperson, there's much more to this technique than simply asking questions and waiting for the answers. An interview is a specialized and formally structured form of interpersonal communication that takes a lot of planning, hard work, and practice. It can be exciting and rewarding or anxiety producing and discouraging.

The previous four chapters have discussed relating to others at an interpersonal level, focusing on verbal and nonverbal communication, and the specialized skill of listening. In no interpersonal communication setting are you required to prepare and utilize your verbal and nonverbal communication skills so effectively as you are in an interview; in no interpersonal communication encounter are you so dependent upon the effective development and practice of your listening skills. This chapter is intended to help you develop your interviewing skills, whether you find yourself in the role of the interviewer or interviewee.

## WHAT IS AN INTERVIEW?

An **interview** is "a form of oral communication involving two parties, at least one of whom has a preconceived and serious purpose and both of whom speak and listen from time to time."[1] This definition highlights several key ingredients of any interview situation.

First, an interview is *primarily* concerned with *face-to-face interactions*. Of course when time, finances, or other factors prevent two parties from meeting personally, an interview can take place over the telephone or by letter. In most instances, however, the participants in an interview meet in person. The fact that they can thus actually observe each other reinforces the importance of nonverbal communication.

Second, an interview *always involves two parties*—not always just two *people*. One person can be interviewed by a group of people, or several people can be interviewed by one person. A common practice

*An interview is more purposeful and planned than other forms of interpersonal communication.*

in higher education is for a committee of faculty members to conduct an interview with a job applicant. Similarly, it is common for a group of journalists to interview two or more political candidates at the same time, as in a presidential debate.

*A preconceived and serious purpose* is the third element that sets an interview apart from other forms of interpersonal communication. Both parties are usually aware of the nature and purpose of the interview before it occurs. This focus on goals usually makes the situation more formal than informal conversations among friends, discussions over lunch, and romantic dinners by candlelight.

*As in other interpersonal situations, interview participants speak and listen at times.*

The fourth important element in the definition is the *sharing of speaking and listening roles*. An interview is generally a series of questions and answers. Both parties must listen carefully and respond appropriately. Although this trading of listening and speaking roles is similar to other interpersonal communication events, an interview requires **more careful listening** and **more focussed responding** than does an informal conversation between friends.

## TYPES OF INTERVIEWS

Physicians need to find out "what's ailing you." Personnel managers need to decide if you're "right for the job." Counselors try to help you with personal problems. Candidates for public office encourage you to vote for them in an upcoming election. These four situations illustrate the four types of interviews, classified according to purpose: information gathering, information sharing, problem solving, and persuading.

In reality, most interviews are conducted with more than one purpose in mind. For example, an employment interview is aimed primarily at information sharing, but each party will attempt to persuade the other as well. An interviewer will attempt to *solve the problem* of finding the right person for the job, and an interviewee will try to gather enough information to answer the question, "Would I want to work for this organization?" Thus, an employment interview generally helps accomplish goals related to all four interview purposes. Nevertheless, to avoid confusion, each type of interview will be examined separately.

### An Information-gathering Interview

The objective of an **information-gathering interview** is to gain specific kinds of information to aid in making a decision or implementing an action. An *exit interview* provides information about a departing employee's reasons for leaving a job. Very often such information is useful to an organization in discovering what improvements

Reporters use information gathering interviews to collect facts that ensure accurate reporting.

in benefits, working conditions, salary, promotion policy, or other factors might help reduce employee turnover. An *opinion poll* gathers information that is useful in developing a plan of action. A marketing researcher may test new or current products, the broadcast industry may assess the popularity of specific programs, and private pollsters may evaluate the public's support for political candidates or government policies.

Physicians, nurses, and other medical personnel use *medical interviews* to gather enough information for the proper diagnosis and treatment of a patient. Police officers and lawyers use *legal interviews* to compile facts related to law enforcement and justice. Finally, reporters conduct *journalistic interviews* to track down and gather the names, places, dates, and other facts that will ensure accurate and timely reporting.

*In information-gathering interviews, an interviewer seeks to gain specific knowledge from an interviewee.*

## An Information-sharing Interview

During an **information-sharing interview** both the interviewer and the interviewee provide and gather information. Sometimes the amount of information shared is nearly equal. Other times one party shares more information than the other.

An information-sharing interview is common in business and industry. In an *employment interview,* an interviewer gathers information about an interviewee's qualifications and motivations. The interviewer offers information about the organization and the position. The

*In information-sharing interviews, both parties question and respond.*

interviewee, in turn, shares information about his or her qualifications and motivations. The interviewee gathers information about the organization's background, benefits, salary scale, and promotion policies. After some time on the job, an employee will probably participate in a *work-appraisal interview*. Its purpose is to share information about job performance, supervisor-subordinate relations, work deadlines, production quotas, and other job-related concerns. An *orientation session* which is often carried out in an interview setting, is intended to introduce newcomers to the established procedures of a business, school, or other organization. The purpose of a *briefing* is to share with established employees information on the implementation of or change in an organization's procedures or policies. The aim of an *instructional interview* is to achieve a desired level of proficiency in a specific technique or skill.

## A Problem-solving Interview

*Problem-solving interviews focus on mutual concerns and resolution of problems.*

A **problem-solving interview** is conducted to discuss and resolve a concern that is important to both parties. An interviewer and interviewee share information and investigate alternatives in an attempt to effectively resolve the difficulty.

Psychiatrists, managers, college professors, and other professionals conduct *counseling interviews* to help find solutions to the personal or professional problems of their clients, students, or subordinates. *Disciplinary interviews* examine corrective action that may be taken in response to the undesired behavior of employees or students. Although disciplinary interviews are generally arranged by interviewers, both parties need to understand the causes and consequences of the problem at hand. Finally, *grievance interviews* encourage open discussion of complaints by individuals or groups. The success of grievance interviews (or any problem-solving interviews) depends largely on the effectiveness of the listening and responding skills of both parties. Both parties need to listen to and understand the problems to be dealt with, examine possible solutions, and resolve the issue in a manner that is mutually satisfactory. Indeed, effective interpersonal communication is especially crucial to the success of the problem-solving interview.

## A Persuading Interview

*Persuading interviews focus on ideas or product acceptance and action.*

The purpose of a **persuading interview** is to gain the interviewee's acceptance of an idea, product, or service and to obtain some subsequent action based on that acceptance. The success of this type of interview can be measured by the performance of the desired behavior.

The most common type of persuading interview is a *sales interview*. That knock on the door or ring of the telephone just as you are sitting

**Review Box**

**Four Types of Interviews**

| *Type* | *Main Objective* | *Examples* |
|---|---|---|
| Information Gathering | To gain specific kinds of information to aid in making a decision or implementing an action | Opinion polls; exit, medical, legal, journalistic interviews |
| Information Sharing | For both the interviewer and the interviewee to provide and gather information | Orientation sessions; briefings; employment, work-appraisal, instructional interviews |
| Problem-Solving | To discuss and resolve a concern that is important to both parties | Counseling; disciplinary, grievance interviews |
| Persuading | To gain acceptance of an idea, product, or service and to obtain some action based on that acceptance | Sales and campaign interviews |

down for dinner may mean that you will soon meet a person who will try to persuade you to purchase a product or service.

In a similar vein, the objective of a *campaign interview* is to "sell" a candidate in an election. The requested action is your vote.

Although their purposes may vary, all interviews have certain elements in common—oral communication, two parties, a preconceived and serious purpose, and the sharing of speaking and listening roles. Furthermore, while their actual subjects and goals may differ, all maintain a basic structure and involve a series of questions and responses. In the next section, you will examine these structural elements, as well as the kinds of questions and questioning sequences most commonly used.

## ORGANIZING AN INTERVIEW

An interviewer maintains primary responsibility for the planning and execution of an interview. It is important to be clear about an interview's purpose, what is expected during the meeting, and the possible outcomes. Therefore an interviewer must prepare, decide on an opening, formulate questions, and think about a conclusion.

## Preparation

*Outlining objectives is vital to effective planning.*

The interviewer, as the primary interview planner, must *be clear about the purpose of the interview.* Is the meeting intended to provide counseling to a worker, to inform the worker of some disciplinary action being taken, or both? Based on this knowledge, the interviewer then *establishes a set of objectives.* If the only purpose of the interview is to inform a worker about a disciplinary action, the interviewer's objectives are (1) to identify the worker's violation of specific rules, (2) to inform the person about the nature and extent of the disciplinary action, (3) to outline the possible consequences of ignoring the disciplinary conditions, and (4) to explain the length and termination of the disciplinary action. If counseling is to be a part of the encounter, the interviewer might plan (1) to discuss the person's past work record, (2) to encourage the worker to discuss possible causes of the undesirable behavior, and (3) to investigate measures to prevent future undesirable behavior. Each of these is a separate purpose that requires an interviewer to develop a separate set of well-defined objectives.

Once an interviewer identifies the objectives of the interview, he or she decides *how* to accomplish them through questioning and effective time management. The interviewer formulates key questions and possible follow-up questions, and arranges them so that (1) the interview will flow smoothly, (2) important questions are not forgotten, and (3) time is used efficiently.

The last point is important. The interviewer effectively structures time to ensure that adequate information will be shared. He or she asks relevant questions and anticipates probable follow-up questions. The interviewer guides the discussion toward the objectives and allows sufficient time to cover all important points. Valuable time is saved by *gathering and evaluating information in advance.* Such research will help to decide which areas of information need further elaboration or clarification, how much time and effort should be put into each topic of discussion, and how to structure the interview to ensure maximum productivity and efficiency. For example, a physician's familiarity with a patient's history can shorten a medical interview and increase its efficiency.

A final step in the preparation stage for an interview is *to select as pleasant, comfortable, and private an environment as possible.* An interviewee may experience a certain amount of anxiety during the

Opening an interview with a firm handshake creates a friendly atmosphere and helps put both interviewer and interviewee at ease.

process. To minimize discomfort, an interviewer can *arrange a physical setting* that is free from auditory and visual distractions, interruptions, and physical barriers. An interviewer who sits behind a huge desk may appear aloof and distant. One who sits opposite an interviewee, without any furniture barriers, can appear encouraging and friendly. Which person would you rather interview with?

*Plan for an interviewee's comfort and privacy.*

## The Opening

The opening of any interview is crucial because it can *create a climate for positive and open communication*. A skilled interviewer begins by *trying to put an interviewee at ease*. He or she briefly discusses the weather, recent events attended by both parties, or other light topics to ease some of the anxiety an interviewee may feel. The interviewer also promotes *a degree of rapport and diplomacy* with the interviewee. Making direct eye contact, smiling, offering a firm handshake (avoid the "Incredible Hulk" and "dead fish" grips), extending a sincere invitation to sit in a comfortable chair all help establish a warm

*Establish a positive climate for communication early.*

atmosphere. The interviewer states that he or she is glad to see the other person and looks forward to talking with her or him.

A skilled interviewer also *provides an orientation to an interview.* Even though an interviewee will usually know why he or she is there, clarifying a meeting's purpose helps both parties to get their bearings and checks their understandings. To pave the way for productive communication, the interviewer must make sure that both parties know the purpose of the interview and that everyone is on the same wavelength before the actual questioning begins.

## Questions

Any type of interview involves the asking of questions by at least one party. If any information is to be gathered or shared, if anyone is to be persuaded, or if a problem is to be solved as a result of an interview, the right questions must be asked and the appropriate answers must be obtained.

If an interviewer has done a thorough job of identifying and clarifying his or her objectives and gathering information in advance, the key questions to be asked are fairly obvious. But what kinds of questions are they?

An interview is conducted as a series of questions and responses. Even though both parties will listen and speak, the interviewer has the primary responsibility for questioning. Interview questions fall into one of four categories: open, closed, probing, or hypothetical.

*Open questions are broad and allow freedom of response.*

**Open questions.**   **Open questions** are broad and basically unstructured. Often they indicate only the topic to be considered and allow interviewees considerable freedom to determine the amount and kind of information they will provide.

Because they encourage the interviewee to share information almost without restriction, open questions are useful to determine opinions, values, and perspectives. Such questions as "What are your long- and short-term career goals?", "Why do you need my help?", and "How do you feel about gun control?" prompt personal and wide-ranging responses.

*Closed questions require short answers.*

**Closed questions.**   **Closed questions** limit the range of possible responses. They may ask for a simple yes or no (Did you see the mugger's face?), or they may allow interviewees to select responses from a number of specific alternatives (How often do you go to the movies? [a] Less than once a month, [b] Once a month, [c] Twice a month, [d] Once a week). Closed questions enable interviewers to gather spe-

## Types of Interview Questions

| | Uses | Example |
|---|---|---|
| **Open Question** | Prompt wide-ranging responses<br>Determine opinions, values, perspectives | Tell me about your previous job duties.<br>How would you describe your son's problems in school? |
| **Closed Question** | Requests simple yes or no response<br>Forces a response from limited options | Have you been skiing in the past month?<br>Which one of the following drinks would you buy?<br>[a] Coke<br>[b] Pepsi<br>[c] Mr. Pibb<br>[d] Diet Coke |
| **Probing Question** | Encourages clarification of or elaboration on previous responses<br>Directs responses in a specific direction | Would you tell me more about the pain in your side?<br>We've talked about your mother. Can you describe how you felt about your father's long absences from home when you were a child? |
| **Hypothetical Question** | Gauges reactions to emotional or value-laden situations<br>Elicits response to a real or imaginary situation | How would you support your opponent if she were elected chairperson of the board?<br>What would you do if your secretary lost an important file? |

cific information, by restricting interviewees' freedom to express personal views or elaborate on responses. Closed questions are most often used when the maximum amount of information is required in a relatively short period of time.

*Probing questions
help to clarify
previous responses.*

**Probing questions.**   **Probing questions** encourage interviewees to clarify or elaborate on partial or superficial responses. Through the use of these questions, interviewers attempt to direct responses. Such questions as "Could you elaborate on your coursework in the area of speech communication?", "Do you mean to say that you already *own* three vacuum cleaners?", and "Will you tell me more about your relationship with your supervisor?" call for further information in a particular area. Probing questions are often spontaneous and are often used to follow up on the key questions that interviewers have prepared in advance.

*Hypothetical
questions often
assess emotions
and/or values.*

**Hypothetical   questions.** Interviewers   use   **hypothetical questions** to describe a set of conditions and ask interviewees what they would do if they were in specific situations. Such questions are generally used either to gauge reactions to emotion-arousing or value-laden circumstances or to discover responses to real or imaginary situations. A police officer might ask an eyewitness to a murder, "What if I told you that the man you identified as the murderer in the line-up was the mayor?" During an exit interview, a personnel manager might ask, "If we promoted you to Chief Sanitary Engineer and paid you four dollars an hour, would you consider staying with Bob's Landfill and Television Repair?"

## Questioning Sequences

Open, closed, probing, and hypothetical questions may be used in any combination, as long as their sequence is thoughtfully planned. Depending on the purpose, these questions may be arranged into four basic sequences: funnel, inverted funnel, quintamensional, and tunnel.[2]

**The funnel sequence.** The **funnel sequence** begins with broad, open questions and proceeds toward more closed questions (see Figure 7–1). The advantage of this format is that it allows an interviewee to express views and feelings without restriction, at least early in an interview. For example, it may be more useful to begin a grievance interview with the question, "How would you describe your relationship with your supervisor?" instead of asking "What makes you think your supervisor treats you like an idiot?" The first question allows the free expression of feelings, while the second question clearly reflects an interviewer's bias, immediately forcing the discussion in a negative di-

**Figure 7–1**
The Funnel Sequence

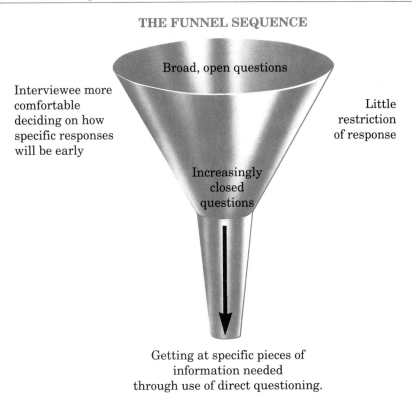

THE FUNNEL SEQUENCE

Broad, open questions

Interviewee more
comfortable
deciding on how
specific responses
will be early

Little
restriction
of response

Increasingly
closed
questions

Getting at specific pieces of
information needed
through use of direct questioning.

rection. The following series of questions provides an example of a
funnel sequence that might be used for a grievance interview:

1. How would you describe your relationship with your supervisor?
2. How do you think your supervisor sees you as an employee?
3. Are you satisfied with the way your supervisor treats you?
4. What do you believe to be the source of the conflict between you
   and your supervisor?
5. What has your supervisor done to make you think that she
   wants to fire you?

The *funnel sequence* is appropriate when an interviewer believes that
an interviewee is more comfortable with questions that allow him or
her to choose general or specific responses.

**Figure 7–2**
The Inverted Funnel Sequence

THE INVERTED FUNNEL SEQUENCE

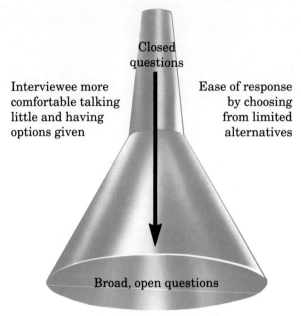

Closed
questions

Interviewee more
comfortable talking
little and having
options given

Ease of response
by choosing
from limited
alternatives

Broad, open questions

Building the "big picture" with
repeated questioning, integrating
previous responses

The inverted funnel sequence.    Just the opposite of the funnel sequence, the **inverted funnel** begins with closed questions and proceeds to more open questions (see Figure 7–2). A grievance interview based on the inverted funnel might include the following series of questions:

1. Do you believe that your supervisor wants to fire you?
2. What makes you think you'll be fired soon?
3. What do you think has caused this problem between you and your supervisor?
4. How has this problem developed?
5. How would you describe the general working climate in your department?

The relatively closed questions that begin the inverted funnel sequence are intended to *encourage an interviewee to respond easily,* because they require only brief answers (yes or no, short lists, and the like). As the sequence progresses, the questions become more open and thus require more elaborate answers and greater disclosure.

The *inverted funnel sequence* is appropriate when an interviewer wants to direct the interview along specific lines and encourage an interviewee to respond with short, easily composed answers. An interviewer can follow up with more general questions to provide increasingly broad information—the "big picture," so to speak.

**The quintamensional design sequence.** *Quintamensional* means "five dimensions." The **quintamensional design sequence**[3] is a five-step series of questions intended to assess an individual's attitudes toward a particular topic and the strength of his or her feelings about the relevant issues. The first step assesses a respondent's knowledge about an issue (awareness). Next, an interviewer asks for an interviewee's general perspective—for example, a description of the nature of the controversy or the important and unimportant elements (uninfluenced attitudes). Third, an interviewer asks for a respondent's personal stand (specific attitude). Fourth, an interviewer wants to know the respondent's reaons for his or her specific attitude or opinion (reason why). Finally, an interviewer assesses the strength of an interviewee's feelings about his or her opinion (intensity of attitude). The five steps and sample questions can proceed as follows:

1. *Awareness:* Tell me what you know about the race for Public Sanitation Engineer in the November elections.
2. *Uninfluenced Attitudes:* What are the issues in this race as you see them?
3. *Specific Attitude:* Which candidate do you plan to vote for in this race?
4. *Reason Why:* What led you to favor this candidate?
5. *Intensity of Attitude:* How strongly do you feel about your choice—strongly, very strongly, definitely not willing to change your mind?

**The tunnel sequence.** Finally, the **tunnel sequence** consists of a series of parallel open or closed questions, or a combination of the two. This sequence has no probing questions; it goes into less depth than the other three sequences. An interviewer may use the tunnel sequence to gather information about attitudes and opinions without regard for the reasons behind an interviewee's answers or the intensity of his or her feelings. The following is a typical tunnel sequence:

1. What are the three major issues in the presidential campaign this year?
2. Which candidate would you vote for if the election were held today?
3. For whom do you think you will vote in the race for U. S. Senator?
4. Are you a registered voter in this state?
5. What do you think of the proposition to set up a nuclear waste dump in this state?

The tunnel sequence is most appropriate when an interviewer wants some general information on a variety of topics in a relatively short period of time.

Although these sequences have been discussed as if they were independent and easily distinguishable, good questioning strategy will probably combine some elements of each. The key to effective interviewing is to prepare a set of questions that will get the needed kinds and amount of information. An interviewer should remain flexible enough to add, subtract, and revise questions as a discussion proceeds. Such an approach ensures accomplishing interviewing objectives.

*Questioning sequences add structure and ensure productive information exchange throughout an interview.*

## The Conclusion

Opinion polls, marketing surveys, and sales pitches often end rather abruptly with a "Thank you for taking the time to help me out." Many other kinds of interviews require follow-up meetings or some form of future contact, however. For this reason, and for reasons of common courtesy, the conclusion of an interview is very important.

A primary function of the conclusion is to summarize the proceedings. All parties should be aware of and agree on what happened during the meeting. To ensure understanding and satisfaction, an interviewer summarizes the highlights of the discussion, asking for and offering clarification, if necessary.

*An effective conclusion includes a summary, a discussion of future actions, and mutual thank you's.*

Another function of the conclusion is to encourage continued friendly relations. The positive communication climate developed during the interview should be carried into the conclusion. Comments such as "I'm so glad we had a chance to talk about this problem" or "It's been a pleasure to serve you" enable both parties to feel that they have had a positive and productive encounter. An interviewer can tell the other party when to expect further contact or action, if appropriate. A job applicant wants to know when to expect a phone call about a follow-

---

*Review Box*

## Organizing an Interview

| Step | Goals |
|---|---|
| Preparation | Review the purpose. |
| | Establish objectives. |
| | Write key questions. |
| | Gather and evaluate preinterview information. |
| | Arrange the setting. |
| | |
| Opening | Put the interviewee at ease. |
| | Establish rapport and diplomacy. |
| | Provide an orientation. |
| | |
| Questions | Use questions appropriate to the interview type and objectives. |
| | Design questioning sequences appropriate to interview purpose and information needs. |
| | |
| Conclusion | Summarize the proceedings. |
| | Encourage friendly relations. |
| | Arrange further contact(s). |
| | Exchange thank you's. |

---

up interview or a job offer. An expert, interviewed by a journalist, wants to know what will be done with her comments and when the story is likely to be published.

At the end of virtually any interview, *both* the interviewer and the interviewee are expected to say thank you. Because an interview is a mutual effort, both parties deserve recognition.

## THE RESPONSIBILITIES OF THE INTERVIEWER

Since an interviewer is typically the person who arranges for an interview, he or she develops the objectives and maintains control over the situation. Regardless of the type of interview, the interviewer has certain responsibilities that must be met if the meeting is to be productive and successful. These include being aware of biases and prejudices, adapting to the interviewee's behavior, dealing with sensitive content, listening effectively, and recording information.

## Being Aware of Biases and Prejudices

*Being aware of biases and prejudices helps reduce communication noise.*

First and foremost, an interviewer must be aware of his or her own biases and prejudices. As was discussed in Chapter 3, each person has a set of experiences, beliefs, attitudes, and values through which that person receives, interprets, and evaluates incoming stimuli. If accurate and useful information is to be shared in an interview, an interviewer must be aware of his or her own perceptual processes so that the interviewer can make accurate and objective interpretations. An otherwise qualified candidate for a job shouldn't be eliminated from consideration just because the interviewer has a bias against redheads.

## Adapting to an Interviewee's Behavior

*Good interviewers adapt to different interviewees and situations.*

Skilled interviewers observe, evaluate, and adapt to the communication behavior of their interviewees. Because no two interviews—and no two interviewees—are exactly alike, interviewers adapt their communication behavior accordingly. A flexible communication style is a necessity. Interviewers should have predetermined plans, but they should not be thrown off balance if an interviewee suddenly turns the tables and asks, "How much money do *you* make for this job?"

Adaptability also includes the use of appropriate language and vocabulary. Interviewers should consciously choose language and vocabulary that interviewees will understand. Little is gained by the use of technical, ambiguous, or vague terms. Words should be straightforward, simple, and specific, but not so simple that interviewees feel "talked down" to. Empathy is important in determining the most appropriate language and vocabulary.

## Dealing with Sensitive Content

*Good judgment is required when sensitive topics arise.*

When planning questions for an interview, consider possible sensitive topics and topics to be avoided. Certain questions—ones about age, marital status, and religion—are illegal in an employment interview. A question such as "Why were you fired from your last job?" will provoke a defensive reaction in a grievance interview. The househusband who answers the doorbell may be mildly offended if the vacuum salesperson asks, "Are you the lady of the house?"

Good judgment and choice of words play crucial roles. One ill-chosen question can destroy the positive and open communication developed in an opening. Effective interviewers avoid potentially troublesome topics and attempt to put interviewees at ease. They discuss sensitive issues *if and only if* they are related to the purpose of the interviews. When a sensitive subject must be discussed, experienced interviewers choose their words carefully. Thus, the question "Why were you fired?" might be rephrased as "How would you describe your relationship with your previous supervisor?"

## Listening Effectively

Effective listening must be at the heart of any interview. No matter how well interviewers have prepared, the time will have been wasted if they are poor listeners. They need strong listening skills to make sure that they are receiving the kind and amount of information they need. They must be able to identify partial or irrelevant responses.

Highly developed listening skills also increase the ability to accurately perceive and interpret unintentional messages and beliefs, attitudes, and values. Interviewers learn a great deal from nonverbal, as well as verbal, communication.

## Recording Information

The information accumulated from an interview is useless if it is not recorded completely and accurately. A partial or inaccurate report can lead to poor decisions and mistaken actions.

*Information should be accurately and completely recorded.*

Interviewers have two options for recording interview data: note taking or tape recording. In either case, interviewees should be advised that the recording process is taking place.

When notes are taken, the notes should be brief, but as complete as possible to ensure accuracy and thoroughness. Interviewers may need to assure interviewees that they are listening closely even though they seem to be focused on their writing. Responses that are not written down during the interview may well be forgotten.

Remember that Murphy's Law ("Anything that can go wrong will, and usually at the worst possible moment") governs any attempt at using electronic recording devices. So take care to test microphone placement in advance and to bring enough recording tape. Also remember that even though you are taping, you must still listen carefully in order to guide the interview successfully.

## THE RESPONSIBILITIES OF THE INTERVIEWEE

Although the bulk of the responsibility for productive interviews fall on interviewers, interviewees must accept the responsibilities of thoughtfully preparing, carefully listening, and seriously responding if they hope to make worthwhile contributions. Good interviewees know

Review Box

## The Responsibilities of an Interviewer

| *Responsibility* | *Contribution to the Interview* |
| --- | --- |
| Being aware of biases and prejudices | Objectivity<br>Increased accuracy of perceptions and evaluations |
| Adapting to an interviewee's behavior | Reduced emotional reaction to unexpected questions or responses<br>Increased understanding through use of proper language and vocabulary<br>Increased empathy |
| Dealing with sensitive content | Avoidance of defensive reactions<br>Elimination of illegal questions<br>Maintenance of a positive communication climate |
| Listening effectively | Increased accuracy and completeness of responses<br>Increased accuracy of perception and interpretation of information<br>Identification of follow-up questions |
| Recording information | Increased usefulness of information received<br>Increased accuracy and permanence of information exchanged |

what to expect in interviews. They prepare responses for common questions, pay close attention to requests for specific information, and answer questions directly and accurately.

## Preparing for an Interview

In most cases, interviewees have some advance knowledge of the purpose and objectives of interviews prior to them. They can therefore anticipate probable topics of discussion. For example, a person who will be attending a grievance or counseling interview can prepare by clearly identifying the problem, its causes, and possible solutions. Someone preparing for a legal interview can focus on the facts of his or her case.

Interviewees may also want to do some research. For example, job applicants can find out as much as they can about the companies with which they are interviewing—the products or services; backgrounds; reputations; and policies on hiring, salary, and promotions. It is generally advisable for students to have some knowledge of degree requirements and class schedules before coming to academic counseling interviews. In most cases, people who have not done some preinterview research will be at distinct disadvantages.

*Thorough preparation promotes active participation and positive impressions.*

Finally, prospective interviewees should plan the management of certain nonverbal behaviors. These include everything from being on time (a matter of courtesy and respect for the interviewers) to maintaining attitudes of interest and consideration, and wearing appropriate clothing. In addition, steady eye contact, attentive body positions, alert facial expressions, and firm handshakes all contribute to positive images.

## Listening Effectively

Listening skills are even more crucial for interviewees than they are for interviewers. Interviewing situations require interviewees to listen for the *amount and depth of information desired*. For responses to be appropriate and useful, interviewees must know what is being requested. If questions are unclear, interviewees should ask for clarification or elaboration. By doing so, they can respond more fully and relevantly.

*Knowing how to respond requires good listening.*

Successful interviewees also practice empathy. Interviewers are people and interviewing situations are interpersonal encounters. Effective interviewees consider situations from interviewers' points of view, listen for unintentional messages, and watch for nonverbal cues. When interviewees listen to all facets of the communication, they can better adapt to the situation.

## Responding Appropriately

Just as questioning is the primary responsibility of an interviewer, responding is the primary responsibility of an interviewee. Keep answers direct, honest, and appropriate in depth and relevance. For example, in response to the question "How would you describe your working relationship with your supervisor?", don't give a 15-minute speech about your problems with your ex-spouse, keeping the children in clothes, and finding a dependable babysitter. To make sure that you give the best possible answer, listen carefully when a question is posed

*Appropriate responses are brief, relevant, and thoughtfully prepared.*

## The Responsibilities of an Interviewee

*Responsibility*

| | |
|---|---|
| Preparing for an interview | Gives an interviewee a chance to clarify purpose and goals<br>Facilitates advanced research, if necessary<br>Allows for proper management of nonverbal behaviors |
| Listening effectively | Allows an interviewee to gauge the amount and depth of the information requested<br>Promotes empathy |
| Responding appropriately | Facilitates responses that are relevant and that contain the appropriate depth<br>Increases understanding through correct language usage<br>Allows an interviewee to be more adaptable to the needs of an interviewer |

and, if necessary, take a few moments to think before you answer. A response that is well thought out, straightforward, and relevant will be much more appreciated than one that is hasty, evasive, and unrelated to the question.

Using language and vocabulary appropriate to the situation is also important. The use of too much slang or technical terminology in an attempt to impress an interviewer can easily backfire by distracting from or distorting clear and open communication. Direct and simple language increases the chances for understanding and sharing.

Finally, be adaptable and flexible to the needs of the interviewing situation. Some interviewers will ask questions to throw you off-guard. When this happens, take a moment to think before you respond. Try to discover the reason for the question and respond to the best of your ability. Listen carefully for content *and* intent of questions so that you provide the information requested, especially when the interviewer changes topics. Flexibility and adaptability depend on good listening, empathy, accurate reading and interpretation of nonverbal communication, and practice. Just remember, "Engage brain before opening mouth."

---

## SUMMARY

An interview is a highly specialized and formal kind of interpersonal communication. Understanding and practicing effective interviewing communication will allow you to contribute to a productive interview.

▶ **Define *interview*.**

An *interview* is a form of oral communication involving two parties, at least one of whom has a preconceived and serious purpose. Both parties speak and listen from time to time.

▶ **Identify the main differences between an interview and other forms of interpersonal communication.**

Unlike other forms of interpersonal communication, an interview (1) always has a preconceived and serious purpose, (2) requires more careful listening and more focused responding, (3) is more formal, and (4) involves a series of questions and responses.

▶ **List and briefly explain four basic types of interviews.**

*Information-gathering interviews* attempt to gain specific kinds of information from one or more interviewees to aid in making a decision or implementing an action. Interviewers do most of the questioning and interviewees do most of the responding. Both an interviewer and an interviewee question and respond in an *information-sharing interview*. As its name implies, the sharing of information among participants is its objective. Discussion and resolution of mutual problems or concerns is the focus of a *problem-solving interview*. All participants share information and investigate various solutions. An interviewer's purpose in a *persuading interview* is to gain an interviewee's acceptance of an idea, product, or service, and to obtain some subsequent action based on that acceptance.

▶ **Plan the four elements of an interview.**

All participants of an interview must thoroughly *prepare* prior to an interview. They should try to establish a positive communication climate during the *opening*. Properly sequenced *open, closed, probing,* and *hypothetical questions,* as well as clear and relevant responses, form the main portion of an interview. The *funnel, inverted funnel, quintamensional design,* and *tunnel sequences* may be used exclusively or in combination to organize information exchange during an interview. Finally, participants summarize the content and results of the interview and express their gratitude during its *conclusion*.

▶Perform the role of an interviewer, using speech communication behaviors that fulfill the five responsibilities of an interviewer.

To be an effective interviewer, a person must (1) remain aware of biases and prejudices, (2) learn to adapt to an interviewee's behavior, (3) effectively deal with sensitive content, (4) listen carefully, and (5) record information accurately and completely.

▶Perform the role of an interviewee, using speech communication behaviors that fulfill the three responsibilities of an interviewee.

In order to make a positive contribution to an interview, any interviewee must (1) thoroughly prepare, (2) listen carefully, and (3) respond relevantly and directly.

---

## KEY TERMS

**Closed question:**  a question that limits the range of possible responses and requires a simple, direct, and brief answer.

**Funnel sequence:**  a questioning sequence that begins with broad, open questions and proceeds toward more closed questions.

**Hypothetical question:**  a question used to gauge an interviewee's reaction to an emotion-arousing or value-laden situation, or to discover an interviewee's reactions to a real or imaginary situation.

**Information-gathering interview:**  an interview conducted to gain specific kinds of information to aid in making a decision or implementing an action.

**Information-sharing interview:**  an interview in which both the interviewer and the interviewee provide and gather information, often sharing information nearly equally.

**Interview:**  a form of oral communication involving two parties, at least one of whom has a preconceived and serious purpose and both of whom speak and listen from time to time.

**Inverted funnel sequence:**  a questioning sequence that begins with closed questions and proceeds with more open questions, intended to encourage an interviewee to respond easily early in the interview.

**Open question:**  interviewing question that is broad in nature, basically unstructured, and allows the respondent considerable freedom to determine the amount and kind of information provided.

**Persuading interview:**  an interview with the objective of gaining the interviewee's acceptance of an idea, product, or service, and of obtaining some subsequent action based on that acceptance.

**Probing question:**  a question that encourages the interviewee to clarify or elaborate on partial or superficial responses, and that usually directs the discussion in a desired direction.

**Problem-solving interview:**  an interview conducted to discuss and resolve a concern that is important to both parties.

**Quintamensional design sequence:**  a five-step questioning sequence intended to assess both what an interviewee's attitudes are and how strongly he or she feels about the relevant issues. The five steps are (1) awareness, (2) uninfluenced attitudes, (3) specific attitudes, (4) reason why, and (5) intensity of attitude.

**Tunnel sequence:**  a questioning sequence that consists of a series of parallel open or closed questions, using no probing questions, resulting in less depth of information on a number of related issues.

## DISCUSSION QUESTIONS

1. How is an interview similar to, and different from, an informal conversation between friends? What characteristics of effective interpersonal communication discussed in chapters 5 and 6 are *most* crucial to a successful interview? Are any of these characteristics *not* important in an interview? Why or why not?

2. Discuss why and how each of the responsibilities of the interviewer should be fulfilled in each of the four types of interviews. Why is each responsibility important to each type? What are some of the negative consequences of not fulfilling each responsibility? What can an interviewer do to increase her or his chances of meeting each responsibility?

3. Discuss why and how each of the responsibilities of the interviewee should be fulfilled in each of the four types of interviews. Why is each responsibility important to each type? What are some of the negative consequences of not fulfilling each responsibility? What can an interviewee do to increase her or his chances of meeting each responsibility?

## SUGGESTED ACTIVITIES

1. Choose a partner and plan an employment or work-appraisal interview of 8 to 10 minutes. Develop a hypothetical or real-life situation and a question-response sequence for the interview. Perform this simulated interview for your class.

2. Select an interviewing situation discussed in this chapter. Develop funnel, inverted funnel, quintamensional design, and tunnel questioning sequences that might be used in the interview. Which set of questions is most effective? Why?

3. Observe a sales interview in a store. Take notes on the nonverbal communication exhibited by the participants: physical environment, eye contact, proximity of participants, and body movements. Then briefly describe how these nonverbal cues may have influenced the success (or failure) of that interview.

4. Working in a group, design an interview. Choose one of the four types: information-gathering, information-sharing, problem-solving, or persuading. Select a situation and outline how the participants would prepare for, open, question and respond during, and conclude the interview.

## *SUGGESTED READINGS*

Gary Hunt and William Eadie (1987). *Interviewing: A Communication Approach.* (New York: Holt, Rinehart & Winston).

Eric W. Skopec (1985). *Situational Interviewing.* (New York: Harper & Row).

Charles J. Stewart and William J. Cash, Jr. (1985). *Interviewing: Principles and Practices,* 4th ed. (Dubuque, IA: William C. Brown).

# Principles
# of Small Group
# Communication

*After studying this chapter, you should be able to:*

▶ Define a *small group* and explain its four main components.

▶ Identify and describe the seven characteristics of a true group after having observed the group in action.

▶ Cite six advantages of working in groups and discuss how each contributes to group effectiveness.

▶ Describe five obstacles to effective small-group discussion and suggest how each may be overcome.

| | |
|---|---|
| *Stacy:* | Let's have a Winter Wonderland theme for homecoming this year. |
| *George:* | What, are you crazy? Texas weather in October is just like summer! |
| *Jane:* | It's the best theme anyone's come up with yet, and I want to get done with this. I've got a hot date in fifteen minutes. |
| *Harry:* | You would be more concerned if you knew how hard we've worked during the three meetings you missed. Can't you be more responsible, especially since you're the program chairperson? |
| *Leslie:* | I was in North Dakota once in October, and it snowed then. It was beautiful. |
| *Stacy:* | Then it's unanimous. We'll use shredded foam rubber for snow on all the floats. |
| *Jane:* | Thank goodness! Jim's going to be mad if I'm late. |
| *George:* | What happened? I thought we were going to pick a theme for homecoming. |

Sound familiar? Unfortunately, probably so. Working in groups doesn't have to be such a hassle, though, *if* you know how to go about it; but that's a pretty big IF.

The purpose of this chapter (and the next) is to reduce the size of that IF. We will shift our focus from the interpersonal level of speech communication to the group level. In this chapter we will discuss what a group is, some of its characteristics, six important advantages of working in groups, and five obstacles to effective small-group discussion. Our focus in the next chapter will be on the application of these principles to a number of small group communication tasks and practices. The emphasis in both chapters is on the way to become a more effective communicator in small groups.

## WHAT IS A SMALL GROUP?

Seven strangers sit at a bus stop reading their morning papers. Is this a group? Fifteen persons stand in the street observing a man perched on a twelfth-story ledge. Is this a group? Eight department managers engage in a spirited discussion over a new salary and promotion program. Is this a group? By definition, only the last of these collections is a *true* group, because it is the only one that displays all four of a group's components.

You will generally find that most groups you must deal with will be composed of between three and ten members. Therefore, we will be

In a small group, where participants can see and hear each other easily, each person influences and is influenced by the others in the group.

talking of this more limited range when we discuss the typical small group. For our purposes, a **small group** is from three to about fifteen or twenty persons who are communicating face to face so that each person influences and is influenced by each other person.

The communication dynamics among three or more persons are different from those between two. In dyadic communication, the message is intended for only one other individual, and he or she is the only person expected to respond. In contrast, in a group, each message has a source and receiver(s), other members serve as an audience for the message, and anyone may listen and respond.

Our definition specifies that members of a group are meeting *face to face*. This feature differentiates group communication from telephone conference calls, television and radio broadcasts, and written communiques. Certainly a number of people can communicate, get to know one another, and mutually influence one another through a variety of means. But feedback is most immediate and complete, and the potential for mutual influence is at its height, in a face-to-face setting.

*Small groups usually meet face to face.*

*The potential for mutual influence* is great in group situations. At a minimum, each member will recognize the presence of each other member. Much more likely, however, each group member will be influenced by other members' personality characteristics, interactions, and contributions to the task at hand. It is often difficult *to resist* being influenced by either the overtalkative group member or the member who sits in the corner and says nothing. The potential for mutual influence decreases greatly, however, when group membership exceeds twenty.

For a number of people to be considered a group, some form of common behavior must tie them together. This behavior is *interaction,* or *speech communication.* Through speech communication, group members come to know each other, influence each other, and generally develop the feelings of group membership. It is through communication that seven strangers sitting at a bus stop decide to meet socially for a drink on Friday night. It is through communication that fifteen persons watching the man on the ledge might join together to "talk the man down." It is through communication that people influence one another and work toward attaining mutually agreed-upon goals. It is through speech communication that individuals link themselves with one another in a group setting.

*The formation, development, and success of a group depends on effective speech communication.*

## THE CHARACTERISTICS OF GROUPS

What do all of the following groups have in common?

company executives deciding on the location of a new plant

students working on a group assignment

city planners wrestling with the way to raise funds for a new sewage-treatment plant

twelve jurors deliberating the guilt or innocence of an accused murderer

All these groups communicate. The amount, types, and content of their messages may be different, but they are influenced by and influence the other six key characteristics of groups to be discussed in this section: group structure, group climate, group task, situation, group phases, and individual traits.

### Group Structure

**Group structure** is the patterned regularities in feelings, perceptions, and actions that develop during the interaction among group members. Members of a group generally develop a set of feelings and perceptions about the way others should contribute to the group, who should or can talk to whom, who the most prestigious members are, and who should lead the group. Although these feelings and perceptions are not always openly discussed, they are often reflected in members'

*Groups develop regular patterns of feelings, perceptions, and actions through communication.*

actions and interactions. Such actions and interactions take on regular patterns as a group develops. For example, members of a newly formed student senate subcommittee elect a chairperson and compose an agenda during their first meeting. During later meetings, certain members become more vocal and others talk little. The chairperson leads the discussion and makes assignments, and others carry out the duties of the committee. Each member interacts more frequently with some members than with others, and selected members are looked upon as experts on certain topics. Each member probably begins to like some colleagues more than others. These patterned regularities of feelings, perceptions, and actions are indicators that a group has developed a structure. This structure can be seen in four areas: roles, status, leadership, and interaction patterns.

Roles.     A **role** is a set of expectations about the way a group member will behave when occupying a certain position. A secretary keeps minutes and takes care of correspondence. A treasurer handles and accounts for monies. A leader leads. Most group members agree, at least in principle, on the way the holder of a given position should behave. In fact, in most cases, key roles are formally identified and defined. Of course, the extent and formality of the role definitions depend on the formality associated with the group.

*Behavioral expectations are associated with most positions within a group.*

In addition, group members may assume informal roles for which expectations have not been clearly defined. These informal roles fulfill key functions that influence the effectiveness of group processes. Thus, they are called **functional roles.** Functional roles may be arranged into three categories: (1) group task roles, (2) group building and maintenance roles, and (3) individual roles.[1]

**Group task roles** are behaviors that assist a group in achieving its purposes and goals. These roles are clearly related to a group's attempts at coordinating the efforts of all group members toward the successful accomplishment of the group task. Such communication behaviors as contributing new ideas or alternative opinions, elaborating on previous discussion or others' ideas, coordinating suggestions or keeping the discussion on track, and encouraging the use of effective procedures assist the group in accomplishing its goals. For example, a member performing the "energizer" role might say, "We already agree on all the major issues in the case, so let's try to figure out how to solve the problem."

*Members who assume group task roles help the group accomplish its goals.*

**Group building and maintenance roles** are behaviors that establish and maintain good interpersonal relationships among the members of a group. They influence the way the group goes about dealing with personality conflicts, the amount and types of communication

*Good member relationships are established and maintained by people who perform building and maintenance roles.*

among group members, and the motivational factors associated with the conduct of the group's interactions. Praising and encouraging participation, mediating disputes and promoting compromise, and evaluating and regulating group activities help to build and maintain effective relationships among group members. For instance, "Marty, that's an excellent idea, and I think we can really use it to help us plan our next meeting" is a statement that might be made by someone in the "encourager" role.

Finally, **individual roles** are behaviors that satisfy individual needs—needs that are associated with neither a group task nor the building and maintenance of good interpersonal relationships. Belittling others or their ideas; arguing only for the sake of argument; using the group for personal recognition, nongroup-oriented confessions, or personal gain; and dominating the group's time or energies through horseplay or excessive aggression are disruptive and counterproductive to effective group functioning. For instance, someone who constantly uses group time to complain about a personal problem is not making a positive contribution to the group process.

As you can see, group task, building, and maintenance behaviors can greatly increase the efficiency and ease with which groups operate while promoting harmony and satisfaction among group members. When you participate in a group, it is important for you to be aware of, recognize, and perform behaviors that will enhance group progress, not delay it. When you notice someone indulging in nonproductive individual roles, bring the behavior to the member's attention and suggest *to the group* that the discussion get back on track.

**Status.**  A group member's **status** is the estimated worth attributed to him or her by a group. The group bases its estimate of worth on the extent to which it believes that an individual's attributes or characteristics contribute to the group's shared values and needs. For example, if an individual knows a great deal about a wide range of computer systems, that individual may be given high status in a group of executives who are charged with choosing a new computer system.

The same person may be assigned high status in one group and relatively low status in another, depending on the needs and values of the two groups. Although the computer expert may be awarded high status in the executive group, he or she may be just another member of the church's finance committee because he or she lacks knowledge of fiscal planning and budgeting.

**Leadership.**  Leadership behavior can be seen in all groups. Note, however, that all groups do not have *a* leader. **Leadership** is

**Functional Roles in Groups**

|  | *Contribution* | *Behaviors* |
|---|---|---|
| **Group Task Roles** | Assist the group in achieving its purpose and goals | Coordinating, contributing, elaborating, stimulating, energizing, orienting, recording |
| **Group Building and Maintenance Roles** | Help to establish and maintain good interpersonal relationships among group members | Praising, encouraging, mediating, evaluating, regulating, motivating, compromising |
| **Individual Roles** | Satisfy individual needs | Belittling, arguing, confessing, dominating, horseplaying, disrupting, pleading |

communication behavior that influences a group to accomplish its goals. Attempts at directing others' thoughts and actions may be exercised by any group member. Such influence is generally directed toward the attainment of the group's goals, although, like functional roles, it may focus on building and/or maintaining positive relationships among group members as well. Leadership is an important part of group structure and is vital to a group's efficiency and productivity. Leadership will be discussed in more detail in the next chapter.

**Interaction patterns.**   **Interaction patterns** are the recurring and predictable ways in which group members communicate or interact with one another as they conduct group activities. These patterns aid in defining the roles, status, and leadership behaviors in a group. One way to identify interaction patterns is to observe who talks to whom. The frequency and content of messages exchanged among certain group members often provide valuable information about the way each member contributes (or fails to contribute) to the effective functioning of the group. Remember that these interaction patterns are just that—*regular patterns*. They do not imply that certain members may talk to some members and not to others or that communication *never* takes

*Regular patterns of who talks to whom and how often help observers identify and understand the way a group functions.*

place between selected members. They only indicate the *relative* frequency with which members communicate with one another. For instance, more communication is generally directed toward a nonconforming group member than toward a conforming member. Can you guess why?

## Group Task

All groups are formed for some reason. That is, all groups have some job to perform. The **group task,** then, is the reason the group was formed or the job the group must perform.

A group's task may be assigned or suggested by an outside source or by the group itself. The nature of the task may be clearly defined before the group is formed, or part of the group's process may be to arrive at a more specific definition of the task. The explicitly stated problem or job that a group is dealing with is its primary task. Efforts to identify and perform group roles, methods of discussion and decision, and criteria for task completion are important secondary tasks.

## Group Climate

The feelings that group members develop toward a group and the other members of the group create the **group climate.** Group climate includes three elements: cohesiveness, norms, and pressure to conform.

*Group cohesiveness influences individual commitment to and satisfaction with a group.*

**Cohesiveness.**    **Cohesiveness** is the "stick-togetherness," degree of solidarity, or identification of the individuals with the group as a whole. It is the forces acting on group members to remain in the group.

You are encouraged to remain in a group as long as you feel that you are accepted, you are attracted to other group members or to the group as a whole, or you feel outside pressure to continue your support. How would you evaluate the cohesiveness of the group under discussion in the following conversation?

*Frank:*   I think we should split into two separate groups. Mary is a real pain, and Jeff never shows up for our meetings.

*Lisa:*   Yeah, and Craig always seems to start arguments with Amy and me.

*Joan:*   But Dr. Biggers said we have to work as a *group* on this project. How is he going to take this?

*Harry:*   He didn't say we couldn't work as subgroups on two different aspects of the project.

*Lisa:*   That could be a problem. First, let's call a required meeting of the whole group, and whoever doesn't show up is out of the group and we'll tell Biggers why.

Certainly the group is encouraged to work together by an external force—Dr. Biggers. This encouragement may not be strong enough, however, for the group to develop a high level of cohesiveness. Personality conflicts, some members' failure to attend meetings, and constant arguing seem to be overpowering the other forces, at least for Frank, Lisa, Joan, and Harry. Unless the conditions that encourage members to remain in the group are stronger than the opposing forces, these members may drop out.

**Norms.** The standards group members have about the way they should behave in a group are called group **norms.** They may be either explicit or implicit. Explicit norms are formal, mutually agreed-on rules for guiding a group's functioning. *Robert's Rules of Order* sets forth a very formal and explicit system for conducting group meetings commonly called *parliamentary procedure.*[2] Federal and state legislative bodies, many student body and faculty groups, and other formal and long-term groups use parliamentary procedure as the standard of conduct for their meetings.

Not all groups use such a formal and clearcut set of norms. For instance, the four students in our previous example tried to set their own norms. This is typical of many groups, both formal and informal. Even at the most casual level, a group of friends may establish punctuality as a norm by saying that anyone who isn't ready to leave for the movie on time will be left behind.

Implicit norms are never actually stated. Nonetheless, when one of these unspoken rules is broken, members' communication behavior—whether verbal or nonverbal—often indicates that they do, indeed, exist. For example, "group members who interrupt others while talking will become targets of long, cold stares" can be an implicit norm developed in a group where one member typically interrupts others.

Norms exist in all groups. These behavioral expectations and members' willingness to follow them are crucial to the efficiency of the group process.

**Pressure to conform.** Just as all groups have norms, all groups attempt to use the communication process to gain a member's compliance. Communication intended to increase the degree to which a group member's behavior corresponds to the norms of the group is called **pressure to conform.** It may take many forms: a cold stare, verbal reprimands, the assignment of boring or difficult tasks, or even expulsion from the group. The amount and nature of pressure to conform may vary according to the norm violated, the status of the nonconformist, and the point in the group's interaction at which the norm is violated. For example, a person who deviates from a norm during a heated argument may receive a sharp reprimand. The same person

*Members use verbal and nonverbal communication to pressure nonconformists into observing group norms.*

deviating from the same norm during an informal conversation might receive little notice or pressure to conform. Similarly, for the same violation, someone of lower status may receive a sharper reprimand than someone of higher status.

## Situation

Although many people define *situation* as "all the conditions that exist in a group at any *one time*," we prefer to define **situation** more specifically as "the physical arrangements in which a group finds itself, including setting and proximity." As discussed in Chapter 4, the characteristics of a physical environment may greatly influence communication behaviors. Lighting, temperature, colors, arrangement of furniture, and placement of group members within the physical setting are all potential influences on interaction.

**Setting.**   One element of a situation, the group **setting,** is the physical surroundings in which a group is meeting at a particular time. Some people prefer to meet in the home of a group member. Others prefer a more formal atmosphere in which to conduct business. Some group tasks lend themselves to members' sitting on the floor, whereas other jobs are more appropriately accomplished around a large conference table. A small conference room with no air conditioning, a bare wooden table, and wooden chairs in mid-July at 3:00 P.M. is likely to encourage group members to conclude their business in a short time. Indeed, the physical surroundings in which a group meets may have a great deal to do with group climate and effectiveness.

**Proximity.**   Another   element   of   the   group   situation   is **proximity**—the arrangement in which the members place themselves (or in which they are placed) in group meetings. Did you know that the Paris Peace Talks to end the Vietnam conflict in 1968 were held up for weeks because of a disagreement over the shape of the conference table to be used and where the representatives of various nations would be seated around the table? "What difference does that make?" you may ask. "Plenty," many people may respond. The person at one end of a rectangular table is often perceived as the leader or the person with the highest status. The group member seated to the right of that person may be perceived as his or her top aide. Furthermore, if certain subgroups sit together, they may be perceived as a force to be dealt with *as a group*. Although they may not *intend* to influence other group members strategically, they may be doing just that.

Proximity is an important element in the group situation. Imagine how this scene might be different if the two most active participants were sitting side by side.

Some people feel more comfortable if they can clearly see the faces of all participants. Such a seating pattern enables all group members to read the facial expressions of all other group members and obtain useful information about feelings and reactions. Other people prefer to place themselves so that they can make direct eye contact with specific or all group members and thus exchange prearranged, but subtle, eye messages during the course of a meeting.

Regardless of when or where you meet in group settings, you'll find that knowledge about, and planning for, an appropriate group situation will enhance your chances of having a productive meeting. Try matching the level of formality and the needs of the members with your meeting situation. You may be amazed at the positive effects the right situation can have on group productivity and satisfaction.

## Group Phases

Groups grow and develop over a moderately long period of time, just as people do. Just as people pass through predictable phases of growth (infancy, childhood, adolescence, adulthood), so do groups. The four usual development phases of task-oriented groups are orientation, conflict, emergence, and reinforcement.[3]

*Groups develop in stages, just as individuals do.*

**Orientation.**   During the orientation stage of group development, members attempt to become familiar with the group and with other group members. A collection of individuals begins to develop a group climate and to settle questions of leadership, norms, status, and group task. The communication in this first phase is characterized by ambiguity and uncertainty about both interpersonal relationships and the way to go about defining and accomplishing the group task. For example, during the initial meeting of an organization's board of directors, the members will spend some time becoming familiar with each other's educational, occupational, business, and personal backgrounds. They will also discuss perceptions of their roles in running the company and share ideas about the way to proceed with elections, operating procedures, and meeting schedules. Few, if any, decisions will be made, however.

**Conflict.**   The conflict phase follows orientation. Typical of this phase are heated and emotional discussions, frequently over interpersonal issues. The group attempts to resolve questions about the task and the way to proceed. Leadership, norms, and roles begin to take shape, and task-related attitudes and ideas are expressed more strongly. In comparison to the first phase, the conflict stage and its accompanying interaction are much less ambiguous and uncertain. The conflict phase of our board of directors' meetings would probably find the members deliberating over the ideal characteristics of a chairperson, attempting to settle procedural matters, and working on a definition of their primary tasks and goals.

**Emergence.**   Expressions of ambiguity arise anew during the third phase—emergence. Unlike the orientation phase, however, the ambiguity in the emergence phase pertains to task-related attitudes and ideas rather than to interpersonal and procedural matters. Conflict is less evident in this phase, although not completely lacking. Issues argued about in the second phase begin to be resolved as minority group members express their ideas and attitudes in ways that show other group members that they are "coming around." Because attitude change is a gradual process, members' comments change slowly from disagreement through ambiguity to agreement. It is during this phase that the group members begin to see "the light at the end of the tunnel." For example, minority members of a board of directors may begin to give up the demand that *their* candidate be elected chairperson, and some members may begin to reduce their support for holding future board meetings in Hawaii. Statements such as "I might go along with that" and "I guess that's not such a bad idea" are typical during the emergence phase.

**Reinforcement.**    During reinforcement, the final stage of group development, emerging attitudes and accomplishments are supported and rewarded. The agreements and decisions that have been reached are recognized and applauded, and personal satisfaction and gratitude are expressed by all group members. A spirit of unity, friendly cooperation, and "pats on the back for a job done well" are most often associated with this final phase. For our board of directors, congratulations to the newly elected chairperson and statements of support would be common. Expressions of mutual satisfaction with the group's accomplishments and mutual appreciation for individual contributions would be heard.

Not all groups pass through these phases in the same order, nor do all groups necessarily pass through all four phases. Longstanding groups often make decisions with a minimum of orientation and/or conflict. Some groups cycle through several conflict and emergence stages as they make decisions on their way to accomplishing a single task.

Moreover, the individual phases are seldom clearly distinguishable, because the transitions between phases tend to be gradual. Nonetheless, most students in our small-group communication classes are able to identify and analyze communication behaviors in these four phases. They find that such analysis helps them to better understand and explain the small-group communication process.

## Individual Traits

Research indicates that people behave differently in groups than they do when alone.[4] Although it is difficult to pinpoint why this is so, this tendency has important implications for, and influences on, communication in groups. Each member's individual traits, such as personality characteristics, group roles, group status, and individual attitudes toward group participation, interact with and influence group communication in subtle and unique ways. We all experience mood changes, have good days and bad days, and we change our communication behavior to coincide with these changes, often without realizing it. Our relative status or the role that we play in a group may change, and chances are good that, in response, our communication will change as well.

*Individual differences among group members make each group a unique and exciting entity.*

The personal characteristics and abilities of any group member influence the group as a whole. Such characteristics as expertise in a particular subject area, age, sex, physical traits, intelligence, personality traits, and popularity all affect the climate, structure, task, development, and communication of a group, making that group different from any other group. For example, if a city planning committee discovers that one of its members is an architect, the other members may look toward that person to lead a discussion of plans for the construction of a new city hall building. The lone male member in a student group may find that he is perceived as an outsider and is considered unqualified to contribute to the group's problem-solving efforts. Older group members are often looked to for support or leadership. The most dependable member, as perceived by a group, will probably be assigned the tasks most crucial to the accomplishment of the group's goals.

The combination of all individual group members' characteristics makes a group unique, so that a group itself is more than the sum of its parts. If any individual in a group changes, or if a group's membership changes in any way, the group itself changes. Even when only one group member is lost or added, all other characteristics of the group—even its process of communication—change. For instance, suppose that a study group is composed of three females and two males, and that one of the males tends to be among the more talkative members of the group. The less talkative male may feel comfortable expressing his ideas because of the presence of the other male, thus leading both males to actively participate (not dominate) in the group process. Then suppose that the more talkative male drops out of the study group. It is entirely likely that the remaining male will become less active in the group, especially given his reluctance to speak up in the first place.

## Communication

*Communication is the tie that binds a group together, influencing and being influenced by all other group characteristics.*

The final characteristic of a group (and the most important) is communication. Through communication, members link themselves with one another, share and use knowledge, and influence one another in an attempt to achieve the goals that they believe to be important. Through communication, groups establish a group structure, develop a group climate, grow and mature through various phases, and solve problems or conduct business.

There is *mutual* influence between the communication in a group and all other group characteristics. The communication influences all other group characteristics—its structure, task, climate, situation, phases, and composition. These characteristics, in turn, determine the types, content, and frequency of the messages produced. Such relationships will be discussed further in the next chapter, but before concluding, this chapter will examine some advantages of working in groups. It will also identify some possible obstacles to effective small

*Review Box*

## The Characteristics of a Group

| Characteristic | Definition | Elements |
|---|---|---|
| Group Structure | Patterned regularities in feelings, perceptions, and actions | Roles<br>Status<br>Leadership<br>Interaction patterns |
| Group Task | Reason the group was formed or the job to be done | |
| Group Climate | Feelings members develop about the group and other members | Cohesiveness<br>Norms<br>Pressure to conform |
| Situation | Physical arrangements of a group | Setting<br>Proximity |
| Group Phases | Predictable stages of group development | Orientation<br>Conflict<br>Emergence<br>Reinforcement |
| Individual Traits | Unique characteristics of members that influence group process | Personality<br>Group roles<br>Group status<br>Attitudes toward group participation<br>Expertise<br>Age<br>Sex<br>Physical traits |
| Communication | Interaction among group members | Linkages among group members<br>Sharing and use of information<br>Vehicle for mutual influence |

group communication. The next two sections will explain *why* working in small groups is superior to working alone when solving problems and making decisions, and *how* to overcome five obstacles to effective small group communication.

## ADVANTAGES OF WORKING IN GROUPS

Given your knowledge of, and past experiences with, working in groups, you may be tempted to ask, "Why assign a task to a group when a well-informed, intelligent individual might perform the task just as effectively alone?" The "might" in this question is a vitally important word that requires further consideration.

Suppose you were asked to nominate a person to run for president of the United States. What criteria would you use for selection? You would probably consider personality traits, knowledge of foreign and domestic affairs, public image, political background and experience, and financial status. But how would you define each of these factors? *Which* personality traits would you be looking for? *How much* knowledge of foreign and domestic affairs? *What kind* of public image? *What type* and *amount* of political experience? *Which* financial status?

Once you have adequately defined your criteria, how might you go about finding a person who meets your criteria as closely as possible? To aid you in this enormous task, you might enlist the assistance of your parents, friends, instructors, and maybe even some political figures, business associates, and people on the street. (What, *you* aren't that "well-informed, intelligent individual who might perform the task just as effectively alone"?) You could even have a meeting with some of these people so that you could all share your perceptions and ideas about the selection process. (Yes—yet another *group!*)

The advantages of working in groups far outweigh the disadvantages. You can have fun working in groups, and you might even meet new people and develop lasting friendships.

In addition to offering many personal benefits, working in groups greatly enhances the processes of solving problems and making decisions. When people work together, they find higher interest in tasks, greater availability of materials, a wider range of issues and alternatives, increased chances for in-depth analysis, greater commitment to the outcome, and higher quality decisions.

### Higher Interest in a Task

When several people have the opportunity to openly and honestly identify a problem, investigate alternative solutions, and come to some decision, the task seems to become more interesting. Participants catch each other's enthusiasm and build on each other's ideas. As a result, a task may hold individual participants' attention longer and lead to a better conclusion.

### Greater Availability of Materials

When group members join forces, they can usually gather a greater variety of information than can one person working alone. The key is effective division of labor—having individual members work on separate aspects of a problem or task and then share their findings. This saves time and increases group efficiency. It can lead to better decisions based on more and higher quality information.

### Wider Range of Issues and Alternatives

Groups uncover a much broader range of opinions, ideas, feelings, issues, and possible solutions than do individuals working alone. There is no question that the cliché "Two heads are better than one" applies. By encouraging all of its members to express themselves honestly and openly, a group develops a valuable resource that enhances the quality of the final outcome.

### Increased Chances for In-Depth Analysis

The diversity of individual perspectives and opinions that exists in a group provides an excellent opportunity for members to closely and critically examine a problem and its possible solutions. When group members take advantage of this diversity to explore, evaluate, and constructively criticize many viewpoints and issues, they can be more confident that they have thoroughly and effectively considered all possible options and have arrived at the best possible solution.

*Groups outperform individuals because they provide more opportunities for in-depth analysis, encourage broader commitment to decisions, and usually produce higher quality decisions.*

### Greater Commitment to the Outcome

When people are allowed to participate in the decision-making process, they are much more likely to support the final outcome. Thus, managers often meet with subordinates to choose a course of action, and politicians often consult with voters before passing a new law.

### Higher Quality Decisions

The final advantage of working in groups—higher quality decisions—results from combining the other five advantages. Groups can collect, synthesize, and analyze a greater amount of information than

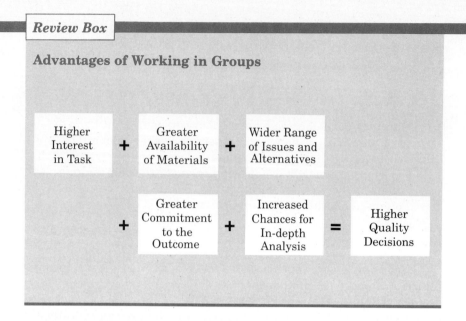

**Review Box**

**Advantages of Working in Groups**

Higher Interest in Task **+** Greater Availability of Materials **+** Wider Range of Issues and Alternatives

**+** Greater Commitment to the Outcome **+** Increased Chances for In-depth Analysis **=** Higher Quality Decisions

can individuals. In addition, when group members take active roles in problem-solving and decision-making tasks, they are more interested in and committed to the task and its outcome. The result is a well-thought-out decision based on a wealth of information, evaluated from many perspectives, and supported by consensus.

Now who do you think could more effectively select a candidate for the president of the United States—you or a group of which you are a part? There is no question that a group would yield superior results; but no group is exempt from obstacles to effective communication.

## OBSTACLES TO EFFECTIVE SMALL GROUP DISCUSSION

As was discussed earlier, effective group communication is characterized by thorough analysis and evaluation of issues, open and honest communication, clearly defined tasks, committed group members, and active participation. When you observe that a discussion lacks some of these traits, you can be sure that the group is experiencing one or more of the following problems: groupthink, defensiveness, hidden agendas, lack of cohesiveness, or unbalanced participation.

## Groupthink

When **groupthink** occurs, members of a group attempt "to minimize conflict and reach a consensus at the expense of critically testing, analyzing, and evaluating ideas."[5] In highly cohesive groups, or in groups with strong, high-status leaders, members often suspend critical judgment and expression of personal opinions to avoid conflict and to preserve a false sense of unanimity. Nonconforming behaviors and ideas are discouraged or ignored, critical analysis of issues and solutions is suspended, and the leader's or the majority's opinion is accepted without dissent. In such cases, open, honest communication becomes impossible, and there is little opportunity to examine a wide range of alternatives and issues.

You can try to overcome groupthink by encouraging the active and open participation by all members. Suggest that the judgment of ideas and solutions be suspended until all of them have been heard and discussed. Insist on critical and thorough analysis of all issues and alternatives. You may want to suggest dividing into subgroups or working individually for a time so that issues may be studied independently. Above all, try to ensure that all group members have a chance to voice their ideas and opinions, and devise a solution or alternative that, as closely as possible, represents the judgments of all group members.

## Defensiveness

Just as partners in an interpersonal relationship may develop defensiveness, so too may members of a group. Real or perceived status differences, nonsupportive or belittling comments, expressions of superiority, and other ineffective communication behaviors may cause members to react defensively. As a result, group discussions will be less effective. Individual withdrawal from participation, personality conflicts, personal attacks, and failure to make progress are frequently observed in groups where one or more members feel defensive.

You can help reduce defensiveness by insisting that the group lay out ground rules for discussion before deliberations begin. Suggest that communication remain focused on issues, not on personality traits or personal conflicts. Promote an attitude of equality among group members, and suggest that everyone has her or his right to be heard and respected, regardless of status or personality differences. If you observe defensiveness in a group member, be supportive of the person as well as his or her ideas and opinions. You don't have to agree, but you can be encouraging and courteous. Mediate disputes if necessary, and try

*To combat defensiveness, be supportive and courteous, mediate disputes if necessary, and keep the discussion issue-oriented.*

to get the discussion back on track. Remind everyone that the group's purpose is to make a decision or solve a problem, not deal with personal conflicts.

## Hidden Agendas

Suppose you have just opened a quick copy-printing service in a new town, and you need contacts to develop your clientele. You might join a civic or social group with the sole purpose of meeting business people and office personnel to whom you can sell your service. You are more interested in this unstated goal than in the goals or activities of the group itself.

When an individual conceals personal goals or needs in hopes of satisfying them through a group's interaction, the individual has a **hidden agenda.** A member with a hidden agenda can detract from a group's effectiveness because he or she will waste the group's time and energy for personal gain.

When you think that a person with a hidden agenda is leading your group off track, try to redirect the discussion to the issue at hand. Remind the group of its task, and suggest that the group's time can be better spent on serious and relevant discussion. You may need to speak with the offending individual in private should the problem persist.

## Lack of Cohesiveness

Some conflict is to be expected and may be constructive, but groups that lack cohesiveness—that don't develop an atmosphere of openness, supportiveness, and friendliness—spend valuable time and energy coping with needless conflict. Personality conflicts, closed-mindedness, pettiness, and inflexibility lead to tense interpersonal relationships, indecision, and declines in motivation and productivity.

To help combat a lack of cohesiveness in a group, promote an atmosphere of supportiveness and friendliness. When divisiveness and hostility occur, suggest a recess, either for a short break or until the next meeting. Reduce tension by telling a joke or attempting to mediate the dispute. Try to refocus attention on the task at hand; encourage participants to remain issue-oriented. Attempt to pull everyone together by emphasizing the group, its goal, and the personal rewards associated with successful task accomplishment.

## Unbalanced Participation

Unbalanced participation may take a number of forms. At one extreme is the *dominating talker*. This person has something to say about everything and attempts to control the discussion. Whether the dominating talker's contributions are useful, he or she diminishes group effectiveness by interfering with the equal participation of all members. At the other extreme is the *nonparticipator*. This person's refusal to take part in group discussion can be just as destructive as the dominator's outspokenness. The idea that the nonparticipator keeps private is lost to the group, and, of course, it may be just the idea that's needed.

Someone who can thwart all but the most assertive participants is the *insensitive group member,* who says what he or she feels, regardless of the way it affects others. Comments such as "That's a stupid idea," "You don't know what you're talking about," and "We already talked about that. Don't you listen?" can inhibit communication, drive members from the group, and create conflict.

The way to deal with unbalanced participation is to be supportive while actively encouraging balanced participation. Statements such as "Jan, we know how you stand on this issue. Let's hear what Denise has to say," or "Jim, how do you feel about this option?" are often useful in drawing nonparticipators into a discussion. By reminding members of the advantages of everyone's active participation, you can sensitize them to the benefits of equality and fairness and may well uncover just the information or solution needed to accomplish the group task.

*When participation is active and balanced, a group stands a better chance of increasing its efficiency and productivity.*

## SUMMARY

Small group communication is a complex, but important, process. Your effectiveness in group settings depends on your understanding and application of the basic principles of small group communication. Knowing how to maximize the advantages of and overcome obstacles to effective small-group discussion will serve you well in social, educational, professional, and personal contexts.

▶**Define a *small group* and explain its four main components.**

A small group consists of three or more persons who are communicating face to face in such a manner that each person influences and is influenced by each other person. In a small group, two or more receivers act as an audience for the message source, and any member may respond at any time. The fact that groups meet in face-to-face settings facilitates immediate and complete feedback. The potential for mutual influence is high in groups, as each member is likely to be affected in some way by each other member's behavior. Speech communication within a group brings individual members together as they become acquainted, influence one another, and develop the feelings of group membership.

▶ **Identify and describe the seven characteristics of a true group after having observed the group in action.**

All groups exhibit seven key characteristics: group structure, group climate, group task, situation, group phases, individual traits, and communication.

*Group structure* is the regular patterns of members' feelings, perceptions, and actions that surface in group interactions. Roles, status, leadership, and interaction patterns are elements of group structure.

*Group task* is the reason the group was formed or the job that must be performed. The task provides the focus for group deliberations.

The feelings that group members have toward each other and toward the group as a whole is the *group climate*. Climate is composed of cohesiveness, norms, and pressure to conform.

The *situation* contributes to the mood of the group. It is the physical arrangements in which a group finds itself at any particular meeting; it consists of setting and proximity.

Groups change and pass through four phases of development: orientation, conflict, emergence, and reinforcement. Topics of discussion and communication characteristics differ in each of these phases.

Groups are composed of individuals, and each individual's traits contribute to all aspects of group communication. Moods, personality characteristics, status, expertise, and sex are just a few of the individual traits that may influence the way groups communicate during a meeting.

Communication, of course, is the crucial element in any group setting. It influences and is influenced by all other characteristics.

▶ **Cite six advantages of working in groups and discuss how each contributes to group effectiveness.**

Group members exhibit higher interest in their task than do individuals. This higher interest promotes enthusiasm, attention, open communication, and better conclusions. By dividing the labor and sharing the workload, group members can gather and process greater amounts and more types of information than can an individual working alone. Through open discussion and active participation, groups have access to a wider range of issues and alternatives than do individuals.

Increased chances for in-depth analysis of issues and alternative solutions grow out of the shared opinions, feelings, and ideas of group participants. Because members share in the problem-solving and decision-making processes, they develop a deeper commitment to the outcome of group discussions and decisions.

▶ **Describe five obstacles to effective small-group discussion and suggest how each may be overcome.**

*Groupthink* is an attempt by group members to avoid conflict by accepting ideas or solutions without critical evaluation and open discussion. To minimize the potential for groupthink, encourage open and thorough discussion of all alternatives, as well as critical and independent thinking.

Defensiveness in a group can result from personality conflicts, aggressive behavior, and expressions of superiority. Resist defensive attitudes by being supportive of all group members and by keeping the discussion issue-oriented, not person-oriented.

Concealed needs or goals that detract from effective small group communication are called *hidden agendas.* When you spot them, point them out to the group and suggest that the discussion return to the task at hand.

Divisiveness, personality conflicts, and hostility indicate that a group lacks cohesiveness. When you detect a lack of cohesiveness, try to promote supportiveness, mediate disputes, focus on the satisfactions and rewards of group work, and direct the discussion to issues.

Unbalanced participation in groups limits the free and open exchange of ideas. To achieve better balance, encourage open, honest, and active participation by all members.

## KEY TERMS

**cohesiveness:**   the "stick-togetherness," degree of solidarity, or identification of the individuals with the group as a whole; the forces acting on group members to remain in the group.

**functional roles:**   informal roles that fulfill key group functions which influence the effectiveness of group processes.

**group building and maintenance roles:**   behaviors that establish and maintain good interpersonal relationships among group members.

**group climate:**   the feelings that group members develop toward the group and the other members of the group.

**group structure:**   the patterned regularities in feelings, perceptions, and actions that develop during interaction among group members.

**group task:**   the reason the group was formed, or the job the group must perform.

**group task roles:**  behaviors that assist the group in achieving its purposes and goals.

**groupthink:**  group attempts to minimize conflict and reach agreement at the expense of critically testing, analyzing, and evaluating ideas.

**hidden agenda:**  personal goals or needs that an individual conceals in hopes of satisfying them through the group's interactions.

**individual roles:**  behaviors that satisfy individual needs at the expense of group effectiveness.

**individual traits:**  personality characteristics, group roles, group status, individual attitudes toward group participation, and other personal characteristics which influence group processes and which make each group unique.

**interaction patterns:**  the recurring and predictable ways in which group members communicate or interact with one another as they conduct group activities.

**leadership:**  communication behavior that influences the group to accomplish its goals.

**norms:**  the standards group members have about how they should behave in a group.

**pressure to conform:**  communication intended to increase the degree to which a group member's behavior corresponds to the norms of the group.

**proximity:**  the arrangement in which the members place themselves or in which they are placed in group meetings.

**roles:**  a set of expectations about how a group member will behave when occupying a certain position.

**setting:**  the physical surroundings in which a group is meeting at a particular time.

**situation:**  the physical arrangements in which a group finds itself, including setting and proximity.

**small group:**  three or more persons who are communicating face to face in such a manner that each person influences and is influenced by each other member.

**status:**  the estimated worth attributed to a member by a group.

## DISCUSSION QUESTIONS

1. Compare and contrast interpersonal communication and small group communication. What are some similarities of the two? What are some differences? What role does interpersonal influence play in groups that many times is *not* present in communication between two people? Why is this so?

2. How would you go about building a good climate in a group to which you belonged? How would you try to build cohesiveness among its members? How would you try to agree on and enforce norms? What kind of and how much pressure to conform would you try to use?

3. Discuss how individual traits of group members can influence effective group processes. How would you go about dealing with an individual who was in a bad mood during a group meeting? What would you try to do if one member were of much higher status and it was obvious to you that the other members were intimidated by that member? Imagine other scenarios and discuss options for effectively dealing with individual differences in group situations.

4. Discuss in detail each of the advantages of working in groups. Why is assigning a task to a group better than having the same number of individuals working on the same task alone? In what groups have you worked where you experienced one or more of these benefits? Do you feel that these groups actually produced higher quality decisions or products than would have been possible by individuals? Why or why not?

## *SUGGESTED ACTIVITIES*

1. Observe a group in its natural setting—a city council meeting, a college or university committee meeting, or a fraternity or sorority meeting. Make notes and diagrams of the situation in which the group is working. How do you think the elements of the situation influenced the group discussion and relationships among group members? What guesses can you make about the influence of status, roles, and leadership on the physical arrangement of the members?

2. Work with five classmates on a problem-solving exercise. (Your instructor might have some interesting exercises you can use.) Observe the deliberations of the group and the contributions of each member as you work together. Note which group task roles, group building and maintenance roles, and individual roles each member performs. How did you know which type of role each was enacting? Which of the observed communication behaviors increased the group's efficiency and productivity? Which of the observed behaviors reduced efficiency and productivity? How might certain roles have been more successfully performed?

3. Observe a group in a natural setting. Pay close attention to the phases of group development as discussed in this chapter. How difficult was it to identify them? Could you tell when the group had left one phase and entered another? What communication behaviors indicated that they had progressed from one phase to another?

4. Observe a group in a natural setting. Look for the occurrence of one or more of the disadvantages of working in groups. How did you know when each occurred? What communication behaviors signaled their presence? What could the group have done to prevent or lessen the negative impact?

## SUGGESTED READINGS

Steven A. Beebe and John T. Masterson. (1986). *Communicating in Small Groups: Principles and Practices,* 2nd ed. (Glenview, IL: Scott, Foresman and Company).

Kenneth D. Benne and Paul Sheats. "Functional Roles of Group Members," *Journal of Social Issues* 4, Spring 1948: 41–49.

Paul A. Hare. (1976) *Handbook of Small Group Research,* 2nd ed. (New York: The Free Press).

Marvin E. Shaw. (1981) *Group Dynamics: The Psychology of Small Group Behavior,* 3rd ed. (New York: McGraw-Hill Book Company).

# Participating in Small Groups

9

*After studying this chapter, you should be able to:*

▶ Distinguish between decision making and problem solving.

▶ Identify and use the nine steps in the problem-solving process.

▶ Use your knowledge of approaches to leadership and styles of leadership to lead a small group through a problem-solving discussion.

▶ Define *conflict,* and identify and use the appropriate style of conflict management in a group situation.

The last chapter introduced some basic principles of small group communication. This chapter will build on those principles by examining some communication behaviors that will improve your effectiveness when working in groups.

First, it is necessary to dintinguish between problem solving and decision making—an important distinction that all group members should understand before working on any task. Then consider the nine problem-solving steps and three methods of making decisions in groups. Next leadership in small groups will be discussed. The objective of this discussion is to enhance your ability to influence and direct a working group. Finally, some ways of managing conflict, a common occurrence in small groups, will be suggested.

You will find that you can apply the general guidelines presented in this chapter to virtually any group situation, be it a school study group, a church fund-raising committee, a civic planning board, or a group of business executives. The focus is on task-oriented groups—specifically those concerned with problem solving and decision making. Such groups are the most common and difficult ones in which to communicate effectively. Participation must be shared and active, leadership must be of high quality, conflict must be resolved, and group needs must be recognized and satisfied. Otherwise, the resulting solutions and decisions are likely to be faulty.

## GROUP PROBLEM SOLVING

*Decision making involves choosing from two or more alternatives; problem solving involves making several decisions.*

Many people use the terms *decision making* and *problem solving* interchangeably. In fact, there is an important and useful distinction between the two. **Decision making** involves choosing from two or more possible alternatives. **Problem solving** is a more complex procedure, involving a series of steps and a number of decisions, through which individuals or groups attempt to change a set of conditions with which they are dissatisfied to a set of conditions with which they are satisfied.

In other words, when you engage in decision making, you identify your options and choose the best one. When you participate in problem solving you proceed through a series of steps, each requiring one or more decisions. These decisions include identifying and clarifying problems, deciding on the conditions that make the situations dissatisfying, generating criteria for evaluating possible solutions, identifying and evaluating possible changes in unsatisfactory conditions, and deciding on the most preferred solution and its implementation. The objective of this process, of course, is to make decisions about the selection and implementation of changes that will result in increased satisfaction with the situation.

This distinction is important because you, as a member of a group, might approach a task differently if your group were selecting a single alternative from a number of possibilities rather than starting with a specific problem, developing a number of possible solutions, and selecting from among them. Problem solving involves making a number of decisions while attempting to improve a situation.

For example, suppose that you face the problem of fitting two years of a foreign language into your four-year degree program in order to fulfill a graduation requirement. On the simplest level, you need to choose from a number of foreign languages. This seems to be a *decision;* but you also have a *problem* that goes deeper than simply selecting from among the available alternatives—you are not good at learning a foreign language. To solve your problem, you might ask yourself a series of questions and make a series of decisions:

| | |
|---|---|
| *Problem:* | How can I most effectively fulfill the two-year foreign language requirement? |
| *Question:* | To *whom* should I turn for guidance? |
| *Decision:* | My academic adviser |
| *Question:* | *Which* foreign language should I take? |
| *Decision:* | Spanish |
| *Question:* | *When* should I enroll in the course? |
| *Decision:* | Summers—it's offered by correspondence then. |
| *Question:* | *What* other courses should I enroll in at the same time so that I will have enough time to study foreign language? |
| *Decision:* | None—I don't need to take any other courses during the summer. |

In this way, you take a systematic approach to identify and clarify the key variables in your situation. You can arrive at the solution that is most advantageous for you.

## Group Decision Making

Groups may arrive at decisions by a variety of methods: (1) by majority vote, (2) by allowing an expert, high-status member, or leader to decide, or (3) by consensus. Each of these methods is commonly used, but the preferred method is the last—consensus. You will see why.

**Decision by majority vote.** Under majority rule, an entire group agrees to accept any decision supported by 50 percent plus one of its members. At first glance this democratic procedure may seem to be the most fair and make the most sense when group members have differing opinions. After all, our nation elects its president in this manner. Closer consideration, however, may reveal that this method is not the most appropriate for true *group* decision making. If the objective is for all members to be satisfied with and committed to a decision (as we believe that they should be), the majority rule method will not suffice. Its inherent problem is that some members "win" while others "lose." Consequently, more likely than not, those who lose will not be completely satisfied with the group's decision and will not be fully committed to support its implementation.

When majority voting decides issues, subgroups often form and bargain with other members or subgroups to gain support for their points of view. As a result, group discussion frequently deteriorates into political or personal battles. Then, when a decision is finally made, members of the minority are likely to withhold their support. In such cases, high-quality decisions are seldom reached and group effectiveness nosedives.

**Decision by experts, high-status members, or leaders.**

*When experts or leaders make decisions, the group surrenders authority and responsibility.*

Decisions reached by experts, high-status members, or leaders are group decisions in name only. Groups often conform to the wishes of such people, or, in some isolated cases, might even *assign* decision-making authority to such group members. When they do this, groups deny their other members any authority or desire to make decisions. They allow themselves to be used merely as sounding boards. Among the many possible negative consequences of such behavior are lack of support for the decisions, failure to use the ideas, opinions, and expertise of other group members, loss of group cohesiveness, and failure to understand the reasons behind the decisions.

**Decision by consensus.**  A decision by **consensus** is a decision

*Group members are more satisfied when consensus is used to make decisions.*

that all group members agree is the best alternative that they can all accept. This does not necessarily mean that *all* members agree that the decision is the *best* possible solution. Rather, it is the best alternative that all members can *agree to accept,* given their individual points of view. In a consensus, no one loses. If all members agree to accept a decision, all members should be at least moderately satisfied with it. Thus, *shared* judgments, ideas, opinions, and responsibility result in *shared* group satisfaction and productivity. When unanimity is not possible in group decision making, consensus is the best alternative.

For example, four friends decide that they would like to go to a movie together. Each person wants to see a different movie—a comedy, a science fiction tale, a drama, and an adventure. After considerable deliberation, the friends decide to attend the comedy, because it is also a spoof of a recent science fiction movie. As part of the decision-making process, the individuals who wanted to see the drama and the adven-

## Methods of Group Decision Making

| Method | How Decision Is Made | Effects on Group |
|---|---|---|
| Majority Vote | Vote is taken by all members; that option receiving more than half the votes is accepted | Some members win; others lose<br>Losers not completely satisfied with or committed to outcome<br>Subgroups often form, dividing group<br>Lower quality decisions |
| Expert, high-status member, or leader | Authority for making decision given to one member of a group | Conformity to the desires of one member<br>Not a group decision<br>Lack of support for the decision<br>Failure to use input of all group members<br>Loss of cohesiveness<br>Failure to understand reasons behind the decision |
| Consensus | All members agree that a decision is the best that everyone can accept | Includes everyone's points of view<br>No one loses<br>Everyone moderately satisfied<br>More commitment to the outcome<br>Higher quality decisions |

ture agree that going to a movie as a group is more important than seeing their preferred kind of movie. In fact, the group agrees to see the other movies sometime in the near future. Although all four friends may not be completely satisfied, they agree that, considering their wide range of preferences, seeing the comedy science fiction movie this time and the drama and adventure in the near future is the best possible alternative *under the circumstances.* A consensus is attained, because all members accept and are at least minimally satisfied with the decision.

## Steps in the Problem-Solving Process

Without order and organization, group problem solving becomes impossible. Here are nine steps that any group can follow to ensure order and organization in its group problem-solving activities.

### Step 1: Working individually, clearly identify and define the group task.

Ask each group member to identify and define the group task prior to the first joint meeting, if possible. This preparation process encourages each member to develop a personal perspective on the problem and to identify possible issues, information needs, and solutions. It also gives each member a well-thought-out position to draw on during the group's deliberations. Make sure that individuals do not attempt to solve the problem or make the decision independently during this step. Coming to the group with strong preconceptions can create inflexibility, and limit free and open discussion.

### Step 2: Prepare for discussion.

Once a personal perspective is developed, suggest that each member prepare for discussion by gathering as much related information as possible. All aspects of a problem should be researched, not just those that support the individual's personal perspective. Each member should be ready to discuss the background of the problem, successful and unsuccessful approaches attempted in the past, the current status of the problem, and criteria for an effective solution. Unless all members have carefully prepared, valuable time and ideas are bound to be lost.

### Step 3: Analyze the problem within the group.

Perhaps the most important step in any problem-solving situation is analyzing the nature of a problem. A group may stumble because it fails to analyze its task completely. If its members have carefully prepared, they will have developed different perspectives and definitions of the situation. These perspectives are discussed and differences are resolved before the group can begin to identify possible solutions. By completing this step early in the problem-solving process, considerable frustration and conflict can be avoided.

To successfully complete this step, share and discuss all individual perspectives. Ask one member to record all definitions and issues during the discussion. Focus on identifying and resolving any differences in individual perspectives by rechecking any written instructions and related information gathered during individual preparation. Resolve, to the satisfaction of all members, any questions about the interpretation of language and the relevance of specific issues. Finally, write a statement of the problem with which all members can agree. Provide a copy of this statement to all participants or display it in plain view to ensure that it serves as the focal point for the remainder of the problem-solving process.

*The first thing a group should do is agree on a single definition of its problem.*

### Step 4: Identify and agree on the set of criteria that will be used to evaluate the acceptability of possible solutions.

Once a group has analyzed and defined the situation, they should identify and agree upon the set of criteria against which the possible solutions will be evaluated. This step ensures that all members will share similar views of what constitutes an acceptable solution. Make sure the criteria for evaluation are generated before the search for solutions so that personal biases and preferences will not enter into the group's decision.

The criteria should arise out of comparisons between the unacceptable conditions in the current situation and the preferred or ideal conditions that would exist if the problem were solved to all members' satisfaction. As a group, state and agree on the unsatisfactory conditions causing the problem. For each of these conditions, devise an alternative condition that helps solve the problem. Compare these pairs of conditions and develop an evaluation criterion for each, stating what must be accomplished for each satisfying condition to be acceptable to all members. As was done with the problem statement, make this set of criteria available to all group members throughout the problem-solving process. If all members accept and use the same set of standards for evaluating alternatives, broad agreement on a final choice should be easier to achieve.

### Step 5: Identify and clarify alternative solutions.

Next, have group members identify and clarify the various solutions available to them. Attitudes of openness, supportiveness, and creativity are necessary prerequisites for the success of this step. Encourage

When a group is supportive and open to new ideas, individuals can share their thoughts and opinions without fear of being ridiculed.

individuals to share ideas and voice opinions freely without fear of being laughed at, criticized, or ridiculed. Seriously consider and accurately record alternatives and possible solutions. No matter how wild an idea may sound initially, give it fair and equal attention. Lighthearted suggestions often provide the seeds for more workable solutions. Although all options should be explored, take care to ensure that the discussion stays on track and time is well spent.

*Brainstorming encourages groups to generate many creative solutions.*

One method of identifying a broad range of creative solutions is **brainstorming.** The goal of this approach is to encourage the production of as many creative ideas as possible by withholding evaluation and criticism *during* the thinking process. To ensure a productive brainstorming session, group members should:

put aside all judgments and criticisms during the brainstorming session;

think of as many solutions as possible—the wilder, the better;

record all ideas and display them for all group members to see;

modify previous ideas to develop new ones;

make sure each group member abides by the rules;

try to draw ideas from all group members;

allow plenty of time for the session; and

evaluate alternatives only after all ideas have been shared, possibly at a later meeting.

Brainstorming may not work for all groups or for all problems. Because it can be time-consuming, it may not be appropriate when time is short. In addition, brainstorming only works well when a problem can be clearly defined. Thus, some problems may be too complex for this technique. Nonetheless, if a group has sufficient time and wants to consider many creative solutions, brainstorming can be a very productive process.

### Step 6: Thoroughly evaluate the alternatives.

The thorough evaluation of alternatives is accomplished by applying the evaluation criteria generated in step 4 to the alternatives generated in step 5. At this point unworkable alternatives are discarded. Discussion during this step is critical but empathic, active but not dominating, cohesive but not overly conforming. Make sure all disagreements are idea-centered, not person-centered. In other words, avoid personality conflicts and personal attacks.

Systematically apply each criterion developed in step 4 to each solution generated during step 5. Keep in mind that your objective is to decide on a set of conditions (a solution) that maximizes group satisfaction, even though perfect agreement may not be possible. First, eliminate any solutions that are clearly unworkable. Then eliminate those that don't conform to a majority of your criteria. Once your list has been reduced to a manageable length, you're ready to select the best solution.

### Step 7: Select from among the alternatives.

Finally you are ready to solve your problem. As in the previous step, caution is the guideline. Resist making hasty decisions and avoid groupthink. Keep discussion free, open, and idea-centered. Encourage contributions from each group member. Remember, a decision that all members can accept is superior to one in which some members "win" and some "lose."

Apply your evaluation criteria to each of the alternatives on your short list. Ask all participants for their personal perspectives, including the possible benefits and drawbacks they foresee. You may want to rank the solutions by applying each one to the problem and visualizing how the situation would change. Ask the group, for each proposed solution, if it could accept the outcome. Remember, your goal is consensus, so make sure that your final choice maximizes group satisfaction.

### Step 8: Implement the solution.

In addition to identifying the solution to a problem, your group may be expected to develop a plan for making the necessary changes. To do so, you will need to discuss how to allocate money, personnel, time, and other resources. During this step, set challenging, but realistic, goals. Make sure that all members support the plan and are committed to its goals. Finally, clearly communicate the plan and its supporting rationale to all people who will share responsibility for its success or failure. Knowing why something is to be done can be just as important as knowing what is to be done, especially when people who were not involved in the decision-making process are responsible for implementation.

### Step 9: Evaluate the success of the solution.

*If implementing a solution is part of a group's task, evaluation of the outcome is a must.*

A final possible step in the problem-solving process is to evaluate the success of the solution. Conduct follow-up studies about the effectiveness of the solution in meeting the criteria and improving the unsatisfactory conditions that were its target. If your group is not directly responsible for the solution's implementation, set up a meeting with the people who are. Find out if the implementation has been completed, if the unsatisfactory conditions have been remedied, and if any changes in the solution or its implementation are needed. You may find that your group will have to meet again to work out changes.

Members of a problem-solving group must share the responsibilities of preparing for discussion; defining the group's task; generating and evaluating alternative solutions; and selecting, implementing, and evaluating the preferred option. The fulfillment of these responsibilities absolutely *requires* that all members be committed to the group and possess effective group communication skills. In addition, to be successful, all groups need two other crucial assets: effective leadership and effective conflict management strategies. These are the main topics of the next two sections of this chapter.

## GROUP LEADERSHIP

Each individual is important to group success and must contribute to the accomplishment of group goals. Getting the most out of every group member is a primary responsibility for those who assume leadership positions; but, as we shall see, effective leadership is shared leadership.

### Leaders Versus Leadership

In Chapter 8, *leadership* is defined as "communication behavior that influences a group to accomplish its goals." This behavior is very often exhibited by several or all members of a group, but not everyone leads at the same time. The person who assumes the leadership role and exerts influence in a particular situation will depend primarily on the *needs of the group at the time.*

A group may have a formal leader, *assigned* that position by another person outside the group. For example, the company president may name the vice-president of marketing to lead a problem-solving group of departmental managers working on a new employee benefits package. In another instance, a group may *elect* its formal leader to his or her position. Thus, the members of a town's Fourth of July fireworks committee may hold an election at their first meeting to select a chairperson who will preside over all their meetings until their task is accomplished. Finally, a group may have an *emergent* leader, a person who is neither assigned nor elected, but to whom all members look for direction and guidance during group deliberations. Most groups that have no formal officers or structure, such as study groups and social groups, don't elect or assign leaders. Their members can readily identify, however, the person they turn to when the group needs direction or help with a difficult decision.

Despite its importance—or perhaps because of it—true leadership rarely resides in a single group member. When *leadership* is effective, all members *share* in the process of identifying the needs of the group, influencing other members to recognize these needs, and assisting the group in meeting them. Any member may influence any other at any point in the group's deliberations and may provide important direction toward the accomplishment of group goals. Such factors as physical setting, group composition, group structure, group needs and goals, and the broader social setting within which the group works all influence who will assume leadership and when. Some leadership behaviors may assist the group in attaining its goals and others may work to smooth interpersonal relations among members. Some may even serve the group in both ways. Effective members develop sensitivity to which leadership behaviors the group needs and when they should be performed.

*Influence and needs satisfaction are keys to effective leadership.*

## Approaches to Leadership

For decades researchers have tried to identify the characteristics of effective leaders. Most have followed one of three basic approaches.

Advocates of the **trait approach** have investigated the vast array of personal characteristics that have been associated with great leaders. They have found that such factors as aggressiveness, height, eye color, talkativeness, charisma, and self-confidence are all characteristics of leaders. They have been unable to identify any one trait or set of traits, however, that can accurately predict leadership. As a result, we can conclude that personal traits don't predict (or make) leaders.

Even in informal groups where roles are not formally assigned, individuals may naturally fall into leadership positions.

A second approach, the **situational approach,** proposes that the only way to understand effective leadership is to examine such contextual factors as group structure, history, norms, composition, and resources. The focus of this approach is on the interrelationships among the leader, the followers, and the situation they are in. Thus, a leader might be effective in one situation, but not in another. The complex relationships among leaders, followers, and the situation determine the effectiveness of leadership in a particular group.

*Initiating, organizing, clarifying, and resolving make for effective functional leadership.*

The **functional approach** is closest to what is termed *shared leadership.* Rather than exploring personal traits or situational factors as prime determinants of leadership effectiveness, the functional approach focuses on behaviors that guide, direct, and influence other group members, regardless of who exhibits the behaviors. If behaviors assist the group in attaining its goals or in building or maintaining good interpersonal relationships among members, they constitute effective leadership. Proponents of the functional approach have found that behaviors such as initiating discussion, organizing group thinking, clarifying communication, and resolving conflict are associated with effective leadership.[1]

Although none of these three approaches is wrong or right, the functional approach seems to be the best description of the way leadership works in groups. Certainly we all know individuals who seem to have a knack for leadership. Most of us have experienced situations that called for a particular type of leader. Generally, however, any group member has the ability to contribute to group success by identifying and helping to satisfy group needs when they occur. *How* that person goes about providing leadership is the subject of the following section.

## Styles of Leadership

People provide leadership in small groups in four main ways: by dictating, by facilitating, by reflecting, and by denying. These four behaviors parallel four common styles of leadership: authoritarian, democratic, group-centered, and laissez-faire.

An **authoritarian leader** allows other group members no freedom or influence in the group. This leader makes all decisions, takes all responsibility for group actions, and imparts knowledge to followers. The military commander who must rapidly evaluate a situation, quickly make a strategic decision, and immediately implement a plan of action is most likely to use an authoritarian style of leadership.

A **democratic leader** allows much more freedom and shared responsibility in a group. Democratic leaders see themselves as facilitators, helpers, and guides in group settings. They may provide some structure and direction to group deliberations, but they leave most of the responsibility for decisions and evaluation to the group as a whole. Democratic leaders may clarify matters and encourage creative and critical thinking, but they avoid personal involvement in issues. For instance, a quality control inspector on an automotive assembly line schedules weekly meetings with assembly-line personnel. The inspector provides structure and direction by reviewing recent deficiency rates and suggesting areas in which the group, as a whole, needs to improve. Then he or she turns control of the meeting over to the group, adding only clarifying and encouraging comments when requested or needed.

A **group-centered leader** refuses to give direction to the group, but, instead, tries to understand what group members are thinking and feeling, and then attempts to reflect these feelings and thoughts back to the group. A group-centered leader works to develop and maintain a positive group climate, good interpersonal relations, and free and open communication. A counselor who gets a therapeutic group started and then offers interpretations of members' ideas and feelings back to the group as a whole is acting as a group-centered leader. The counselor may also encourage quiet members to speak up or may point out conflict that the group needs to deal with. Despite such occasional interventions, the counselor allows the group to set its own agenda and make its own decisions.

A **laissez-faire leader** takes noninvolvement one step further. This kind of leader makes contributions only when asked and denies

**Review Box**

## Styles of Leadership

| *Style* | *Key Characteristics* |
|---|---|
| Authoritarian | Group members have no influence in the group |
| | Leader makes all decisions |
| | Leader takes all responsibility for group actions |
| | Leader imparts all knowledge |
| Democratic | Leader facilitates, guides, helps |
| | Leader provides structure and direction |
| | Responsibility for decisions and evaluation lies with members |
| | Leader avoids personal involvement in issues |
| | Leader may clarify and encourage |
| Group-centered | Leader gives no direction to the group |
| | Leader attempts to understand the thinking and feelings of group members and reflects them back to the group |
| | Leader works to develop and maintain positive group climate, good interpersonal relations, and free and open communication |
| Laissez-faire | Leader denies any responsibility for group action |
| | Leader makes contributions only when asked |
| | Leader exists in name only |

any responsibility for group action. Such a leader avoids participation and maintains an attitude of total indifference toward other group members. One might say that a laissez-faire leader is a leader in name only. A committee chairperson who merely calls a meeting to order and asks for a motion for adjournment, without participating in between, is practicing a laissez-faire style of leadership.

Imagine a platoon of Marines under fire whose group-centered leader decided to conduct a meeting to ask how members felt and what they'd like to do next. Those marines would fare much better with an authoritarian approach by an officer—right or wrong. Imagine that you have been put in charge of a group of physicists who are selecting the best time to launch a manned moon vehicle. If you lack expertise in scheduling rocket launches, don't know how physicists go about making such decisions, and prefer not to slow the progress of the group by asking a lot of questions, you might just call the meeting to order, sit back, listen, and hope that you will learn something useful. From these examples, you can tell that no single style of leadership works in every situation.

The authoritarian style of leadership is most appropriate when decisions need to be made quickly, and when a knowledgeable and responsible person is present to do so. Many groups, for one reason or another, find that time pressure or emergency conditions require quick action with little or no group interaction. Such conditions, however, may limit the quality of the decision.

Democratic leadership can be used under most circumstances. Because this style assigns responsibility for decision making and evaluation directly to the group as a whole, each individual has the chance to facilitate, guide, and provide structure and information. As a result, each person has an equal opportunity to perform a variety of roles and carry out several functions as that person works with other members to satisfy group needs.

Groups in conflict or in need of improved interpersonal relationships require a group-centered leader. Such a leader can also help members become more aware of their own muddled thinking. Reflecting on feelings and thinking processes often aids members in recognizing that personality conflicts, unbalanced participation, lack of group cohesiveness, and groupthink must be overcome before progress can be made on the group task.

Finally, laissez-faire leadership may be appropriate at two times. The first is when group members have become too dependent on a designated leader. To counteract this tendency, the leader assumes a laissez-faire style, forcing the group to accept more responsibility for its own progress. The second is when limited knowledge or experience in the group's task area may leave the laissez-faire style as a leader's sole option.

What, then, do effective leaders *do?* Good leaders *recognize* the needs of groups and attempt to *satisfy* them. Good leaders *summarize* the progress of groups and *encourage* individuals and groups to strive for bigger and better things. They *actively participate* in all aspects of group functioning, *facilitate* balanced participation by all group members, and *solicit* input from less vocal members. Effective leaders *relieve tension* in groups by telling jokes or suggesting breaks when necessary; they *direct* group interaction toward the attainment of group goals. They *prepare* for group discussion and *contribute* the results of their preparation. They *seek* information and opinions from others, and *coordinate* and *clarify* information and opinions when needed.

When leading a group, don't be afraid to *mediate* and *harmonize* disputes and personality conflicts. *Pay close attention to* and *reflect* the thinking and feelings of other group members. Finally, *set* a good example and *orient* the group toward positive interpersonal relationships and productive goal achievement.

## GROUP CONFLICT

Not all group members get along well together, nor do they always see eye-to-eye. When disagreements occur groups inevitably experience conflict. Many group members believe that conflict is objectionable and should be avoided at all costs; in fact, when handled well, conflict can be productive, enlightening, and even fun. Thus, it is not the *presence or absence* of conflict that is important—it is *the way it is managed* that counts, especially in group situations.

### What Is Conflict?

**Conflict** may be defined as the disagreement between two or more parties about the acceptance of some idea, action, or goal. A conflict is either perceived or real. It is only *perceived* when individuals misunderstand, inaccurately perceive, or personally dislike one another, but actually agree on the relevant issues. On the other hand, a conflict is *real* when individuals fully understand, accurately perceive, and even like one another, but find that they still disagree. Even when people merely *perceive* that they disagree, a conflict exists.

*Conflict may be either perceived or real, and involves two or more interdependent parties.*

Just as they say "it takes two to tango," it takes at least two parties to make a conflict—*parties* instead of *individuals,* because many conflicts involve two or more *groups* of people. These parties must also *be interdependent,* because parties who are *independent*—whose actions or ideas have no effect on one another—will seldom have a conflict. Finally, the focus of a conflict may be any idea, action, or goal, from "What movie should we go see tonight?" to "Who owns the land on the west bank of the Jordan River?" Whatever the basis of a conflict, its acceptance must affect all parties involved. Those ideas, actions, or goals that don't affect at least one other party in some way will not promote a conflict.

### Styles for Dealing with Conflict

There are five common styles for dealing with conflict: withdrawing, smoothing, forcing, compromising, and problem solving. Although most people use one style predominantly, the situation, parties involved, and timing influence which style will be used in a specific instance.

Some people prefer **withdrawing,** avoiding conflict at all costs. As you can imagine, such people will, more likely than not, feel cheated and insecure in dealings with others, because they don't even try to get some of what they want. They just give up!

People who use **smoothing** as an approach to conflict will give in to others' demands or opinions, preferring to concede rather than face a disagreement. People who give in to others time after time accumulate negative feelings that are bound to surface sooner or later.

A third method of dealing with conflict is **forcing,** the desire to have one's own way, regardless of the consequences. Forcers use manipulative communication techniques, intimidation, and competitive strategies to gain an advantage. Have you ever been browbeaten by someone who just wouldn't take no for an answer? That person was probably a forcer.

A more acceptable approach to conflict is **compromising,** agreeing to trade something important for something equally important from the other party. Labor negotiations, treaty negotiations, and sales negotiations usually involve compromising. In such cases, each party wins something and loses something at the same time. Compromising is generally accepted as an excellent method of dealing with conflict. It is perfectly acceptable in our society for people to ask for more than they expect so that, in the end, they feel that they have "won," even though they have had to make certain concessions.

*Everyone wins and loses as a result of compromising.*

**Problem solving** can be more productive and satisfying than compromising, because it attempts to arrive at a resolution to the conflict that satisfies all parties to the greatest extent possible, without "playing games" or inflating their demands at the outset. It offers the potential for all parties to win and for no one to lose. This approach combines the best of problem-solving methodologies, interpersonal communication, and group cooperation and productivity. When conflicting parties practice problem solving, they develop a sincere concern and responsibility for maximizing the gains and minimizing the losses of all parties, not just themselves. Open, honest, and responsible communication is practiced, and an attitude of mutual respect and sincerity is maintained throughout the process. The result of this method—ideally, at least—is a decision that all parties can agree is the best possible, and that maximizes the gains and minimizes the losses for everyone.

Of course, the problem-solving approach is an ideal. Not all conflicts can be resolved so that all parties are 100-percent happy with the outcome. It is *preferable* to the other four methods *because of its focus on maximizing the gains and minimizing the losses of all parties concerned.* It is an ideal to aim for, keeping in mind that some compromises may be necessary along the way.

*Problem solving maximizes gains and minimizes losses for everyone.*

### Styles of Dealing with Conflict

| *Style* | *Characteristics* | *Results* |
| --- | --- | --- |
| Withdrawing | Avoidance of conflict at all costs<br>Conflict never gets resolved | Feelings of being cheated<br>Insecurity in dealing with others |
| Smoothing | Giving in to others' demands or opinions<br>Concessions preferred to open disagreement | Negative feelings toward others build<br>Sudden emotional blow-ups |
| Forcing | Use of manipulative communication techniques, intimidation, and competitive strategies to gain an advantage<br>Desire to win at any cost | Hard feelings toward forcers<br>Possible termination of relationships |
| Compromising | Agreement to trade something you want for something the other party wants | Each party wins and loses something |

## Effective Conflict Management

As stated earlier, your attitude toward conflict influences how you will choose to deal with it. Negative attitudes and poor conflict management can lead to hard feelings, dissatisfaction with outcomes, reliance on power, manipulation, threats, and serious losses. On the other hand, positive attitudes and constructive management can result in positive feelings toward others, mutual satisfaction with outcomes, minimal losses, and a genuine sense of cohesiveness and success. Conflict is *not* naturally good or bad. Its value is related to the effectiveness with which it is managed through speech communication. You will ensure the best results if you follow seven basic guidelines.

| *Style* | *Characteristics* | *Results* |
|---|---|---|
| Compromising (continued) | Often begins with inflated goals and demands<br>Use of manipulative strategies to win as much as you can | Less than open, honest settlement of the conflict |
| Problem Solving | The ideal style of dealing with conflict<br>Sincere concern for maximizing gains and minimizing losses of all parties<br>Attempt to arrive at a solution that satisfies all parties to the greatest extent possible<br>Requires open, honest, and responsible communication, as well as mutual respect and sincerity from all | Everyone wins and no one loses<br>A decision that all parties agree is the best possible<br>All parties are maximally satisfied |

## Take your time.

To avoid poor outcomes, take your time when dealing with conflict. Don't rush to reach an agreement while under pressure or to get it over with. Tackle conflict when you have the time, energy, and attitude that will allow all parties to think clearly and discuss the issues thoroughly.

## Remain issue-oriented.

Stick to the issues; don't let the discussion degenerate into a clash of personalities or a shouting match. Resist the urge to make personal comments or bring up irrelevant issues. If you notice that your deliberations are becoming too heated or too personal, redirect the discussion to the issues or call for a recess.

**Establish common ground early in the conflict resolution process.**

First identify and clarify points on which all parties *agree*. Then deal with other issues. You may find that the situation you perceived to be hopeless isn't all that bad.

**Listen and respond effectively.**

Chapter 6 discussed the importance of listening carefully and responding effectively. These communication behaviors are especially important when dealing with conflict. Take time to clarify issues and positions; make sure that everyone's understanding is clear before you proceed.

**Don't be afraid to admit that you are wrong.**

Although it may be difficult, recognize and say that you may have been mistaken about a point or that you now understand and agree with a previously unacceptable position. Honesty and mutual respect are vital to dealing with conflict and conflicting parties effectively.

**Clarify your agreement.**

When the conflict is resolved, clarify all areas of agreement to make sure that everyone is satisfied and thinking along the same lines. Clear up any uncertainties or possible misinterpretations before concluding the discussion. Check that everyone understands and agrees on what has been decided and what each party is supposed to do next.

**Assess the outcome.**

As with any good problem-solving or decision-making process, implement the solution and evaluate its success later. A solution that doesn't effectively deal with a conflict might be as bad as no solution at all.

Becoming an effective group participant takes time and practice. By studying the principles of group communication and participating in decision-making and problem-solving groups, you can develop a set of communication skills that will serve you well in career and social settings throughout your life.

## SUMMARY

Problem solving, leadership, and conflict management are three mainstays of successful communication in small groups. Gaining knowledge and experience in these three areas will greatly enhance your effectiveness.

▶ **Distinguish between decision making and problem solving.**

Decision making consists of selecting one alternative from among many. Problem solving is a process that involves many decisions as a group attempts to change a set of conditions with which it is dissatisfied to a set of conditions with which it is satisfied. In a group, decisions are usually made (1) by majority vote, (2) by an expert, a high-status member, or a leader, or (3) by consensus.

▶ **Identify and use the nine steps in the problem-solving process.**

Successful problem solving requires that groups use the following process:

1. Individually identify and define the group task.
2. Prepare for discussion.
3. Analyze the problem within the group.
4. As a group, agree on a set of criteria to be used to evaluate possible solutions.
5. Identify and clarify alternatives.
6. Evaluate the alternative solutions.
7. Select from among the alternatives.
8. Implement the solution.
9. Evaluate the success of the solution.

▶ **Use your knowledge of approaches to leadership and styles of leadership to lead a small group through a problem-solving discussion.**

The leader of a small group must be able to identify group needs and direct the behavior of individuals and the group as a whole toward meeting those needs. A person who understands approaches to studying leadership and styles of leadership will be better equipped to adjust his or her leadership behavior as the situation demands.

Researchers have used three approaches to studying leadership. The *trait approach* focuses on personal characteristics that have been associated with great leaders. The *situational approach* examines contextual factors, such as group structure, history, norms, composition, and resources, as determinants of effective leadership. The *functional approach* focuses on behaviors that guide, direct, and influence other group members, regardless of who exhibits the behaviors. Of these three perspectives, the functional approach most fully explains how leadership works in groups.

The four most common styles of leadership are authoritarian, democratic, group-centered, and laissez-faire. Authoritarian leaders make all decisions, take all responsibility for group actions, and impart knowledge to followers. Democratic leaders provide some structure and direction to group deliberations, but leave most of the responsibility for decisions and evaluation to the group as a whole. Group-centered leaders refuse to give directions to the group. They try to understand what group members are thinking and feeling, and then attempt to reflect those feelings and thoughts back to the group. Finally, laissez-faire leaders make contributions to group process only when asked and deny any responsibility for group action. All four leadership styles have their place in groups, depending on the situation, group composition, group task, and needs.

▶Define *conflict,* and identify and use the appropriate style of conflict management in a group situation.

A *conflict* is a disagreement between two or more parties about the acceptance of some idea, action, or goal. Individuals and groups typically use one of five styles to deal with conflict: withdrawing, smoothing, focusing, compromising, and problem solving. People who use the withdrawing style dislike conflict and attempt to avoid it at all costs. Smoothers give in to others' demands or opinions, preferring to concede rather than face a disagreement. Those who prefer a forcing style use manipulative communication techniques, intimidation, and competitive strategies to gain an advantage. Compromisers agree to trade something they want for something equally important to the other party. People who prefer the problem-solving approach to dealing with conflict develop a sincere concern and responsibility for maximizing the gains and minimizing the losses of all parties. They attempt to arrive at a resolution of the conflict that satisfies all parties to the greatest extent possible, without playing games or inflating their demands at the outset. Although problem solving is the ideal or preferred method, each of the others may be acceptable in some situations.

## KEY TERMS

**authoritarian leader:**  a leader who makes all decisions, takes all responsibility for group actions, and imparts knowledge to followers.
**brainstorming:**  a method of generating a wide range of problem solutions by encouraging the production of as many creative ideas as possible by withholding evaluation and criticism during the thinking process.
**compromising:**  a style of dealing with conflict in which people agree to trade something they want for something equally important from the other party.

**conflict:** disagreement between two or more parties about the acceptance of some idea, action, or goal.

**consensus:** a decision that all group members agree is the best alternative that they can all accept.

**decision making:** choosing from two or more possible alternatives.

**democratic leader:** a leader who may provide some structure and direction to group deliberations, but leaves most of the responsibility for decisions and evaluation to the group as a whole.

**forcing:** a style of dealing with conflict in which people use manipulative communication techniques, intimidation, and competitive strategies to gain an advantage.

**functional approach:** an approach to studying leadership that focuses on behaviors that guide, direct, and influence other group members, regardless of who exhibits the behaviors.

**group-centered leader:** a leader who refuses to give direction to the group, but tries instead tries to understand what group members are thinking and feeling, and then attempts to reflect these feelings and thoughts back to the group.

**laissez-faire leader:** a leader who makes contributions only when asked and denies any responsibility for group action; a leader in name only.

**problem solving:** a procedure involving a series of steps and a number of decisions, through which individuals or groups attempt to change a set of conditions with which they are dissatisfied to a set of conditions with which they are satisfied.

**problem solving (approach to dealing with conflict):** a style of dealing with conflict in which people develop a sincere concern and responsibility for maximizing the gains and minimizing the losses of all parties. They attempt to arrive at a resolution of the conflict that satisfies all parties to the greatest extent possible, without "playing games" or inflating their demands at the outset.

**situational approach:** an approach to studying leadership that proposes that the only way to understand effective leadership is to examine such contextual factors as the group's structure, history, norms, composition, and resources.

**smoothing:** a style of dealing with conflict in which people give in to others' demands or opinions, preferring to concede rather than face a disagreement.

**trait approach:** an approach to studying leadership that focuses on the vast array of personal characteristics that have been associated with great leaders.

**withdrawing:** a style of dealing with conflict in which people dislike conflict and/or dealing with conflict, so they avoid it at all costs.

## DISCUSSION QUESTIONS

1. Discuss the advantages and disadvantages of each of the three methods of making decisions. How would the use of each method affect the communication that takes place during group discussion? How would each method make individual group members feel after a decision is made?

2. Evaluate the importance of the nine steps in the problem-solving process. At which step in the process is a group most likely to experience conflict or other problems? Which of the steps is a group most likely to skip over or forget? What can you do to assist a group in using this problem-solving process most effectively?

3. Imagine situations in which each of the four styles of leadership are used. What circumstances within each situation influence your choice of leadership style? If you were to change one group characteristic in each situation (task, structure, status differences, setting, individual personalities, or expertise), would you change the preferred style of leadership?

4. How do you usually handle conflict situations? Do you use different styles with different people? Do some situations require styles that you don't like? How can you improve your personal style of dealing with conflict?

## SUGGESTED ACTIVITIES

1. Working with four or five classmates, identify a problem that needs solving. It might be a personal problem, a college or university problem, or a social problem. Using the nine-step problem-solving process as a framework, list the decisions that must be made in order to reach an effective solution. You don't necessarily need to solve the problem; just outline the problem-solving strategy by identifying the decisions that need to be made along the way.

2. Form a discussion group on the topic, "What can be done to decrease the use of illicit drugs in high schools?" Direct each member to think of his or her own solution to the problem—the wilder the better. When each participant has come up with a personal solution, have the group discuss the problem and possible solutions for ten to fifteen minutes. Each group member should argue only for the acceptance of his or her own solution

during this time. For the next ten to fifteen minutes, have the group attempt to reach a consensus, using all the guidelines for effective group communication outlined in this chapter. At the end of this second period, discuss the relative effectiveness of the two approaches to solving the problem—individual versus group. Which perspective was more effective? Which was more enjoyable for the participants? Which promoted more conflict and hard feelings?

**3.** Observe a community or school group as it discusses a controversial issue. Take notes on each member's communication. Then try to identify each one's predominant style of dealing with conflict: withdrawing, forcing, smoothing, compromising, or problem solving. What communication behaviors helped you identify each member's style? Did any participant frequently use more than one style? What, if any, style of conflict management was used *by the entire group?*

## SUGGESTED READINGS

Steven A. Beebe and John T. Masterson. (1986) *Communicating in Small Groups: Principles and Practices,* 2nd ed. (Glenview, IL: Scott, Foresman and Company).

John K. Brilhart. (1986) *Effective Group Discussion,* 5th ed. (Dubuque, IA: Wm. C. Brown Publishers).

Dennis S. Gouran. (1982) *Making Decisions in Groups: Choices and Consequences.* (Glenview, IL: Scott, Foresman and Company).

Julia T. Wood, Gerald M. Phillips, and Douglas J. Pedersen. (1986) *Group Discussion: A Practical Guide to Participation and Leadership,* 2nd ed. (New York: Harper & Row).

**PART**

3

# EFFECTIVE PUBLIC COMMUNICATION

# 10 Speech Preparation: Getting Started

*After studying this chapter, you should be able to:*

▶ Outline the six steps to follow in speech preparation and presentation.

▶ Use appropriate criteria to select and narrow a topic for a speech.

▶ Discover information about your audience that will help you adapt your speech to its needs and interests.

▶ Identify the general purpose of your speech and write a corresponding specific purpose and thesis statement.

▶ Take steps to improve your credibility as a speaker.

You probably began speaking before the age of two; yet, speaking to an audience may strike you as difficult and maybe even a little scary. That's not unusual, and that's why this final portion of the book explains how to prepare and deliver a public speech.

Public speaking is different from other levels of communication for both speakers and listeners. The most obvious difference is that, during public communication, one person is speaking while other people are listening. This format requires a more formal approach than do small group discussion and interpersonal communication, because speakers direct their messages to many people at one time. They need to identify beforehand the common attitudes, beliefs, values, and needs of their audiences. The listeners, too, identify their expectations beforehand; they have more specific expectations for speakers in public communication settings than they do for speakers in interpersonal settings. Public speakers have greater control over the communication process.

This chapter examines the public speaking process by presenting six key steps for preparing and presenting speeches. These steps will be expanded in the chapters ahead. To help you get started, the chapter will explain how to select a topic and develop a speech purpose, tell how to analyze an audience, and provide some pointers for enhancing your credibility.

## AN OVERVIEW OF SPEECH PREPARATION AND PRESENTATION

You're sitting at your desk. You have a speech to deliver. You're not sure how to get started. What do you do first? How do you progress from staring at a blank piece of paper to standing before an audience and delivering your message? Actually, the process is not so difficult if you approach it systematically. All you need to do is follow six basic steps.

### Step One: Select a Topic

For many people, selecting a topic is frustrating. In trying to identify that one best idea, they come up empty. Nothing grabs them because their desire to find the ideal topic is so strong that they become overly critical of themselves.

If you find this happening to you, audience analysis and taking an inventory of your own interests can help. Usually, the best ideas for speeches come from your own experiences. What issues do you feel strongly about? Have you had any interesting or unusual jobs? What

*The best speech topics will often stem from your own interests and experiences.*

topics have struck you while reading or watching television? What subjects seem to be suggested by the speaking occasion? Specific strategies of topic selection will be discussed later in this chapter.

## Step Two: Analyze Your Audience

As a public speaker, you want your audience to listen to your message. To accomplish this, you try to choose a topic that your audience will be interested in. You try to approach your topic in ways that will hold your audience's attention. Of course, this is easier said than done unless you are already familiar with the audience and have examined its nature—unless you have performed an audience analysis.

When you analyze your listeners, your objective is to understand how they are going to react to you and your message. How will they respond to your topic? Will they be impressed with you and your speech? Knowing as much as you can about your listeners and their expectations will help you make many important decisions as you prepare your speech.

## Step Three: Develop a General Purpose, a Specific Purpose, and a Thesis Statement for Your Speech

Once you have chosen your topic and analyzed your audience, you need to decide on your purpose. Every speech should have a general purpose and a specific purpose.

*The three possible general purposes of a speech are to inform, to persuade, and to entertain.*

A **general purpose** is the overall objective of your message. There are three possible general purposes: *to inform* (to teach, describe, or explain), *to persuade* (to change or reinforce attitudes, beliefs, values, or behavior), and *to entertain* (to present a message with humor, interesting stories, and illustrations). Usually in a speech communication class your instructor will determine the general purpose of your assigned speech.

After determining your general purpose, you will need to develop a specific purpose. A **specific purpose** is a finely tuned statement identifying what you want your audience to do, feel, or know after listening to your speech. For example, if you have decided to talk about antiques your general purpose is to inform. Your specific purpose may be that your audience, after listening to your speech, will be able to identify three characteristics of Fiestaware.

Once you have specified your general and specific purposes, prepare a thesis statement. A **thesis statement** is a one-sentence summary of your speech. It identifies the essence of your message. The following

The speaker in this car maintenance class will want to anticipate the audience's expectations and design the speech to meet those expectations. How might a speech directed at a mixed group of men and women be different?

is a thesis sentence for the speech about Fiestaware: Fiestaware can be identified by the concentric circles found on the front of the plate, the use of bright colors, and the distinctive "Genuine Fiesta" stamp on the back of the plate.

## Step Four: Gather Supporting Material

Once you have developed your general and specific purposes and a clear thesis statement, you are ready to begin gathering material to support and develop your speech's main ideas. Of course, you have probably been thinking about possible sources of information since you first considered your topic, but now you can begin gathering supporting material with clear goals in mind.

**Supporting material** consists of the definitions, examples, statistics, testimony, illustrations, and analogies that verify, amplify, and clarify the main ideas of your speech. You cannot just string a series of ideas together. Instead, you need to fill out your thoughts with definitions, explanations, facts, personal and hypothetical examples, analogies, statistics, and testimony from a variety of sources. Your selection of supporting material has an important effect on your ability to maintain your audience's interest in your speech. Almost any subject can be made interesting with supporting material that commands the attention of the audience. *Specific, personal,* and *concrete* supporting materials are best for gaining and maintaining audience attention.

## Step Five: Organize Your Speech

Careful organization can enhance the probability that your talk will be well received. Audience members will also remember more of your presentation if you announce your organizational plan early and then stick to it. In addition, you will feel more comfortable delivering your speech if you have systematically thought it out in advance.

*A speech has three main parts: an introduction, a body, and a conclusion.*

There are three essential parts to any speech: the introduction, the body, and the conclusion. The introduction catches the audience's attention and provides an overview of the speech. The body is the longest part of the message. It presents the key ideas and fully develops them by citing supporting material. The conclusion mainly summarizes the speech ideas in a concise and interesting way.

Although it may seem that the most logical way to prepare a speech is to conduct some research and then sit down and write everything out, progressing from beginning to end, such an approach is not advisable for several reasons. First, you must take into account that there are differences in style between oral communication and written communication. Specifically, an oral style is more *personal,* more *informal,* and more *repetitious*. Second, as you prepare a speech, you must constantly bear in mind that, although a reader can stop, reflect, or reread for additional clarity, a listener does not have these advantages. Finally, it is difficult to prepare an introduction for a speech before you know what you'll say in the body and the conclusion.

For these reasons, we recommend that you begin to organize a speech by working on an outline of the body. Then develop the conclusion and, finally, work on the introduction. Chapter 12 will discuss the organization of speeches in much greater detail.

## Step Six: Rehearse and Deliver Your Speech

Once you have prepared your speech outline, introduction, and conclusion, you will be ready to work on your delivery. Effective delivery includes direct eye contact with listeners, an audible voice with natural variations in pitch, nondistracting gestures, and appropriate posture. During the early part of this century, elocutionists, the forerunners of today's speech teachers, believed that delivery was more important than content. Thus, speech training consisted largely of exercises for improving posture, movement, and vocal quality. While contemporary speech teachers certainly don't discount the importance of speech delivery, they prefer a more balanced approach.

The best way to polish your delivery is to spend some time rehearsing. You will get the most out of your rehearsal if you recreate as closely as possible the actual environment in which you will be speaking. For example, practice standing up and using a lectern (or a

> **Review Box**
>
> ## Six Steps in Preparing and Presenting a Speech
>
> 1. Select a topic.
> 2. Analyze your audience.
> 3. Determine your general purpose, specific purpose, and thesis statement.
> 4. Gather supporting material.
> 5. Organize your speech.
> 6. Rehearse and deliver your speech.

substitute for a lectern) if you will be using a lectern when you actually deliver your message. More specific hints for rehearsal and delivery will be presented in Chapter 13. But first, now that you have a general idea of the six steps for preparing and presenting a speech, let's return to the beginning and systematically examine each step in more detail.

## SELECTING AND NARROWING A TOPIC

When you are asked to speak, unless you are assigned a specific subject, selecting a topic will probably be your most immediate concern. If no topic immediately leaps to mind, the best starting point is your own interests and background. Take a personal inventory by answering the following questions:

1. What are your major and minor fields of study?
2. What are your hobbies?
3. What organizations do you belong to?
4. Have you taken any interesting trips or vacations? (Or, would you like to travel to a particular destination?)
5. What interesting jobs have you held or do you wish to hold?
6. What television programs do you watch? How do those reflect your interest?
7. What kind of music do you listen to?
8. What books or magazines do you read for pleasure?
9. What special skills or talents do you have?
10. Who are some interesting people that you know?
11. What movies or plays do you enjoy?

Such questions should get you started thinking about your interests, likes, and dislikes. You will find that when you really care about a topic, your audience will probably catch your enthusiasm.

Another approach is to survey news programs, talk shows, newspapers, and magazines for timely and thought-provoking topics that mesh with your own interests. Do not simply translate an article into a speech. Instead, bring some personal experience to it. With additional research and self-examination, you should be on your way to developing an engaging presentation.

Brainstorming may also help you develop an appropriate speech topic. To adapt the group technique discussed in Chapter 9 to an individual level, begin with a blank sheet of paper or speak into a tape recorder. List as many possible speech topics as you can. Don't evaluate them. Just keep the ideas coming. Once you have twenty or fifty or eighty ideas, you can start to evaluate them. For each potential speech topic, ask: Is this a topic I'm interested in? Can I find resources and information to develop my ideas? Do I have some personal experiences that would add greater interest to this topic? Would my audience be interested in this topic? If you can answer yes to each of those questions, you are on the right track.

*You will often need to narrow your topic to cover a manageable amount of information within your assigned time limit.*

In most cases, your initial idea for a speech topic will be quite general. Thinking in broad terms is fine at the beginning because it leaves more possibilities open. Once you have chosen a general field of interest, however, you will need to narrow your focus to fit your assigned time limit and to avoid being overly vague. Restricting yourself to a more specific subject will also help you to use your research time more efficiently.

The best way to begin narrowing your topic is to think of the various subtopics it encompasses. For example, if you'd like to talk about soccer, you might consider discussing soccer's history, its rules, the life of a famous soccer star, or how your favorite soccer franchise was started. Even your subtopic may need to be narrowed, depending on its complexity, the nature of your speaking assignment, your time limit, and the characteristics of your audience. Using the worksheet on page 239 should help you to narrow your topic to suit your specific circumstances.

## ANALYZING AN AUDIENCE

The most effective public speakers are audience-centered—that is, they are sensitive to their listeners' needs and interests, and try to adapt their message accordingly. They recognize that an audience is, in fact, a collection of individuals, each with a unique point of view. So before they speak, they try to find out as much as possible about their listeners, both as individuals and as a group. This process of discovery is called audience analysis.

## Key Categories of Information

An audience may be analyzed from three different perspectives: demographic, attitudinal, and environmental. When analyzing an audience it is useful to discover as much as you can about the interests, background, likes, and dislikes of your listeners.

**Demographic information.** In a **demographic analysis,** a speaker attempts to learn about an audience by collecting and interpreting basic information about members' ages, sex, race, religion, education, and social and political affiliations. This process enables a speaker to identify similarities and differences in listeners' backgrounds and make some assumptions about their probable likes, interests, and needs.

Among the key questions to ask in a demographic study are the following:

1. What is the age level of the audience?
2. How many males and females are in the audience?
3. What is the education level of the audience?
4. What is the racial makeup of the audience?
5. What are the religious affiliations of the audience?
6. What are the political biases of the audience?
7. What is the income level of the audience?
8. Are most members of the audience married or single?
9. What do members of the audience do for a living?
10. What kind of career goals do members of my audience have?

**Attitudinal information.** An **attitudinal analysis** attempts to identify an audience's attitudes, beliefs, and values about specific issues and ideas. Such information can be helpful in gauging how receptive the listeners will be to a given topic or approach and how likely they are to be won over. For example, people are least likely to change their values, more likely to change their beliefs, and most likely to change their attitudes. Thus, if you know something about your audience's attitudes, beliefs, and values, you can either choose a matching topic or construct a counterargument that will have maximum impact.

One important bit of information to discover at this time is your audience's probable attitude toward you. What does your audience expect from you? Do they expect to be entertained, informed, bored? Are you the sole reason for their attendance, or are you going to be sandwiched between a business meeting and a refreshment hour? The answers to these questions can help you with every aspect of speech preparation and delivery, but will be particularly useful as you choose a topic and select supporting materials.

*In audience analysis, your goal is to discover how your listeners are likely to react to you and your message.*

You will also want to assess the way your listeners feel about the topic you have selected. Are they informed about your topic? Are they interested, apathetic, or neutral? If your topic is controversial, are they for it or against it? For example, if you have decided to speak in favor of expanding the state prison system, you should know whether your listeners are likely to agree with your proposal. What are their attitudes about increased taxes to pay for more state-supported prisons? Do they believe that crime is a serious problem in your state?

An attitudinal analysis can provide answers to the following questions:

*Questions About You, the Speaker*

Does my audience believe I am knowledgeable?
Does my audience believe I can be trusted to give them accurate information?
Does my audience expect me to be interesting and worthy of attention?

*Questions About the Speech Topic*

What strong attitudes does the audience hold about my subject?
What underlying values does the audience hold?
What are the audience's underlying beliefs?
Will my audience find this topic interesting?
What does my audience already know about this topic?
What does my audience need to know in order to support my point of view?

**Environmental information.**   Finally, you will want to do an **environmental analysis**—a study of the speech occasion and the physical surroundings in which you will be speaking. For example, will you be speaking in a large room with a public address system, or will it be a small room with chairs arranged in a circle? Will a lectern be available for your use? How is the room decorated? Is it well lighted and well ventilated?

Of course, there are limits to what you, as a speaker, can change in the physical environment; but you can be prepared to compensate for any factors that may make it more difficult for your audience to attend to your message. Your topic choice, the kinds of examples and illustrations, and your delivery style can help you reach an audience in an environment that is working against you. For instance, you may need to use more stories, visual aids, and personal examples to hold an audience's attention.

---

**Review Box**

**Kinds of Audience Analysis**

| | |
|---|---|
| Demographic Analysis | Interpreting the age, sex, race, religion, education, and social and political affiliations of your audience |
| Attitudinal Analysis | Identifying audience members' attitudes, beliefs, and values about you and your message |
| Environmental Analysis | Investigating the speech occasion and the physical surroundings in which you will be presenting the speech |

The following questions will help you assess your speaking environment:

1. What are the physical arrangements for the speaking situation? (How will the chairs be arranged?)
2. How many people are expected to attend the speech?
3. Will you be expected to speak from a lectern and use a microphone?
4. Will the room be adequately lighted and ventilated?
5. At what time of day will you speak?
6. What is the total program and what events precede and follow your presentation?

Audience analysis, like the communication process itself, is continuous. Keeping your audience in mind as you select a topic and a purpose, and as you research, organize, and rehearse your speech is important. It is also crucial to analyze your audience while delivering your speech, observing listener's reactions to your presentation. Audience analysis is a thread that is woven through the entire fabric of speech preparation and delivery.

## Methods of Audience Analysis

You may choose to analyze your audience either informally or formally. In an **informal analysis,** you gather data about your listeners by simply observing them or casually chatting with them. In a **formal analysis,** which is much more structured, you design and administer a questionnaire to obtain more precise and uniform information.

You can gather valuable information about your audience and its members just by observing them either before or during your speech.

*Informal audience analysis may begin with the person who asks you to speak.*

**Informal audience analysis.**   One of the easiest ways to begin finding out about your audience is simply to ask some basic questions. Often the best source of information is the person who invited you to speak. He or she can usually give you basic demographic data and insights into strongly held attitudes, beliefs, and values. This person may also be familiar with the room in which you will be speaking—its size and arrangement.

You may also gather valuable information by directly observing your audience. For example, you might try to attend a meeting of the group well in advance of your speaking date. One advantage of speaking to your classmates is that you have had many opportunities to observe them and probably have some idea of their interests, needs, and perspectives.

You will want to observe your audience during your speech as well. Are they making eye contact and paying attention, or do they look restless, fidgety, and bored? If you are not getting the response you want, you may need to change the content or delivery of your speech. Increasing your volume, eye contact, or vocal enthusiasm can help to keep your audience interested. Or you may need to add more examples and anecdotes to clarify your points. Sharp observation of your audience both before and during your speech can greatly enhance the effectiveness of your presentation.

**Formal audience analysis.**   In addition to informally observing and asking questions, you may decide to examine your audience formally through the use of a questionnaire. You can find out demographic information by asking such simple multiple-choice questions as:

*Formal audience analysis may be used to expand on information gathered during informal analysis.*

1. I am classified as a
   a. freshman
   b. sophomore
   c. junior
   d. senior
   e. graduate student
2. I am from
   a. the Midwest
   b. the South
   c. the East
   d. the West
   e. other
3. My highest degree earned is a
   a. high-school diploma
   b. bachelor's degree
   c. master's degree
   d. doctor's degree

One of the most popular techniques to examine audience attitudes is a Likert scale, on which audience members tell whether they strongly agree, agree, are undecided, disagree, or strongly disagree with a series of statements. For example:

Circle the response that best reflects your attitude toward each statement.

1. The state should pass a law requiring everyone to wear seat belts.
   a. Strongly agree
   b. Agree
   c. Undecided
   d. Disagree
   e. Strongly disagree

2. Casino gambling should be legalized in our state.
   a. Strongly agree
   b. Agree
   c. Undecided
   d. Disagree
   e. Strongly disagree

Multiple-choice questions may be used to explore attitudes.

Which one of the following statements best describes your position on capital punishment?

**1.** I support capital punishment.
**2.** I am against capital punishment.
**3.** I am undecided about capital punishment.

Finally, audience members can summarize their attitudes toward a particular issue by answering an open-ended question such as: What are your feelings about capital punishment? Because the answers to open-ended questions tend to be longer and more unpredictable, they can be difficult to summarize, but they will usually provide greater insight than will other methods.

## DEVELOPING SPEECH PURPOSES AND A THESIS STATEMENT

Thoughtfully formulate your general purpose, specific purpose, and thesis statement; they will form the foundation for the research and drafting of your speech. Care taken at this stage will help you focus your efforts and make the most of your time as you progress through the later steps of the speech-development process.

### The General Purpose

As mentioned earlier, a general purpose is the overall objective of a speech. The three general speech purposes are to inform, to persuade, and to entertain. When the purpose is to inform others, a speaker intends to teach, define, illustrate, clarify, or elaborate on a topic. Speaking to inform is usually the general purpose of a presenter of lectures, seminars, and workshops. Someone who demonstrates how to build something is also usually speaking to inform, as is a person who explains a new invention or describes how something works. (We will discuss strategies of informative speaking in Chapter 14.)

A second general purpose of public speaking is to persuade. In such cases, a speaker hopes to change or reinforce the audience's attitudes, beliefs, values, or behavior. Political speeches, advertisements on radio and TV, and sermons are typical examples of speeches to persuade. (We will explain this form of speech in Chapter 15.)

A speaker may also deliver a speech to entertain. Typically, a speech that entertains does so with humor. After-dinner speeches and comedy monologues are examples of speeches that entertain. Often the keys to a truly entertaining speech lie in a speaker's delivery, and his or her selection of stories, examples, and illustrations. Although we will not devote much time to entertaining speeches, you will note that speakers who effectively entertain apply many of the same communication principles that we discuss in other contexts. Although it is possible to distinguish among the three general purposes, it is not unusual for a speech to include a combination of two, or even all three.

## The Specific Purpose

While listening to a speech, have you ever nudged the person next to you and whispered, "What's this person talking about, anyway? I don't understand the point?" You may have had some idea of the general topic and a hint of the general purpose, but the gist of the message escaped you. Usually a speaker has failed to narrow the topic and develop a specific purpose. As defined earlier, a *specific purpose* is a finely tuned statement of what a speaker wants an audience to do, feel, or know after listening to his or her speech.

*If a speaker's specific purpose is unclear, the entire speech is likely to be unclear.*

Narrowing a topic and developing a specific purpose go hand in hand. Suppose, for example, that you have chosen to speak on the broad topic of consumer economic problems. After considering your audience and your time limits, you decide to focus more narrowly on the local housing shortage, but even this narrower topic needs more specific direction. This can be achieved by deciding exactly what you want your audience to be able to do, feel, or know when you finish your speech. Explicitly state this as your specific purpose. Thus, your speech about the housing shortage might have the following specific purpose:

> *At the end of my speech, the audience should be able to identify two causes and two effects of the current housing shortage in our community.*

Note how this statement defines exactly what you want the audience to be able to do: identify two causes and two effects of the housing shortage. It is then your responsibility as a speaker to communicate the two causes and two effects of the housing shortage so clearly that your audience can definitely name them. Using action words such as *identify, define, restate,* and *list* will help make your specific purpose statement more precise. The following are some other examples of specific purpose statements:

> *At the end of my speech, audience members will be inspired to write their town council members to express their opposition to the mayor's approach to rising crime in our community.*

*At the end of my speech, the audience should be able to list three reasons why pit bulls pose a serious danger to children.*

*At the end of my speech, the audience should be able to define* cryogenics *and describe the steps involved in the cryogenic process.*

Once you have formulated your specific speech purpose, write it on a piece of paper or a note card and keep it in front of you as you gather information on your topic. Your specific purpose will guide your research efforts and help you to eliminate irrelevant material. As you continue to read and learn more about your topic, you may decide to modify your specific purpose. The important point to remember is that you should have *some* purpose in mind at all times during the preparation of your speech.

## The Thesis Statement

Once you have your specific purpose, you can develop a clear **thesis statement**—a one-sentence summary that identifies the essence of the message you will share with your audience. In the following examples, note the relationships among the speech topic, the general purpose, the specific purpose, and the thesis statement.

| | |
|---|---|
| *Topic:* | Stamp Collecting |
| *General Purpose:* | To inform |
| *Specific Purpose:* | At the end of my speech, the audience should be able to describe two different kinds of Chinese stamps. |
| *Thesis Statement:* | Chinese stamps can be classified by their postmarks—those postmarked from ships and those postmarked from cities. |

| | |
|---|---|
| *Topic:* | Dude Ranches |
| *General Purpose:* | To inform |
| *Specific Purpose:* | At the end of my speech, the audience should be able to identify the four types of entertainment at popular dude ranches in Texas. |
| *Thesis Statement:* | Texas dude ranches offer four main types of entertainment—horseback riding, hiking, swimming, and camping. |

The worksheet on page 239 is designed to guide you through the first three steps in the speech-development process.

## Developing a Speech Purpose

1. General Speech Purpose: (Circle one)

        To inform           To persuade           To entertain

2. Possible Speech Topics

    _____    _____    _____

    _____    _____    _____

    _____    _____    _____

    _____    _____    _____

3. Narrowing the Topic

   General Topic

   _____

   Possible Subtopics

   _____

   _____

   _____

   _____

   _____

   _____

4. Specific Purpose Statement
   At the end of my speech the audience

   _____

   _____

5. Thesis Statement

   _____

   _____

   _____

   _____

| Review Box |
| --- |

**Speech Purposes**

| *General Purpose* | *Specific Purpose* | *Thesis Statement* |
| --- | --- | --- |
| The overall objective of a speech | A finely tuned statement of what a speaker wants an audience to do, feel, or know after listening to his or her speech | A one-sentence summary that identifies the essence of a speaker's message |
| Examples: | | |
| To Inform | At the end of my speech, the audience should be able to list three ways to classify nonverbal communication. | The three ways to classify nonverbal communication are sign language, action language and object language. |
| To Persuade | At the end of my speech, the audience should take a class in speech communication. | Taking a class in speech communication will improve your skill in communicating with others. |
| To Entertain | At the end of my speech, the audience should identify three locations for meeting someone in a supermarket. | The three best places to meet someone in a supermarket are the frozen food section, the bakery, and the checkout line. |

## BECOMING A CREDIBLE SPEAKER

So far we have presented specific advice about choosing a speech topic, analyzing an audience, and developing the foundation statements upon which to build a speech. In addition to these mechanical aspects of speech making, consider a more intangible aspect—the image you project to listeners. It is time to take a closer look at the notion of credibility and examine ways in which you can improve your credibility as a speaker.

**Credibility** is the extent to which a listener perceives a speaker to be competent, trustworthy, and dynamic. The more credibility a listener attributes to a speaker, the more likely it is that he or she will respond favorably to the speaker's message. Thus, credibility is not something that a speaker possesses or lacks. It is an *attitude* that a *listener* has. A listener gives credence to a speaker's message if he or she believes the speaker displays the key characteristics of competence, trustworthiness, and dynamism.

1. *Competence* refers to a speaker's knowledgeability and expertise. Is the speaker experienced and does he or she possess the background to be considered an expert on the subject?
2. *Trustworthiness* stems from a speaker's honesty and believability. Is the speaker someone who inspires confidence?
3. *Dynamism* is the energy, enthusiasm, and charisma that a speaker projects. A person with charisma possesses a personal magnetism or dynamism that makes that person attractive and appealing. Thus, a dynamic person exudes a forcefulness that commands an audience's attention and respect.

## Three Phases of Credibility

Because your success as a speaker depends on the strength of your credibility, you will want to do all you can to be perceived as competent, honest, and dynamic. This task will be simplified if you approach credibility in terms of three phases.

**Phase 1: Initial credibility.** **Initial credibility** is the attitude that a listener has toward you before you begin your speech. Most listeners develop some preconceived notions about a speaker even before the speaker starts talking. Such impressions are based on the speaker's personal appearance and reputation, comments that others have made, and the nature of the introduction that the speaker receives. To enhance your initial credibility:

*Even before you begin to speak, listeners begin to form impressions about your credibility.*

1. Make sure your physical appearance does not violate the expectations of your audience. Don't dress too informally, for example, if your audience expects more formal attire.
2. Well in advance of your speech, contact the person who will introduce you to make sure he or she has all the information needed to project a positive image of you to the audience.
3. Don't rush to the lectern and immediately start speaking. Appear confident by establishing eye contact with your audience before you begin your speech.

*A well-prepared speech will greatly enhance your derived credibility.*

**Phase 2: Derived credibility.   Derived credibility** is the attitude a listener develops while you are presenting your speech. To firmly establish your credibility during the second phase:

1. Maintain eye contact with your audience. Looking at your listeners communicates your interest in them.
2. Vary your vocal inflection to express interest, enthusiasm, and sincerity.
3. Use posture and gestures to convey your energy and conviction. Don't slouch on the lectern, lean on a table, or distract the audience with unmeaningful gestures.
4. Present a well-organized message. Establish an overview of your main ideas, present the body of your speech, and summarize your key thoughts during the conclusion.
5. Use appropriate grammar.
6. Pronounce words clearly and accurately.
7. Use appropriate evidence to support your conclusions.
8. Thoroughly research your topic so your audience will see that you are informed and qualified.

*Terminal credibility is the product of initial and derived credibility.*

**Phase 3: Terminal credibility.   Terminal credibility** is the attitude that a listener holds toward you after your speech is concluded. It is the result of your initial and derived credibility. If you are unknown to your audience at the start of your speech, your initial credibility will be low. Nonetheless, if you present a well-organized, well-researched, and well-delivered message, you can count on derived credibility to enhance your image. Then, if the audience reflects on your message and decides that your conclusions are sound and consistent with their own views, your terminal credibility will be high.

Sometimes a phenomenon called the *sleeper effect* comes into play. The **sleeper effect** is a change in a listener's attitude caused by the passage of time. Through the sleeper effect, an idea may gain appeal if a listener has a chance to think about it. Thus, at first hearing, your listeners may reject your point of view, but, if given some time for consideration, they may come to recognize its value. As a result of the sleeper effect, your credibility and the acceptability of your ideas, like fine wine, may improve with age.

To boost your credibility during this final phase:

1. End your speech on time. If you violate your audience's expectations about the length of your speech, the only thing they may remember is that you talked too long.
2. End with eye contact. When you finish your speech, look directly at the audience and accept their applause graciously. The

*Review Box*

## Three Phases of Credibility

| *Phase One* *Initial Credibility* | *Phase Two* *Derived Credibility* | *Phase Three* *Terminal Credibility* |
|---|---|---|
| *Description:* Attitude listeners hold before you speak. | *Description:* Attitude listeners develop while you are speaking. | *Description:* Attitude listeners hold after you speak. |

| *Suggestions* | *Suggestions* | *Suggestions* |
|---|---|---|
| 1. Monitor your appearance. | 1. Maintain eye contact. | 1. End your speech on time. |
| 2. Prepare to be introduced. | 2. Vary your vocal inflection. | 2. End your speech with eye contact. |
| 3. Don't rush up to the lectern. | 3. Use appropriate posture. | 3. Be prepared for questions. |
| 4. Establish eye contact before you speak. | 4. Organize your message logically. | |
| | 5. Use appropriate grammar. | |
| | 6. Pronounce words properly. | |
| | 7. Use evidence to support your conclusions. | |
| | 8. Do enough research to appear informed and qualified. | |

amount of applause you receive can influence listeners' attitudes toward you and your message.

3. **Be prepared for questions.** Even if no formal question-and-answer session is scheduled, you should be ready to respond to listeners' queries. If you can't answer basic questions about your topic, your credibility will erode.

Credibility, then, is an attitude that you can cultivate in your listeners. The more favorably you are perceived by your listeners, the more effectively you can pursue your speech purpose. If you carefully consider how you can enhance all phases of your credibility, you will make a more positive and lasting impression on your audience.

## *SUMMARY*

When you think about public communication, you probably picture someone presenting a speech to an audience. Speech delivery is only one small fraction of the entire public speaking process, however. A truly effective speaker spends much more time on tasks an audience never sees. The speaker knows that care spent on the early steps of speech planning and development pays off in greater confidence and polish during the actual presentation.

▶**Outline the six steps to follow in speech preparation and presentation.**
The six basic steps in the speech-making process are the following: (1) select a topic; (2) analyze your audience; (3) develop a general purpose, a specific purpose, and a thesis statement for your speech; (4) gather supporting materials; (5) organize your speech; and (6) rehearse and deliver your speech.

▶**Use appropriate criteria to select and narrow a topic for your speech.**
The best speech topics will probably stem from your own interests and background. Thus, taking a personal inventory and brainstorming are likely to help you to identify some general subject areas. You will then want to narrow your topic to fit your assigned time limit and avoid being overly vague. As you refine your topic, you will want to consider the amount of interest it is likely to generate, its applicability to your audience, and the availability of outside sources of information.

▶**Discover information about your audience that will help you adapt your speech to their needs and interests.**
To find out as much as possible about the audience, both as individuals and as a group, an experienced speaker usually performs several kinds of audience analysis. A *demographic analysis* yields basic information about audience members' ages, sex, race, religion, and the like. Such data enable a speaker to identify similarities and differences in listeners' backgrounds and make assumptions about their probable

likes, interests, and needs. An *attitudinal analysis* attempts to identify an audience's attitudes, values, and beliefs about specific issues and ideas. Armed with such information, a speaker can evaluate listeners' probable receptivity to a given topic or approach and the likelihood of their being won over to a different point of view. Finally, in an *environmental analysis,* a speaker studies the speech occasions and the physical surroundings of the event. The speaker can then be prepared to compensate for any physical factors that may interfere with the audience's ability to concentrate on the message.

A speaker may gather information about an audience either informally or formally. In informal analysis, the speaker either observes audience members or casually chats with them. In formal analysis, a much more structured approach, the speaker uses a questionnaire to obtain more uniform and precise data.

▶**Identify the general purpose of your speech and write a corresponding specific purpose and thesis statement.**

The three general purposes of public speaking are to inform, to persuade, and to entertain. An informative speech is intended to teach, define, illustrate, clarify, or elaborate on a topic. A persuasive speech attempts to change or reinforce an audience's attitudes, beliefs, values, or behavior. A speech to entertain is designed for audience enjoyment and usually incorporates humor.

A specific purpose is a finely tuned statement of what a speaker wants an audience to do, feel, or know after listening to his or her speech. Narrowing a topic and developing a specific purpose are closely related. Both limit the scope of the topic and help a speaker focus his or her thoughts and research efforts on a limited area. Ultimately, when precisely thought through, they should help a speaker communicate more clearly with the audience.

Finally, a thesis statement is a one-sentence summary of the essence of a speech's message. An outgrowth of the specific purpose, it adds further structure to the development and presentation of a speech.

▶**Take steps to improve your credibility as a speaker.**

Credibility is the extent to which a listener perceives a speaker to be competent, trustworthy, and dynamic. You can enhance an audience's perception of you by recognizing the three phases of credibility and using them to your advantage.

*Initial credibility* is the attitude that a listener has toward you before you begin your speech. You can improve your initial credibility by paying attention to your appearance, having an introducer list your qualifications, and appearing calm and interested in your audience.

*Derived credibility* is the attitude a listener develops while you are presenting your speech. To enhance your credibility at this stage, maintain eye contact with your audience, vary your vocal inflection, speak clearly and grammatically, and use appropriate posture and gestures. Also make sure that your message is well organized and supported by strong evidence.

*Terminal credibility* is the attitude that a listener holds toward you after your speech is concluded. It is the product of your initial and derived credibility. To leave your audience with a good lasting impression, end your speech on time, look directly at your listeners as you close, and be prepared to answer questions about your speech's content.

Finally, never underestimate the power of the sleeper effect. Even though your listeners may at first seem to reject your ideas, if given time for consideration, they may eventually accept your point of view.

---

## KEY TERMS

**Attitudinal analysis:**  the identification of audience members' attitudes, beliefs, and values about specific issues and ideas.

**Credibility:**  the extent to which a listener perceives a speaker to be competent, trustworthy, and dynamic.

**Demographic analysis:**  the collection and interpretation of basic information about audience members' ages, sex, race, religion, education, social and political affiliations, and the like.

**Derived credibility:**  the attitude that a listener develops toward a speaker while the speaker is presenting the speech.

**Environmental analysis:**  a study of the speech occasion and the physical surroundings of the event.

**Formal audience analysis:**  the gathering of precise and uniform information about listeners by designing and administering a questionnaire.

**General purpose:**  the overall objective of a speech; the three possible general purposes are to inform, to persuade, and to entertain.

**Informal audience analysis:**  the gathering of information about listeners by simply observing them or casually chatting with them.

**Initial credibility:**  the attitude that a listener has toward a speaker before he or she begins to speak.

**Sleeper effect:**  a change in a listener's attitude caused by the passage of time.

**Specific purpose:**  a finely tuned statement of what a speaker wants an audience to do, feel, or know after listening to his or her speech.

**Supporting material:** the definitions, examples, statistics, testimony, illustrations, and analogies that verify, amplify, and clarify the main ideas of a speech.

**Terminal credibility:** the attitude that a listener holds toward a speaker after the speech is concluded.

**Thesis statement:** a one-sentence summary that identifies the essence of a speaker's message.

## DISCUSSION QUESTIONS

1. What are the key criteria to use when selecting a speech topic?
2. Discuss the advantages and disadvantages of formal and informal methods of analyzing your audience.
3. What are the differences among a speech's general purpose, specific purpose, and thesis statement?
4. Suggest three specific methods of enhancing your initial, derived, and terminal credibility as a speaker.

## SUGGESTED ACTIVITIES

1. Select a speech that has been reprinted in a recent edition of *Vital Speeches in America*. Identify the general purpose, specific purpose, and thesis sentence. Also, identify the speech's introduction, body, and conclusion, as well as the main ideas presented.
2. Write a short paper in which you summarize demographic, attitudinal, and environmental information about your classmates and your speaking environment for your next speech. You may decide to develop a brief questionnaire or survey and distribute it to your audience to help you gather information.
3. Identify a nationally prominent speaker whom you perceive to be credible. Identify the specific communication strategies and behaviors that have enhanced his or her credibility as competent, trustworthy and dynamic.
4. Attend a speech delivered on campus or in your community. Write a short paper in which you describe the initial, derived, and terminal credibility as either high, medium, or low. Were there differences in the initial, derived, and terminal credibility of the speaker? What specific behaviors helped to influence your

attitude toward the speaker during each phase of credibility development? Two weeks after hearing the speech, what was your impression of the speaker? Was there a "sleeper effect" in your evaluation of the speaker?

## SUGGESTED READINGS

Ehninger, D., Gronbeck, B.E., McKerrow, R.E. and Monroe, A.H. (1986). *Principles and Types of Speech Communication* (10th edition). (Glenview, Illinois: Scott, Foresman and Company).

Brooks, W.T. (1988). *High Impact Public Speaking.* (Englewood Cliffs, New Jersey: Prentice-Hall).

Sprague, Jo and Douglas, Stuart (1984). *The Speaker's Handbook.* (San Diego: Harcourt Brace Jovanovich, Publishers).

Doolittle, Robert J. (1984). *Professionally Speaking: A Concise Guide.* (Glenview, Illinois: Scott, Foresman and Company).

# Supporting Materials

*After studying this chapter, you should be able to:*

▶ Identify six kinds of supporting materials and assess their effectiveness.

▶ List at least four general sources of supporting materials and tell how to evaluate their usefulness.

▶ Use four different methods to collect supporting materials.

▶ Effectively use supporting materials to prepare and present speeches.

*"Five to seven minutes! I'll never be able to talk that long. What am I supposed to say for five minutes?"*

After having learned the six steps in preparing a public speech and after having studied the first three steps in detail, are you still wondering whether you can actually speak for five minutes? Are you still questioning whether you can say anything useful or interesting to your audience? Question no more! This chapter will help you find, evaluate, and present relevant, interesting, and valid information.

## TYPES OF SUPPORTING MATERIALS

*Supporting materials help to verify, amplify, and clarify main ideas.*

As you discovered in Chapter 10, *supporting materials* consist of the definitions, examples, statistics, testimony, illustrations, and analogies that verify, amplify, and clarify your main ideas. Each supporting statement is relevant and obvious in its applicability and clarity of expression.

Imagine that you and a friend have just finished viewing the film *The Day After,* which depicts the aftermath of a nuclear attack in a midwestern town. As you talk about your feelings, you and your friend find that you disagree over the possibility of such events ever happening in the United States. Your friend believes that such a situation could never occur, while you insist that the film was very realistic, maybe even a prophecy. You become so fascinated that you decide to investigate the likelihood of a successful nuclear attack on the United States and use your findings to fulfill one of your speech assignments. Where do you start? What kind of information do you need to reach a conclusion about the probability of such an event?

Because you've already mastered the material in previous chapters of this book, you'd probably want to make sure that you and your audience share a common frame of reference. Thus, you'd begin by defining the critical terms on the topic, such as *nuclear attack, survival, nuclear proliferation,* and *Strategic Defense Initiative (SDI* or *Star Wars).* Then you would probably want to uncover any examples of nuclear proliferation and results of previous nuclear attacks. You might find stories or anecdotes dealing with philosophical and moral issues related to nuclear attacks and/or disarmament, and you'd probably try to make some comparisons between present conditions and previous or hypothetical situations. You would also need some statistics about numbers and strength of warheads held by potential attackers, survival rates of victims of previous nuclear attacks, and quantity and quality of defense systems. Finally, you would probably read and use opinions of experts in the fields of medicine, political science, and nuclear physics. In the process, you would examine the six basic kinds of supporting materials commonly used in public speeches: definitions, examples, illustrations, analogies, statistics, and testimony.

## Definitions

As you know from Chapter 3, the success of the communication process depends on shared meaning through shared language usage. As a public speaker, make sure your audience members know the meanings of any technical or unfamiliar terms required by your topic and understand any familiar terms or concepts that you may use in an uncommon manner.

Most of us know that a **definition** is simply a statement of the meaning of a term or concept. A literal definition can be found in a variety of dictionaries, such as the *Oxford English Dictionary,* the *Random House Dictionary of the English Language, The Dictionary of Philosophy,* and *The Dictionary of Finance and Investment Terms.* Such reference books not only give the specific meanings of a word but also its *etymology*—tracing its development from other languages. Knowing the history of a particular term or concept can assist both you and your listeners in better understanding it. It can also make your speech more interesting.

*Definitions are the most basic way to explain unfamiliar concepts or uncommon usages of words.*

You might want to expand on a dictionary definition. Citing specific uses of a term, explaining what its meaning includes and does not include, and comparing and contrasting the term with similar terms can help audience members to grasp the specific intent. For example, most Americans are probably familiar with the term *Republican,* but do they really know all its meanings? If you were talking about the civil war in Nicaragua, you would probably need to define the term *republican* so that audience members were not confused. You would have to explain why the Contras were fighting for a *republican* form of government and how that form differs from the current form of government in that country.

Despite their great utility—or perhaps because of it—definitions can be overused. Merely defining a word with other words may not be very interesting to your audience. To avoid this problem, define words and new or uncommon concepts when you need to, but stay away from topics that are so technical that they create speeches filled with nothing but definitions.

## Examples

When you use an **example,** you provide a specific instance that clarifies or dramatizes a point. An example can be very brief or quite lengthy. For instance, you can clarify what you mean by "problems of violent crime" with a few one- or two-word examples—murder, rape, armed robbery. On the other hand, if you are preparing a speech on violations of human rights in foreign countries, you may spend a great deal of time detailing such violations in one country, or you may provide detailed descriptions of specific instances in several countries.

One of the most effective ways to hold people's attention is to use **personal examples**—firsthand experiences that clarify or dramatize your point. Most audiences will enjoy hearing you tell relevant personal stories. Firsthand experience with a topic often adds to your credibility.

Another good way to expand on a topic and maintain listeners' interest is through the use of a hypothetical example such as the one that began the discussion about kinds of supporting materials earlier in this chapter. A **hypothetical example** is a purely fictional incident that is devised to illustrate a given point. It is never presented as if it were true: rather, it usually begins with a phrase such as "Imagine yourself in the following situation . . ." or "What would you do if . . .?" Phrases like these indicate to your audience that, while your example might be quite believable, it never actually happened.

A key to using examples—whether true or hypothetical—is to make them come alive to your listeners by appealing to their senses. Describe the sights, sounds, smells, and textures you want your audience to imagine. The more concrete and vivid your examples are, the more likely it is that you will gain and maintain audience interest and attention. The more likely it is that you will also be perceived as a competent and qualified speaker.

## Statistics

*Statistics are useful for summarizing facts.*

**Statistics** are numerical data that summarize facts or examples. They are often used as evidence to emphasize the significance of problems, to demonstrate how widespread situations are, and to compare and contrast similar phenomena.

One often-used statistic is a **percentage,** which indicates proportion. A speaker can succinctly indicate the extent of unemployment by saying that "Today 7 percent of the able-bodied people of working age are without jobs."

Another popular kind of statistic is the **average.** An average is a single value that represents the middle point among a number of unequal values. This statistic is a useful means of summarizing facts, but it can easily mislead an audience if not used properly. When you give someone an average, unless you also provide some indication about the variation in the numbers used to reach the average, the figure can be misleading. For example, the average of 2, 3, 4, 2, 2, and 22 is 5.8. The number 22 makes the average of the six numbers higher than all but one of the numbers. Thus, this average does not accurately represent all six scores.

While statistics can lend substance and credibility to your presentation, their overuse can overwhelm and bore listeners. Fortunately, there are ways to increase the meaningfulness of statistics for your audience. For example, you can make any statistic less abstract by comparing it to something that your audience can visualize. Rather than just saying that 55,000 people were killed in auto accidents last year, you might state that the equivalent of the entire population of Palo Alto, California (or some town of similar size that is familiar to your audience), was wiped out by traffic accidents last year. Using round numbers will also aid listeners' comprehension and recall, unless you have to be very precise. In the auto-accident example, 55,000 was not the exact number of traffic fatalities last year, but it is easier to recall than 55,156. Because statistics can add interest and clarity to your speech, it is important to learn to use them cautiously and appropriately.

## Testimony

**Testimony** is a statement made by a third party to support an idea or position that you are trying to develop. The best testimony, of course, does not come from just anyone. It comes from a person or group whom your audience will recognize as qualified and knowledgeable.

There are two basic kinds of testimony. **Peer testimony** is a statement made by an ordinary person who has firsthand knowledge of a subject. For example, a former heroin addict's description of withdrawal from drugs is peer testimony. **Expert testimony** is a statement made by a specialist. For instance, if you are developing a speech opposing increased defense spending by the federal government, you may choose to quote from a recent Senate Armed Services Committee report that criticizes the amount of money wasted on poorly designed tanks.

When using testimony to support your position, make sure that the person or group you quote (1) is knowledgeable in the field to which the comment applies, (2) is not biased, (3) will be respected by your listeners, and (4) is quoted by a reputable source, such as the *Congressional Report* or a national news magazine. A physician, a lawyer, an elected official, and a business person or salesperson are all reputable sources in their respective areas of expertise.

*Credible, well-known individuals are good sources of testimony.*

When you select testimony for your presentation, make sure it is accurate. Take care to quote it word for word. Choose a passage that faithfully represents the content of the total message, not one that distorts the speaker's or writer's true intent. Finally, keep track of the source of your selection—you'll need to make a precise reference to it when you use it in your speech.

**Kinds of Supporting Materials**

| *Material* | *Uses* | *Examples* |
|---|---|---|
| Definition | Clarify unfamiliar terms or concepts<br>Explain uncommon uses of familiar words | Citing dictionary definitions<br>Expanding on dictionary definitions<br>Tracing word origins<br>Comparing and contrasting with similar or familiar words<br>Explaining your unique use of a word or concept |
| Example | Clarify or dramatize a point<br>Expand on a topic<br>Hold listeners' attention | Sharing firsthand experiences (personal examples)<br>Suggesting purely fictional incidents (hypothetical examples) |
| Statistics | Summarize facts or examples<br>Show how significant a situation is<br>Compare and contrast similar phenomena | Comparing percentages<br>Citing averages |

## Illustrations

An **illustration** is a story, fable, or anecdote having a theme, moral, or purpose that supports a point you wish to make in your speech. An illustration can be humorous, serious, or even tragic. It can be part of your personal experience. One student delivered a speech intended to persuade the audience to contribute to the Muscular Dystrophy Association. He emphasized his plea by telling the story of the long and painful deterioration of his brother, who was a victim of the disease.

Don't assume that the moral or purpose of your illustration will be so clear that you need not state it explicitly. Provide a preview that tells your listeners what to look for; or, if you prefer not to identify your theme beforehand, make your point after you tell your story.

*If in doubt about your listeners' understanding of an illustration, explain your reason for using it.*

| *Material* | *Uses* | *Examples* |
|---|---|---|
| Testimony | Add authority to a point or position | Quoting a recognized expert on the topic<br>Citing a respected book, periodical, or report |
| Illustration | Make a point more memorable<br>Encourage audience involvement<br>Evoke an emotional response | Telling a humorous fable with a moral that supports a key thought<br>Telling a dramatic story to emphasize the importance of taking immediate action |
| Analogy | Compare one object, concept, or principle to another<br>Show similarities or differences<br>Clarify relationships among familiar and unfamiliar concepts | Using a literal analogy to compare or contrast things of the same class<br>Using a figurative analogy to compare or contrast things of different classes |

## Analogies

Another word for **analogy** is *comparison*. With an analogy, you support a point by comparing one object, concept, or principle to another.

There are two types of analogies—literal and figurative. A **literal analogy** compares or contrasts things of the same class. Comparing the voting records of two senators in terms of relative conservatism is an example of a literal analogy. A **figurative analogy** compares or contrasts things of different classes. In an attempt to make the process of nuclear fission more understandable to his audience, the commentator of a TV science program used a room filled with spring-loaded mousetraps. Each mousetrap had two ping-pong balls resting on it. When the commentator tossed another ping-pong ball into the room, he set off a chain reaction, releasing the mousetraps and filling the air with ping-pong balls. "This," said the commentator, "is similar to what happens in the nuclear fission process, when the nucleus of an atom is bombarded with another charged particle, thus setting off a chain reaction and releasing vast amounts of energy."

*Don't try to prove a point with a figurative analogy.*

A figurative analogy is a good tool for clarifying relationships and adding interest, but beware of trying to *prove* any point with only a figurative analogy for support. Comparing and contrasting things of different classes may aid listeners' understanding, but an analogy based more on imagination than on fact is likely to undermine your credibility. Balancing creativity with reality is the key to developing an effective figurative analogy.

As you can see, you have a wide variety of supporting materials to choose from as you prepare a speech. You can mix kinds and use any number that you need to support the points you are trying to make. As long as your definitions, examples, statistics, testimony, illustrations, and analogies (1) are relevant to the point you are trying to make, (2) increase clarity and comprehension for your listeners, and (3) verify and lend credibility to your speech ideas, you can use them liberally.

## SOURCES OF SUPPORTING MATERIALS

So far, we have talked about the basic kinds of supporting materials, have briefly noted some of their benefits, and have pointed out how they can be used and misused. But we have yet to discuss their sources. In this age of what many people call the information explosion, materials to verify, clarify, amplify, and illustrate your speech are everywhere. Nevertheless the location, evaluation, and integration of these supporting materials will depend on your specific purpose, will require some amount of diligent research, and must be logically and psychologically adapted to your general and specific purposes. The four most common sources of supporting materials are personal experience, printed resources, visual and audio resources, and other people.

### Personal Experience

What are people like? How do they act and react in different situations? What do they know and how do they know it? What are their feelings on different topics? All these and other questions are at least partially answerable through *personal observation*. Both formal and informal observations of the world around you can contribute to your credibility.

All kinds of printed matter, from popular magazines to specialized newspapers, may provide supporting materials for your speech.

Your *reading* and *education* are other personal experiences that may provide support material. Your courses can furnish a multitude of topics and volumes of support for your speeches. Any reading you do, whether for classes, for pleasure, or for personal enrichment, is a gold mine of supporting materials. In fact, you'd probably be foolish not to tap these resources, considering the time and effort you spend in such pursuits.

Finally, it's difficult to imagine a *job* or job-training program that didn't, in some way, furnish some knowledge that you could use as an illustration, example, or analogy for any number of speech topics. Your personal experiences in the business arena are a vast and valuable storehouse of supporting materials that you can draw on whenever it is relevant.

*Telling relevant personal experiences adds interest and credibility to your speech.*

## Printed Resources

Much of the information we acquire comes from *printed resources*. Books, newspapers, magazines, technical journals, indexes, and encyclopedias all provide a wide variety of support materials.

Dictionaries and encyclopedias are good sources of *definitions*. Specialized dictionaries define terms for individual disciplines and scientific fields, such as philosophy, physics, social sciences, and chemistry.

Almost unlimited numbers and kinds of *examples* can be found in books—fiction or nonfiction, textbooks or recreational reading, reference works or biographies. Survey results published in magazines and technical journals, reports published by the federal government, and articles in newspapers are good sources for *statistics*.

*Testimony* can be found in many types of publications, such as biographies, newspaper and magazine articles, reproductions of speeches and interviews, and books written on specific technical and/or controversial topics. Many printed resources are also excellent sources of *illustrations*. Fiction and nonfiction books, newspapers, magazines, and printed speeches (such as those found in *Vital Speeches of the Day*) can provide a multitude of stories and anecdotes. Finally, source material for *analogies* may be found in many of the same printed materials, or you may develop them yourself, based on a combination of readings. In short, printed resources can provide virtually any kind of supporting material if you know what to look for and are willing to dig for it.

## Visual and Audio Resources

Perhaps the second most widely available sources of potential supporting materials are the audiovisual media. Television is probably the most frequently used medium, but films, slide presentations, records, audiotapes, compact discs, and videotapes can also be extremely useful. News broadcasts, documentaries, movies, and interview programs such as "Issues and Answers" and "Meet the Press" are just a few of the information-rich sources available through the media.

No speech on classical music is complete without at least one musical segment played from a tape or record. The replay of a portion of a videotaped interview or documentary lends strong support to a speech on American foreign policy in the 1980s, especially if the interviewee is a recognizable foreign policy expert who is respected by your listeners. Even speakers who do not use such aids during a speech find that audiovisual resources still provide much information that is useful during the speech-development process.

## Other People

Informal or formal discussions with *other people* can furnish you with useful information. How other students view the parking problem on campus, a police officer's perspective on campus security, or an instructor's opinions about the way to reduce the federal deficit can become the bases for appropriate speeches. You can even conduct your own opinion survey to collect evidence for a speech.

---

*Review Box*

**Sources of Supporting Materials**

| *Source* | *Examples* |
|---|---|
| Personal Experience | Firsthand observations<br>Reading<br>Education<br>Jobs |
| Printed Resources | Books, newspapers, magazines, technical journals, indexes, encyclopedias, dictionaries<br>Fiction or nonfiction, textbooks or recreational reading, reference works or biographies<br>Government documents<br>Reproductions of speeches and interviews |
| Visual and Audio Resources | Television<br>Films, slide presentations, and videotapes<br>Records, audiotapes, compact discs<br>News broadcasts, documentaries, movies, and interview programs |
| Other People | Formal or informal discussions<br>Interviews<br>Personal opinion surveys |

## Evaluating Sources of Supporting Materials

In your search for supporting materials of all kinds, take care to evaluate the quality of every potential source. First and foremost, *relate all material to your topic and your specific purpose.* Irrelevant or tangential information will not only distract listeners from important points, but will also reduce your effectiveness as a speaker. You will want to maintain your credibility by using credible sources. Make sure your sources are reputable and accurate, and report your findings honestly and precisely. The *Reader's Digest* once published a condensed version of a feature-length article about violence during the 1980 riots in Miami, Florida. Although the trouble was indeed serious, the way the article was condensed made the entire Miami area sound like a war zone. In reality, only a small portion of the city was directly affected.

Make sure that your sources are *timely*. It is seldom acceptable to quote ten-year-old statistics to support the present state of affairs.

*Use only credible sources that will clearly help you achieve your specific purpose.*

*Find the most recent information available and adapt it to the level of your audience.*

Times change, and so do world conditions. To preserve your credibility, you must present the most recent and accurate information you can find.

Finally, ensure that your sources and supporting materials *are appropriate to your audience.* A general audience will rarely be interested in complex diagrams or numerous statistics. By the same token, children's bedtime stories are probably not your best choice of illustrations when presenting serious moral or ethical issues to college students. Adapt your level of difficulty by choosing supporting materials that coincide with the knowledge and sophistication of your audience. Effective audience analysis can assist you in this regard.

## FINDING SUPPORTING MATERIALS

Once you have some idea of the kinds of supporting materials you will need and their sources, you will be ready to start searching them out. The four best places to search for materials are libraries, interviews, classes, and broadcast and recorded media.

### Libraries

As a student, you are undoubtedly familiar with libraries. You are probably aware that the holdings of most *public* libraries include more fiction, a greater number of popular periodicals, more general interest reference works, and fewer technical journals than do *college or university* libraries. Depending on your speech topic, the level of sophistication of your audience, and your treatment of the topic, you will want to select the kind of library that will best suit your needs.

Once inside, head for the card catalog. It is still your best means of locating books, reference works, and pamphlets. Most card catalogs are indexed by subject, author, and title.

Nearly all libraries subscribe to the *Reader's Guide to Periodical Literature*—the index of most general interest periodicals. Many public libraries, and nearly all college and university libraries, carry more specialized indexes for a variety of academic areas, such as the *Social Science Index, Education Index,* and *Psychological Abstracts.* These indexes identify more technical information in specialized areas of research.

Collections of quotations, song lyrics, poems, jokes, fables, and statistics are also available in most libraries. Such publications can be rich sources of examples, definitions, illustrations, and statistics.

Just as crucial to your search as the card catalog is the reference librarian. Don't hesitate to ask this person to help you find government

The Library is one of the four best places to search for supporting materials.

documents, archives, audiovisual materials, and other publications. Public and college libraries contain a nearly limitless supply of information. With a librarian's assistance, you should be able to tap this valuable resource for more information than you'll be able to use in a lifetime of speeches.

## Interviews

An interview is a terrific way to gather supporting material for a speech, *if* your speech topic lends itself to first-hand testimony and *if* suitable people are available. Both peer and expert testimony can be compiled through interviewing. For example, if you are giving a speech in favor of coed dormitories on your campus, you can gather peer testimony by interviewing students on a campus that already has coed dorms. If you are speaking on the need for a change in federal fiscal policy to reduce the national debt, you can collect expert testimony by interviewing a specialist in the field of economics. Any number and kinds of interviews can be used to gather supporting material for speeches. Just be sure to evaluate the credibility of your sources and the probable usefulness of their responses before spending the time and effort that can be consumed by interviewing.

*Interviewing the right people can yield original and persuasive expert or peer testimony.*

## Classes

As we have already suggested, your classes can be valuable places to gather supporting material. Both your instructors and your textbooks are potential sources of expert testimony. Bibliographies used in classes or published in textbooks may suggest additional readings to be investigated. Through your classes, you may discover topics that you'd like to develop into speeches.

## Broadcast and Recorded Media

As mentioned earlier, the mass media can be excellent places to look for information. Television programs, films, and multimedia presentations can supply examples, illustrations, testimony, and statistics that may be extremely useful to the development of a speech. The most important thing to remember in gathering supporting material from the media is that you must record (in electronic or written form) the information *accurately* and *completely*. To ensure precision, video- or audiotaping is preferred, but remember that such recording *must be for your personal use only*. Many libraries have collections of films and tapes that you may check out or examine on the premises. Regardless of the way you gather or use supporting material from the media, it is important to abide by the law and conform to ethical standards.

If you have a personal collection of records and tapes, you have a ready-made research base. An additional source for audiovisual aids is commercial rentals or sales. Ask at your public or college library for catalogs from commercial rental or sales agencies, or visit your local video rental and sales store.

## USING SUPPORTING MATERIALS EFFECTIVELY

At this point, you may feel overwhelmed by the number and variety of options available to you as you research supporting materials and develop your topic into an interesting and coherent speech. You can take control of the situation if you are cautious, organized, and selective. The following guidelines should help you to select productive supporting materials based on careful analysis of your audience, your topic, your specific purpose, and your personal needs and speaking style.

*Supporting materials must be directly related to your specific purpose.*

1. First and foremost, *let your specific purpose guide your research efforts.* Write your topic, specific purpose, and thesis statement on a sheet of paper and keep them within sight at all times

during the research process. If a piece of information will not directly verify, illustrate, amplify, or clarify one of your main points or subpoints, don't use it. *Directly* means any material that is clearly relevant to the point or subpoint it is intended to support, without furthering your cause of informing or persuading your listeners on the selected topic.

2. Closely related to choosing material that clearly supports your specific purpose is making sure that all material is *logically and psychologically adapted to your communication goals and specific purpose.* Any example, illustration, statistic, or analogy may support a variety of ideas or points in a speech. The key is to select the one kind and specific piece of support material that will assist you in making a given point most clearly and effectively. If necessary, you may even want to point out its relevance during your speech. Your audience should always have a clear idea of the way all the elements of your presentation are related.

*Help your audience understand how your speech content relates to your communication objectives.*

3. Select the supporting material that will be *most interesting and understandable to your listeners.* Don't ignore the previous two guidelines, but if you have a choice among several equally effective and relevant pieces of information, choose those that are most likely to hit home with your audience members. For example, if you accept an invitation to present your college classroom speech entitled "The Peaceful Uses of Nuclear Power in the 1990s" to a seventh-grade class, you will need to make some changes. The level of interest and understanding will be different.

4. *Use a variety of supporting materials.* Variety breeds interest— novelty breeds attention. Thus, presenting a combination of recent unemployment statistics, testimony from the Secretary of Labor, and examples of local layoffs while discussing current problems of unemployment is more likely to hold your listeners' attention than is citing a long string of statistics. In addition, such variety indicates thorough research, which boosts your credibility.

5. As you make decisions about specific supporting materials, make sure that the sources you use are *reliable* and that your information is *accurate.* Neglecting either of these criteria will undermine your credibility and hamper your ability to attain your speaking goals and specific purpose. Even if none of your listeners catches an inaccurate statement or recognizes a questionable source, you'll know, or someone will realize your error later. The result is the same.

*Check your sources for credibility and accuracy before using them in your speech.*

*Uphold your ethical responsibilities by citing your sources completely and accurately.*

6. Finally, when using supporting material, it is crucial to *cite your sources in your speech*. Citing outside sources adds to your credibility. In addition, good speaking ethics *absolutely require* you to give credit where credit is due and to notify your listeners of ideas that are not originally yours.

Source citations should always be brief and accurate. You may cite a definition simply by saying *"The Oxford English Dictionary* defines *democracy* as. . . ."* You may refer to a personal interview with a comment such as, "In a personal interview, Robert Money, Professor of Economics at Fiscal University, said that. . . ." Magazine articles often require more detail, but the citation can still be brief: "In the April 14, 1987, issue of *Time* magazine, Vice-President George Bush was quoted as saying. . . ." Other citations may be composed and included in an equally brief, but accurate manner. Some references may sound clumsy when spoken aloud, but "clumsy" is preferable to "missing."

Supporting materials are an essential element of every well-crafted speech. Much information and many choices are at your disposal if you investigate thoroughly. Strive for interest, attention, relevancy, and credibility. Fulfill your ethical responsibilities by citing your sources, and use variety and accuracy to support your ideas.

## SUMMARY

Supporting material is the substance of any speech. If carefully researched, selected, and integrated into a presentation, it promotes attention, interest, understanding, and acceptance among audience members.

▶**Identify six kinds of supporting materials and assess their effectiveness.**

Speakers may use examples, definitions, illustrations, analogies, statistics, and testimony to verify, clarify, amplify, and illustrate their main points. To be effective, supporting material should be relevant to the topic, increase clarity and comprehensibility, and verify and lend credibility to a speech.

▶**List at least four general sources of supporting materials and tell how to evaluate their usefulness.**

Any of the six kinds of supporting materials can be developed from personal experience, printed resources, visual and audio resources, and other people. When evaluating possible sources, make sure that the material is related to your topic, that the sources will be perceived as credible, that the information is recent, and that the amount, kind, and complexity of the material is appropriate for your listeners.

 **Use four different methods to collect supporting materials.**

Libraries are the commonest and richest starting point for speech research. Any number and kind of supporting materials can be obtained in public and college and university libraries. An important part of library research is knowing whom and how to ask for help. You may also use your interviewing skills to compile peer and expert testimony for a speech. Information you gain from classes and instructors may greatly add to your storehouse of supporting materials and suggest ideas for speech topics. Finally, an almost unlimited amount and variety of supporting materials can be obtained from broadcast and recorded media. As with all supporting material, information recorded or quoted from the media must be accurate, complete, and properly documented in your speech.

▶ **Effectively use supporting materials to prepare and present speeches.**

In researching supporting materials for a speech, make sure the information you select will amplify, clarify, or verify your specific purpose. Adapt material so that your listeners can make clear and unambiguous connections between it and your specific purpose. Use a variety of supporting materials to make your speech more interesting and understandable to your audience members. Use the most accurate and credible sources you can find, and be sure to fulfill your ethical responsibilities by citing your sources in your speech.

## *KEY TERMS*

**analogy:** a comparison or contrasting of one object, concept, or principle with another.

**average:** a single value that represents the middle point among a number of unequal values.

**definition:** a statement of the meaning of a term or concept.

**example:** a specific instance that clarifies or dramatizes a point.

**expert testimony:** a statement made by a specialist in the topic of interest.

**figurative analogy:** a comparison or contrasting of things from different classes.

**hypothetical example:** a purely fictional incident that is devised to clarify or dramatize a point.

**illustration:**   a story, fable, or anecdote that has a theme, moral, or purpose that supports a point a speaker wishes to make.

**literal analogy:**   a comparison or contrasting of things from the same class.

**peer testimony:**   a statement made by an ordinary person who has firsthand knowledge of a subject.

**percentage:**   a statistic that indicates proportion.

**personal example:**   a firsthand experience that clarifies or dramatizes a point.

**statistics:**   numerical data that summarize facts or examples.

**supporting material:**   the definitions, examples, statistics, testimony, illustrations, and analogies that verify, amplify, and clarify the main ideas of a speech.

**testimony:**   a statement made by a third party to support an idea or position that a speaker is trying to develop.

## DISCUSSION QUESTIONS

1. Why does using a variety of types of supporting materials help you as a speaker? How does such variety boost your credibility? How does it help you maintain listener attention and interest?

2. How might your choices of types and sources of supporting materials differ for informative and persuasive speeches on the same topic? What types of supporting materials are most important to a successful speech in each case? How might your approach to locating effective supporting materials for each speech be different?

3. Think about a speech you have heard recently. Apply the six guidelines for using supporting materials effectively to that speech, and decide how well the speaker followed those guidelines. What should the speaker have done differently to effectively meet those six guidelines?

## SUGGESTED ACTIVITIES

1. Imagine that you have selected "The Value of a College Education" as a topic for your next speech. You have tentatively decided that your main points for this informative speech will be the following:

    I. Dealing with the real world
    II. Being an informed citizen
    III. Preparing for a career

List three definitions, examples, illustrations, analogies, statistics, or pieces of testimony that you may possibly use to develop these three main points. Why would each be necessary or useful in your attempt to convey the benefits of a college education to your listeners?

2. Select one item from each of the six kinds of supporting materials you listed in activity 1. For each of these six items, find and record two personal examples, two printed resources, two audio or visual resources, and two other people that can provide supporting material. Using the four criteria for evaluating sources of supporting materials, decide whether each of these twelve sources is acceptable for your speech.

3. Find and record eight items of supporting material for the speech described in activity 1—two each from a library, interviews, classes, and broadcast or recorded media. Be sure to record complete and accurate citations for each item.

4. Using the six guidelines in the final section of the chapter, assess the work that you have done in activities 1–3. How well did you conform to these guidelines as you researched and selected information for this hypothetical speech? What would you do differently if you actually had to complete this assignment for a classroom speech?

## SUGGESTED READING

William A. Haskins and Joseph M. Staudacher. (1987). *Successful Public Speaking: A Practical Guide.* (Glenview, IL: Scott, Foresman and Company).

John H. Powers. (1987). *Public Speaking: The Lively Art.* (Belmont, CA: Wadsworth Publishing Company).

Rebecca B. Rubin, Alan M. Rubin, and Linda J. Piele. (1986). *Communication Research: Strategies and Sources.* (Belmont, CA: Wadsworth Publishing Company).

# 12 Organizing Your Speech

*After studying this chapter, you should be able to:*

▶ List five advantages of effective speech organization.

▶ Properly use five patterns of speech organization.

▶ Develop a complete and well-structured outline for a speech.

▶ Compose and deliver an effective conclusion for a speech.

▶ Compose and deliver an effective introduction for a speech.

▶ Compose and properly use effective speech transitions.

So, you have a speaking engagement coming up. Like any effective public speaker, you've analyzed your audience, selected a topic, identified your specific purpose, and researched your subject area. Your next step is to combine all these preparatory steps into an organized and understandable whole, which will be your speech. In this chapter, you will learn why speech organization is an important part of speech development, as well as how to accomplish your overall objective—the presentation of an effective public speech.

The following sections will offer some suggestions for effective speech organization. They will present some general guidelines for organizing, examine several tried-and-true patterns of speech organization, and discuss several formats for structuring your thoughts on paper. Because any good speech must have a beginning and an end, some techniques for planning speech conclusions and introductions will be discussed, along with ways to tie your entire presentation together by using transitions. The first step in this process, however, is to investigate *why* organization is such a crucial step in speech preparation.

## THE IMPORTANCE OF ORGANIZING

Have you ever had someone tell you a story by starting at the end and then going back to the beginning to fill you in on the details? If so, you probably had considerable trouble following the pattern of events; and you probably had some difficulty recalling the story if you tried to retell it. These problems that arise from disorganized messages can be compounded in public speaking situations. Therefore careful organization is a "must" in five crucial areas: speech development, audience recognition of key ideas, information management, audience memory and recall, and time management.

### Speech Development

Human beings are logical, rational, thinking animals. When their thoughts and behaviors lack order, they feel uncertainty, ambiguity, and anxiety. This extends to speech preparation and presentation. Speakers who know what to say, in what order, and what to use to supplement and support their main points feel great confidence. Their audiences can follow along with greater ease and comprehension.

*Good organization benefits both a speaker and an audience.*

The objective of speech organization is to coordinate the main points with the specific purpose, and to support and expand on the main points using the information gathered during the research process. A careful planning process allows you to examine the relationships among your main points, your subpoints, and your supporting materials. It allows you to arrange them into a sequence that will enhance understanding and recall.

## Audience Recognition of Key Ideas

Human speech communication is temporary. Unless you record it and play it back, it is gone within a fraction of a second and can never be recaptured. Your purpose in speaking in public is to convey information or to influence beliefs, attitudes, values, and behavior over a period of time. If your attempts to inform or persuade are to be successful, your audience must be able to recognize your key ideas, identify the logical relationships between these ideas and your speaking purpose, and remember what you have said. Effective speech organization assists you in this regard.

## Information Management

Have you ever been a member of a group that was discussing a topic with which you were unfamiliar? The discussion was fast and furious, and other group members introduced new information faster than you could handle it. If you felt frustrated and anxious, you were probably experiencing information overload.

In a public speaking situation, unlike a small group or interpersonal situation, you can't (or shouldn't) stop a speaker and ask for a definition of terms or a summary of the last five minutes. You must hope that the speaker effectively defines terms that might be unfamiliar to you and includes internal summaries and point-to-point transitions so that you can follow what he or she is saying. In these and other ways that will be discussed later in the chapter, you can manage the information that is presented.

## Audience Memory and Recall

If you want your speech to have a lasting effect on your listeners, you must use techniques to help them remember what you have to say. The use of repetition and restatement, internal summaries, and transitions (telling listeners what is important and when you are going on to another point) must be well planned out and thoughtfully incorporated into your speech. These techniques will be discussed later in this chapter.

## Time Management

A faculty member once told of a major corporation that gave paid speakers a strict time limit for speeches at their meetings. A speaker's violation of the limit by more than thirty seconds one way or the other virtually ensured that he or she was not invited back. Although time limits for speeches may seem artificial and useless, they make you a more effective speaker.

Good organization aids time management by structuring segments of a speech so that (1) all material can be covered, (2) all main points can have balanced treatment, and (3) adequate time can be allotted for the introduction, conclusion, and a question-and-answer period if necessary. Good preparation and practice enhance time management, but if your organization is weak, all the rehearsal in the world won't help you to meet minimum or maximum time limits.

Both you and your listeners benefit when your speech is well organized. The remainder of this chapter will provide some specific suggestions to help you accomplish this task.

## GENERAL GUIDELINES FOR ORGANIZING A SPEECH

Depending on your general purpose, your topic, and your audience, each speech that you prepare should have a *unique* specific purpose. As you learned in Chapter 10, your specific purpose is your focal point for researching and selecting supporting materials. It should also serve as your focus as you organize your speech.

Once you have composed your specific purpose, write your thesis statement. This summary of your message will give direction to your speech-development efforts and provide a gauge against which to check how well your finished product has stayed on track. For example, if you are preparing an informative speech on the value of eating health foods to members of the Uptown Athletic Club you will organize and research differently from the way that you will if you are preparing a persuasive speech on the same topic for a group of expectant mothers. You will expect each audience to have different knowledge about health foods and different reasons for wanting to know more about them. In response, you will want to tailor your main ideas and supporting materials to fit each group's special needs. Each of these speeches will require a unique approach to organizing similar, but slightly different, ideas and supporting materials.

### The Sequence of Speech Development

Chapter 10 explained a six-step sequence of speech preparation. Step 5 proposed that you organize first the body of your speech, then the conclusion, and finally the introduction. This step emphasized that

*Organize a speech's body first, then the conclusion, and finally the introduction.*

*Remember [SPOBCIT] = GO when preparing a speech.*

speech preparation is a *process*—a series of interrelated steps, some of which might need reviewing and refining as each later step is completed. The following formula may help you understand this interrelatedness as it applies to the speech organization process:

$$[SPOBCIT] = GO$$

where

[ ] = take the elements within the brackets as an interrelated whole

SP = *Specific Purpose*

OB = *Organized Body*

  C = *Conclusion*

   I = *Introduction*

  T = *Transitions*

GO = *Good Organization*

Take a moment to notice several important features of this formula. First, *all* steps in the speech preparation and delivery process are not included. This chapter is about *speech organization,* so the elements of the formula pertain specifically to that task. This does not mean that the other steps are unimportant! It simply means that these are the most important elements when it comes to speech organization. Second, note that all elements within the brackets are to be taken as an interrelated whole. This means that each component is equally important to GO—Good Organization. All elements must be related to one another, must be constantly reviewed and refined, and must form a logical, understandable, and unique presentation based on your general and specific purposes, your topic, your audience, and your personal style. Third, the elements are arranged in the order in which we suggest you tackle them.

1. Your specific purpose, as *the objective* for your speaking engagement, must precede the other organizational components.
2. Once you have completed your research, you should organize the body of your speech. The body should come first because you can't introduce or conclude something if you don't know its contents.
3. Your conclusion should be tentatively composed next because, as your summary and final chance to impress the audience, it must follow logically and dramatically from the ideas you presented in the body.
4. The introduction, gauged to preview your speech and gain attention, comes next, as it is generally related to the concluding remarks.

**5.** Finally come the transitions: the connectors between the introduction and the body, between the body and the conclusion, and between the main points in the body. They are usually the last elements composed in the organization step because the speech must be nearly complete before you can connect all the pieces effectively and creatively.

Last, notice that this formula can be pronounced as a word (an acronym): [SPOBCIT] = GO. If you remember this acronym, you'll never forget how to organize a speech.

## Assembling and Sorting Ideas

The next two sections will present some patterns of speech organization and some ways to arrange your thoughts on paper. You will find those two tasks easier if you first take the following steps to assemble and sort your ideas:

**1.** After you finalize your specific purpose, write down as many related ideas as you can, each on a separate note card. This will make it easier to eliminate nonessential ideas and to organize the remaining ones.

**2.** Record *each* piece of supporting material on a separate note card along with complete and accurate information about its source. As a result, you will find it easier to shuffle data from pile to pile as you make decisions about the selection, ordering, and support of the main points in the body of your speech.

**3.** Keep *everything* related to your speech together and in good shape until after your presentation. You never know when you'll change your mind and need those note cards you threw in the garbage the night before. In addition, keeping everything together will reduce the possibility that important materials will get lost or accidentally discarded with last week's grocery list.

**4.** When you've finished your search for supporting materials, sit down with all your note cards, read each one thoroughly, and compose and write down new main points or ideas, if appropriate. Then, *and only then,* begin to select and organize ideas for the body of your speech. You must know what you have to work with before you can make any decisions about the inclusion or exclusion of ideas or materials and how to arrange them as main and supporting points.

The most important piece of advice is to *be as accurate, complete, and thorough as you possibly can be.* The need for accuracy, completeness, and thoroughness is primary if you are to be an effective speaker.

*Be as accurate, complete, and thorough as you can be while preparing a speech.*

## PATTERNS OF ORGANIZATION

No matter what methods you use in preparing a speech, you must eventually choose some pattern of organization. Such structure assists you in speech development and delivery, and assists your audience in listening, comprehending, and remembering what you have said. This section will present five of the most common patterns of speech organization. Remember that each may be used to provide structure for a variety of speech purposes and approaches. Use the pattern (or combination of patterns) that will work best for you.

### The Chronological Pattern

*The chronological pattern is organized around time sequences.*

As you might guess, the **chronological pattern** arranges ideas according to a time sequence. A how-to presentation or an explanation of a historical event or a social or political movement frequently fits well into a chronological pattern. Any series of ideas that listeners will best understand and follow in terms of time is best organized in this fashion.

Suppose you have just been asked to present a twenty-minute speech entitled "How to Secure Investment Capital for Starting Your Own Business" at the monthly luncheon meeting of your local Rotary Club. You know that there are five basic steps in the process and that you will need to cover all of them in your presentation. You search your memory for the five steps and write them down as you think of them: closing the deal, identifying potential sources of money, writing a business plan, making contacts and selling your plan, evaluating and ranking potential sources.

The body of your speech is now organized, right? WRONG! All five steps are recorded, but most of your listeners will get lost early in the speech if you maintain the order of your ideas as you've listed them. Instead try a chronological pattern of organization:

    I.  Writing a business plan
   II.  Identifying potential sources of money
 III.  Evaluating and ranking sources
 IV.  Making contact and selling your plan
   V.  Closing the deal

### The Spatial Pattern

Imagine that you have been successful in obtaining a loan to build a new building for your manufacturing enterprise and that you are scheduled to make an oral presentation to a group of architects to explain how you want your building designed. How would you organize this speech?

Try the **spatial pattern,** which uses geographical or physical layout as its organizing principle. Your organization for the speech may look something like this:

*Speeches organized around physical layout use a spatial pattern.*

    I. Northeast corner—office, with an entrance for office staff and customers on one wall
   II. Northwest corner—restrooms, employee lunchroom and lounge, shop foreman's office
 III. Southwest corner—tool room and parts area
 IV. Southeast corner—shipping and receiving
   V. Remainder of south half of building— assembly and finishing areas

By systematically describing your imagined floor plan, you can help the architects visualize the space and how you plan to use it.

## The Topical Pattern

When a speech's content doesn't neatly follow either a chronological or a spatial pattern, try a topical pattern. A **topical pattern** organizes an idea based on order of importance (most important to least important), an acronym (KISS, Keep It Short and Simple), a formula ([SPOBCIT = GO), or some other logical, understandable, and meaningful device.

*The topical pattern may use importance, an acronym, or a formula as the organizing principle.*

Suppose that you had not yet decided *where* each department should be located in your new building. You might then choose to use a topical pattern of organization to detail only the needed departments and the approximate space requirements for each. In that case, the outline of your main points might look something like this:

    I. Office space (1500 square feet)
   II. Assembly and finishing (5000 square feet)
 III. Restrooms/Lounge/Shop (200 square feet)
 IV. Tools/Parts Room (500 square feet)
   V. Shipping/Receiving (1000 square feet)

From this presentation, the architects can understand your needs and begin to develop some appropriate designs.

It is important that you include in your topical pattern all the main points in a sequence that will *not* confuse or distract your listeners. If an acronym, formula, or other creative device can be used, fine. Otherwise, simply make sure that you explain all the important points in an organized and effective manner.

## The Problem-Solution Pattern

The **problem-solution pattern** of organization can be used appropriately for either informative or persuasive speeches. At a minimum, this pattern includes the statement of a problem and the presentation of at least one possible solution.

Suppose you were giving an informative speech to a production team in a large corporation. You might want to identify a problem with the quality of one of your products, emphasize its seriousness by citing some examples, and list some probable causes. You might suggest some possible solutions, but your objective would be to have the team solve the problem on its own. In other words, you would want to *inform* the production managers about the problem, rather than *persuade* them that a particular solution was the right one. Such a speech might be organized as follows:

    I. Breakage of plastic chair casters
   II. Returns from twenty-seven customers in last six months
 III. Possible solutions
     A. Change supplier for plastic casters
     B. Change to metal casters
     C. Redesign chair legs

You may also use the problem-solution pattern in a persuasive speech. Then you would want to persuade your listeners that a particular solution would be most effective for eliminating a problem and motivate them to take the steps that you suggest. Thus, if you were dealing with the same product-quality dilemma described earlier, after defining the problem, you might try to persuade the production team to change the design of the chair legs to reduce stress on the casters. In this situation, your speech outline may look like this:

    I. Fragile plastic chair casters
   II. Returns from twenty-seven customers in last six months
 III. Possible solutions
     A. Change supplier for plastic casters
     B. Change to metal casters
     C. Redesign chair legs
 IV. Defense of redesign as best solution
     A. High quality of present casters
     B. Stress caused by design of chair legs
     C. Redesign as simplest and least expensive solution

Presenting the problem and then supporting a particular response is an equally acceptable form of the problem-solution pattern of organization.

## The Cause-Effect Pattern

When you describe a past, present, or future situation and discuss one or more causes of that state of affairs, you are using the **cause-effect pattern** of organization. When this pattern is used, it does not matter whether causes or effects are mentioned first.

For example, in an informative speech entitled "Clean Air in the United States by the Year 2000," you might first discuss three predominant *causes* of decreasing air pollution over the last ten years. Then you would probably want to detail one or more *effects* of decreased air pollution. In such a case, your outline would be constructed as follows:

I. Causes of decreasing air pollution
   A. Increased awareness of air pollution
   B. More car pooling
   C. Stricter enforcement of the Clean Air Act
II. Effects of decreased air pollution
   A. Less lung disease
   B. Higher energy costs

Your topic and specific purpose may indicate that effects should be discussed before causes. For instance, suppose that you want to persuade a group of parents to seek help for their teenagers if certain danger signs arise. You may begin by pointing out the increasing suicide rate among adolescents and teenagers and citing some statistics and examples *(effects)*. Then, you might suggest several of the presumed *causes* of these increases and cite the behaviors identified as possible danger signs. Finally, you might provide a list of people and organizations that are available for help. An outline of your speech would include:

I. Troubled behavior in adolescents and teens
   A. Increasing rate of adolescent suicide
   B. Increasing percentage of adolescents reporting experience with drugs
   C. Higher percentage of teenagers with arrest records
II. Causes of troubled behavior
   A. Increased peer pressure
   B. Decreased parental discipline
   C. Wider availability of drugs
III. People and organizations that can help

**Patterns of Speech Organization**

| *Pattern* | *Organizing Principle(s)* |
|---|---|
| **Chronological** | Arrange main points in the order that events or steps occur in time. |
| **Spatial** | Arrange main points according to geographical or physical layout. |
| **Topical** | Arrange main points in a logical order according to their importance. Arrange using a memorable acronym, formula, or some other understandable and meaningful device. |
| **Problem-Solution** | Arrange main points, stating a problem and at least one possible solution. In an informative speech, include the existence of the problem, support for its existence, and a number of possible solutions. In a persuasive speech, include support for the problem's existence, a number of possible solutions, and the preferred solution and support for its acceptance. |
| **Cause-Effect** | Arrange main points by describing a situation or set of conditions and discussing one or more causes of that state of affairs. Discuss cause(s) first and then effect(s), or effect(s) first, followed by cause(s). |

Note that the cause-effect pattern is still present. Only the *order* is changed.

You probably noticed that the final point in this speech to parents offers one possible *solution* to the problem of increasing teenage suicide—enlisting the assistance of outside individuals and organizations. Thus, its design actually combines the cause-effect *and* the problem-solution patterns of organization. This practice is not unusual. It is frequently necessary or advisable to combine two patterns, because you may find that one is not exactly what you need. Be creative! Use whatever works best for you, given your particular topic and perspective.

## ORGANIZING THE BODY

Once you understand and can use the organizational patterns, you're ready to start arranging your speech on paper. You can just list everything you want to say in the order you want to say it or, to express yourself most effectively, you can provide more structure. As you speak, you'll need to know what's related to what, what to emphasize and deemphasize, and when and how to get from one point to another. One of the most common and easy-to-understand methods of providing this structure is an outline.

### Fundamentals of Outlining

An **outline** is a written, formally structured set of interrelated ideas and information used to describe the contents of a written or oral presentation. The simplest outline for a presentation takes the following form:

*The preferred way of organizing ideas is to do an outline.*

I.  Introduction
II. Body
III. Conclusion

Of course, this outline is not very helpful because it's so vague. It doesn't tell anything about the topic, the organizational pattern of the body, or the content of the speech. A truly useful outline will give all the detail a speaker needs to deliver a successful presentation.

*Main points* form the most general level of speech structure. Thus, ideas designated with Roman numerals can be identified quickly as main points. Each main point is usually explained, illustrated, or supported in some manner by subpoints, and those subpoints, in turn, are usually supported by even more specific subpoints. The levels of support and support-for-support that you will use in your speech can be organized into an outline using the following set of indentions and symbols:

I. _____
  A. _____
  B. _____
    1. _____
    2. _____
      a. _____
      b. _____
        (1) _____
        (2) _____
          (a) _____
          (b) _____
II. _____

Note that good outlining form requires that if you have an A, you *must* have a B, and if you have a 1, you *must* have a 2. Subpoints A and B *subdivide* and *support or explain* Roman numeral I; you can't subdivide something into *one* piece.

The ideas in an outline can be written in *one* of three forms: complete sentences, phrases, or words. A single idea expressed in these three forms would look like this:

    Sentence:  Good cooks know how to select spices that
                      complement the foods they are cooking.
    Phrase:     Selection of spices
    Word:       Spices

Be consistent in your form. If you start with complete sentences, use complete sentences throughout.

## Three Principles of Outlining

In addition to using the correct system of symbols and maintaining a single form of expression throughout, make sure that your outline conforms to the principles of division, subordination, and parallelism.

*Division means only one idea to an entry.*

**Division.**  According to the principle of **division,** each entry in an outline must contain one and only one idea. Thus, if you decide to divide the body of your speech into four main points, each one must be presented in a separate entry (numbered I, II, III, IV) and discussed separately.

As you develop your outline, double-check your use of the words *and* and *or*. Make sure that you aren't unintentionally combining two points into one. For example, you are outlining a speech entitled "Investing in Thoroughbred Horses" and one of your main points is *buying and training horses*. You haven't conformed to the principle of division, because *buying* and *training* are two distinct ideas. You need to treat them as two separate points.

**Investing in Thoroughbred Horses**

Incorrect:
   I.  Buying and training thoroughbred horses
Correct:
   I.  Buying thoroughbred horses
  II.  Training thoroughbred horses

This principle holds true for subpoints as well. If you're going to support a point using two examples, you must put each example in a separate subpoint.

After gathering your notes, you will want to organize your thoughts into an outline.

**Subordination.** Effective outlining also requires that you observe the principle of **subordination**—that is, each subpoint at any level of an outline is related to and adds more specific information about the more general point above it. In the previous example, if your first main point is *I. Buying thoroughbred horses,* subpoints A and B might be *Identifying sellers* and *Criteria for selection.*

*Each subpoint adds more specific information about the point preceding it.*

### Investing in Thoroughbred Horses

Incorrect:
    I. Buying thoroughbred horses: identifying sellers
    II. Buying thoroughbred horses: criteria for selection
Incorrect:
    I. Buying thoroughbred horses: identifying sellers
      A. Criteria for selection
Correct:
    I. Buying thoroughbred horses
      A. Identifying sellers
      B. Criteria for selection

Both of these subpoints are more *specific* and *add further information about* the process of buying thoroughbred horses. Thus, points A and B are *subordinate* to point I.

**Parallelism.**   Finally, according to the principle of **parallelism,** all items at the same level of an outline must be at approximately the same level of specificity. This requirement does *not* imply that all main points must be developed to the same level of detail, nor does it suggest that all points must have the same number of subpoints. It simply means that *all A's, B's, and C's must contain information that has a similar amount of detail.* Likewise, all 1s, 2s, and 3s must be similar in their level of specificity.

For instance, in your speech about investing in thoroughbred horses, the following outline does not conform to the principle of parallelism:

  I. Buying thoroughbred horses
   A. Identifying sellers
   B. Criteria for selection
  II. Training thoroughbred horses
   A. Daily exercise routines
   B. Prerace exercise routines

Points IIA and IIB add much more specificity to point II than points IA and IB add to point I. Much more goes into training horses than just exercise. The following outline of points I and II more closely conforms to the principle of parallelism:

  I. Buying thoroughbred horses
   A. Identifying sellers
   B. Criteria for selection
  II. Training thoroughbred horses
   A. Boarding the horses
   B. Exercising the horses

Subpoints A and B under II coincide more with the level of detail in subpoints A and B under I.

A complete outline for the body of our example would look like this:

### Investing in Thoroughbred Horses

  I. Buying thoroughbred horses
   A. Identifying sellers
   B. Criteria for selection
   C. Price expectations
  II. Training thoroughbred horses
   A. Boarding the horses
   B. Exercising the horses

   III. Racing thoroughbred horses
      A. Racing classifications
      B. Selecting race locations
      C. Finding jockeys
   IV. Making the most of your investment
      A. Costs of investing
      B. Profit expectations
      C. Investment-related taxes

## Checking Your Outline

Once you have completed a preliminary outline for the body of your speech, check to make sure that you have met the following criteria:

1. Do all items in the outline contribute to the successful accomplishment of your oral presentation?
2. Are all subpoints relevant to and explain, illustrate, or in some way support the more general points above them?
3. Is the form of all items (sentence, phrase, or word) consistent throughout the outline?
4. Do all items in the outline contain *one and only one idea* (division)?
5. Does each subpoint and sub-subpoint contain *more detail and a higher degree of specificity* than the more general point above it (subordination)?
6. Do all items *at the same level* provide *the same amount of detail and specificity* (parallelism)?

If you can answer these questions positively, your outline will put you well on the road to a successful speaking performance.

## CONCLUDING YOUR SPEECH

Your **conclusion** is your final chance to reinforce the ideas you covered in the body and to leave the audience with a memorable impression. As a general rule, your conclusion should take up no more than 5 to 10 percent of your total speaking time. This means that it will be relatively short in comparison to the body. Given the many things you need to accomplish and the short amount of time you have, you will need to plan your conclusion carefully.

## The Functions of a Conclusion

To be most effective, your speech conclusion should serve four functions. It should:

1. restate your main points;
2. relate your main points to the specific purpose;
3. dramatically implant your central idea in your listeners' minds; and
4. tell your listeners what you want them to think or do.

*A conclusion restates the main points and relates them to the specific purpose.*

In any speech, you'll have three opportunities to reinforce your main ideas—in the introduction, in the body, and in the conclusion. Because the conclusion comes last, it is your final chance to drive your message home. You will therefore want to *restate your main points* briefly but clearly. At the same time, you can *relate your main points to your specific purpose.* For example, suppose that the four main points in your speech about investing in thoroughbred horses were the following:

I. Buying thoroughbred horses
II. Training thoroughbred horses
III. Racing thoroughbred horses
IV. Making the most of your investment

If your specific purpose is "At the end of my speech, the audience should be able to give four reasons why investing in thoroughbred horses can be fun and profitable," you will want to emphasize that in your conclusion. Thus, you might say:

> *Purchasing horses can be educational, training is a lot of fun, and racing your horses can be a thrilling experience. But you must use wisdom and caution if you want to make the most of your investment. Overall, investing in thoroughbred horses is one of the most exciting and profitable ventures that I can imagine.*

You also want to use your conclusion to *dramatically place your main idea in the minds of your listeners.* Thus, to plant an unforgettable image in your audience's imagination, you might add:

> *Nothing can beat the thrill of seeing your own horse cross the finish line first, unless it's collecting the first-place purse.*

Finally, you want to *tell your listeners what you want them to think or do.* Given your informative purpose, you may finish your conclusion by saying:

> *The thrill of victory is an unforgettable feeling. I hope you can see why I think thoroughbred horses are a good investment, at least for me.*

## Concluding Devices

There are a number of strategies for concluding a speech. Certainly a review of your main points and a restatement of your specific purpose is a dependable standby. By using your creativity, however, you can design a conclusion that performs the required functions while also increasing the interest and impact of your speech. The six most common concluding devices are summaries, illustrations, humorous statements, quotations, appeals to emotions, and appeals to action. In most cases, you will want to combine two or more of these devices in your conclusion.

**Summaries.**   A summary offers one or more statements that bring together the main content of a speech. The following is a concluding summary for an informative speech on applying for financial aid:

> *Applying for financial aid can be a time-consuming and frustrating task. If you know where to look for sources, fill out the forms correctly the first time, and maintain contact with financial offices, however, success will be yours.*

**Illustrations.**   Chapter 11 discussed the way to use an illustration as supporting material. An illustration may also be used to conclude a speech. Recall that an *illustration* is a story, fable, or anecdote that has a theme, moral, or purpose that supports a point you wish to communicate or reinforce. Given that one of your goals in a conclusion is to reinforce previously stated ideas, an appropriate illustration may be very helpful. For instance, a speech encouraging students to participate as volunteers in the "Meals on Wheels" program may be concluded as follows:

> *A friend of mine has worked as a volunteer in this program for two years. Once, when he was delivering evening meals, an elderly woman opened her door with tears in her eyes. My friend discovered that she had forgotten to buy her son a birthday card. Because he was nearly done with his route, he offered to stop at the drugstore. When he returned with the card, the woman was so grateful that she told him to keep the change. Seventy-one cents was a less important reward for my friend than the woman's broad smile and warm thank-you. At times like these, the intangible rewards are immeasurable.*

**Humorous statements.**   Not everyone can tell a joke well, and not all speech topics lend themselves to humorous endings. If a humorous comment is related to your topic and if you can deliver the

George Bush making an appeal to his listeners' emotions.

comment effectively, you will probably leave your audience with a favorable impression. Thus, in closing a speech about seeking and using legal advice you might say:

> *Remember, check your local bar association for information about the reputation and specialties of lawyers in your area. Don't forget to shop for price, as well. Anyone who has ever talked to a lawyer knows that talk doesn't come cheap.*

**Quotations.**   Extracts from literature or others' speeches often make strong endings. For instance, the words of the late president John F. Kennedy might add power to the conclusion of a recruiting speech for the Peace Corps:

> *Government service provides excellent opportunities for foreign travel, superior salary and retirement benefits, and exciting work. In addition, you will be serving your country in one of the most prestigious ways possible. "And so my fellow Americans," as John F. Kennedy said, "ask not what your country can do for you; ask what you can do for your country."*

**Appeals to emotions.**   Many speeches can be effectively concluded with appeals to listeners' feelings of fear, sympathy, patriotism,

William Jennings Bryan
on the campaign trail,
inspiring his audience to
action.

or excitement. Such emotional appeals are especially useful when a
speaker hopes to encourage a specific way of thinking or acting. A
speech soliciting donations to an African hunger relief fund might close
with the following appeal to emotions:

> *Listen to the cries of the thousands of hungry children in Africa,
> and remember the photo of the village children with bloated
> bellies who subsist on dry rice and contaminated water.
> Remember the thousands of children who die every day of hunger
> and malnutrition.*

**Appeals to action.**   Much like appeals to emotions, appeals to
action encourage listeners to become involved. In these cases listeners
are asked to take specific actions. Campaign, recruiting, and fund-
raising speeches commonly attempt to inspire audience members to
action. For instance, a campaign speech might conclude as follows:

> *Remember, a vote for Smith is a vote for lower taxes, reduced
> defense spending, better social programs, and truth in
> government. If you want to keep more of your hard-earned
> dollars in your own pocket, on election day pull the lever for
> Smith.*

As you organize your speech, you may find that the best approach is to write several different conclusions and select the one that best suits your topic, your audience, and your specific purpose. Then be sure to practice your conclusion until you can present it without notes. You want to put all your energy into delivering your closing remarks, not into trying to remember them.

## INTRODUCING YOUR SPEECH

Even a speech with a beautifully polished body and conclusion may falter if it lacks a purposeful introduction. A strong opening is crucial, because a speaker who loses an audience's attention at the start will probably have a hard time regaining interest as time passes. You can avoid this problem if you understand the basic functions of an introduction and use them to your advantage.

### The Functions of an Introduction

Much like a conclusion, an introduction serves four functions:

1. to gain listeners' attention;
2. to state a speech's specific purpose;
3. to preview a speech's content; and
4. to establish a speaker's credibility.

The overall success of your speech greatly depends on your ability to construct an introduction that serves these four functions.

Most audience members automatically tune in to a speaker in the beginning and tune out later. To entice your audience into listening to your entire speech, your opening comments need to be so compelling that everyone wants to hear more. "Imagine that you could make $10,000 a year in part-time work." This would certainly *capture your listeners' interest* right away!

Once you have the audience's attention, you can *define your specific purpose* and *outline the main ideas to listen for in your speech.* As you did in your conclusion, try to create a clear, but concise, series of comments that consumes no more than 5 to 10 percent of your total speaking time. For example, you might continue your introduction by saying:

> *I find investing in thoroughbred horses exciting and profitable, and I hope that you'll soon understand why I feel that way. Buying horses, training them, getting them on the racetrack, and trying to make the most of my investment are all exciting challenges for me.*

Finally, *establish your credibility as a speaker on your topic* with your introduction. Refer to the amount of research you have done or the amount of training or experience you have in the field.

> *My father has raced thoroughbreds for more than ten years. In the three years that I've been training and racing Quickfoot, I've earned nearly $25,000.*

A good introduction will preview your speech and help you establish credibility.

## Introductory Devices

Some of the devices discussed in the section on conclusions may also be used in introductions. Remember, the keys to a good introduction are to *pique interest* and *provide a preview.* You can often accomplish both tasks by using startling statements, questions, illustrations, and personal experiences.

**Startling statements.**   Citing emotion-laden or unusual statistics or facts is often a good way to gain attention. At the same time, take care not to shock or offend your listeners, as this may cost you their attention. In a speech about the advantages of using seat belts, you might use a fact discussed in the previous chapter:

> *The equivalent of the total population of Palo Alto, California, died in traffic accidents last year. Yes, 55,000 people died in automobile accidents in one year, and it is estimated that 20 to 25 percent of them would have been alive today if they had been wearing seat belts. Seat belts can save your life, or at least reduce the severity of your injuries, but only if you use them.*

**Questions.**   Another way to encourage your audience's involvement is to ask them thought-provoking questions that preview your speech's content. Thus, you might open by saying:

> *How much is it worth to you to prolong your life by one year? By two years? By five years? By possibly ten years? A regular program of exercise can not only prolong your life, but also increase your alertness and your resistance to some common illnesses.*

**Illustration.**   Stories of various kinds, if they are related to your topic, can fulfill several functions of an introduction. If used properly, they can gain attention, establish your specific purpose, preview your main points, and establish your credibility.

> *Last summer I worked as an intern in a dentist's office. One day a woman brought her seven-year-old daughter in for her first*

*checkup ever. During the exam, I could see that many of the girl's teeth were decayed or missing, and her gums were red and swollen. By the end of that appointment, I was convinced that proper dental hygiene and regular dental checkups prevent tooth decay and gum disease, enhance personal appearance, and preserve general health by enabling proper eating. And I hope that soon you, too, will be convinced.*

**Personal experience.**   Personal experiences used in an introduction can establish your credibility and gain attention. For example, in a speech to a group of parents to encourage their involvement in the local PTA, you might open by telling a personal experience:

*When I was in elementary school, our playground was bare. We had no basketball hoops, no ladders or gym bars, and no hard surfaces to play games on—at least, not until several parents and teachers joined together to raise funds for playground improvements. The birth of the PTA and the activities it sponsored made my later grade-school years enjoyable and memorable. I'll never forget what fun we had both during school hours and after. You, too, can take an active role in making your school children's days enjoyable and memorable by becoming involved in the activities of the Washington Elementary School PTA.*

## MAKING TRANSITIONS

*Transitions link ideas and direct thinking processes.*

**Transitions** are words, phrases, or sentences that join ideas together, show relationships between two or more ideas, and direct listeners' thought processes in the direction you want them to go. They are the cement that hold speeches together. Thus, transitions are another vital component of an effective presentation.

Transitions may *join ideas together* by providing links between two main points and the specific purpose, or between two subpoints and a main point. For example, in explaining why the national trade deficit must be reduced, an economist might change from talking about lower unemployment to discussing the value of the dollar by saying:

*A reduction in our trade deficit will* not only *lower unemployment,* but *will* also *increase the value of the dollar abroad.*

In other cases, transitions *show the relationship between ideas*. If a school board member were trying to muster voters' support for a new high school, the school board member might use transitions to list related ideas:

> There are three reasons why *we need to build a new high school: overcrowding, safety, and location*. First, *West High School is designed for only eight hundred students, and its current enrollment exceeds nine hundred*. . . .

Finally, effective transitions help *signal that a speaker is changing ideas* and *that the listeners should pay particularly close attention if they hope to follow the speaker's train of thought*. If a transition is used to draw attention to a *speaker's* change in thought, it should automatically point *listeners'* thought processes in the appropriate direction. For example, a mayor may help town council members follow along by saying:

> We have considered *two reasons why we need an increase in property taxes,* so we'll go on to discuss *the third: our community's need for increased public transportation*.

## Transitional Devices

You may not have considered the words *but, because,* and *however* as transitions; nonetheless, they are. Note the way the previous sentence works as a transition. First it directs your attention to the three words *but, because,* and *however*. Then it encourages you to examine your thinking about those three words. Finally it uses the word *nonetheless* as a transition to point your thought processes in the desired direction. Of course, there are far too many possible transitions to include in this book, but the following are some of the most common words and phrases that will help you tie your thoughts together:

| | | |
|---|---|---|
| on the other hand | for example | likewise |
| however | again | so |
| but | in addition | while |
| all in all | then | since |
| also | therefore | specifically |
| finally | because | yet |
| although | nevertheless | in other words |

The most crucial positions for effective transitions are between the introduction and the body, and between the body and the conclusion.

Returning to the example, "Investing in Thoroughbred Horses," an effective transition between the introduction and the first main point in the body—*buying thoroughbred horses*—might be as follows:

> *My father has raced thoroughbreds for more than ten years. In the three years I've been training and racing Quickfoot, I've earned nearly $25,000.*
> *The first crucial step in smart investing is learning how to buy the right horse. . . .*

Similarly, the audience can be alerted that the last subpoint is finished and the conclusion is beginning.

> *Smart investing practices and knowledge of the current tax laws can minimize your end-of-the-year outlay to the IRS. And that makes all the long hours of training, traveling, and bookkeeping well worth the effort.*
> *Purchasing horses can be educational, training is a lot of fun, and racing your horses can be a thrilling experience. . . .*

Your audience members must recognize when you change ideas and be able to follow your train of thought. The best way to ensure that they grasp key relationships in your speech is to use clear transitions.

## SUMMARY

Effective speech organization aids both speakers and listeners. No matter what the nature of your topic, your audience, your general and specific purposes, and your supporting material, a coherent pattern of organization is absolutely essential.

▶ **List five advantages of effective speech organization.**

Effective organization helps a speaker develop a speech, assists listeners to recognize key ideas, enables a speaker to manage information more effectively, aids audience memory and recall, and makes it easier for a speaker to manage speaking time.

▶ **Properly use five patterns of speech organization.**

Your pattern of organization should be carefully matched to the nature of your topic and the approach you plan to take. The *chronological sequence* works well when your main points can be arranged according to time. The *spatial pattern* may be appropriate if it is important for your audience to understand geography or physical layout. The *topical pattern* organizes ideas according to order of importance, an acronym, a formula, or some other logical device. The *problem-solution format* identifies a source of concern and suggests at least one possible response. With this format, you may leave the final choice of solution up to the audience or explicitly advocate a specific course of action. And finally, the *cause-effect pattern* describes a situation and discusses one or more of the factors that led to its existence. Depending on the topic, either causes or effects may be examined first.

As you organize your speech, you may find that no single pattern perfectly suits your purposes. In that case, you may want to combine two or more patterns.

▶ **Develop a complete and well-structured outline.**

An outline is a written, formally structured set of interrelated ideas and information. It is the preferred method of speech development and organization, because it forces a speaker to consider relationships among ideas and their order. A good outline conforms to the principles of division, subordination, and parallelism.

▶ **Compose and deliver an effective conclusion.**

For an effective conclusion include four ideas: restate your main points, relate your main points to the specific purpose, dramatically implant your central idea in your listeners' minds, and tell your listeners what you want them to think or do. You may close your speech with a summary, illustration, humorous statement, quotation, appeal to emotions, or appeal to action.

▶ **Compose and deliver an effective introduction.**

A good introduction will gain listeners' attention, state your specific purpose, preview your speech's content, and establish your credibility. Startling statements, questions, illustrations, and personal experiences, in addition to the devices commonly used in concluding, may all contribute to a strong introduction.

▶ **Compose and properly use effective speech transitions.**

*Transitions* are words, phrases, or sentences that join ideas together, show relationships between ideas, and direct listeners' thinking. The most critical places for transitions are between the introduction and the body, between the body and the conclusion, and between main points. Clear transitions are also needed whenever a change in ideas occurs.

## KEY TERMS

**cause-effect pattern:** a pattern of speech organization that describes a past, present, or future situation and discusses one or more causes of that state of affairs.

**chronological pattern:** a pattern of speech organization that arranges ideas according to a time sequence.

**conclusion:** the final chance a speaker has in a speech to summarize and reinforce the ideas covered in the body of the speech and to leave the audience with a memorable impression.

**division:** a principle of outlining which requires that each entry in an outline contain one and only one idea.

**outline:** a written, formally structured set of interrelated ideas and information used to describe the contents of a written or oral presentation.

**parallelism:** a principle of outlining which requires that all items at the same level of an outline be at approximately the same level of specificity.

**problem-solution pattern:** a pattern of speech organization that includes the statement of a problem and the presentation of at least one possible solution.

**spatial pattern:** a pattern of speech organization that uses geographical or physical layout as its organizing principle.

**subordination:** a principle of outlining which requires that each subpoint at any level of the outline be related to and add more specific information about the more general point above it.

**topical pattern:** a pattern of speech organization that organizes ideas based on order of importance, an acronym, a formula, or some other logical, understandable, and meaningful device.

**transition:** words, phrases, or sentences that join ideas together, show relationships between two or more ideas, and direct listeners' thought processes in the direction a speaker wants them to go.

## DISCUSSION QUESTIONS

1. How do you respond to a speaker who seems to aimlessly go from point to point? In contrast, how does effective speech organization assist you in understanding and remembering key points in a speech?

2. When using an outline to prepare for a speaking assignment, you are forced to use the visual mode of communication. What effect does using the visual mode have on organizing your thinking and orally presenting your speech? What advantages

and disadvantages does this dependence on the visual mode provide when delivering your speech?

3. How are specific concluding and introductory devices related to your speech topic? What questions about your topic should you ask yourself to help you make productive decisions about the specific devices to use? How would your choice of specific devices differ for informative and persuasive speeches on the same topic?

## SUGGESTED ACTIVITIES

1. Select a speech topic from the list.
     Nuclear Power Plants
     Inflation
     Term Life Insurance
     Higher Education
     AIDS
     Political Campaigns
     Crime in Your Community
   a. Write a specific purpose statement and a thesis statement for the topic.
   b. Identify at least three main points for the topic.
   c. Select an appropriate pattern of organization for the speech.
2. Find a transcript of a speech in a recent edition of *Vital Speeches of the Day* or a similar publication. Outline the speech in proper form and identify its pattern of organization.
3. Using the speech topic you chose in activity 1, write three possible conclusions, each using a different concluding device.
4. Using the speech topic you chose in activity 1, write three possible introductions, each using a different introductory device.
5. Using the results of activities 1–4, write effective transition statements between the introduction and first main point, between each succeeding pair of main points, and between the last main point and the conclusion.

## SUGGESTED READINGS

James Gibson. (1971). *Speech Organization: A Programmed Approach.* (San Francisco: Rinehart Press.).
Judy L. Haynes. (1981). *Organizing a Speech: A Programmed Guide,* 2nd ed. (Englewood Cliffs, NJ: Prentice-Hall).

# 13 | Delivering Your Speech

*After studying this chapter, you should be able to:*

▶ Outline the advantages and disadvantages of four styles of speech delivery.

▶ Use nonverbal codes to complement your verbal message.

▶ Select and use visual aids that will enhance your presentation.

▶ Rehearse a speech both physically and mentally.

The first five elements of planning and preparing a speech—audience analysis, topic selection, general and specific purposes, supporting materials, and patterns of organization—have already been covered. This chapter will discuss the actual, physical presentation of a speech—various styles of delivery, some nonverbal cues that enhance delivery, the use of visual aids, and several specific tips on effective speaking.

## STYLES OF DELIVERY

Students who are new to public speaking frequently ask two questions: "Do we have to write our own speeches?" and "Do we have to memorize them?" These questions reflect expectations based on the type of public speaking to which people are most frequently exposed—the televised political speech. Indeed, politicians often appear to be reading their speeches or to have memorized their material. (In the latter case, they are probably reading from a teleprompter.)

While some speeches may be appropriately read or memorized, most speaking situations call for styles of delivery that are more flexible and adaptable. The three styles of delivery in addition to reading are memorization, impromptu speaking, and extemporaneous speaking.

### Reading

The most important reason that politicians read their speeches is that politicians are speaking for the public record. Often they have provided copies of their speeches to members of the media beforehand. Excerpts will be quoted in newspapers or played on television and radio news programs (or, at least, so the politicians hope). In such situations, it is crucial that words be chosen carefully and delivered faithfully. The written and spoken texts of the speech must match, because the audience includes not only those present, but those not present.

*A written manuscript is important only when you are speaking for the public record.*

This style of delivery (also called **manuscript speaking** because it relies on a full written transcript of the speech) is important to master *only* if it is likely that you will be speaking for the record. Otherwise, you are best advised to avoid it, because its disadvantages usually far outweigh its benefits.

The greatest disadvantage of speaking from a manuscript is that it locks you into a single structure and time limit. Any experienced public speaker knows that the amount of time allotted to a speech is not always predictable, particularly if there are several speakers on the program. In this case, the words of one of our former professors seem to provide the only guidance: "The amount of time you have to speak varies inversely with your position on the program."[1] A thirty-minute manuscript is difficult to deliver in the seven-minute spot remaining at the end of a multispeaker meeting.

Second, it is extremely difficult to speak well when relying on a manuscript. Central to an effective public speech is the relationship between a speaker and an audience. When a speech is read, a third element—a manuscript—is introduced into the relationship. A speaker's attention must then be divided between the audience and the written text. As a result, eye contact is usually greatly reduced; there is a loss of rapport and speaker credibility. The speaker's ability to monitor the audience's response and adapt accordingly is diminished as well. In short, listeners may feel alienated because a speaker is reading *to* them, rather than speaking *with* them. These are not desirable outcomes, and only the most skilled manuscript speakers are able to avoid them.

*Spoken English is different from written English.*

Finally, there is a difference between written and spoken language that must be overcome if a manuscript speech is to sound like anything other than an "essay on its hind legs." To experience the difference between speaking and writing, try to read one of your term papers aloud in a way that sounds as if you are speaking spontaneously, as if you have just thought of the words for the first time. Chances are you will be unable to.

You do not normally write as you speak. If you have ever seen unedited transcripts of an interview or testimony in a hearing, you have seen a dramatic illustration of this. If you *must* prepare a manuscript from which to speak, there are certain characteristics that you can incorporate to make it sound more like naturally spoken English. These include:

> short and simple words;
>
> short and simple sentences;
>
> more use of questions;
>
> more personal pronouns;
>
> more contractions of words;
>
> more use of colloquial expressions;
>
> frequent use of transitions;
>
> repetition;
>
> internal summaries; and
>
> more direct adaptation to the immediate audience.[2]

## Memorization

There was a time when virtually all formal public speeches were memorized. In the days before radio, television, and motion pictures became commonplace, public speaking was a primary source of entertainment. Oratory was considered an art form; training consisted of studying the great orators, memorizing their speeches, and emulating their movements and gestures. While there is some merit to the notion that observing and practicing new behaviors improves one's own delivery, the usual result of this old-fashioned training is a more or less mechanical performance, one that looks more like a caricature of a speech than a speech itself.

Today, audiences find memorized words and gestures phony, unless they are delivered so artfully that they appear natural—a level of achievement reached by very few. Also, like a manuscript speech, a memorized speech lacks flexibility and adaptability. Finally, there is the danger of forgetting part of the speech, a danger that can only increase a speaker's anxiety level. Therefore, in most cases, memorizing a speech is just as unsatisfactory as reading it.

*Memorized speeches tend to sound stilted and unnatural.*

## Impromptu Speaking

**Impromptu speaking** is delivering a speech using no notes or preparation. If you think about it, you'll realize that this is really the most common form of public speaking. When you state your position at a meeting or answer a question in class, you are actually making a short impromptu speech—a speech for which you have had little or no time to prepare, no chance to do research, and no opportunity to rehearse. These situations test your ability to think on your feet, and to organize and present your thoughts effectively.

The one advantage to the impromptu style of delivery is its spontaneity—you are unlikely to sound stale or overrehearsed. In addition, impromptu speaking ability can be of considerable value to you during question-and-answer periods following a speech. The lack of adequate time to analyze an audience, research, and prepare, however, argue against the use of this style in formal speaking situations, except in emergencies.

## Extemporaneous Speaking

In **extemporaneous speaking,** a speaker prepares remarks in advance, but delivers them without relying on a manuscript or memorization. Because the extemporaneous style of delivery combines the

## Review Box

### A Summary of Delivery Styles

*Reading*

| | |
|---|---|
| Advantages: | Assurance that written and spoken texts will match when speaking for the record |
| | Need for thorough preparation |
| Disadvantages: | Loss of flexibility in language and timing |
| | Division of speaker's attention between manuscript and audience |
| | Loss of spontaneity; threat of sounding stale |
| | Tendency for language to be too formal to be spoken conversationally |

*Memorization*

| | |
|---|---|
| Advantages: | Same as for reading |
| Disadvantages: | Loss of flexibility and spontaneity |
| | Possibility that speaker may forget part of the speech |
| | Increased anxiety as a result of fear |
| | Tendency to sound overrehearsed and unnatural; difficult to sound conversational |

*Impromptu Speaking*

| | |
|---|---|
| Advantages: | Spontaneity |
| Disadvantages: | Lack of adequate time to analyze audience, do research, prepare |

*Extemporaneous Speaking*

| | |
|---|---|
| Advantages: | Time to prepare—analyze the audience, research the topic, prepare supporting materials and visual aids, organize ideas, and rehearse |
| | Flexibility and adaptability |
| | Spontaneous and conversational tone |
| Disadvantages: | None |

best of the other styles while avoiding their disadvantages, it is the most appropriate for most speaking situations.

With time to prepare, you can analyze the size and composition of your prospective audience, research your topic, prepare supporting materials and visual aids, organize your ideas, develop an outline, and rehearse your speech. Then at the appointed hour, you will be ready to deliver your speech, either with or without notes.

Unlike speeches that are memorized or read, an extemporaneous speech is spontaneous, flexible, and adaptable. When you are not locked into a manuscript, either written or memorized, you are free to focus fully on the audience and the ideas you are trying to convey. Then, if you see that audience members don't understand fully, you can re-phrase and repeat your ideas. If time grows short, you can accelerate or condense your speech. Your language will be spontaneous, rising out of the present moment, adapted to the reality of the situation, rather than tied to the situation as you imagined it during your preparation.

Flexibility, adaptability, spontaneity, and preparation make extem-poraneous delivery the most effective style for most situations. This does not rule out the possibility, or even the desirability, however, of using a combination of styles.

*The extemporaneous style combines the best of the other styles without their disadvantages.*

## Mixing Styles of Delivery

It is to your advantage to develop skills in all four styles of delivery, because, depending on the situation, any and all of these methods may be appropriate. For example, during an extemporaneous speech you may wish to use a lengthy quotation from another source. You will then need skill in reading from a manuscript. In the same speech you may tell a joke that relies on a specific play on words. In this case memorization is a must, because there is nothing worse than going to your notes for a punch line. Any speaking situation may call for im-promptu remarks; a listener may ask a question or a subject may arise that you hadn't anticipated.

Having a repertoire of styles that can be adapted to changing sit-uations is the essence of effective public speaking delivery. Developing such a repertoire requires a small amount of ability and a large amount of practice. The primary skill to be developed is the ability to effectively reinforce what you say with what you do—the coordination of verbal and nonverbal codes.

## COORDINATING VERBAL AND NONVERBAL CODES

The art of public speaking is to be so well prepared, both mentally and physically, that the act of speaking appears effortless, as if it occurred naturally, without preparation. This is the phenomenon of freedom through discipline. This seeming paradox (freedom and dis-cipline appear to be conflicting concepts) is not limited to public speaking, but is to be found in all the arts and sciences. Musicians master their technique through countless hours of practicing scales and arpeggios. Artists study the fundamentals of perspective before trying to paint perfect landscapes. Einstein struggled through calculus long before arriving at his monumental insight that $E = MC^2$. Even a wide receiver, who seems to have the perfect knack for being in the right place at the right time, actually learned that knack through endless repetitions, running routes on the practice field, and training his body and mind to respond quickly to defensive formations and moves by the defensive back.

*Minimize noise to maximize effectiveness.*

Your job as a public speaker is to be understood. The probability that you will be understood increases as your nonverbal codes are brought into harmony with your verbal code. To encourage such harmony, most public speaking assignments in communication courses are followed by feedback sessions in which the instructor and class members comment on a speaker's nonverbal behaviors. Often videotape playback is used for the same purpose. To prepare you for these sessions, look at the way many of the nonverbal codes introduced in Chapter 4 relate to effective public speaking.

## Eye Contact

*Eye contact signals that communication channels are open.*

Eye contact is one of the most important nonverbal elements of public speaking. If you have already completed a speaking assignment, you have no doubt heard your instructor comment on the importance of eye contact. If not, you will. When you were younger, did anyone ever say to you, "Look at me when I'm talking to you!"? From a very early age, at least in contemporary North American culture, eye contact is the signal that communication channels are open, that it is time either to speak or to listen.

Do you know how to avoid talking with that person in the airport who wants to give you a flower, awaken your spirituality, and collect your money? It's simple. Never establish eye contact, because once you have, you will feel obligated to communicate. Do you see the connection with public speaking? Your eye contact holds the attention of the audience; it connects you with them.

There is another, equally important function of eye contact. It enables you to monitor the effects you are having on your audience. Only by observing your listeners can you read their behaviors. Only through eye contact can you tell whether they're happy or sad, confused or enlightened. In other words, most of the feedback you receive (besides laughter and applause) comes through eye contact.

Clearly, maintaining eye contact with an audience is a critical skill; but a number of things may interfere. The most common obstacle, especially among beginners, is a set of notes. When speakers feel insecure, they want a crutch; the crutch frequently takes the form of extensive notes. Of course, when they have too many notes, they tend to use them, and when they're looking at their notes, they can't maintain eye contact.

Effective use of eye contact, which comes with practice, should allow each person in your audience to feel that you are speaking directly to him or her. If your audience is small enough, this can be accomplished by sweeping the group, allowing your eyes to rest on each person from time to time. With a larger audience, this is impossible. In such a case, focus on sections of the audience—first on one section, then another.

## Body Posture

The way you stand affects the way you speak. Your body posture signals to you, and to others, your readiness for activity (or inactivity). If you doubt this, try delivering a dynamic speech while staring at your fingernails and relaxing in a comfortable recliner. It is virtually impossible to generate enthusiasm in yourself or an audience while sitting in a chair. Your words may say that you're excited, but your body contradicts them.

Remember that nonverbal messages are generally more believable than verbal messages. Therefore, your posture should indicate that you are alert, but not tense. You should stand erect, with your weight distributed evenly over both feet. Do not lock your knees, as this tightens the rest of your body and creates a rigid look. Instead, place one foot slightly in front of the other. Such a position will help you avoid rocking from side to side, which is particularly important if you are using a microphone or being videotaped.

Practice until you find the body position that is right for you. There is a balance between relaxation and readiness for action that you will find with practice.

## Movement

Movement adds variety to your speech and helps to hold an audience's attention. Furthermore, you can use movement to decrease the physical, and therefore emotional, distance between you and your audience. Leaving the lectern to move closer to an audience can increase both your listeners' liking for you and your credibility.

To create a positive impression, movement must be naturally motivated. If movement appears contrived, it becomes a source of noise.

There are also times when you should not move more than a few inches. For example, when using a microphone and speaking before a

*Body movement should amplify and reinforce your words.*

stationary video camera, you must keep movement to a minimum to ensure that the volume level on the public address system remains constant and that the image of your head remains in camera range.

As with many of the elements of effective delivery, movement is a question of balance. Some movement is good, but too much may become a source of noise. Keep movement to a minimum until you develop some sense of control. Again, it's a question of freedom through discipline—once you're comfortable speaking while standing still, it's time to start adding some motion.

## Gestures

Knowing what to do with your hands while speaking is like knowing what to do when someone points a camera at you and says, "Now just act natural, and hold it." You become self-conscious and have no idea of how to "act natural." The first few times you speak in public, you will probably do one of two things: either you will wave your hands wildly or you will forget you have hands.

Gestures express your emotions. They are natural occurrences that, if controlled, can dramatically improve your effectiveness. In this instance, again, freedom through discipline is the key. It is impossible to concentrate simultaneously on the ideas you want to express verbally and the gestures you want to make with your hands, face, and shoulders. Therefore, the first step is to become aware of what your body is doing and to bring it under control. If you don't know what to do with your hands, rest them on the lectern—without gripping the sides. As you gradually become comfortable with only limited gesturing, allow your body to move more freely.

Gesturing is something you automatically know how to do. When you are not self-conscious, it will flow naturally from your emotions. The key lies not in knowing when to gesture, but in knowing when not to.

## Vocal Cues

Your voice—apart from the words it conveys—carries a great deal of meaning. Whether your voice is smooth and rich or shrill and strident will affect the way your audience receives your ideas. Indeed, as much as 38 percent of the social meaning in normal, human communication may be stimulated by vocal cues.[3]

Knowing that your voice is such a powerful instrument of communication should help you to use it effectively. The three vocal characteristics that you need to focus on are rate, pitch, and volume.

**Rate** is the speed at which you speak. Be aware of a rate that is too fast for an audience to follow or one that is too slow to hold attention.

When you limit movement and gesturing as this speaker is doing by putting her hands in her pockets, vocal cues become even more important to the effectiveness of your speech.

**Pitch** refers to the highness or lowness of your voice. Pitch is used to complement and clarify verbal communication. For example, you usually end a question with a rise in vocal pitch. To be most effective, keep vocal pitch under control.

Often, when beginning speakers are nervous, they lose some pitch control because of shallow breathing. As a result, they maintain a pitch that is higher than normal. Such a problem can be overcome through relaxation techniques and proper breathing.

**Volume** is the loudness or softness of the voice. Difficulties with volume are common among inexperienced speakers and can be especially annoying to listeners. Some speakers, when they are nervous, lower their volume to make themselves less conspicuous. Other speakers simply do not know how to project their voices. In such cases, learning to breathe properly usually solves the problem. At the other extreme are speakers who shout their speeches. This can wear out an audience in no time at all, especially in a small room. The answer, as always, is balance—a voice that is not too loud and not too soft.

## Variety

Vocal variety is crucial to effective public speaking. There is always some variety in normal speech—your pitch rises and falls, you speed up or slow down according to your enthusiasm or energy level, you whisper sweet nothings and shout your approval. In public speaking,

*Variation of rate, pitch, and volume helps to hold audience attention.*

though, normal variety is not enough. The variety of rate, pitch, volume, movement, and gesture all needs to be amplified to compensate for the increased distances and the larger number of listeners. You have undoubtedly heard speakers who never varied their rate, who spoke evenly, at the same volume, with little inflection, who didn't move, who used few gestures, and who spent most of their time reading from their notes. The most interesting material in the world cannot overcome such static delivery. The plodding monotony will put any audience to sleep. In contrast, variety in speaking adds emphasis and creates feelings of motion and novelty that stimulate an audience to pay close attention.

Like so many aspects of public speaking, adding variety to your delivery style is merely a matter of taking what comes naturally at other levels of communication and amplifying and formalizing it. The more you practice, the better you'll get.

## USING VISUAL AIDS

To deliver an effective speech, you must polish your basic verbal and nonverbal communication skills. You can add even more impact and variety to your delivery if you know how to use visual aids.

*Visual aids should do what the spoken word alone cannot do.*

A **visual aid** is any kind of instructional material, such as a picture, chart, or diagram, that relies on sight to clarify a point. Visual aids can make your speech more memorable and credible. They can also help your audience to comprehend and retain your message. They can effectively and dramatically clarify a point.

### Kinds of Visual Aids

When you show something to your audience, you reinforce your message and help your audience remember the information you present. It is important, however, to know what visual aid to use. If you are talking about playing the trombone, bring your trombone to class. Sports equipment, cooking utensils, and macramé wall hangings are just a few of the objects that you can share with an audience. To be most effective, objects should be large enough to be seen by all audience members and small enough to be handled easily.

**Models.**  If the object you would like to show your audience is too large, difficult to handle, or otherwise impossible to bring to your speaking date, consider finding or making a model of it. Models that actually work are particularly interesting. Just make sure that your model will be large enough to be seen clearly.

**Diagrams.** Diagrams can be useful means of illustrating the parts of a whole or the steps in a process. Of course, as with objects and models, diagrams that are too small to be seen clearly will frustrate your audience.

**Flip charts.** A *flip chart* is a series of posters or diagrams that are assembled on an easel and displayed one at a time. A flip chart may consist of diagrams prepared in advance or blank sheets of paper that you write on with a dark-colored marker as you speak. A flip chart is usually easier to handle than individual sheets of poster paper. It is important to practice with your flip chart before you give your speech so that you feel comfortable using it.

**Chalkboards.** Most classrooms, lecture halls, and conference rooms have a chalkboard on which you can draw or write largely enough for all to see. A chalkboard is an excellent place to display individual words, short phrases, and brief diagrams. But because stopping to write or erase can break the flow of your presentation, more elaborate content should be displayed on other kinds of visual aids. If you intend to use a chalkboard, be sure to rehearse with it before you give your speech. As most teachers can testify, it takes practice to use a chalkboard with skill.

**Pictures.** Large pictures or posters can help your audience visualize objects, scenes, or locations. The key is to make them big enough to be seen by all. Of course, poorly used or poorly chosen pictures can hinder more than they help. To make sure that your pictures do not distract your audience's attention, do not reveal them until they are needed, and make sure that they are not so fascinating that your audience prefers to focus on them instead of on your message.

**Slides.** Projected photographic slides can be used for dramatic effect. With the additional technology, however, come the additional problems of extension cords, screens, projector bulbs, and remote control. Because slides require a darkened room, you will lose some eye contact with your audience too. Sometimes it helps to have someone else run the projector; but, whether you work the projector yourself or have a helper, it is crucial that the slides on the screen correspond to your comments. If necessary, turn off the projector or insert blank slides so that your spoken message will be synchronized to the appropriate visual images.

**Movies.** If you have ample time, short movies at the beginnings or ends of speeches can make topics come alive. Of course, in short speeches movies are likely to consume too much time. The same advice applies for movies as it does for slides—it is usually wise to have someone help you operate the projector.

**Videotapes.**   Now that video cassette recorders are widely available, the use of videotape is becoming increasingly common in classrooms and lecture halls. One advantage that videotape has over slides and film is that the room usually does not have to be darkened unless you are using a large screen image. Original videotape or excerpts from a professionally prepared video can add interest to presentations.

**Overhead projectors.**   When you use an overhead projector, you can prepare your visuals in advance and add to them while you're speaking. In addition, the room need not be completely dark, so you can maintain eye contact with your audience. Be sure to practice with the overhead projector before your speech; check to see that the images are in focus and clearly visible from the back of the room.

**Handouts.**   Many business and technical speakers rely heavily on handouts to supplement their oral presentations. Nonetheless, some public speaking teachers discourage their use because such materials can be distracting. If a handout covers the same material as a speech, listeners have less motivation to pay attention because all they need know is already written out for them.

If you need to give your listeners written material, guide them through it by pointing out what they should focus on during your speech. If you see that they are too engrossed, tell them that they will have time to read later. Another approach is to wait until the end of your presentation to provide a handout. This works particularly well if you are the last speaker; but, if others must speak after you, they may not appreciate your giving their listeners something to occupy their attention.

**Audio aids.**   Music may be used to demonstrate a point or to set a mood at the beginning or ending of a speech. You can also play a short excerpt of a tape-recorded interview. Rather than read a quotation, you can play a tape of your expert delivering the comment in his or her own words. When selecting audio aids, bear in mind that tape recorders and compact disc players are easier to cue up than phonographs.

**Yourself.**   Don't forget that you are a visual aid. Not only does your use of gestures, posture, eye contact, and vocal inflection help communicate your message, but your appearance or costume can en-

Projected images, timed to match your comments, will help your audience remember important points.

hance the message you wish to convey. Wearing tennis clothes while teaching how to serve or modeling a garment that you have made can add interest to your presentation.

## Using Visual Aids Effectively

Once you have chosen your visual aids, you will want to use them effectively. Following are some factors that will affect the impact of your visual aids.

*Visual aids that are too small, poorly used, or badly timed can detract from your presentation.*

**Size.**  Make sure your visual aids are large enough to be seen clearly by everyone in your audience. Visuals that are too small are extremely frustrating for listeners. If you think your visual aid may be difficult to see and your audience is small, you can bring it closer to the group to ensure that the details will be clear. If that solution is unworkable and if no other speakers are scheduled, you may invite your listeners to see your visual after your presentation.

**Timing.**  By displaying your visual aids at the proper time, you can control your audience's attention. If possible, try to conceal your

*The beginning and the end of your speech are important times to make a strong impression.*

visual aids until you are ready to refer to them. If you display all of your diagrams, posters, and models before you speak, some of their impact may be lost. When using an overhead projector, for instance, turn the projector on when you want your audience to refer to your statistics or diagram. When you move to another point, turn the projector off, so the audience will focus on you and the point you are making. If you have an elaborate drawing you wish to display on the chalkboard, prepare it ahead of time, but keep it covered so the audience won't be distracted by it before you are ready to refer to it. Both the beginning and the ending of your speech are good times to use visual aids to call your listeners' attention to key thoughts.

**Rehearsal.**   Prepare your visual aids in advance and use them as you practice your speech. Picture the room in which you will be speaking and think about the way your visual aids will fit in. Will you need extension cords? How will you display your poster? Do you have chalk and an eraser? Consider the variety of details that pertain to your visuals. Then practice your speech from start to finish just as you will deliver it to your audience. During this stage it is also wise to make contingency plans in case your visual aids malfunction. What will you do if the bulb on the overhead projector burns out during your talk? What if your model breaks when you pick it up? If you should develop a problem with your visuals, don't complain to your audience. Just keep going.

**Simplicity.**   Charts and diagrams will be more legible if you draw them with dark markers and keep them simple. It is better to use two or three simple posters than to try to cram everything you need onto one poster. Don't worry that your visual aids won't be polished enough. Visuals can be effective without being as slick as a Broadway production.

**Variety.**   Consider using several kinds of visual aids if they will help you gain and maintain audience attention. For example, you might first show a small object to your audience and then use an enlarged diagram to explain it further.

**Focus.**   Don't just show your visual aids—integrate the visual with the verbal. Direct your audience's attention to the important facts or statistics on a chart or poster you display; then explain them thoroughly. Don't expect your audience to know why you are showing the chart without any help from you.

*Review Box*

**Visual Aid Check List**

As you prepare a speech, use this check list to make sure you are using visual aids effectively.

_____ Are your visuals large enough to be seen clearly?
_____ Is the writing on each visual made with a dark marker?
_____ Are your visuals relevant to the point you are making?
_____ Do you have appropriate equipment (projectors, extension cords, and the like)?
_____ Have you practiced your speech using all of your visuals?
_____ Do you have appropriate transitions to and away from your visuals?
_____ Will your visuals distract from your message?
_____ Will you maintain eye contact with your audience and not your visual?
_____ Will you talk about your visuals rather than just show them?
_____ Will you show your visuals at the proper time?
_____ Have you tried to incorporate a variety of visuals?
_____ Are you optimizing the impact of your visuals by interacting with them and encouraging your audience to do the same?

**Eye contact.**   Talk to your audience and not to your visual aid. It may be tempting to read your chart or poster, but you should be familiar enough with it so that you can summarize its highlights without prolonged breaks of eye contact with your listeners. If necessary, you may want to make notes of key information so that you can glance at them rather than at a chart or poster on the wall behind you.

**Interaction.**   When you are using visual aids, don't just point to them—interact with them. For example, if you are sharing an antique spinning wheel from your collection, show your listeners how it works. At the same time, communicate with your listeners. Ask them such questions as "Can you see the spindle work?" "Can those of you in the back row see the texture on the wheel?" You may also invite people from the back of the room to come in for a closer look if you fear they can't see your demonstration. Interacting with your visual aids and encouraging your audience to do the same ensures optimal impact.

## SOME FINAL TIPS ON DELIVERY

This chapter concludes with a few tips on public speaking that don't fit neatly into other categories. These tips, nevertheless, address some common concerns about delivery.

1. *Apologies.* You often hear speeches that begin something like this: "When I was asked to speak here tonight, I really didn't know what I would talk about or why anyone would want to hear what I've got to say." You have also heard speakers waste time explaining why their slides didn't arrive from Cleveland or why they couldn't prepare adequately. Such behavior is self-defeating. Speakers who apologize for what they are going to say create the impression that they are unprepared and unworthy. Why, then, would an audience want to listen to them?

2. *Rehearsal.* One of the best ways to build your self-confidence is through rehearsal. This involves both physical and mental practice.

    Physical rehearsal can take many forms: delivering a speech to friends or family members, rehearsing in front of a mirror, using audio- or videotape for self-analysis, and practicing in the actual location in which you will speak. If possible, visit the site of the speech. Check out the size of the room, the acoustics, the availability of electrical outlets, and other factors that will affect your choices about delivery.

    As important as physical rehearsal is mental rehearsal. To practice mentally, think about all the ways in which you can accomplish your speaking objectives. Take the audience's point of view and picture yourself speaking. Then imagine the questions the audience may ask. Visualizing the room, the audience, and the whole speaking situation will help you feel more comfortable with the actual event, because you will have "already been there." An advantage of mental rehearsal is that it can be done anywhere, without disturbing others.

3. *Using Jokes.* According to one old wives' tale, a speaker should first loosen up an audience by telling a little joke ("A funny thing happened on my way to . . ."). Unfortunately, this approach can backfire, because there are few greater public embarrassments than a poorly told joke. Some people are gifted joke tellers. They have a sense of good taste and timing. For these persons, sharing a laugh with an audience may well be a good way to build rapport. Most of us lack this talent, however, and, as a result, will create a better first impression if we do not try to force a laugh.

*If you're not good at telling jokes, it's best not to try.*

---

### Rehearsing a Speech

Use the following guidelines for both mental and physical preparation:
1. Review the outline of your speech, noting the organization and arrangement of ideas. Then put the outline away.
2. Close your eyes and imagine the situation in which you'll be speaking. Picture the room, the audience, and the occasion. Imagine a person introducing you as the speaker. Take a slow, deep breath, exhale completely to relax your stomach muscles, rise, and prepare to begin your speech.
3. Imagine that the audience is sitting before you. Pause before beginning your introduction and sweep the audience with your eyes. Start strongly. Practice until you can present your entire introduction without using notes.
4. Practice your whole speech without stopping. If you make a mistake, find a way to recover and go on. Don't start over.
5. When you have finished your speech, note the time. Did your presentation run too long or too short? Why? Is the amount of material appropriate for the time allotted? Is your rate of speech too fast or too slow?
6. Review your outline, checking it against your practice speech. Reflect on your posture and gestures. What will you do differently next time?
7. Repeat the process until you are comfortable and confident with the flow of ideas in your speech.

---

Of course, even if you're not a gifted comedian, you can still use humor in your speech. When well chosen, amusing stories and anecdotes can both hold your audience's attention and support the ideas in your speech. Therefore, while we would caution against using jokes routinely as introductions, we would encourage you to explore the use of humor throughout a speech, when it suits your topic.

4. *Time.* A good sense of time is important, but time can be hard to keep track of when you're caught up in the excitement of addressing an audience. That is why what is scheduled as a twenty-minute presentation will often last anywhere from ten to fifty minutes.

With practice, you will learn to relate the amount of material you wish to cover to the amount of time you are allotted. (Members of the clergy, for example, usually know how to make a sermon fit perfectly into a twenty-minute time slot.) In most situations, it is better to err on the short side of the time allotted, because when you speak longer than expected, the audience tends to become restless and lose interest. If there are other speakers on the program, it is particularly important to respect time limits. If the first three speakers take too long, they put the fourth at a serious disadvantage.

5. *"In Conclusion. . . ."* Finally, avoid using the words *in conclusion* to signal your closing remarks. In response, your audience may turn their attention to other things as they prepare to depart— gathering their belongings, putting their shoes back on, talking to friends. Nonetheless, if you feel that you must use this phrase, you should mean it. How many times have you heard speakers say "In conclusion, . . ." or "Finally, . . ." and then ramble on for another twenty minutes?

## SUMMARY

All the hours a speaker spends on planning and preparation are distilled into the few minutes he or she actually addresses an audience. To make the most of this time, a speaker must master the verbal and nonverbal, physical and mental aspects of speech delivery.

▶**Outline the advantages and disadvantages of four styles of speech delivery.**

There are four styles of delivery: reading (also called manuscript speaking), memorization, impromptu speaking, and extemporaneous speaking. Reading and memorization both permit ample preparation, but each is limited by loss of flexibility, adaptability, and spontaneity. Impromptu speaking is an important skill for question-and-answer periods, but lack of preparation time makes it inappropriate for most speaking situations. Extemporaneous speaking allows a speaker time to prepare as well as flexibility, adaptability, and spontaneity. It is thus the best style of delivery for most occasions.

▶**Use nonverbal codes to complement your verbal message.**

Effective speakers use nonverbal behavior to enhance their credibility and boost the impact of their messages. In particular, they maintain eye contact with audience members; stand, move, and gesture forcefully; and vary the rate, pitch, and volume at which they speak. To ensure success, they practice their verbal and nonverbal behavior until the two flow together smoothly and naturally.

▶**Select and present visual aids that will enhance your communication.**

When used properly, visual aids can strengthen your speech by amplifying your verbal message, gaining and holding your audience's attention, and focusing interest on important points. Among the most common visual aids are objects, models, diagrams, flip charts, chalk-boards, pictures, slides, movies, videotapes, overhead projectors, and handouts. You may also want to use audio aids, such as records and tapes. To ensure maximum impact, make certain that your visuals are large and simple enough to be clearly seen by all audience members. Then rehearse their use so that you will display them at the proper time and explain them easily while maintaining eye contact with your listeners. By using a variety of visual aids and enthusiastically inter-acting with them, you can encourage your audience to become actively involved in your presentation.

▶**Rehearse a speech both physically and mentally.**

Thorough rehearsal will help you to build confidence and polish your delivery. You can rehearse physically by practicing your speech in front of a mirror, friends, or family members; recording yourself on audio- or videotape; and visiting the location where you will speak. In addition, you will want to prepare mentally by visualizing the entire speaking situation—the room, the audience, and the way you will look as you talk. Taking the audience's point of view and imagining the questions they may ask will help you anticipate problems and avoid being thrown off by unforeseen circumstances.

## *KEY TERMS*

**extemporaneous speaking:** the delivery of a speech that is pre-pared in advance, but presented without relying on a manuscript or memorization.

**impromptu speaking:** the delivery of a speech off the cuff, with no notes or preparation.

**manuscript speaking:** the delivery of a speech using a full, written transcript.

**pitch:** the highness or lowness of the voice.

**rate:** the speed at which one speaks.

**visual aid:** any kind of instructional material, such as a picture, chart, or diagram, that relies on sight to clarify a point.

**volume:** the loudness or softness of the voice.

## DISCUSSION QUESTIONS

1. In what situations are each of the four styles of speech delivery most appropriate? When might you use all four styles in one speech?

2. In chapter 4 you learned that nonverbal behavior may be divided into five categories—emblems, illustrators, affect displays, regulators, and adaptors. How might a public speaker use nonverbal cues from each of these categories?

3. What do you see as the most important elements of speech delivery? Voice? Posture? Gesture? Eye contact? Variety? Movement? How would you rank order these? Are there other important elements you can identify? Are there situational differences that might change your order? Why?

4. How would you vary your presentational style when speaking to a small, informal group or a large audience at a formal occasion? What aspects of delivery would you adjust and how would you change them?

## SUGGESTED ACTIVITIES

1. Identify the kinds of visual aids that would be most appropriate and helpful for speeches on the following topics:
   —The Internal Combustion Engine
   —A Buyers' Guide to Mutual Funds
   —The Art and Science of Diamond Cutting
   —Making the Perfect Quiche
   —The Joy of Miniature Golf
   —The Selling of a Candidate
   —Why You Should Go to Graduate School
   —Quitting Smoking

   What criteria guided your choice of visual aids? Why are some types of visuals more appropriate to certain topics? What are the advantages and disadvantages of the aids you selected?

2. Attend a public speech and concentrate on the delivery style of the speaker. Based on your observations, answer the following questions:
   a. What style—reading, memory, impromptu, extemporaneous— did the speaker employ? Was the style appropriate to the situation? Why?

   b. How did the speaker use eye contact? Did you feel that the speaker was talking directly to you, or was his or her style more impersonal? How did eye contact affect you as an audience member?

   c. Did the speaker sound enthusiastic about the topic? What created your perception of the speaker's interest in the topic? How did the speaker use vocal rate, pitch, volume, and variety to influence your perception?

   d. How did the speaker look? Was his or her posture and use of gestures appropriate to the topic and situation? Why or why not? Did the speaker have any distracting mannerisms? What were they?

Based on these observations, write three specific recommendations that you would give to the speaker if he or she asked for some feedback about ways to improve.

**3.** Obtain a videotape of one of your own speeches. Answer questions *a* through *c* from activity 2. Make three recommendations to yourself on ways to improve your speaking style. Rehearse your next speech incorporating these recommendations. Again, review the videotape. Were you successful in correcting the weaknesses in your style? Write three new recommendations for yourself based on your observations. Again, rehearse your next speech incorporating these recommendations. Repeat the process until the behaviors have been corrected. Then move on to new aspects of your speaking style that you want to improve.

---

## SUGGESTED READING

Gronbeck, B., Ehninger, D. and Monroe, A. (1987). *Principles of Speech Communication,* 10th edition. (Glenview, IL: Scott, Foresman and Company).

Powers, J. (1987). *Public Speaking: the Lively Art.* (Belmont, CA: Wadsworth Publishing Company).

# 14 Speaking to Inform

*After studying this chapter, you should be able to:*

▶ Describe four methods of informing others.

▶ Adapt the six steps of speech preparation and presentation to the creation of an informative speech.

▶ Identify five basic principles of informing others.

▶ Begin to understand and manage any speech anxiety you may feel.

In the course of your life, you have probably heard more informative speeches than any other kind. From your first look at such programs as "Sesame Street" to your college lectures, people have been attempting to impart information to you. No doubt you have found some efforts boring and ineffective while others have been quite interesting. Have you ever thought about what makes the difference?

This chapter will explain exactly how to prepare an informative speech that will both catch and hold listeners' attention. First will be discussed the methods of informing others: defining, describing, narrating, and demonstrating. Next the steps of speech preparation and presentation as they apply to informative speaking will be reviewed. Then five basic principles of informing others will be identified. Finally, you will get some pointers on managing speech anxiety.

## METHODS OF INFORMING OTHERS

As noted in Chapter 10, the general purpose of an **informative speech** is to teach, define, illustrate, clarify, or elaborate on a topic. When you present an informative speech, your challenge is to find a method of teaching new information in an interesting and effective way. The four most common ways of introducing new information are by defining, describing, narrating, and demonstrating.

*You can present new information by defining, describing, narrating, and demonstrating.*

### Defining

A **definition** is a statement of the meaning of a term or concept. Such basic information ensures listeners' understanding and creates the foundation for more complex thoughts. Therefore, you will want to make sure that your definitions are simple and clear. Here are some ways to use definitions to your advantage.

1. *Consult a dictionary.* The easiest and most obvious way to explain a term is simply to use its dictionary definition. Although this is a good starting point and ensures accuracy, you will find that most dictionary definitions are too dry and technical to use alone.
2. *Put the definition in your own words.* After consulting dictionaries you may decide that the best way to make a term clear to your audience is to define it in your own words. Try to identify what the word means to you.
3. *Cite examples.* "Do you remember seeing the large tree with the long branches in front of our building as you came to class today? That is a ficus tree." The more familiar your audience is with an example, the clearer your definition by example will be.

4. *Note opposites.* Using antonyms or stating opposite meanings can help clarify a term for your listeners. Thus, you could say, "A good teacher is not boring, unfair, or rude."

5. *Offer an operational definition.* An **operational definition** explains how something works or how it is made or measured. For example, the term *temperature* can be defined as "the degrees of heat as measured on a thermometer." An operational definition might also explain a process, thus providing a more precise definition. *Rock tumbling* is "a four-step process of cleaning stones, turning them in a motorized barrel with coarse grit, tumbling them with fine grit, and washing them during a final rinse cycle."

## Describing

To make your speech come alive, you will need to accurately and interestingly describe people, places, things, and ideas. When you **describe,** you provide new information in much the same way a news reporter does. Thus, consider who, what, where, why, and when. As you formulate your description, these five basic questions will help you organize your thoughts.

*A word picture helps your audience visualize what you are describing.*

The key to describing things to your audience is to present concrete word pictures. A **word picture** is a description that helps an audience see a specific image in their mind's eye. Help your audience visualize the thing you are describing by appealing to their senses. Describe its size, shape, color, texture, and weight to make it seem more concrete. Saying that something has the texture of alligator hide or weighed as much as a pickup truck are better descriptions than merely saying that something was rough or heavy. In the process, appeal to what your listeners can touch, feel, or taste in addition to what they can see. Strive to eliminate vague, ambiguous, and general language in order to make your speeches sing with vivid description.

## Narrating

A **narration** is a story that communicates an idea. Everyone likes a good story. Stories are interesting because they are concrete and can help your audience visualize what you are talking about. Mark Twain, Will Rogers, and Bill Cosby are known for being good story tellers. Developing similar skills can greatly add to your interest as a public speaker.

Think of a narrative as having four parts: (1) *the opening,* (2) *the complications,* (3) *the development,* and (4) *the conclusion.* Most stories follow a chronological order. As you open the story, set the stage. Use

Narration is an important skill for on-the-spot reporters who describe the opening, complications, development, and conclusion of news events as they occur.

your skill in describing to provide a word picture of what the audience should see as the curtain goes up. "It was a black murky night. I had just finished my night class and was heading for the parking lot. A cold stinging wind was blowing and I felt alone." With this opening you have set the stage, described what was happening, and provided an image for the audience to visualize.

*A narrative has four parts: the opening, the complications, the development, and the conclusion.*

The complications follow your description of the opening scene. At this point you describe some difficulty, conflict, or problem. This arouses interest and keeps your audience in suspense. "As I was walking to my car I heard footsteps behind me. I quickened my pace. The footsteps kept pace with me. It was too dark to see who was following me, but I knew someone or something was there. I called out 'Who's there?' but I heard no answer. I began to tremble with fear. Someone was following me!"

After presenting the complications, you develop the story further. You may expand on the complications in greater detail and you may begin to identify some possible outcomes for the story. "As I began running toward my car I heard the footsteps run behind me. I ran faster. I was afraid to look back. If I could only reach my car, hop in, and lock the door, all would be well."

In the fourth stage of narration, the conclusion, you tie up the loose ends and provide a satisfying finale. Your conclusion should be brief and make a point. "I saw my car at the far end of the parking lot. It was then I heard a voice behind me call my name. It was my teacher. He wanted to give me a book I had left in class. That night I learned that not all unknown footsteps in the dark are threatening."

Using suspense can add interest to most stories and ensure that listeners stay tuned for the conclusion or main point. Humor can have the same effect. Also, where possible, include dialogue in your story. Rather than just reporting what someone said, use the words that would actually have been spoken: "Report to the lifeboats," came the announcement on the intercom. "This is the captain speaking. We are experiencing slight engine trouble. For your safety we are going to abandon ship."

Besides telling original or personal stories, you can also include stories from TV, motion pictures, plays, or books to make a point and hold audience interest. The four stages of plot development still apply. Set the stage, identify the complications, develop the story, and then head for your conclusion. Above all, make sure the audience understands the point of your story. Don't just tell a story and move on. Link your story to the idea you want your listeners to remember.

## Demonstrating

When you **demonstrate,** you show your audience how to do something or how something works. Often when you demonstrate how to do something, you want your audience to be able to perform the same function. How to run a computer program, bake a cake, build an aardvark cage, knit a sweater, or play a slide trombone are all good subjects for a demonstration.

If your objective is to teach your listeners to perform a new task (such as sewing on a button), you need to analyze their current skill and knowledge levels in order to determine how much background information to provide. Then you should plan to thoroughly describe and demonstrate each step of the task in chronological order.

*Talking while handling visual aids takes practice.*

Because systematic demonstrations can be time consuming, you must be mindful of your assigned time limit. To make sure that your speech will not run too long, time yourself as you practice. Keep practicing until you can handle your visual aids smoothly and efficiently.

The greatest advantage of a demonstration is its strong visual impact. A process seen in operation is easier to understand and recall than a process that is described. Thus, showing how to use a hand-held video camera is more effective than a mere description.

## Review Box

### Methods of Informing Others

| Method | Description | Suggestions |
|---|---|---|
| Defining | Explaining the meaning of unfamiliar words and concepts | 1. Consult a dictionary.<br>2. Put the definition in your own words.<br>3. Cite examples.<br>4. Note opposites.<br>5. Use an operational definition. |
| Describing | Specifying who, what, when, where, and why | 1. Use word pictures.<br>2. Appeal to listeners' five senses. |
| Narrating | Telling a story | 1. Set the stage with the opening.<br>2. Describe the complications.<br>3. Develop the plot.<br>4. Bring the story to a conclusion. |
| Demonstrating | Showing how to do something or how something works | 1. Use visual aids to illustrate your message.<br>2. Use a chronological sequence to organize your thoughts. |

As much as possible, encourage your audience to participate in the process you are demonstrating. Let them do, see, smell, feel, hear, even taste what you are talking about. Keep the following maxim in mind when you give a demonstration speech:

*I hear—I forget;*
*I see—I remember;*
*I experience—I understand.*

## PREPARING AN INFORMATIVE SPEECH

Chapter 10 outlined the six basic steps of speech preparation and presentation. Now it is important to look at those steps as they apply to informative speeches.

## Selecting a Topic

G. K. Chesterton once said, "There is no such thing as an uninteresting topic, only uninterested people." When lectures and other informative presentations seem uninteresting, it is often because their topics are not developed with the audience in mind. The best informative speech topic considers both the speaker's interests and the audience's interests. The following are some topics that might be adapted to appeal to a wide range of speakers and listeners:

How to improve your grades

Optical illusions

Plagiarism

The dangers of owning a pit bull

Organized crime

How I started my own business

The biggest mistake of (Revolutionary War, Civil War)

How a microwave oven works

The farm crisis

How to protect your home from burglary

Rights of smokers (or nonsmokers)

My collection of (stamps, coins, antiques, books)

The best teacher I have had

How to prepare for (a hurricane, tornado, earthquake)

New diets

How the stock market works

Differences between an MBA and an MA degree

How our local government works

Liberation theology

The best speaker I have heard

The national debt

How political campaigns are financed

My hometown

My most unusual relative

The spread of terrorism

Boating safety

Gymnastics (or another Olympic event)

How to be a better listener

How to bake . . .

## Analyzing Your Audience

Once you've chosen a topic, you need to discover what your audience already knows about it. If, for example, you decide to talk about the way to select a graduate school, you can't automatically assume that all of your listeners will want to go to graduate school and are familiar with the related terminology. You will want to find out how many of your listeners intend to go to graduate school, what kinds of schools they're interested in, and how much research they've done on their own.

Consider both formal and informal methods of assessing demographic, attitudinal, and environmental aspects of the audience and the occasion. If you choose an informal approach, you can simply chat with various audience members and ask them how much they know about your topic. If you take a more formal approach, you can design a questionnaire and ask for written responses to a series of more detailed questions.

## Developing a Specific Purpose and a Thesis Statement

Because you already know that your general purpose is to inform, you need to formulate only a specific purpose and a thesis statement. What do you want your audience to be able to do when you finish your speech? Often your objective will correspond to the method you select to inform (define, describe, narrate, or demonstrate). If you will be primarily defining words and concepts, your specific purpose will be for your audience to be able to define the words and concepts you present. If you are demonstrating how something works, your specific purpose will state that your audience should be able to perform or describe the process or activity you demonstrated. Your thesis statement will summarize the content of your speech in a single well-worded sentence. Consider the following examples:

| | |
|---|---|
| *General Purpose:* | To inform |
| *Topic:* | Polaroid camera |
| *Specific Purpose:* | At the end of my speech the audience should be able to describe how a Polaroid instant camera works. |
| *Thesis Statement:* | A Polaroid camera uses special film which contains chemicals that permit photographs to be developed in less than a minute. |
| *General Purpose:* | To inform |
| *Topic:* | Rising health insurance |

| *Specific Purpose:* | At the end of my speech the audience should be able to discuss two reasons why health insurance rates have increased faster than the rate of inflation. |
| *Thesis Statement:* | Health insurance rates have increased dramatically in the past five years because of the high cost of new medical technology and an increase in malpractice suits against medical professionals. |

## Gathering Supporting Materials

The supporting material for an informative speech should help an audience understand and remember a speaker's main points. It is important to find ways to make abstract ideas more concrete. One student wanted to teach her class the value of whole wheat bread over white bread. To illustrate that whole wheat bread contains more wheat germ, she used her audience as her visual aid. She had her listeners imagine that the room in which they were gathered was a loaf of white bread and that they represented individual wheat germs within the bread. "Now imagine," she said, "that there are twice as many people in this room. That gives you some idea of the increased number of wheat germs in a loaf of wheat bread and why it is better than white bread." By involving her audience in her illustration, she vividly drove home her point.

## Organizing Your Speech

*Long speeches need to be chunked into easy-to-remember segments.*

As discussed in Chapter 12, your audience will retain your message more readily if you have identified a limited number of main ideas and organized them logically. The longer your speech is, the more important it becomes to "chunk" it into manageable segments based on your main ideas. The exact number of points will depend on the length of your speech and the topic you have selected, but almost any thesis statement can be divided one of three ways: (1) by logical categories, (2) by reasons, or (3) by identifying steps. For example, a speech about the federal government can be chunked by talking about the three main branches— executive, legislative, and judicial. A speech about the evils of drunk driving can be organized around the reasons that drunk driving is harmful. A speech that teaches computer programming can be divided by stating what must be learned first, second, and third. Whatever your topic, make sure that you have developed a logical way to chunk it into main ideas and subordinate ideas.

Once you have your main ideas and subordinate ideas well organized, you should consider how you can provide smooth transitions from one point to the next. Audience members should never have to wonder why you're talking about a particular idea at a given place in your speech.

One way to make a clear transition is to offer a brief internal summary and a preview of what is yet to come. Note what you have said thus far and identify what the audience still needs to know.

Another technique is to use a *rhetorical question*—that is, a question to which you expect no answer. You might say, "We've talked about some of the causes of cancer, but perhaps you're wondering, 'What are some of the methods of curing cancer today?' That brings me to my next point." You do not need formal transition statements between every minor point in your speech. Transitions should be explicit between the introduction and the body of your speech, and between the body and the conclusion.

*Internal summaries and rhetorical questions make strong transitions between main ideas.*

## Rehearsing and Delivering Your Speech

As discussed in the last chapter, the key elements in speech delivery include eye contact, posture, movement, gestures, and vocal cues. When speaking to inform use these delivery cues to communicate your interest and sincere enthusiasm about your topic.

If you are presenting lots of technical or statistical information, allow ample time for rehearsal so that you will not rely too heavily on your notes during your presentation.

You will also want to emphasize key ideas and information. One way to let your audience know that an idea is important is simply to tell them so. For example, you may declare, "This next point is one of the most important things I want to say" or "Of all the information I have shared with you today, the following idea is the one I want to emphasize and the one I hope you won't forget." Such explicit emphasis is important to use in long speeches, because it signals the information that is most significant. On the other hand, because verbal emphasis can lose some of its impact if overused, employ it only when you really want your audience to remember a key idea.

You can also add emphasis through nonverbal cues. Well-placed and meaningful hand gestures can indicate that the information you're sharing is significant. If you have been delivering your speech from behind a lectern, coming out and standing closer to your audience can signify a change in emphasis. Raising or lowering your voice can also underscore a phrase or idea.

# PRINCIPLES OF INFORMING OTHERS

As you can no doubt testify, some speakers are more effective than others in presenting informative talks. Some seem to know how to prepare presentations that are interesting and memorable and some don't. The difference is that effective speakers actively apply five basic principles of informative speech design. These are the following:

**Early in your speech, establish a motive for your audience to listen to you.**

Don't assume that your listeners will be sitting on the edge of their seats, waiting to hang on every word you say. On the contrary, in most cases, you'll need to tell your audience why they should be interested in you and your topic. You will need to motivate them to listen. If you have done an effective job of analyzing your audience, you will have some useful insights into their interests and needs, and thus know how to appeal to them.

**Seek ways to build repetition into your speech.**

*Tell listeners what you are going to tell them, tell them, then tell them what you told them.*

Your English professor probably warned you about being too repetitive in your term papers. You were counseled not to restate ideas, to write them only once. This is good advice for written communication, but it is not necessarily appropriate for oral communication. You can always go back and reread written communication if it is not clear or if you need to refresh your memory. Such is not the case with oral communication, unless you are tape recording or taking detailed notes. Therefore, to ensure maximum comprehension, you need to build a certain amount of redundancy into your speech. A popular piece of advice for beginning public speakers is *tell them* what you're going to tell them, *tell them,* then *tell them* what you told them. In other words, in the introduction to your speech give a preview of your main ideas, in the body of your speech restate and develop your ideas, and as you conclude provide a summary of your main ideas. Then, when you have finished your speech, your audience should have no doubt about what your main points were and should have heard them enough times to recall them.

**Simple ideas and phrases are more easily remembered than complex ideas.**

Chapter 6 identified one of the barriers to effective listening as information overload. When you try to say too much, the audience often

---

| **Review Box** |
| --- |

**Principles of Informing Others**

1. Establish a motive for your audience to listen to you.
2. Build in redundancy.
3. Use simple ideas and language.
4. Associate the new with the familiar.
5. Pace the flow of information.

---

gets tired of listening and eventually tunes out. Thus, when you are trying to inform others, carefully select the information you wish to share. Simplify, edit, and condense. Rather than dividing your speech into eight main subtopics, find a way to organize it around four. Try to use simple words instead of complicated ones. In every aspect of your speech, the simpler the better.

*Use simple words and phrases to enhance listeners' recall and understanding.*

### Associate the new with the familiar.

Most of you learn by associating new information with information that you already know. For example, when you meet someone for the first time you may find yourself noting how he or she reminds you of someone you already know. When you visit a new town you may note how it is similar to or different from the town in which you live. Because you attempt to make sense of your world by associating the old with the new, you can improve your listeners' understanding by building on previous knowledge. Thus, you might begin to explain the advantages of computerized word processing by asking the audience to think about the functions of a typewriter.

*Build on what listeners already know.*

### Pace the flow of information.

Organize your informative speech to ensure that new information and ideas are evenly distributed throughout. If you present too much new information too quickly, you may overwhelm your listeners and interfere with their comprehension. Thus, the more difficult or technical your topic, the more care you should take to make sure that your audience has time to process your information. Your success as an informative speaker depends not on the quantity of information that you pack into your speech but on the quality of learning that takes place among your listeners. Be sure to allow time to support your information with a variety of examples, illustrations, and explanations.

# MANAGING SPEECH ANXIETY

*Most people feel nervous when they have to deliver a speech.*

The focus thus far has been on the mechanics of speech preparation and presentation. It is important, however, to also discuss how you may feel about giving a speech. It's normal for most people to feel nervous about speaking to others. A recent survey found that fear of speaking in public was the number-one fear of most people, with 41 percent of the respondents reporting that public speaking was their most significant fear.[1] In comparison, fear of death ranked only sixth! In reality, **speech anxiety**—the feeling of nervousness that you experience before and during public speaking—is related to your intrapersonal communication. Your perception of the speaking assignment, your self-image, and your self-esteem interact to create anxiety. You want to do well, but you're not sure that you can or will. Your body responds to this conflict by increasing your breathing rate, producing more adrenalin, and pumping more blood through your veins. In short, it creates more energy to help you deal with the challenge you are facing. You experience physiological changes because of your psychological state. That's why you may have a rapidly beating heart, shaking knees and hands, a quivering voice, increased perspiration, and butterflies in your stomach. While you may perceive these symptoms as hindrances to your performance, your body is simply trying to help you with the task at hand. You may feel more comfortable if you remember that:

1. *You are going to feel more nervous than you look.* After her first speech, Susan sat down and asked, "Couldn't you tell how nervous I was?" Several of her classmates responded, "You were nervous? You sure didn't look nervous to me." That's because you rarely appear as nervous as you think you do. Worrying about appearing nervous may, in fact, unnecessarily increase your anxiety. In response, your body will provide more physiological changes to deal with the psychologically induced state that you have created for yourself.

2. *Realize that almost every speaker experiences some degree of nervousness.* What do Carol Burnett and Abraham Lincoln have in common? If you guessed that they both experienced the fear of public speaking, you are right. Almost everyone experiences some anxiety when speaking. Your goal should not be to eliminate speech anxiety but to manage it so that it does not become such a strong psychological or physiological burden that you do not speak well.

3. *Some anxiety can be beneficial to your performance.* The anxiety that you experience is designed to help you with an important

Don't let anxiety keep you from giving a speech. The physical symptoms of anxiety, such as butterflies in your stomach and quivering hands are only your body's way of giving you more energy to help you deal with the task at hand.

task. Your body can actually function better in the heightened state of readiness that it has created. The increased energy that results can help you get "up" for your speech performance.

4. *Speech anxiety rarely keeps a speaker from speaking.* Even though you may feel your anxiety is so intense that you will not be able to start, let alone finish, your speech, take comfort in knowing that few speakers become so overwhelmed that they are unable to speak. Don't let your anxiety persuade you that you could not possibly give a speech.

## Suggestions for Managing Speech Anxiety

Although you may not be able to eliminate your fear of speaking, you can take some concrete steps to keep it in control.

1. *Select an appropriate topic.* Select a topic with which you are familiar or with which you have had some personal experience. It is rarely a good idea to pick a topic simply because you can find a lot of information about it.
2. *Be familiar with your audience.* If you know your audience, you will feel more comfortable because you will understand

*Rehearse your speech while standing up and imagining that your audience is present.*

how to evoke a positive response from them. (See Chapter 10 to review the methods for analyzing your audience.)

3. *Rehearse while recreating the speech environment.* Practice your speech in a setting that is as similar as possible to the one in which you will be speaking. Rehearse standing up. Imagine that your audience is present. Picture what the room looks like and what time of day it is. Practice rising from your seat, walking to the lectern (if you will be using one), and beginning your opening remarks. Such practice will help you feel more comfortable when it's time to actually give your speech.

4. *Work on speech organization.* You will feel more comfortable and confident delivering a speech that is well-organized, with appropriate transition phrases and summaries.

5. *Become very familiar with your introduction and conclusion.* You will probably feel the most anxiety during the opening moments of your presentation. If you are very familiar with your introduction, you will feel better about delivering the entire speech. If you are comfortable with your conclusion, you will have a reference point to turn to if you should lose your place. If it summarizes your main ideas, it may help you remember where you are and get back on track. If you need to end your speech for any reason, a well-delivered conclusion can let you make a graceful exit and give you the comfort of knowing that you closed your presentation effectively.

6. *Use deep-breathing exercises to help you relax.* To distract your focus from your anxiety, consider taking a few slow deep breaths before you rise to speak. This can be done unobtrusively and can help slow down your physiological responses to your anxiety. While breathing deeply, try to relax your entire body.

7. *Consider incorporating movement into your speech.* Movement can help channel some of the energy produced by your anxiety. Writing on a chalkboard or overhead projector, or pointing to parts of a poster can put that energy to good use and help take the focus off your anxiety. Consider incorporating meaningful gestures to emphasize key ideas.

8. *Seek opportunities to speak more often.* It may sound contradictory to suggest that more public speaking will result in less communication anxiety, but that is indeed the case. The more experience you have speaking in public, the more comfortable you will feel. With each success, you will gain a bit more confidence.

**Review Box**

### Suggestions for Managing Speech Anxiety

1. Select an appropriate topic.
2. Be familiar with your audience.
3. Rehearse while recreating the speech environment.
4. Present a logically organized speech.
5. Know your introduction and conclusion well.
6. Use deep-breathing exercises.
7. Consider incorporating meaningful movement into your speech.
8. Seek more opportunities to speak.
9. Act calm to feel calm.
10. Focus on communicating your message to your audience rather than focus on your fear.

**9.** *Act calm and you will feel calm.* It is possible to induce certain emotions by acting them out. Therefore, if you want to feel greater peace and calmness, act as if you already are peaceful and calm. Don't fidget as you wait to be introduced. Walk to the front of the room purposefully and confidently. Rather than blurting out your opening phrase, take a moment to look at your audience and seek out the most friendly, supportive faces. Then begin your speech. *Think* calm and *act* calm in order to *feel* calm.

**10.** *Focus on the message you have prepared rather than on your fear.* Instead of telling yourself how anxious you are, concentrate on what you are going to say. Before you rise to speak, mentally rehearse your main ideas, your introduction, and your conclusion. Then you'll be too busy to worry about anything else.

*As you speak, look for friendly and supportive faces in your audience.*

Understanding your anxieties and taking concrete steps to alleviate them should greatly increase your comfort in front of an audience. But if you feel you need additional help, don't hesitate to consult your instructor or a counselor. Some universities have special programs designed to help you manage the fear of public speaking. The most widely used approach, called systematic desensitization, teaches the speaker to relax while visualizing various stages of speech preparation and delivering a speech to an audience.

# A SAMPLE INFORMATIVE SPEECH

This speech by Amy Gillespie was a winner in the Interstate Oratorical Association contest. Note how it incorporates the basic principles presented in this and the preceding chapters.

| | |
|---|---|
| *General Purpose:* | To inform |
| *Specific Purpose:* | At the end of the speech, the audience should be able to describe the importance of listening, explain why most people don't listen well, and identify three ways of improving their own listening skill. |
| *Thesis Statement:* | Most people don't listen well because they do not realize that they have a listening problem and they do not attempt to improve their listening skill. |

## LISTEN UP!
### Amy Gillespie
### St. Olaf College, Minnesota[2]

The speaker creates an imaginary situation to pique listeners' curiosity.

Good evening, and welcome to ABC Newsbrief. Top stories in the news include the hijacking of a Swiss airliner late Thursday evening by armed Iranian extremists. The terrorists are holding 23 hostages in Paris. Also in the news, Congress votes down defense spending cuts, but not before 5000 protest in front of the Pentagon. And the weather outlook for tomorrow indicates warmer temperatures, with a slight chance of precipitation in the early morning hours. This has been Newsbrief, now these words.

By asking questions, Amy invites listeners' participation and establishes their need for her information.

We hear news reports like this one every day. But how carefully do we listen to them? Let's find out. See if you can answer the following questions. Number one, what country did the hijacked airplane belong to? Number two, when was it hijacked? And three, where did people protest?

Amy explicitly defines her terms.

I ask these questions to illustrate something we usually take for granted—listening. What is listening? That may sound like an elementary question, but too often we confuse listening with simply hearing. Hearing involves the vibration of sound waves on our eardrums. But listening is the interpretation and evaluation of what we hear.

She wraps up her introduction with a clear preview of what she will talk about.

Today I'd like to talk about listening. First, I'll establish its importance in our society and show the problems that can arise when it breaks down. Then I'll examine the causes of our bad listening habits;

and finally, offer some solutions for them, which can be implemented in our nation's school systems and in our daily lives.

First of all, we need to understand how important listening really is. Says Robert Montgomery, author of *Listening Made Easy,* "We listen more than we do any other human activity except breathe." And the *American School Board Journal* of September, 1981, reports that the average adult spends 80 percent of his or her time communicating—45 percent of that time is spent listening. As for college students, we spend 70 percent of our class time listening.

Unfortunately, despite the fact that we spend so much time doing it, we are atrocious listeners. According to the *Executive Health Newsletter* of December, 1981, "Immediately after listening to a ten-minute presentation, the average listener had heard, correctly understood, properly evaluated and retained approximately half of what was said." Fifty percent is lost forever. After 48 hours, that figure jumps to 75 percent. How about you? Did you know the answers to my questions? Here they are. The hijacked plane was Swiss. It was attacked late Thursday evening. And 5000 people protested in front of the Pentagon. If you got one or more of these wrong, you're not alone. The *Executive Health Newsletter* estimates "most people make more than one listening mistake every day."

The problems that arise from our poor listening affect every aspect of our lives, from our jobs to our personal relationships. A University of Minnesota study reports that "in the business world, nearly 60 percent of misunderstandings can be traced to poor listening." Listening expert Dr. Lyman Steil notes, "Because of listening mistakes, letters have to be retyped, appointments rescheduled, shipments rerouted. Productivity is affected and profits suffer." Another listening expert, Dr. Ralph Nichols, says that if ineffective listening "could be tallied in terms of dollars and cents," (it would) "undoubtedly cost our nation's industry millions of dollars a year."

Not only is good listening essential in the corporate world, but it is vital in our personal lives as well. In the home, says Montgomery, "Poor listening leads the list of causes of marital conflict." The Family Service Association of America asked husbands and wives, "What are the major conflicts in your married life?" Eighty-seven percent responded, "Poor communication . . . My spouse doesn't listen to me." How many times have we complained about that boyfriend or girlfriend who simply doesn't listen! The day-to-day friction between roommates and families that is caused by poor listening makes its personal cost very great.

Before I explain what we can do to improve our listening, it will be helpful to understand the cause of poor listening. The main reason we are bad listeners is the attitude in our society that takes listening for granted. After all, we've been listening since we were born!

The speaker makes a smooth transition from the introduction to the body and *establishes a motive for listening to the entire speech.*

Amy presents a quotation and some statistics to support her point. Note that she always cites her sources.

Amy builds her case with another quotation and more statistics.

Once again, Amy invites involvement.

Amy identifies poor listening as a serious problem and begins to list its effects.

Amy continues to build her credibility by citing expert testimony.

The speaker uses more quotations and statistics to emphasize the far-reaching effects of poor listening.

With this transition sentence, Amy helps listeners to follow her train of thought.

<table>
<tr><td>

The speaker changes her focus to the main reason for poor listening, thus establishing a clear cause-effect relationship.

Amy cites a series of supporting examples.

The speaker makes a transition from identifying the problem to suggesting a solution.

Amy begins to spell out a course of action.

She supports her recommendation with a quotation and research results.

The speaker makes a clear transition from solutions for children to solutions for audience members themselves.

Amy enumerates her suggestions, using the words *first*, *second*, and *third* to help her audience follow along.

</td><td>

Unfortunately, most educators wrongly believe that, just because we know how to listen, we are good at it. Thus listening is not taught in schools the way other communication skills like speaking, reading, and writing are. In fact, of those four skills, listening is used the most, but it is taught the least.

To make matters worse, our educators actually go out of their way to make listening easy on us. "Teachers routinely repeat instructions and directions, so students come to expect it and don't listen the first time," says Dr. Nichols. This coddling is continued throughout our lives, with radio and TV announcements that are simplified and repeated. The result is lazy listeners with poor listening habits.

Although our bad habits are ingrained from the outset, there is a cure for poor listening, and that is instruction and practice. Good listening won't come about by itself; it must be taught and worked on. First of all, it must be begun with our nation's school children. According to Dr. Nichols, "Our best listeners . . . (are) primary school children. (But) as the grade level increases, the caliber of listening performance . . . falls." If we can teach people good listening habits when they're young, they will retain their natural listening abilities all their lives.

The January, 1985, issue of the *International Listening Association Newsletter* encourages teachers to incorporate listening in their regular school curricula by coordinating subjects like English or social studies to focus on listening skills.

The results of school listening programs are tremendous. Says Dr. Steil, "In schools where listening is taught, listening comprehension has as much as doubled in a few months." In one study reported by the *Journal of Educational Research*, fifth graders were given specific training in listening for main ideas, details, and inferences: "Not only were gains in these skills significant, but other skills, such as getting word meaning and following directions, also showed improvement."

Clearly, then, a listening program is well worth the time and effort on the part of our nation's schools.

Even though the rest of us are beyond our grade school days, Dr. Steil tells us there are three ways in which we too can improve our listening.

The first way is to try to find some personal benefit in what we hear. Often when a seemingly irrelevant topic is introduced, we automatically shut our ears. For example, how many of us really listen to the safety instructions on an airplane anymore? After our first few flights, we tend to just tune out the flight attendant's instructions. But think if there were an emergency. Could you properly use the safety equipment? If we try to find this kind of value in what is floating into our ears, we will pay better attention and thus be better listeners.

</td></tr>
</table>

A second tip Steil clues us in on is to make use of the fact that thought is faster than speech. Now I'm speaking at a rate of about 125 words per minute. You are thinking four times that fast. This discrepancy, known as a time lag, leaves a lot of time for spare thinking. But what do we do with that time? Too often we become bored or distracted by our own thoughts. So Steil proposes that instead of daydreaming, we use that extra time to our advantage: to mentally summarize what the speaker has said, to weigh the facts and evidence presented, or to anticipate the upcoming ideas or arguments. This will keep us from drifting off and also give us a better understanding of what is being said.

*Amy personalizes her message by asking her listeners to examine their own behavior.*

A third way to improve our listening is to actually practice it by consciously pursuing difficult listening material. Two examples would be presidential debates or a program like "Meet the Press," which has a lot of facts to be digested and judgments to be made. We'll find that with practice, we will all become better, more effective listeners.

*The speaker dramatizes her point by calling on listeners to imagine an emergency.*

*Amy uses the current situation as an example.*

When we see what can and does go wrong every day due to our own listening errors, it becomes clear that our listening is an area in which we need to work. . . .

*The speaker now makes a transition between the body and the conclusion.*

Remember the questions I asked at the beginning of my speech? You know how many answers you got right. If you're not satisfied with your tally, I challenge you to start today, to find something of personal benefit in even the dullest conversations. Use the time lag effectively, and refrain from tuning out if subject matter becomes a bit difficult or technical. Force yourself to listen.

*Finally, by referring to her introductory questions, she asks her audience to use the information she has shared.*

---

## SUMMARY

When you inform others you assume the role of a teacher. Skilled teachers are able to develop a meaningful message that listeners will remember by following the principles and suggestions in this chapter.

▶**Describe four methods of informing others.**

The four most common methods of informing are defining, describing, narrating, and demonstrating. *Defining* is clarifying the meaning of an unfamiliar word or concept by quoting the dictionary, explaining in your own words, citing examples, noting opposites, or using an operational definition. *Describing* is presenting the who, what, when, where, and why about something. *Narrating* is story telling. A narration has four parts: the opening, the complications, the development, and the conclusion. *Demonstrating* is showing how something works, often using visual aids.

▶**Adapt the six steps of speech preparation and presentation to the creation of an informative speech.**

The six steps of speech preparation and presentation can be easily adapted to an informative presentation. First, select a topic that is of interest to both you and the audience. Second, analyze your audience, giving special attention to the information that they already know; build upon existing audience knowledge. Third, given that your general purpose is to inform, you need to develop a specific purpose statement that indicates what you want the audience to be able to do or know at the end of your speech. You also need to develop a clear thesis sentence. Fourth, gather supporting materials that create interest and clarify your major ideas. Fifth, logically organize your speech using well-worded transition phrases. Finally, rehearse and deliver your speech, giving verbal and nonverbal emphasis to key ideas.

▶**Identify five basic principles of informing others.**

The principles of informing others are the following:

1. Establish a motive for your audience to listen to you early in your speech.
2. Find methods of building redundancy into your speech; tell them what you are going to tell them, tell them, tell them what you told them.
3. Use simple ideas and phrases to help your listeners remember your message.
4. Build on what your audience already knows; associate the new with the familiar.
5. Strive to distribute new information evenly throughout your speech; pace the flow of the information you present.

▶**Begin to understand and manage any speech anxiety you may feel.**

It is normal to feel anxious about delivering a speech, but you can manage your nervousness by taking a few simple, concrete steps. Begin by selecting a topic with which you are already familiar. Then research your audience so that you can tailor your comments to interest them. When rehearsing, try to visualize the situation exactly as it will be. Boost your confidence by making certain that your speech is logically organized. In addition, become so familiar with your introduction and conclusion that you can present them without notes. Before you speak, relax by doing deep-breathing exercises. Then during your speech, use meaningful movement to burn off excess nervous energy. You will find that if you act calm, you will feel calm. Focusing your attention on your message will help you forget your discomfort.

## KEY TERMS

**Definition:** a statement of the meaning of a term or concept.
**Demonstrating:** showing an audience how to do something or how something works.
**Describing:** informing others about the who, what, when, where, and why of a term, concept, idea, thing, or person.
**Informative speech:** an oral presentation that is designed to teach, define, illustrate, clarify, or elaborate on a topic.
**Narration:** a story that communicates an idea or has a point.
**Operational definition:** a way of defining something by explaining how it works or how it is made or measured.
**Speech anxiety:** the feeling of nervousness that many speakers experience when preparing for and delivering a public speech.
**Word picture:** a verbal description that helps an audience visualize a specific image.

## DISCUSSION QUESTIONS

1. Suggest ten appropriate topics for an informative speech. Would each lend itself best to defining, describing, narrating, demonstrating, or some combination of methods?

2. What techniques can be used to motivate an audience to listen to your message?

3. Why does a speech need to be more redundant than a written message?

4. Why do most people experience speech anxiety?

5. What is your most effective method of managing speech anxiety?

## SUGGESTED ACTIVITIES

1. You will be assigned to a group with three or four other students.[3] Each group member will be given a copy of *Time, Newsweek,* or another similar magazine. Your task, as a group, is to develop a five-minute informative speech based on information that you find in the magazines. Specifically, you should (1) choose a topic, (2) write a specific purpose and thesis statement, (3) write a brief outline using at least three different sources (three different articles from the available magazines), (4) draft an introduction, (5) draft a conclusion, and (6) elect one group member to present the speech to the class.

2. Watch a documentary on TV and analyze its application of the basic principles of informative speaking. Consider such questions as: Was a motive for listening established? Was the pace of the presentation of information appropriate? Were terms and concepts clearly defined? Were clear transition phrases used?

3. Interview someone who does a lot of public speaking, such as a professor, a minister, or a politician. Has this person ever suffered from speech anxiety? What techniques does he or she use to manage anxiety?

4. Develop a three- to five-minute informative speech in which your key purpose is to define, describe, narrate, or demonstrate. Prepare an outline and a bibliography that includes at least three references. In addition to the speech, write a two- to three-page paper in which you describe the principles of informative speaking that you used (such as how you used transitions, how you established a motive for listening, your method of organizing your information, and the rationale for your choice of supporting materials).

## SUGGESTED READINGS

Powers, John H. (1987). *Public Speaking: The Lively Art.* (Belmont, California: Wadsworth Publishing Company).

Eisenberg, Abne M. and Gamble, Teri Kwal. (1982). *Painless Public Speaking.* (New York: Macmillan Publishing Company).

Katula, Richard A. (1987). *Principles and Patterns of Public Speaking.* (Belmont, California: Wadsworth Publishing Company).

Haskins, William Z. and Staudacher, Joseph M. (1987). *Successful Public Speaking: A Practical Guide.* (Glenview, Illinois: Scott, Foresman and Company).

Hanna, Michael S. and Gibson, James W. (1987). *Public Speaking for Personal Success.* (Dubuque, Iowa: Wm. C. Brown).

# Speaking to Persuade

**15**

*After studying this chapter, you should be able to:*

> Define *persuasion* and explain how it occurs.

> Select an appropriate topic for a persuasive speech.

> Adapt a persuasive speech to a friendly, neutral, or hostile audience.

> Use proof to construct sound arguments.

> Organize a persuasive speech based on the motivated sequence.

Think about the number of radio, TV, billboard, newspaper, and magazine advertisements you have seen or heard today. Consider how many times your friends, family members, employer, co-workers, and instructors have made requests of you. It has been estimated that you are exposed to over 600 persuasive messages every day!

Because the persuasive appeals that you hear strongly affect both your opinions and your behavior, it is important to understand their guiding principles. Then you will be a more informed consumer of persuasion as well as a more powerful persuader.

This chapter will examine the many aspects of persuasion, including exactly what it is and how it occurs. It will present some specific techniques for preparing a persuasive appeal, with particular attention to adapting a message to an audience and choosing the most purposeful supporting materials. Finally, it will present the motivated sequence, an especially effective way of organizing a persuasive speech.

## WHAT IS PERSUASION?

The television screen shows the image of a tall, frosty glass of orange juice. The announcer intones, "Florida orange juice. Brimming with flavor. Cool, delightful, and delicious. Refreshing. It's not just for breakfast anymore." After seeing this television commercial, you are quite aware those who prepared the commercial certainly want to change your behavior—they want you to buy Florida orange juice. Yet when you examine the message, on the surface it appears to be informative. At no time does the announcer say, "Buy it," or "Try it today." The announcer simply describes a glass of orange juice and implies that many people are drinking it at times other than breakfast. It is clear, however, that the advertiser is not paying over $100,000 for 30 seconds of air time just to inform you about the virtues of orange juice.

An encyclopedia salesperson at your local shopping mall may get your attention by offering a drawing for a free set of books. Before you leave, the salesperson will have emphasized the value of the product and encouraged you to purchase a 32-volume library for your home.

The indirect appeal of the commercial and the direct appeal of the salesperson are examples of persuasion. **Persuasion** is the process of changing or reinforcing an attitude, belief, value, or behavior through the use of verbal or nonverbal messages.

## HOW DOES PERSUASION OCCUR?

Why do people change their attitudes and behavior in response to something someone else says? One explanation is based on the idea that people need harmony and consistency in their lives.

## Dissonance Theory

**Dissonance theory** is based on the notion that humans strive for consistency in their thoughts and actions.[1] The theory suggests that each person operates from an organized, logical set of thoughts about him- or herself, other people, and everything with which that person comes into contact. The person attempts to organize thoughts about the world so that each attitude and belief is consistent with all other attitudes and beliefs. Each time the person is presented with information that is inconsistent with the way he or she has organized thoughts, the person experiences a state of disorganization called **cognitive dissonance.** Such disorganization is uncomfortable and prompts the person to reestablish consistency and balance.

*You strive for consistency in your thoughts and actions.*

Restoring balance to mental processes is similar to restoring balance to physical processes. If you are injured, your body moves to correct the problem. Whether it is through the production of more white blood cells, a rise in temperature, or a change in respiration, your body attempts to restore physiological balance. This is the same type of process that, according to dissonance theory, occurs psychologically. Someone who attempts to change your attitudes, beliefs, values, or behavior usually begins by pointing out a certain problem or need that you have. Then the persuader offers a solution to that problem. Thus, the persuader first creates imbalance and then attempts to restore balance by recommending a change. The recommended solution is, of course, the specific attitude, belief, value, or behavior that the persuader wants you to adopt.

A politician who aspires to the presidency of the United States usually tries to remind listeners of the various problems confronting the country—inflation, unemployment, and energy needs. Once the dissonance has been created, the candidate suggests that the problem can be alleviated, or at least somewhat diminished, if he or she is elected president. The candidate in effect says, "If I become president, I can restore balance to the country." The implication is that the voters will feel more peace of mind if they agree to support his candidacy.

Thus, according to dissonance theory, persuasion is more likely to occur if listeners first experience cognitive dissonance. Then the persuader will suggest how listeners can reorganize their thoughts and reachieve balance by adopting his or her proposal.

## Responding to Dissonance

When you experience dissonance, you may attempt to restore psychological balance in several ways.[2] First, you may *attack the credibility of the source* of the troublesome information. If, for example, a speaker says that the university you attend does not offer a high-quality edu-

---

| Review Box |

### Responding to Dissonance

When you experience cognitive dissonance you can respond in one of the following ways:

1. Attack the speaker's credibility.
2. Reinterpret what you hear to fit your existing position.
3. Seek new information to support your position.
4. Avoid listening to the dissonant information.
5. Accept the new point of view.

---

cation, you will probably experience some dissonance. In response, you may attack the speaker's credibility by concluding that the speaker does not know what he or she is talking about. If your speech instructor gives you a grade that you feel significantly underestimates your speaking ability, you may conclude that he or she is inept. Such a conclusion makes you feel better by reducing your dissonance.

A second response to dissonance is to *reinterpret* the speaker's statement so that you hear what you want to hear. You focus on the part of the message that does not create dissonance. For example, if you smoke you may be more likely to reject evidence about the health dangers of cigarette smoking. You will want to believe the claim that smoking does not pose a health threat.

Third, you may *seek new information* to support your position and refute the position of the individual who created the dissonance. Imagine that you have just purchased a new car. Then you read that a consumer organization has found that model unsafe for highway travel. In reaction, to help reduce your dissonance, you may seek additional information about the safety of your new car to support your original decision to buy it.

A fourth possible response is to *avoid listening* to the information that is creating the dissonance. If your English teacher gave you a failing grade last semester, you would probably not attend ceremonies honoring him or her as teacher of the year.

A fifth way of responding to dissonant information is with the response desired by the persuader. That is, you may *change your attitude, belief, value,* or *behavior* to support the position that he or she is advocating. If the candidate for mayor persuades you that your city government is in a mess and only she can correct the problem, you may decide to support her instead of the candidate whom you were originally backing. If the deodorant commercial persuades you that perspiration odor will invite scorn from all your friends and associates, you may decide to purchase that brand.

The objective of the persuader is to cause listeners to experience dissonance that will motivate them to support the particular change that the persuader is advocating. To accomplish this, the persuader must be perceived as believable enough to withstand attacks on his or her credibility. The message must be clear enough that listeners cannot selectively reinterpret it to suit their own interests. The information must be compelling enough that listeners feel equipped to make a choice in favor of the persuader.

## PREPARING A PERSUASIVE SPEECH

Now that you have become aware of some basic principles of persuasion, it is time to focus on the way to prepare a persuasive speech. You will follow the same steps introduced in Chapter 10:

1. Select a topic.
2. Analyze your audience.
3. Develop a general purpose, a specific purpose, and a thesis statement.
4. Gather supporting material.
5. Organize your speech.
6. Rehearse and deliver your speech.

As noted earlier, speech preparation and delivery is a process. Therefore, these steps, of necessity, overlap.

### Selecting a Topic

The best topic for a persuasive speech is one about which you feel strongly. If you talk about an attitude, belief, value, or action that you are truly committed to, you will be much more convincing. Controversial issues also make good speech topics. When selecting a topic for a persuasive speech, use the method discussed in Chapter 10: assess your own interests, attitudes, beliefs, and values and then brainstorm to come up with a creative angle.

*Controversial subjects about which you feel strongly make good persuasive speech topics.*

Another good source of ideas for persuasive speech topics is the media. What are some of the current issues on your campus, in your community, in your state, or in the country? Read editorials in newspapers and magazines like *Time, Newsweek,* and *U. S. News and World Report* to find out what people are interested in and talking about. Tune in to talk shows on radio and TV. Any topic that ignites people's emotions is likely to make a good basis for a persuasive speech.

The following list of topics may help you think about some of the issues that exist where you live. Depending on time limits, some of these topics may need to be narrowed.

| | |
|---|---|
| Too much violence on TV | A college degree for everyone |
| Record companies censoring their own recordings | Changing the state liquor laws |
| A limit on liability insurance suits | Legalizing casino gambling |
| Why you should buy a computer | More discipline for children |
| Why you should exercise more | A course in parenting for every parent |
| Stop jogging today | Stricter gun control laws |
| Why you should major in the liberal arts | Legalizing drugs |
| Public speaking as a requirement | Term papers—an (in)effective method of learning |
| Reducing our sugar intake | Permitting (or prohibiting) prayer in public schools |
| Reducing our salt intake | Higher salaries for teachers |
| Reducing our fat intake | Listening to *X* kind of music |
| We should lose weight | Reading a newspaper every day |
| Spending less on national defense | The parking problem on campus |
| Volunteer for . . . | Halting drugs (or alcohol) on campus |
| Spend less money on . . . | |
| Nuclear power plants—unsafe | |
| Changing the presidential election process | |

## Audience Analysis: Adjusting Ideas to People and People to Ideas

*A persuasive message must be adapted to listeners' beliefs, attitudes, and values.*

Successful persuasion depends on shrewd audience analysis. Each listener has certain attitudes, beliefs, and values that will affect his or her receptivity to a persuasive message. Unless you know what those attitudes, beliefs, and values are, you cannot hope to appeal to them. Unless you can adjust to your audience's ideas, you cannot hope to persuade them to adjust to yours.

### Strategies for Adapting Your Persuasive Message to Your Audience

Your audience's attitude toward you and your message plays a key role in the way you prepare your persuasive presentation. You will want to address an audience that is friendly toward you and your ideas

Successful persuasion depends on your ability to analyze your audience and adapt to their ideas.

differently from one that is neutral or hostile. The following sections will consider several specific strategies for adapting to friendly, neutral, and unreceptive audiences.

   **Adapting to a friendly audience.**   Of course, all speakers wish that they could always speak to friendly and responsive audiences. Following are five ways in which you can build on your audience's friendliness in order to achieve your persuasive goal:

### Clearly state why you have come to speak and what you want your audience to do.

If your listeners are already favorably disposed to you and your message, you can explicitly tell them what your objective is and what you want them to do. For example, if you know that most people in your audience share your desire to ban nuclear weapons, you may begin by saying that you have come to promote attendance at a ban-the-bomb rally on Saturday.

### Emphasize the degree of similarity between you and your audience. Identify with them.

If you are speaking to people who have children, and you have children of your own, mention this common bond if it is relevant to the issues you are addressing. What else do you have in common—interests, education, stands on other issues, religion, hometown, ethnic origin?

### Don't be afraid to make strong appeals to your listeners' emotions.

If your listeners are already convinced of the logic of your position, you can often move them to take action by appealing to their emotions while reminding them of the evidence that supports your conclusion. How to use emotional appeals will be discussed in greater detail later in this chapter.

### Suggest that listeners take specific and immediate action.

If you are trying to persuade your audience that a new library should be built in your community, you can conclude your speech by inviting your listeners to sign a petition in support of your proposal. If you don't have a petition to be signed, you can ask those who support your proposal to raise their hands. Successful salespersons know that the best time to get people to buy something is immediately after they have described the virtues of their product.

### If your audience is already committed to your position, ask them to reinforce one another to show their support.

If you are trying to motivate audience members to lose weight (and you know that they want to lose weight), ask them to encourage one another. They can be invited to exchange phone numbers and develop a support network. They can agree to meet again so that they can celebrate victories over the battle of the bulge or hear confessions from those who have had less willpower. Weight Watchers and other similar diet organizations use this technique successfully.

*An audience's neutrality may stem from lack of information.*

**Adapting to a neutral or apathetic audience.**     While it would be great if most of your audiences were initially supportive of your ideas, many will be somewhat neutral or apathetic. This may occur for at least three reasons. First, your audience may not have enough information on your subject to take a position. If you are trying to persuade them that biofeedback is useful, you will first have to explain what biofeedback is. Second, although listeners may have enough information, they may be undecided. If you are trying to persuade your audience to take another class in communication, they may already know the pros and cons, but they may hesitate to commit themselves before they choose their other courses for next semester. Third, audience members may be unable or unwilling to take a stand because they fail to see how your topic affects them. If your listeners can be convinced that the water shortage in the Southwest may eventually affect them, they may be more willing to accept your contention to conserve water now in your community.

Following are four specific steps you can take to adapt your message to a neutral audience:

## Make sure you have your listeners' attention.

It is going to be more difficult for you to get your audience to focus on your message if they are not really interested. Incorporating some of the following factors into your speech can help you gain and maintain audience attention.[3]

*Activity or movement.* Physically move around or tell a story that involves action and change.

*Reality.* Do everything possible to make your topic seem real, tangible, and concrete.

*Proximity.* Refer to events and examples that directly affect your audience—situations that are close at hand and current.

*Familiarity.* Remember that things, people, and events common to your audience are easy for them to visualize and relate to.

*Novelty.* Use something unusual, such as a story, personal example, or visual aid, to pique your audience's curiosity.

*Suspense.* Withhold the key idea until the end of the story. If the audience knows it's coming, they'll keep listening.

*Conflict.* Introduce conflict of ideas, personalities, or philosophies.

*Humor.* Lighten a moment or drive a point home by making a humorous comment.

*The Vital.* Remember that anything that affects a person's life, happiness, satisfaction, property, or employment is likely to strike a respondent chord.

## Make sure listeners know how your subject affects those they love.

If you are trying to win support for the city's new water fluoridation process, you can tell your listeners that such a process would help make their family and loved ones healthier.

## Realize that the response from a neutral audience is not going to be as immediate or favorable as that from a friendly audience.

Persuasion rarely occurs all at once or at the first hearing of arguments and evidence. It often takes several attempts to reach a neutral audience. Be patient and allow time for the sleeper effect to work in your favor.

| Review Box |
| --- |

## Adapting Your Persuasive Message to Your Audience

| *Situation* | *Suggestions* |
| --- | --- |
| Adapting to a Friendly Audience | Clearly state your objective.<br>Establish your similarity to your audience.<br>Use emotional appeals.<br>Encourage specific and immediate action.<br>Ask listeners to reinforce one another to show their support. |
| Adapting to a Neutral or Apathetic Audience | Make sure you have your listeners' attention.<br>Make sure your listeners know how the subject you are addressing affects them or those they love.<br>Bear in mind that a neutral audience is not going to respond as immediately or favorably as a friendly audience would.<br>Refer to attitudes, beliefs, and values your listeners have in common. |
| Adapting to an Unreceptive or Hostile Audience | Don't tell your audience that you are planning to change their attitudes or behavior.<br>Don't ask for a dramatic change in attitude or behavior.<br>Emphasize areas of agreement before you discuss those issues upon which you disagree.<br>Acknowledge hostile audience members' points of view.<br>Present both sides of the issue that you are addressing.<br>Take steps to establish your credibility. |

### Refer to interests your listeners have in common.

What issues or topics does your audience find exciting or important? At a meeting of the local Parent Teachers Association, speaking about the need for improved reading skills is a better idea than talking about a recent vacation trip.

Adapting to an unreceptive or hostile audience.   The toughest audience to persuade is one that is unreceptive or hostile toward you, your topic, or your stand on the issues. If the audience is hostile because they do not like your stand on the topic, keep in mind the following six suggestions:

### Don't tell your audience that you are planning to change their attitudes or behavior.

If you do, you may make them defensive. Imagine that you are a Democrat speaking at a Republican party meeting. You hope to win some converts to your political point of view. If you announce at the outset that you plan to change your listeners' attitudes, they will probably mentally say, "Oh, yeah? Just try!" If you are more subtle—saying, for example, that you have come to share some new points of view—you will be less likely to arouse their resistance.

### Don't ask for a dramatic change in attitude or behavior.

If you do, it can backfire and make your audience even more hostile. Set a realistic limit on what you can achieve. Don't be overly timid in your approach, but realistically assess your objective.

### Emphasize areas of agreement before discussing areas of disagreement.

Even if the group you are facing is not in favor of abortion and you are, you can at least all agree that the issue is controversial and evokes strong feelings on both sides. Your audience will probably also agree that individual freedom of choice is an important right. Once you help your audience to understand that you share some common ground, they may be more attentive when you explain your position, even though it is at odds with their own.

### Acknowledge hostile audience members' points of view.

Being objective will demonstrate your readiness to accept the reasonableness of people holding differing opinions. Do not belittle your audience for taking a different stand from yours. If an audience member criticizes your logic, respond courteously. Even if your critic grows rude, your ability to stay calm and respectful will win you sympathy and support.

### Present both sides of the issue you are addressing.

If you present only your side of the issue, hostile audience members will be thinking about their side anyway. You can often defuse this tendency by noting other points of view and then citing evidence to support the advantages of your position.

**Firmly establish your credibility.**

Credibility is always important, but it becomes especially crucial when your audience is hostile. Don't boast about your qualifications. Simply let your listeners know that you have the experience, interest, and skills required to address your topic knowledgeably.

Audience analysis is vital to the success of your persuasive efforts. Your ability to adapt your message to your audience will often determine whether you achieve your persuasive objective.

## Developing a Specific Purpose and Thesis Statement

After you have selected a topic and analyzed your audience, you need to "fine tune" your speech objective. If you already know that your general purpose is to persuade, you need only develop a specific purpose and a thesis statement. The specific purpose for a persuasive speech should follow the same format recommended in chapter 10: it should specify what you want your audience to be able to do when you have finished your speech. For example, if you intend to advocate strict discipline for children, your specific purpose might read: "At the end of my speech, the audience members should agree that effective discipline is important to their children." Your thesis statement, or one-sentence summary of your speech, could then read: "Children need discipline from their parents so that they can learn the implications of their behavior and follow the rules of society."

## Developing Supporting Material

Just as you gathered examples, statistics, illustrations, and other supporting material for your informative speech, so, too, will you seek appropriate supporting material for your persuasive speech. Your goal will be to select the material that will have the strongest persuasive impact on your audience. Of course, the attitude your audience has toward you and your topic will help determine what kinds of support will work best.

*Aristotle believed that audiences are persuaded by three methods: ethos, logos, and pathos.*

Aristotle, the famous Greek philosopher, believed that audiences were persuaded through three primary methods. First, they supported an idea if the speaker or those who supported the speaker were ethical and credible; Aristotle used the term **ethos.** Second, they were more

> **Review Box**
>
> ## Methods of Persuading
>
> **Ethos**        The character and ethics (credibility) of a speaker
>
> **Logos**        The reasoning and evidence a speaker uses to support
>                  arguments
>
> **Pathos**       The appeal to listeners' emotions

likely to support a proposition if it was logically sound and supported with appropriate evidence; Aristotle called this *logos.* Finally, they were apt to be persuaded if the speaker appealed to their emotions to support a particular issue; the term Aristotle used was *pathos.* Let's examine supporting materials in terms of Aristotle's three categories.

   **Ethos.**   *Ethos* refers to a speaker's ethics or character. If a speaker is perceived as believable, trustworthy, and accurate, an audience is more likely to respond favorably to a request for action or change. Today the term *credibility* is used to describe a speaker's ethics and character.

   In addition to assuring your audience that you are a credible speaker, you need to select supporting material that your audience will find believable, valid, and trustworthy. To make certain that the sources of your supporting material are credible, ask yourself the following questions:

1. Is my supporting material from reliable sources?
2. If I am using expert opinion, will my audience find my source well-qualified and unbiased?
3. Will the source of my information be perceived as believable?

   **Logos.**   **Reasoning** is the process of drawing a conclusion from evidence. **Evidence** consists of the definitions, examples, statistics, and other supporting materials that pertain to a specific situation. Together, reasoning and evidence form **proof.** To persuade your listeners, you must provide the right proof—the right combination of evidence and reasoning—to change their beliefs, attitudes, values, or behavior. Your evidence will be the supporting materials you've chosen to present, as discussed in Chapter 11. Your reasoning will be the thought processes you use to lead your listeners from each piece of evidence to the conclusion you'd like them to draw. The three general patterns of reasoning are inductive reasoning, deductive reasoning, and causal reasoning.

*Inductive reasoning.* **Inductive reasoning** is a thought pattern that moves from specific information to a general conclusion. The specific information typically consists of facts, examples, statistics, or comparisons. In the following example, note how the speaker leads the audience from specific examples and reliable statistics to the desired general conclusion:

> *Karl wore a seat belt during his recent auto accident and was not seriously injured. Dorothy, who also wore her seat belt, wasn't hurt when she had an auto crash, either. Steve, another seat belt wearer, came out of his accident unscratched as well. These examples, plus recent statistics from the National Safety Council which show that 10,000 accident victims who wore seat belts had significantly fewer serious injuries than did 10,000 who did not wear seat belts, point to the conclusion that seat belts help to prevent serious injuries.*

When reasoning inductively to a generalization, keep the following questions in mind:

**a.** Are there enough instances to prove your point?
**b.** Are the instances typical?
**c.** Are the instances recent?

*Deductive reasoning.* Deductive reasoning is just the opposite of inductive reasoning. In **deductive reasoning,** your thought pattern moves from a general statement to a specific conclusion. Such reasoning is often organized as a **syllogism,** a form of argument that has three key elements: a major premise, a minor premise, and a conclusion. To formulate a syllogism, begin with a general statement.

Excessive campaign spending is undesirable.

This general statement is called your **major premise.** Next, move to a more specific statement, such as

Media campaigning requires that excessive amounts of money be spent.

This more specific statement is called a **minor premise.** In reasoning deductively, you need to make sure that your major and minor premises can be proven or supported with evidence. Based on your general statement and your more specific statement, you then infer a necessary consequence, or **conclusion.** In this example, your conclusion would be

Therefore, media campaigning is undesirable.

*Inductive reasoning moves from specific information to a general conclusion*

*Deductive reasoning occurs when you draw a specific conclusion from a general statement.*

Inductive, deductive or causal reasoning can help you lead your listeners from each piece of evidence to the conclusion you'd like them to draw.

Following are additional examples of deductive reasoning cast in the form of syllogisms:

*Major Premise:*     All economics professors are highly intelligent.
*Minor Premise:*     Dr. Salem is an economics professor.
*Conclusion:*     Dr. Salem is highly intelligent.

*Major Premise:*     All state sales taxes are unfair to low income families.
*Minor Premise:*     Our state is proposing a new state sales tax.
*Conclusion:*     Our state's proposed sales tax is unfair to low income families.

If you plan to use deductive reasoning, ask yourself:

**a.** Is the major premise true?
**b.** Have I chosen the best possible conclusion from the major premise?

*Causal reasoning.*    **Causal reasoning** is a thought process that attempts to establish a cause-effect relationship between two or more events. You may reason from *cause to effect,* moving from a known factor to a predicted result, or from *effect to cause,* starting with the result and trying to figure out what produced it. For example, in reasoning from cause to effect, you may conclude that last year's shortage of rainfall and the resulting drop in the water table are probably the causes of the sinkholes that have formed in your community recently.

*Causal reasoning attempts to establish a cause-effect relationship between two or more events.*

**Review Box**

## Types of Reasoning

| Type | Definition | Example |
|---|---|---|
| Inductive Reasoning | Thought pattern that moves from specific information to a general conclusion | Because San Antonio and Miami crime rates decreased when handgun permits were required, all communities in the United States should require handgun permits. |
| Deductive Reasoning | Thought pattern that moves from a general statement to a specific conclusion | All handguns laws that restrict the purchase of handguns are effective (major premise). Our state senator is proposing a new law that would restrict handgun purchases (minor premise). The senator's proposed law will be effective (conclusion). |
| Causal Reasoning | Thought pattern that relates two or more events to prove that one or more of the events caused the other | Since the new law requiring a permit to purchase a handgun went into effect, the crime rate has decreased. |

In reasoning from effect to cause, you may note that stock market prices are down and then go on to speculate that the reason for the drop is the high national debt.

Doublecheck your reasoning to make sure that you are not inadvertently using a reasoning fallacy. You should also monitor the persuasive messages you hear to make sure you are not swayed by another person's reasoning fallacy.

**Pathos.**   As you are leafing through a magazine, you come across a picture that catches your attention. It shows a young girl with big, beautiful penetrating eyes; but she is sad—she has tears glistening in her eyes. The caption at the bottom of the picture reads, "Don't turn this page. Respond to the needs of starving children like this one. Send your check to Save Our Children today." It is not logic or evidence that makes you respond to this promotion, but rather, emotion. Your emotions strongly influence your responses. Thus, using pathos, or emotional appeals, is one way in which a speaker may try to motivate you to change your beliefs, attitudes, values, or behavior.

*Pathos ignores evidence and logic in favor of emotion.*

**Emotional appeals** are statements, examples, opinions, and visual and auditory stimuli that trigger strong feelings. They may be verbal, describing in words what may happen if seat belts are not fastened, or nonverbal, the picture of the child in the magazine ad or the music that accompanies a pep rally.

Most psychologists believe that human behavior is motivated by needs. These needs are tied to deep-seated emotions. Knowing this, a persuasive speaker may appeal to one of these needs in order to evoke an emotional reaction. One insurance company, for example, bases its television advertising campaign on the audience's need for security. The appeal is *not* made through facts or statistics, but through the portrayal of a young, busy family whose provider sighs happily, "They need me." He (and, the company hopes, the audience as well) is greatly relieved that he has life insurance to meet his family's needs, even if he should die.

A speaker may also appeal to values to stimulate an emotional reaction. Thus, mentioning the following goals would motivate many Americans to respond: a comfortable life; equality; an exciting, stimulating life; family security; freedom; happiness; inner harmony; mature love; national security; pleasure; salvation; self-respect; a sense of accomplishment; social recognition; true friendship; wisdom; a world of beauty; and a world of peace.[4]

How can you use emotional appeals in a speech to motivate audience members to respond to your message? Perhaps the best way is to use examples and illustrations to which your listeners can relate. Imagine that you want to encourage college-age audience members to make regular deposits in their savings accounts. You will be more successful if you tell them how their savings can benefit them in the immediate future (for example, they can use them for a down payment on a car), rather than try to persuade them to save for retirement. On the other hand, an older audience may find an appeal to save money for retirement more persuasive because they are closer to retirement age.

The Roman orator Cicero contended that if you want a listener to experience a certain emotion, you should experience and demonstrate the emotion as you speak. Thus, if you want your audience to be excited and enthusiastic about a particular proposition, try being excited and enthusiastic about it as you talk to them. If you want them to be sad, communicate your sadness with your emotions.

The language that a speaker uses also affects a listener's emotional state. Certain words and phrases can arouse an audience. For example, "America—love it or leave it" was often used to evoke a strong emotional response during the Vietnam war. Patriotic slogans, such as "Remember the Alamo" or "Remember Pearl Harbor," have also evoked strong emotional responses in audiences.

A speaker can try to motivate listeners through threats or fear.[5] A strong fear-arousing approach such as "You will get lung cancer and die if you don't stop smoking," is more likely to succeed if a speaker is perceived as highly credible. Thus, a doctor providing medical advice and a lawyer providing legal advice are among those who can use strong fear appeals to maximum benefit.

On the other hand, if a speaker is not a highly credible source, he or she should probably try to arouse only a moderate level of fear. If a speaker attempts to arouse fear too intensely, the listeners may find the message unbelievable or think that it does not apply to them. As a result, they may totally ignore what the speaker has to say.

Finally, the success of a fear appeal relies partly on how immediate the particular threat is to an audience. For example, if people rarely travel by airplane, they are unlikely to be aroused by descriptions of the many near collisions in the skies over major airports. If people don't smoke, they will not be interested in a speech about the danger of lung cancer caused by smoking.

Emotional appeals can be effective if they are carefully planned to address the needs, values, and motives of an audience. Appealing to such basic emotions as pride, fear, love, hope, or loyalty can be highly persuasive.

## Organizing Persuasive Messages

*The organization of your ideas and arguments can enhance or detract from your ability to persuade others.*

The order in which you present your main ideas to your audience can have a significant impact on your communication effectiveness. Of the approaches discussed in Chapter 12, the problem-solution and cause-effect patterns are particularly effective for presenting persuasive information. Following are some other thoughts to bear in mind as you organize your persuasive presentation:

1. Use the introduction of your persuasive speech to emphasize areas of agreement between you and your listeners. This helps to establish common ground between you and your audience to accept your arguments.

2. If you feel your audience may be hostile to your point of view, place your strongest arguments first. If you save your strongest arguments until the end, your listeners may close their minds early and lose interest.

3. If you feel you need to state specific conclusions to your audience to move them to take action, it is better to do so toward the end of your speech. They will more likely take action after you have described the problem and presented your evidence for change.

In addition to these specific suggestions, a five-step plan developed by Alan Monroe can help you to organize a persuasive speech. Monroe's **motivated sequence** is an expanded version of the problem-solution pattern of organization that is based on the principles of cognitive dissonance discussed earlier in the chapter.[6] A speech that is organized using the motivated sequence includes five steps: (1) attention, (2) need, (3) satisfaction, (4) visualization, and (5) action.

*The motivated sequence consists of five steps: attention, need, satisfaction, visualization, and action.*

1. *The Attention Step.* As in any speech, you should first capture your audience's attention, called by Monroe the **attention step.** A personal or hypothetical example, startling statement or statistic, rhetorical question, or well-chosen analogy often piques an audience's curiosity. For example, one speaker began a speech advocating increased use of government wiretaps with the question, "What if your brother or sister's life depended on the use of an FBI wiretap?" Such an opening sentence sparked the audience's attention and also introduced the problem.

2. *The Need Step.* The next step, the **need step,** is to describe the problem and, by showing how it affects the listeners personally, establish their need for concern. You can relate your topic to your audience's interests by citing facts and statistics to suggest its scope. Personal examples and expert opinions can also be used to identify the problem and emphasize its immediacy. For example, a speaker who wanted to illustrate the problem of organized crime in America cited evidence of illegal activity in her community. An effectively prepared need step should bring the problem home to your listeners.

   Professor Harold Hill in the musical *The Music Man* effectively convinced the people of River City, Iowa, that the parents of the community needed to purchase band uniforms and instruments from him. He had an effective need step for his persuasive sales campaign. In one of the notable songs from the musical he told them they had "trouble right here in River City." He convinced them their youngsters were frequenting the pool halls and needed more wholesome diversions such as participating in a marching band. An effective need step brings the problem home to the listeners.

3. *The Satisfaction Step.* Once you have identified your listeners' need for concern, you should satisfy it by presenting a solution, identified as the **satisfaction step.** Perhaps passing a new law, electing a specific political candidate, or buying a certain product will solve the problem. At this point in your speech you need not go into great detail about your solution. Just make sure that your audience understands your proposal. You can also cite examples of the way your solution has worked in other situations.

4. *The Visualization Step.* Your aim in the **visualization step** is to help your listeners see how your solution will satisfy their need. What will the future be like if your solution is adopted? How will life be better, the community safer, or the country stronger? Think of the many TV and magazine advertisements that help you visualize what it is like to enjoy a certain product. Smiling, happy people are shown enjoying the promoted soft drink. A cheerful, well-scrubbed family is pictured enjoying hamburgers and french fries in a fast-food restaurant. You can use the same kind of positive visualization to appeal to the pleasure, pride, and security of your listeners.

   You may also use a negative visualization to appeal to your listeners' fears and insecurities. You can explain how a problem will continue or get even worse if your solution is not adopted. Think of the TV ad that shows a mom who, because she used the wrong detergent, forced her family to endure the humiliation of wearing dingy clothes. Imagine a politician who uses negative visualization to claim that the problems facing voters will get even worse unless the politician is elected to office.

5. *The Action Step.* Finally, in the **action step,** you ask your audience to take specific action to implement the solution that you have suggested. Tell your audience what you want them to do so that the positive image of the visualization step can be achieved or the negative implications can be avoided. While the specific action will depend on your problem and solution, possible actions include signing a petition, raising hands to show support, meeting with you after your speech for more information, placing an order for a product or service, calling or writing to register a complaint, signing up for a class, or trying a new hobby.

The motivated sequence is a guide, not an absolute formula to apply in the same way to every persuasive speech that you deliver. You may find that you will need to modify it to suit your needs for a particular audience. If, for example, you are speaking to a hostile audience, you may not include a specific action for them to take. If you can get a

| Review Box |
| --- |

## The Motivated Sequence

| Step | Purpose | Method |
| --- | --- | --- |
| Attention | To get the audience to listen to your message | Rhetorical question<br>Unusual fact<br>Unusual statistic<br>Quotation<br>Analogy<br>Personal example<br>Hypothetical example<br>Illustration |
| Need | To describe the problem and relate it to the audience's personal concerns | Documentation of a problem using facts, statistics, and examples |
| Satisfaction | To present a solution that satisfies the audience's need | Description of the way a problem can be solved |
| Visualization | To help the audience see how the solution will solve the problem | *Positive visualization:* showing an audience how great it will be if your solution is adopted<br>*Negative visualization:* showing an audience how terrible it will be if your solution is not adopted |
| Action | To call for personal commitment and deeds | Specific, detailed instructions about the way your audience should respond to your persuasive message |

hostile audience to recognize that there is a problem (need step) and that your solution (satisfaction step) may have some positive benefits (visualization step), you will have achieved your purpose. If you are speaking to an audience that is apathetic toward your speech objective, you may need to emphasize the attention and need steps and not ask them to take specific action.

## Rehearsing and Delivering Your Speech

The final step in the process of persuasive speaking is to rehearse and deliver your speech. Follow the steps outlined in Chapter 13. Remember that eye contact, appropriate vocal delivery, and effective use of movement and gestures will help persuade your audience of your enthusiasm and commitment to your proposition and encourage them to follow your lead.

## A SAMPLE PERSUASIVE SPEECH

Note how the following sample speech by Linda Loehr incorporates the basic principles of persuasive speaking. Applications of her persuasive technique are identified in the left-hand margin.

| | |
|---|---|
| *General Purpose:* | To persuade |
| *Specific Purpose:* | At the end of the speech, audience members should enroll in a first-aid course. |
| *Thesis Statement:* | Many lives can be saved if only more people know how to administer first-aid. |

### IGNORANCE KILLS[7]
### Linda Loehr
### University of Southern Colorado

The speaker immediately grabs her audience's attention with a dramatic, real-life example (step 1 of the motivated sequence).

Last summer on a Sunday afternoon, seven-year-old Michael James was swimming at a public pool. As a precocious seven year old, he decided to dare the big slide that looked like so much fun. He entered the water, became winded, and lost consciousness. Unnoticed by the lifeguard, he floated into a group of children playing dead man's float. One of the children saw that Michael wasn't coming up for air. He called to the lifeguard, and Michael was soon pulled from the water. His face was blue; his breathing had stopped. The pool staff quickly administered artificial respiration, and I'm happy to report that Michael James is alive and well today. But, unfortunately, not all story endings are this happy.

Linda uses a second, even more dramatic example to emphasize her point and introduce the problem she will address.

Andrew Miller was eating dinner with his wife one night when suddenly a piece of meat lodged in his throat. He tried to cough it up but could not, and he passed out. His face became discolored. His wife panicked and called the neighbors, but no one knew the correct procedure. More neighbors were called. Finally, an ambulance was summoned. It was too late, Andrew Miller died in front of his wife and 13 of his friends and loved ones. Was the cause of death chicken fried steak? No—Ignorance!

The names Michael James and Andrew Miller are fictitious, but their stories are very real. More importantly, their lives or deaths depended on one thing—the quickness and accuracy of first-aid given to them by those around them.

Michael James was fortunate; he was in a controlled situation with trained people who knew what to do. He lived. Andrew Miller was not; he died. Couldn't we find a way of bringing this first-aid care into our homes for our loved ones?

To a pool staff, first-aid courses are a common event, but to most families and students these courses are almost nonexistent.

Thousands of lives are saved each year because of simple application of first-aid techniques, but double the number of lives are lost because people simply don't know what to do. Ignorance kills.

Do you realize that the difference between life and death is five minutes? A mere five minutes because five minutes of no oxygen to the brain produces brain damage and, more often than not, death! In emergencies, do you really want to wait for professionals to arrive? Can we learn to act on our own?

Ignorance of first-aid is a serious problem in our society today. We must look at this problem, discuss its consequences, and look to some probable solutions.

The problem stems from the lack of any real dissemination of quality first-aid information in our society today. First-aid education is simply not a requirement within our system.

We must look at this lack of education on all three levels of its existence—the levels of secondary education, of higher education, and, finally, of home and family education.

First, on the level of secondary education, there is usually some type of required "health" course in all schools. But, according to Mark J. Kittleson and Bruce M. Ragon, these courses are inadequate. Kittleson and Ragon found in their recent survey of *What High School Students Know About First-Aid,* that school politics, uninformed administrators, and poorly designed programs caused the first-aid courses to be less than complete. Most students' knowledge is based on simple factual data that they cannot apply. The students' understanding of the functions, processes, and implications of this material is highly inadequate.

Many studies have shown that although students can master facts for simple classroom testing, they cannot apply what they have learned. One study suggested that the simple mastery of facts for normal classroom testing was a far cry from the knowledge needed in real-life situations.

Linda asks a question that appeals to listeners' concern for loved ones. In the process, she begins to identify the problem and relate it to listeners' personal interest (step 2 of the motivated sequence).

The speaker cites a simple statistic to underscore the seriousness of the situation.

She continues to build her case by noting the small difference that separates life from death. She then asks her listeners to picture themselves in a life-threatening situation.

In this transition, Linda previews three of her main points— the problem, its consequences, and some solutions.

She uses causal reasoning to link lack of education with ignorance of first aid.

Once again, the speaker uses a transition sentence to preview her next few points.

Linda cites expert testimony to support her opinion.

The speaker helps her listeners draw an appropriate conclusion from the research she has presented. Then she leads them to her next point.

Linda uses more causal reasoning to develop the scope of the problem. Note how she presents both sides of the issue— first citing an opposing opinion and then citing an opinion that supports her own view.

Linda provides a brief internal summary before moving on to her next thought.

She once again draws in home and family.

Linda asks a rhetorical question to remind audience members of their personal vulnerability.

Linda begins a clear statement of the solutions to the problem (step 3 of the motivated sequence).

She lists the steps in her solution, highlighting them with the terms *first, second,* and *third.*

As you can see, on the secondary education level, we are providing the facts but not the applications. Thus, we are, in essence, giving these students useless knowledge. Unfortunately, health education on the higher educational levels is not much better. Only 10.7 percent of all universities in the United States require health education.

The reasoning for this was given in a recent study entitled *Health Education Requirements in American Universities.* College administrators have pointed out that "health" is non-academic in nature, is taught on the secondary level, and is less relevant than other courses which the students might take.

But many professionals disagree and state that any field of knowledge should be considered academic. In light of what we've seen about how poorly designed the high-school "health" courses are, what course could possibly be more relevant to anyone than that which preserves life?

Now we have observed two levels of formal education and have discovered a lack of first-aid education.

The home-and-family scenario is just as bad. Only one out of every fifty families in the United States participates in some type of first-aid course together. The American Red Cross stated that family apathy toward first-aid is a significant problem because most accidents occur in the home, and families have very little education about what to do.

Having observed all levels of education, we have yet to discover any real, quality first-aid training.

The consequences are astounding. Do you realize that what you don't know puts you at the highest risk? Heart disease, which afflicts one out of every five people in the United States has reached epidemic proportions and is now the leading cause of death. Death from heart attack is preventable, but prevention is not being taught on a wide basis.

There are several possible solutions to the lack of first-aid education. Although they may not be glamorous, they are practical, and they will help solve the problem.

First, we need an attitude change in our society. We must cease to believe that first-aid is solely the responsibility of others. We must take the responsibility upon ourselves.

The second part of the solution lies with education. The ideal would be to implement programs in all high schools and universities, and to require all students to take those courses. Changing the curriculum is not a farfetched solution; for example, there has been a recent upsurge of interest in heart health knowledge for school-aged children. But, curriculum change takes time and needs support. And we need action now!

You and I can take the necessary action which would be the third part of the solution. We are all in some way connected with the school systems in our society, and we need to make the need for programs clear. Request these courses at your university. If you have children, inquire about the quality of their school's health programs. We must make the schools know that we are concerned and that we need action.

> Linda tells her listeners exactly what they can do to solve the problem (step 5 of the motivated sequence).

The third and most timely solution lies at the family level and with you. You can take direct action. Sign yourself and your family up for a first-aid course. Such courses are readily available in most communities at community centers or local fire stations. For example, in a nine-hour cardiopulmonary resuscitation course, you will learn everything from clearing an airway to reviving someone after a heart attack.

> She drives her point home by returning to the theme of family.

No household can exempt themselves from the need for first-aid training. Over 3000 people died last year because of obstructed airways. Take a first-aid course, and make it a family night. It can be a lot of fun for you and your family. I signed myself and my family up for a course, and we had a lot of fun.

> She uses a personal example to encourage positive visualization (step 4 in the motivated sequence).

Take a first-aid course, and you will feel better about your family's safety. They will too.

Remember Michael James? I sure do because I was the lifeguard who gave Michael James artificial respiration. He lived. Remember Andrew Miller? He died. Why? Because of ignorance. If these two stories were yours, which story ending would you have? It's up to you. But remember ignorance kills!

> Linda closes her speech by returning to her initial examples. She combines an emotional appeal with an appeal to action.

## SUMMARY

Armed with principles of persuasive communication you will be better prepared to respond to the over 600 persuasive messages you receive each day. Your skill as a speaker should also grow as you learn to apply the persuasive strategies in this chapter.

▶**Define *persuasion* and explain how it occurs.**
*Persuasion* is the process of changing or reinforcing an attitude, belief, value, or behavior through the use of verbal or nonverbal messages. One attempt to explain how the persuasion process works, dissonance theory, is based on the notion that humans strive for consistency in their thoughts and actions. When we receive new information that is inconsistent with the way we organize our thoughts, we experience cognitive dissonance. Because dissonance is uncomfortable, we seek to reestablish balance, often by changing an attitude, belief, value,

or behavior to be consistent with the new information. Thus, a speaker may purposely create cognitive dissonance in order to persuade listeners to accept his or her proposal.

Of course, listeners do not always respond as a speaker hopes. Instead of accepting the new information, they may (1) attack the speaker's credibility, (2) reinterpret what they hear to fit their own position, (3) seek new information to support their position, or (4) avoid listening to the dissonant information.

▶**Select an appropriate topic for a persuasive speech.**

The best topic for a persuasive speech is one about which you feel strongly. To find a topic that will work for you, inventory your own interests, attitudes, beliefs, and values and then brainstorm to come up with a creative angle based on your own experience. Good persuasive speech topics can also be found by perusing magazines and newspapers or tuning in to TV and radio programs.

▶**Adapt a persuasive speech to a friendly, neutral, or hostile audience.**

With a friendly audience you should clearly state your speech goals, emphasize areas of agreement between you and your audience, use strong emotional appeals, suggest that listeners take specific and immediate action, and ask them to reinforce one another's attitudes. With a neutral or apathetic audience you should immediately gain their attention, relate your topic to those they love, don't expect a favorable response right away, and refer to common interests. With an unreceptive or hostile audience don't announce that you will change their attitudes, don't expect dramatic changes, emphasize areas of agreement, acknowledge hostile listeners' points of view, present both sides of the issue, and firmly establish your credibility.

▶**Use proof to construct sound arguments.**

To persuade your listeners, you must have the right *proof*—that is, the right combination of evidence and reasoning. Evidence consists of the definitions, examples, statistics, and other supporting materials that pertain to your position. Reasoning is the process of drawing conclusions from evidence. The three general patterns of reasoning are inductive, deductive, and causal. *Inductive reasoning* is a thought process that moves from specific information to a general conclusion. Both generalizations and analogies are forms of inductive reasoning. In *deductive reasoning,* the thought process moves from a general statement to a specific conclusion. Such an argument often takes the form of a syllogism, which has three key elements: a major premise, a minor premise, and a conclusion. Finally, causal reasoning attempts to establish a cause-effect relationship between two or more events. It may progress from cause to effect or from effect to cause.

**Organize a persuasive speech based on the motivated sequence.**

The motivated sequence is a flexible guide that may be modified to suit a wide variety of topics and audiences. An expanded version of the problem-solution pattern of organization, it proceeds through five steps. In the attention step, you spark your audience's interest in your topic. In the need step, you describe a problem and create concern by relating it to your audience's interests, wants, and desires. In the satisfaction step, you propose a course of action that will solve the problem and satisfy your listeners' concerns. In the visualization step, you paint word pictures of the positive results of accepting your solution or the negative results of rejecting it. And finally, in the action step, you ask your audience to perform specific deeds to implement your plan.

## KEY TERMS

**Action step:**  the fifth step in the motivated sequence—calling for action to implement the speaker's solution to the problem.

**Attention step:**  the first step of the motivated sequence—capturing the audience's interest right from the beginning.

**Causal reasoning:**  a thought process that attempts to establish a cause-effect relationship between two or more events.

**Cognitive dissonance:**  the sense of disorganization that prompts a person to change when new information conflicts with previously organized thought patterns.

**Conclusion:**  in a syllogism, the necessary consequence of the major and minor premises.

**Deductive reasoning:**  a thought process that draws a specific conclusion from a general statement.

**Dissonance theory:**  a theory which contends that because humans strive for consistency in their thoughts and actions, new or contrary information can result in a reevaluation of existing attitudes, beliefs, values, and behavior.

**Emotional appeal:**  a statement, example, opinion, or visual or auditory stimulus that triggers strong feelings.

**Ethos:**  a speaker's ethics or character, referred to as credibility.

**Evidence:**  the definitions, examples, statistics, and other supporting materials that pertain to a specific situation.

**Inductive reasoning:** a thought process that draws a general conclusion from specific information.
**Logos:** the use of logic and reasoning to persuade an audience.
**Major premise:** the general statement that is the first element of a syllogism.
**Minor premise:** the specific statement that is the second element of a syllogism.
**Motivated sequence:** a strategy for organizing a persuasive speech that proceeds through five steps: attention, need, satisfaction, visualization, and action.
**Need step:** the second step of the motivated sequence—describing the problem and establishing the audience's need for concern.
**Pathos:** the use of emotional appeals to persuade an audience.
**Persuasion:** the process of changing or reinforcing an attitude, belief, value, or behavior through the use of verbal or nonverbal messages.
**Proof:** evidence plus reasoning used to support a persuasive argument.
**Reasoning:** the process of drawing a conclusion from evidence.
**Satisfaction step:** the third step of the motivated sequence—presenting the solution to the problem that has been identified.
**Syllogism:** a deductive argument that has three key elements: a major premise, a minor premise, and a conclusion.
**Visualization step:** the fourth step of the motivated sequence—picturing the positive results that will occur if the recommended solution is adopted or the negative results that will occur if the solution is not implemented.

## DISCUSSION QUESTIONS

1. Provide examples of the way attempts to persuade can be either subtle or direct.
2. How does the theory of cognitive dissonance help you understand how people are persuaded?
3. If you were trying to persuade listeners to increase school taxes so that new educational programs could be implemented, how would your strategy differ when speaking to a friendly, an apathetic, or a hostile audience?
4. What are the differences among the persuasive methods of ethos, logos, and pathos?
5. Discuss how the theory of cognitive dissonance explains the effectiveness of the motivated sequence.

## *SUGGESTED ACTIVITIES*

1. Identify three nationally recognizable people who, in your opinion, are highly credible public speakers. Analyze their credibility based on the three factors discussed in this chapter. Are they qualified, knowledgeable, and competent? Are they trustworthy, honest, and sincere?

2. Prepare and deliver a five-minute persuasive speech in which you argue against your own convictions. Search for examples, statistics, and testimony to support your speech purpose. Were you believable to your audience? Was it difficult to develop arguments for a speech about which you did not feel strongly?

3. After you have presented a persuasive speech in which you argued against your feelings, present a second persuasive speech in which you take the position you actually support. Again, search for strong evidence to support your position. Compare your audience's response and your own feelings about the two presentations.

4. Select five television or magazine advertisements and analyze the persuasive strategies they use to evoke a response. Consider use of evidence, message organization, emotional appeals, type(s) of reasoning, and adaptation of the message to the needs of the listener.

5. Listen for the five steps of the motivated sequence (attention, need, satisfaction, visualization, and action) in the sales presentations that you hear. Also, look for the five steps in TV and magazine advertisements, sermons, and political speeches.

## *SUGGESTED READINGS*

Andrews, J.R. (1983). *The Practice of Rhetorical Criticism.* (New York: Macmillan Publishing Company).

Bostrom, R.N. (1983). *Persuasion.* (Englewood Cliffs, New Jersey: Prentice-Hall).

Dance, F.E.X. and Zak-Dance, C.C. (1986). *Public Speaking.* (New York: Harper & Row).

Larson, C.U. (1986). *Persuasion: Reception and Responsibility.* (Belmont, California: Wadsworth Publishing Company).

Kahane, H. (1986). *Logic and Contemporary Rhetoric.* (Belmont, California: Wadsworth Publishing Company).

Simons, H.W. (1976). *Persuasion: Understanding, Practice, and Analysis.* (Reading, Massachusetts: Addison-Wesley).

# Notes

## Chapter 1

1. *Careers in Communication Arts and Science*. (Falls Church, VA: Association for Communication Administration, 1985).
2. T. Watzlawick, J. Beavin Bavelas, and D. Jackson, *The Pragmatics of Human Communication*. (New York: W.W. Norton, 1967).

## Chapter 2

1. K. Horney, *Neurosis and Human Growth*. (New York: W.W. Norton & Co., 1950), 17.
2. W. James, *Principles of Psychology*. (New York: Henry Holt and Company, 1890).

## Chapter 3

1. Bernard Berelson and Gary A. Steiner, *Human Behavior,* Shorter Edition (New York: Harcourt Brace Jovanovich, 1967), 141.
2. Robert W. Leeper, "The Role of Motivation in Learning: A Study of the Phenomenon of Differential Motivational Control of the Utilization of Habits," *Journal of Genetic Psychology* 46 (1935): 3–40.
3. Alfred Korzybski, *Science and Sanity,* 2nd ed. (Lancaster, PA: Science Press, 1941).
4. Joe McGinnis, *The Selling of the President, 1968* (New York: Trident Press, 1969), 91–92.
5. F. K. Heussenstann, "Bumper Stickers and Cops," *Transaction,* 35 (1971): 32–33.

## Chapter 4

1. A. Mehrabian, *Nonverbal Communication* (Chicago: Aldine-Atherton, 1972), 108.
2. P. Ekman and W. V. Friesen, "The Repertoire of Nonverbal Behavior: Categories, Origins, Usage, and Coding," *Semiotica* 1 (1969): 49—98.
3. G. Leathers, *Successful Nonverbal Communication: Principles and Applications* (New York: Macmillan Publishing Company, 1986), 162.
4. A. Kendon, "Some Functions of Gaze-Disection in Social Interaction," *Acta Psychologica* 26 (1967): 22–63.
5. Paul Ekman, W. V. Friesen and S. S. Tomkins, "Facial Affect Scoring Technique: A First Validity Study," *Semiotica* 3 (1971): 37–58; P. Ekman and W. V. Friesen, *Unmasking the Face* (Englewood Cliffs, N J: Prentice-Hall, 1975).
6. E. T. Hall, *The Hidden Dimension* (Garden City, New York: Doubleday & Company, Inc., 1966); R. Shuter, "Proxemics and Tactility in Latin America," Journal of Communication 26 (1976): 46–52.
7. A. Hare and R. Bales, "Seating Position and Small Group Interaction," *Sociometry* 26 (1963): 480–486; L. T. Howells and S. W. Becker, "Seating Arrangement and Leadership Emergence," *Journal of Abnormal and Social Psychology* 64 (1962): 148–50.
8. A. H. Maslow and N. L. Mintz, "Effects of Esthetic Surroundings: I. Initial Effects of Three Esthetic Conditions upon Perceiving 'Energy' and 'Wellbeing' in Faces," *Journal of Psychology* 41 (1956): 247–54.
9. A. Mehrabian, *Public Places and Private Spaces* (New York: Basic Books, 1976).

10. See: J. Kelly, "Dress as Non-Verbal Communication," Paper presented to the annual conference of the American Association for Public Opinion Research, May 1969; M. Lefkowitz, R. Blake, and J. Mouton, "Status Factors in Pedestrian Violation of Traffic Signals," *Journal of Abnormal and Social Psychology* 51 (1955): 704–6; J. Mills and E. Aronson, "Opinion Change as a Function of the Communicator's Attractiveness and Desire to Influence," *Journal of Social Psychology* 1 (1965): 73–77; J. E. Singer, "The Use of Manipulative Strategies: Machiavellianism and Attractiveness," *Sociometry* 27 (1964): 128–51.
11. W. Wells and B. Siegel, "Stereotyped Somatypes," *Psychological Reports,* 8 (1961): 77–78.
12. M. Lefkowitz, R. Blake, and J. Mouton, "Status Factors in Pedestrian Violation of Traffic Signals," *Journal of Abnormal and Social Psychology,* 51 (1955): 704–6.
13. See: A. Montague, *Touching: The Human Significance of the Skin* (New York: Harper & Row, 1978).
14. Nancy M. Henley, *Body Politics: Power, Sex, and Nonverbal Communication* (Englewood Cliffs, N J: Prentice-Hall, Inc., 1977).
15. P. Ekman, "Communication Through Nonverbal Behavior: A Source of Information About an Interpersonal Relationship," in *Affect, Cognition and Personality,* ed. S. S. Tomkins and C. E. Izard (New York: Springer, 1965).
16. A. Mehrabian, *Nonverbal Communication.*
17. See: M. L. Knapp, *Nonverbal Communication in Human Interaction* (New York: Holt, Rinehart and Winston, 1978): 418.

## Chapter 5

1. Sarah Trenholm, *Human Communication Theory,* (Englewood Cliffs, NJ: Prentice-Hall, 1986), 144.
2. Joseph A. DeVito, *The Interpersonal Communication book,* 4th ed. (New York: Harper and Row, 1986), 5.

3. Thanks for this example go to our friend and colleague, Phil Backlund.
4. Robert B. Zajonc, "Attitudinal Effects of Mere Exposure," *Journal of Personality and Social Psychology* 9 (1968): 1-29.
5. Gerard Egan, *Encounter: Group Processes for Interpersonal Growth.* (Belmont, CA: Brooks/Cole Publishing Company, 1970).
19. Adapted from Jack R. Gibb, "Defensive Communication," *Journal of Communication* 11 (1961): 141-8.

## Chapter 6

1. L. Barker, R. Edwards, C. Gaines, K. Gladney, and F. Holley, "An Investigation of Proportional Time Spent in Various Communication Activities of College Students," *Journal of Applied Communication Research,* 8 (1981): 101–9.
2. Douglas Ehninger, Alan H. Monroe, and Bruce E. Gronbeck, *Principles and Types of Speech Communication* (Glenview, IL: Scott, Foresman and Company, 1978), 128.
3. Ralph G. Nichols and Leonard A. Stevens, "Six Bad Listening Habits," in *Are You Listening?* (New York: McGraw-Hill, 1957).
4. See: Ralph G. Nichols and Leonard Stevens, *Are You Listening?* (New York: McGraw-Hill, 1957).
5. Adapted from: Lyman K. Steil, Larry L. Barker, and Kittie W. Watson, *Effective Listening: Key to your Success* (Reading, MA: Addison-Wesley Publishing Company, 1983): 72–73.
6. Adapted from A. Wolvin and C. G. Coakley, *Listening Instruction* (Urbana, IL: Eric Clearinghouse on Reading and Communication Skills, 1979).

## Chapter 7

1. R.S. Goyer, W.C. Redding, and J.T. Richey, *Interviewing Principles and Techniques: A Project Text.* (Dubuque, IA: Wm. C. Brown, 1968), 6.

2. C.J. Stewart, and W.B. Cash Jr., *Interviewing Principles and Practices,* 2nd ed. (Dubuque, IA: Wm. C. Brown.)
3. Gallup, G. (1947). "The quintamensional plan of question design." *Public Opinion Quarterly,* 11 (Fall), 385–93.

## Chapter 8

1. Kenneth D. Benne And Paul Sheats, "Functional Roles of Group Members," *Journal of Social Issues* 4 (Spring 1948): 41–49.
2. Henry M. Robert, *Robert's Rules of Order, Newly Revised* (Glenview, IL: Scott, Foresman and Company, 1981).
3. B. Aubrey Fisher, "Decision Emergence: Phases in Group Decision-Making," *Speech Monographs* 37 (1970): 53–66.
4. Marvin E. Shaw, *Group Dynamics: The Psychology of Small Group Behavior,* 3rd ed. (New York: McGraw-Hill, 1981), 46.
5. Steven A. Beebe and John T. Masterson, *Communicating in Small Groups: Principles and Practices,* 2nd ed. (Glenview, IL: Scott, Foresman and Company, 1986), 138.

## Chapter 9

1. Dean C. Barnlund and Franklyn S. Haiman, *The Dynamics of Discussion* (Boston: Houghton Mifflin, 1960).

## Chapter 13

1. Thanks, and a tip of our hats to Professor Frank E.X. Dance of the University of Denver.
2. Frank E.X. Dance and Carol Zak-Dance, *Public Speaking* (New York: Harper and Row, 1986), 65.
3. A. Mehrabian and M. Wiener, "Non-Immediacy Between Communicator and Object of Communication in a Verbal Message," *Journal of Consulting Psychology* 30 (1966).

## Chapter 14

1. Survey conducted by R.H. Bruskin Associates published in *Spectra,* 19 (December 1973): 4.
2. Amy Gillespie, "Listen Up!" *Winning Orations.* (The Interstate Oratorical Association, 1985): 48-51.
3. Adapted from: Melanie Booth-Butterfield, "Many-Heads-Make-Light-the-Work Speech" (Group Speech Development), *The Idea Book: For Teaching the Basic Speech Communication Course.* (Glenview, Illinois: Scott, Foresman and Company, 1986), 20.

## Chapter 15

1. Leon Festinger, *A Theory of Cognitive Dissonance* (Evanston, UL: Row, Peterson, 1957).
2. For additional discussion, see Wayne C. Minnick, *The Art of Persuasion* (Boston: Houghton Mifflin Company, 1967), 114.
3. Douglas Ehninger, Alan H. Monroe, and Bruce Gronbeck, *Principles and Types of Speech Communication,* 10th ed. (Glenview, IL: Scott, Foresman and Company, 1987), 131–35.
4. Milton Rokeach, *Beliefs, Attitudes and Values* (San Francisco: Jossey-Bass, 1969), 124.
5. For a discussion of fear appeal research, see Irving L. Janis and Seymour Feshbach, "Effects of Fear Arousing Communications," *Journal of Abnormal and Social Psychology,* 48 (January 1953): 78–92; Frederick A. Powell and Gerald R. Miller, "Social Approval and Siapproval Cues in Anxiety-Arousing Situations," *Speech Monographs,* 34 (June 1967): 152–59; and Kenneth L. Higbee, "Fifteen Years of Fear Arousal: Research on Threat Appeals: 1953–68," *Psychological Bulletin,* 72 (December 1969): 426–44.

6. For an extensive discussion of the motivated sequence, see Douglas Ehninger, Alan H. Monroe, and Bruce E. Gronbeck, *Principles and Types of Speech Communication,* 10th ed., (Glenview, IL: Scott, Foresman & Company, 1987).

7. Linda Loehr, "Ignorance Kills," *Winning Orations.* (The Interstate Oratorical Association, 1985): 3–7.

# Glossary

**action step (Chapter 15):** the fifth step in the motivated sequence—calling for action to implement the speaker's solution to the problem.

**adaptor (Chapter 4):** a nonverbal behavior that helps to satisfy a personal need and to adapt to immediate surroundings.

**affect display (Chapter 4):** a nonverbal cue that communicates emotions.

**allness statement (Chapter 3):** a simple but untrue generalization.

**analogy (Chapter 11):** a comparison or contrasting of one object, concept, or principle with another.

**attending (Chapter 6):** the sequel to selecting; focusing on one sound.

**attention step (Chapter 15):** the first step of the motivated sequence—capturing the audience's interest right from the beginning.

**attitude (Chapter 3):** a learned tendency to respond positively or negatively to a given stimulus.

**attitudinal analysis (Chapter 10):** the identification of audience members' attitudes, beliefs, and values about specific issues and ideas.

**authoritarian leader (Chapter 9):** a leader who makes all decisions, takes all responsibility for group actions, and imparts knowledge to followers.

**average (Chapter 11):** a single value that represents the middle point among a number of unequal values.

**Baker Model (Chapter 5):** a model of interpersonal communication that is based on silence as the aim of communication.

**belief (Chapter 3):** the conviction that something is true.

**brainstorming (Chapter 9):** a method of generating a wide range of problem solutions by encouraging the production of as many creative ideas as possible by withholding evaluation and criticism during the thinking process.

**bypassing (Chapter 3):** a barrier to communication that arises when the same word is interpreted in different ways.

**causal reasoning (Chapter 15):** a thought process that attempts to establish a cause-effect relationship between two or more events.

**cause-effect pattern (Chapter 12):** a pattern of speech organization that describes a past, present, or future situation and discusses one or more causes of that state of affairs.

**channel (Chapter 1):** a pathway through which message-signals pass between source and receiver.

**chronological pattern (Chapter 12):** a pattern of speech organization that arranges ideas according to a time sequence.

**closed question (Chapter 7):** question that limits the range of possible responses and requires a simple, direct, and brief answer.

**closure principle (Chapter 3):** the tendency to perceive complete wholes, even when some of the parts are missing.

**cognitive dissonance (Chapter 15):** the sense of disorganization that prompts a person to change when new information conflicts with previously organized thought patterns.

**cognitive function (Chapter 4):** the function of eye contact that provides information about thought processes.

**cohesiveness (Chapter 8):** the "stick-togetherness," degree of solidarity, or identification of the individuals with the group as a whole; the forces acting on group members to remain in the group.

**communication competence (Chapter 5):** knowledge of social rules and understanding of communication as it relates to those rules.

**competence (Chapter 5):** your knowledge of the rules in a communication setting.

**complementarity (Chapter 5):** the degree to which two persons are compatibly different from each other.

**compromising (Chapter 9):** a style of dealing with conflict in which people agree to trade something they want for something equally important from the other party.

**conclusion (Chapter 12):** the final chance a speaker has in a speech to summarize and reinforce the ideas covered in the body of the speech and to leave the audience with a memorable impression; (Chapter 15) in a syllogism, the necessary consequence of the major and minor premises.

**conflict (Chapter 9):** disagreement between two or more parties about the acceptance of some idea, action, or goal.

**connotative meaning (Chapter 3):** the individual, unique level of meaning.

**consensus (Chapter 9):** a decision that all group members agree is the best alternative that they can all accept.

**content aspect (Chapter 1):** the portion of communication that is the verbal message.

**context (Chapter 1):** the entire communication environment; (Chapter 5) the situation in which communication occurs.

**credibility (Chapter 10):** the extent to which a listener perceives a speaker to be competent, trustworthy, and dynamic.

**decentering (Chapter 6):** stepping away from your own thoughts and attempting to experience the thoughts of another person.

**decision making (Chapter 9):** choosing from two or more possible alternatives.

**decoding (Chapter 1):** the interpretive process of assigning meaning to messages.

**deductive reasoning (Chapter 15):** a thought process that draws a specific conclusion from a general statement.

**defensive communication (Chapter 5):** messages and behavior that are likely to arouse defensiveness in another person.

**definition (Chapter 11; Chapter 14):** a statement of a term's meaning or concept.

**democratic leader (Chapter 9):** a leader who may provide some structure and direction to group deliberation, but leaves most of the responsibility for decisions and evaluation to the group as a whole.

**demographic analysis (Chapter 10):** the collection and interpretation of basic information about audience members' ages, sex, race, religion, education, social and political affiliations, and the like.

**demonstrating (Chapter 14):** showing an audience how to do something or how something works.

**denotative meaning (Chapter 3):** the level of meaning at which all members of a language group agree.

**derived credibility (Chapter 10):** the attitude that a listener develops toward a speaker while the speaker is presenting the speech.

**describing (Chapter 14):** informing others about the who, what, when, where, and why of a term, idea, thing, or person.

**developmental/relational perspective (Chapter 5):** a view of interpersonal communication as the result of a developmental, evolutionary process within a relationship.

**DeVito Model (Chapter 5):** a descriptive model that identifies the principal components and processes of interpersonal communication.

**displacement (Chapter 2):** the mental ability to step outside of the present moment.

**dissonance theory (Chapter 15):** a theory which contends that because humans strive for consistency in their thoughts and actions, new or contrary information can result in a reevaluation of existing attitudes, beliefs, values, and behavior.

**division (Chapter 12):** a principle of outlining which requires that each entry in an outline contain one and only one idea.

**dyadic (Chapter 5):** occurring between two persons (a dyad).

**dyadic effect (Chapter 5):** mutual relationship-building process in which disclosure by one person leads to disclosure by another.

**effect (Chapter 5):** the consequence of communication.

**emblem (Chapter 4):** a nonverbal cue that acts as a substitute for oral communication.

**emotional appeal (Chapter 15):** a statement, example, opinion, or visual or auditory stimulus that triggers strong feelings.

**empathic listening (Chapter 6):** a combination of listening skills and feedback skills that enhances the ability to identify and respond to the feelings of another person.

**empathy (Chapter 5):** the ability to understand what another is thinking or feeling.

**encoding (Chapter 1):** the process through which messages are cast into a system of signals.

**environmental analysis (Chapter 10):** a study of the speech occasion and the physical surroundings of the event.

**ethos (Chapter 15):** a speaker's ethics or character, referred to as credibility.

**evidence (Chapter 15):** the definitions, examples, statistics, and other supporting materials that pertain to a specific situation.

**example (Chapter 11):** a specific instance that clarifies or dramatizes a point.

**expectation (Chapter 3):** in perception, the tendency to see what is anticipated.

**expert testimony (Chapter 11):** a statement made by a specialist in the topic of interest.

**expressive function (Chapter 4):** the function of eye contact that indictes feelings and emotions.

**extemporaneous speaking (Chapter 13):** the delivery of a speech that is prepared in advance, but presented without relying on a manuscript or memorization.

**fact-inference confusion (Chapter 3):** a barrier to communication that occurs by responding to something as if it were observed when, in reality, it was merely a conclusion.

**feedback (Chapter 1; Chapter 6):** a receiver's response to a message that enables a sender to gauge whether he or she has been understood.

**field of experience (Chapter 5):** the sum total of all the facts and events you've ever observed.

**figurative analogy (Chapter 11):** a comparison or contrasting of things from different classes.

**forcing (Chapter 9):** a style of dealing with conflict in which people use malipulative communication techniques, intimidation, and competitive strategies to gain an advantage.

**foreground/background screening (Chapter 3):** a selection process based on the relationships among objects and sounds in the environment.

**formal audience analysis (Chapter 10):** the gathering of precise and uniform information about listeners by designing and administering a questionnaire.

**functional approach (Chapter 9):** an approach to studying leadership that focuses on behaviors that guide, direct, and influence other group members, regardless of who exhibits the behaviors.

**functional roles (Chapter 8):** informal roles that fulfill key group functions which influence the effectiveness of group processes.

**funnel sequence (Chapter 7):** a questioning sequence that begins with broad, open questions and proceeds toward more closed questions.

**general purpose (Chapter 10):** the overall objective of a speech; the three possible general purposes are to inform, to persuade, and to entertain.

**general semantics (Chapter 3):** the study of how language affects attitudes and behavior.

**group building and maintenance roles (Chapter 8):** behaviors that establish and maintain good interpersonal relationships among group members.

**group-centered leader (Chapter 9):** a leader who refuses to give direction to the group, but tries instead to understand what group members are thinking and feeling, and then attempts to reflect these feelings and thoughts back to the group.

**group climate (Chapter 8):** the feelings that group members develop toward the group and the other members of the group.

**group communication (Chapter 1):** interaction that occurs when from three to fifteen or twenty persons meet, and, by exchanging views, attempt to accomplish some mutually agreed-upon task or goal.

**group structure (Chapter 8):** the patterned regularities in feelings, perceptions, and actions that develop during interaction among group members.

**group task (Chapter 8):** the reason the group was formed, or the job the group must perform.

**group task roles (Chapter 8):** behaviors that assist the group in achieving its purposes and goals.

**groupthink (Chapter 8):** group attempts to minimize conflict and reach agreement at the expense of critical discussion.

**hearing (Chapter 6):** the physiological process of receiving sound waves through the ear and the auditory nerve.

**hidden agenda (Chapter 8):** personal goals or needs that an individual conceals in hopes of satisfying them through the group's interactions.

**hypothetical example (Chapter 11):** a purely fictional incident that is devised to clarify or dramatize a point.

**hypothetical question (Chapter 7):** a question used to gauge an interviewee's reaction to an emotion-arousing or value-laden situation, or to discover an interviewee's reactions to a real or imaginary situation.

**illustration (Chapter 11):** a story, fable, or anecdote that has a theme, moral, or purpose that supports a point a speaker wishes to make.

**illustrator (Chapter 4):** a nonverbal behavior used to add meaning to an accompanying verbal message.

**immediacy cues (Chapter 4):** nonverbal cues that communicate liking or affection.

**immediacy principle (Chapter 4):** the tendency to move closer to persons and things you like and to avoid or move away from persons and things you dislike.

**impromptu speaking (Chapter 13):** the delivery of a speech off the cuff, with no notes or preparation.

**individual roles (Chapter 8):** behaviors that satisfy individual needs at the expense of group effectiveness.

**individual traits (Chapter 8):** personality characteristics, group roles, group status, individual attitudes toward group participation, and other personal characteristics which influence group processes and which make each group unique.

**inductive reasoning (Chapter 15):** a thought process that draws a general conclusion from specific information.

**informal audience analysis (Chapter 10):** the gathering of information about listeners by simply observing them or casually chatting with them.

**information-gathering interview (Chapter 7):** an interview conducted to gain specific kinds of information to aid in making a decision or implementing an action.

**information overload (Chapter 6):** a listening barricade that occurs when the accumulated quantity of words becomes so great that you suffer from listening fatigue.

**information-sharing interview (Chapter 7):** an interview in which both the interviewer and the interviewee provide and gather information, often sharing information nearly equally.

**informative speech (Chapter 14):** an oral presentation that is designed to teach, define, illustrate, clarify, or elaborate on a topic.

**initial credibility (Chapter 10):** the attitude that a listener has toward a speaker before he or she begins to speak.

**interaction patterns (Chapter 8):** the recurring and predictable ways in which group members communicate or interact with one another as they conduct group activities.

**interpersonal attraction (Chapter 5):** the amount of liking you feel toward another person.

**interpersonal communication (Chapter 1; Chapter 5):** face-to-face interaction between two persons, with the potential for immediate feedback.

**interpretation (Chapter 3):** the assigning of meaning to perceptions.

**interview (Chapter 7):** a form of oral communication involving two parties, at least one of whom has a preconceived and serious purpose and both of whom speak and listen from time to time.

**intimate space (Chapter 4):** zone of space within 0 to 1½ feet of an individual, where the most intimate personal communication occurs.

**intrapersonal communication (Chapter 1):** speech communication within an individual.

**inverted funnel sequence (Chapter 7):** a questioning sequence that begins with closed questions and proceeds with more open questions, intended to encourage an interviewee to respond easily early in the interview.

**laissez-faire leader (Chapter 9):** a leader who makes contributions only when asked and denies any responsibility for group action; a leader in name only.

**leadership (Chapter 8):** communication behavior that influences the group to accomplish its goals.

**liking (Chapter 4):** dimension of nonverbal meaning that communicates interest and attraction; conveyed through eye contact, touch, forward lean, and reduced space between people.

**linguistic competence (Chapter 5):** knowledge of the rules, vocabulary, and structures of language.

**listening (Chapter 6):** the process of making sense out of what you hear; includes the four stages of selecting, attending, understanding, and remembering.

**listening barricade (Chapter 6):** an obstacle that keeps you from listening well.

**literal analogy (Chapter 11):** a comparison or contrasting of things from the same class.

**logos (Chapter 15):** the use of logic and reasoning to persuade an audience.

**Major premise (Chapter 15):** the general statement that is the first element of a syllogism.

**manuscript speaking (Chapter 13):** the delivery of a speech using a full, written transcript.

**mass communication (Chapter 1):** communication that is mediated, through television, radio, newspapers, billboards, or motion pictures.

**material self (Chapter 2):** a composite of all the physical elements that reflect who you are.

**message (Chapter 1):** the product of encoding; any signal or stimulus to which a receiver assigns meaning.

**metacommunications (Chapter 1):** communication about communication.

**minor premise (Chapter 15):** the specific statement that is the second element of a syllogism.

**monitoring function (Chapter 4):** the function of eye contact that provides feedback about another person's response.

**motivated sequence (Chapter 15):** a strategy for organizing a persuasive speech that proceeds through five steps: attention, need, satisfaction, visualization, and action.

**narration (Chapter 14):** a story that communicates an idea or has a point.

**need step (Chapter 15):** the second step of the motivated sequence—describing the problem and establishing the audience's need for concern.

**noise (Chapter 1):** anything that interferes with the clear reception of a message.

**nonverbal communication (Chapter 4):** communication behavior other than written or spoken language that creates meaning to someone.

**norms (Chapter 8):** the standards group members have about how they should behave in a group.

**open question (Chapter 7):** interviewing question that is broad in nature, basically unstructured, and allows the respondent considerable freedom to determine the amount and kind of information provided.

**operational definition (Chapter 14):** a way of defining something by explaining how it works or how it is made or measured.

**organization (Chapter 3):** the mental arrangement of objects into a recognizable pattern.

**outline (Chapter 12):** a written, formally structured set of interrelated ideas and information used to describe the contents of a written or oral presentation.

**parallelism (Chapter 12):** a principle of outlining which requires that all items at the same level of an outline be at approximately the same level of specificity.

**paraphrasing (Chapter 6):** restating in your own words what you think another person has said.

**pathos (Chapter 15):** the use of emotional appeals to persuade an audience.

**peer testimony (Chapter 11):** a statement made by an ordinary person who has firsthand knowledge of a subject.

**percentage (Chapter 11):** a statistic that indicates proportion.

**perception (Chapter 3):** the process by which people select, organize, and interpret sensory stimulation into a meaningful picture of the world.

**performance (Chapter 5):** your actual behavior as you speak, listen, and adjust to a variety of situations and contexts.

**personal example (Chapter 11):** a firsthand experience that clarifies or dramatizes a point.

**personal space (Chapter 4):** zone of space between 1½ and 4 feet from an individual, where most social conversations take place.

**persuading interview (Chapter 7):** an interview with the objective of gaining the interviewee's acceptance of an idea, product, or service, and of obtaining some subsequent action based on that acceptance.

**persuasion (Chapter 15):** the process of changing or reinforcing an attitude, belief, value, or behavior through the use of verbal or nonverbal messages.

**physiological selection (Chapter 3):** the filtering of stimuli that stems from the natural limitations of the sensory organs.

**pitch (Chapter 13):** the highness or lowness of the voice.

**polarization (Chapter 3):** barrier to communication that occurs when something is

described in terms of extremes, such as good or bad, beautiful or ugly, positive or negative.

**power (Chapter 4):** dimension of nonverbal meaning that communicates status and influence; conveyed through protected space, increased distance, relaxed posture, and status clothing.

**pressure to conform (Chapter 8):** communication intended to increase the degree to which a group member's behavior corresponds to the norms of the group.

**probing question (Chapter 7):** a question that encourages the interviewee to clarify or elaborate on partial or superficial responses, and that usually directs the discussion in a desired direction.

**problem-solution pattern (Chapter 12):** a pattern of speech organization that includes the statement of a problem and the presentation of at least one possible solution.

**problem solving (Chapter 9):** a procedure involving a series of steps and a number of decisions, through which individuals or groups attempt to change a set of conditions with which they are dissatisfied to a set of conditions with which they are satisfied.

**problem solving approach to dealing with conflict (Chapter 9):** a style of dealing with conflict in which people develop a sincere concern and responsibility for maximizing the gains and minimizing the losses of all parties. They attempt to arrive at a resolution of the conflict that satisfies all parties to the greatest extent possible, without "playing games" or inflating their demands at the outset.

**problem-solving interview (Chapter 7):** an interview conducted to discuss and resolve a concern that is important to both parties.

**proof (Chapter 15):** evidence plus reasoning used to support a persuasive argument.

**proximity (Chapter 8):** the arrangement in which the members place themselves or in which they are placed in group meetings.

**proximity, contact, and interaction (Chapter 15):** the actual, physical availability of other people.

**psychic tension (Chapter 5):** the discomfort you feel when there is misunderstanding or conflict.

**psychological selection (Chapter 3):** a perceptual screening process based on beliefs and selective attention.

**public communication (Chapter 1):** communication that is generated by one individual and directed toward an audience.

**public space (Chapter 4):** all territory more than 12 feet beyond an individual, in which the most formal and intentional communication occurs.

**quintamensional design sequence (Chapter 7):** a five-step questioning sequence intended to assess both what an interviewee's attitudes are and how strongly he or she feels about the relevant issues. The five steps are (1) awareness, (2) uninfluenced attitudes, (3) specific attitudes, (4) reason why, and (5) intensity of attitude.

**rate (Chapter 13):** the speed at which one speaks.

**reasoning (Chapter 15):** the process of drawing a conclusion from evidence.

**receiver (Chapter 1):** any individual or group toward whom communications are intentionally or unintentionally directed.

**reciprocal identification (Chapter 5):** the degree of similarity and understanding between two (or more) persons.

**regulator (Chapter 4):** a nonverbal cue that helps control the flow of communication between people.

**regulatory function (Chapter 4):** the function of eye contact that controls the back-and-forth flow of conversation and signals whether communication channels are open or closed.

**relationship aspect (Chapter 1):** verbal or nonverbal information about the way the content aspect of communication should be received.

**remembering (Chapter 6):** the process of recalling past events.

**responsiveness (Chapter 4):** dimension of nonverbal meaning that communicates active interaction; conveyed through eye contact, varied vocal quality, animated facial expression, and forward lean.

**role (Chapter 2; Chapter 8):** a set of expectations about how to behave when you occupy a certain position.

**satisfaction step (Chapter 15):** the third step of the motivated sequence—presenting the solution of the problem that has been identified.

**selecting (Chapter 6):** the process of sorting through competing sounds in the environment in preparation for focusing on one sound.

**selective attention (Chapter 3):** the tendency to filter out unwanted or unneeded information.

**selective exposure (Chapter 3):** the tendency to be open to some experiences and not to others.

**self-concept (Chapter 2):** your relatively consistent set of beliefs about yourself.

**self-disclosure (Chapter 5):** sharing information about yourself that would not otherwise be known.

**self-esteem (Chapter 2):** how you feel about your view of yourself.

**self-fulfilling prophecy (Chapter 2):** a prediction that comes true because you expect it to come true.

**self-image (Chapter 2):** your view of yourself in a particular situation.

**self-reflexiveness (Chapter 2):** your uniquely human ability to think about what you're doing as you do it and to think about what you're saying as you say it.

**sensory stimulation (Chapter 3):** the nervous system's response to the environment.

**setting (Chapter 8):** the physical surroundings in which a group is meeting at a particular time.

**similarity (Chapter 5):** the degree to which two persons are alike.

**situation (Chapter 8):** the physical arrangements in which a group finds itself, including setting and proximity.

**situational approach (Chapter 9):** an approach to studying leadership that proposes that the only way to understand effective leadership is to examine such contextual factors as the group's structure, history, norms, composition, and resources.

**situational perspective (Chapter 5):** a view of interpersonal communications as a particular context or level in which human competition occurs.

**sleeper effect (Chapter 10):** a change in a listener's attitude caused by the passage of time.

**small group (Chapter 8):** three or more persons who are communicating face to face in such a manner that each person influences and is influenced by each other member.

**smoothing (Chapter 9):** a style of dealing with conflict in which people give in to others' demands or opinions, preferring to concede rather than face a disagreement.

**social self (Chapter 2):** the self in interaction with others.

**social space (Chapter 4):** zone of space spanning 4 to 12 feet from an individual, where most business communication takes place.

**source (Chapter 1):** the point at which information originates.

**spatial pattern (Chapter 12):** a pattern of speech organization that uses geographical or physical layout as its organizing principle.

**specific purpose (Chapter 10):** a finely tuned statement of what a speaker wants an audience to do, feel, or know after listening to his or her speech.

**speech anxiety (Chapter 14):** the feeling of nervousness that many speakers experience when preparing for and delivering a public speech.

**speech communication (Chapter 1):** a human process through which we make sense out of the world and share that sense with others.

**spiritual self (Chapter 2):** your process of introspection as well as your moral and spiritual aspirations.

**static evaluation (Chapter 3):** a statement failing to recognize that everything is in process.

**statistics (Chapter 11):** numerical data that summarize facts or examples.

**status (Chapter 8):** the estimated worth attributed to a member by a group.

**stereotype (Chapter 3):** a generalized grouping of people that overemphasizes presumed similarities and ignores individual differences.

**subordination (Chapter 12):** a principle of outlining which requires that each subpoint at any level of the outline be related to and add more specific information about the more general point above it.

**supporting material (Chapter 10; Chapter 11):** the definitions, examples, statistics, testimony, illustrations, and analogies that verify, amplify, and clarify the main ideas of a speech.

**supportive communication (Chapter 5):** messages and behavior that encourage openness to others.

**syllogism (Chapter 15):** a deductive argument that has three key elements: a major premise, a minor premise, and a conclusion.

**symbol (Chapter 2):** an arbitrary representation of a thing or idea that bears no resemblance to that which it represents.

**terminal credibility (Chapter 10):** the attitude that a listener holds toward a speaker after the speech is concluded.

**testimony (Chapter 11):** a statement made by a third party to support an idea or position that a speaker is trying to develop.

**thesis statement (Chapter 10):** a one-sentence summary that identifies the essence of a speaker's message.

**topical pattern (Chapter 12):** a pattern of speech organization that organizes ideas based on order of importance, an acronym, a formula, or some other logical, understandable, and meaningful device.

**trait approach (Chapter 9):** an approach to studying leadership that focuses on the vast array of personal characteristics that have been associated with great leaders.

**transition (Chapter 12):** words, phrases, or sentences that join ideas together, show relationships between two or more ideas, and direct listeners' thought processes in the direction a speaker wants them to go.

**tunnel sequence (Chapter 7):** a questioning sequence that consists of a series of parallel open or closed questions, using no probing questions, resulting in less depth of information on a number of related issues.

**understanding (Chapter 6):** the process of assigning meaning to the stimuli to which you attend.

**value (Chapter 3):** a judgment about the relative importance of something.

**visual aid (Chapter 13):** any kind of instructional material, such as a picture, chart, or diagram, that relies on sight to clarify a point.

**visualization step (Chapter 15):** the fourth step of the motivated sequence—picturing the positive results that will occur if the recommended solution is adopted or the negative results that will occur if the solution is not implemented.

**volume (Chapter 13):** the loudness or softness of the voice.

**withdrawing (Chapter 9):** a style of dealing with conflict in which people dislike conflict and/or dealing with conflict, so they avoid it at all costs.

**word picture (Chapter 14):** a verbal description that helps an audience visualize a specific image.

# Acknowledgments

Page 98, "The DeVito Model" from *The Interpersonal Communication Book*, 4th edition by Joseph A. DeVito. Copyright © 1986 by Joseph A. DeVito. Reprinted by permission of Harper & Row.

Page 101, From "The Theory of Silence" by Sidney J. Baker, *Journal of General Psychology,* 53, pp, 145-167, 1955. Reprinted with permission of the Helen Dwight Reid Educational Foundation. Published by Heldref Publications, 4000 Albemarle St., N.W., Washington, D.C. 20016. Copyright © 1955.

Pages 134-135, "A Comparison of Good and Bad Listening Habits" from *Effective Listening: Key to Your Success* by Lyman K. Steil, Larry L. Barker and Kittie W. Watson. Copyright © 1983 by Random House, Inc. Reprinted by permission.

Pages 334-37 and 362-65, From 1985 *Winning Orations of the Interstate Oratorical Association.* Reprinted by permission.

## Photo Credits

All photos not credited are the property of Scott, Foresman and Company.

| | | |
|---|---|---|
| Page | 1 | Mark Antman/The Image Works |
| Page | 7 | Jean-Claude Lejeune |
| Page | 15 | Comstock |
| Page | 25 | Tom McCarthy/Hillstrom Stock Photo |
| Pages | 32, 50 | Jean-Claude Lejeune |
| Page | 57 | The Museum of Modern Art/Film Stills Archive |
| Page | 65 | Inkblot courtesy Anthony B. Ciminero |
| Page | 71 | Michael Sullivan/TexaStock |
| Page | 93 | Jean-Claude Lejeune |
| Page | 97 | Hennepin County Public Affairs |
| Pages | 127, 139 | Jean-Claude Lejeune |
| Page | 149 | Gale Zucker/Stock, Boston |
| Page | 153 | Rhoda Sidney/Leo de Wys, Inc. |
| Page | 173 | Frank Siteman/The Picture Cube |
| Page | 181 | Howard Dratch/Leo de Wys, Inc. |
| Page | 204 | Dan Chidester/The Image Works |
| Page | 208 | Gans/The Image Works |
| Page | 223 | Jerry Berndt/Stock, Boston |
| Pages | 227, 234 | Alan Carey/The Image Works |
| Page | 257 | Hugh Rogers/Monkmeyer Press Photo Service |
| Page | 261 | Howard Dratch/Leo de Wys, Inc. |

Page 281   Betsy Cole/The Picture Cube
Page 286   Paul Conklin/Monkmeyer Press Photo Service
Page 287   Library of Congress
Page 305   Rocky Welden/Monkmeyer Press Photo Service
Page 309   Leo de Wys, Inc.
Page 331   Bill Grimes/Leo de Wys, Inc.
Page 347   Alan Carey/The Image Works
Page 355   Howard Dratch/The Image Works

# Index

Accenting, as nonverbal communication function, 82–83
Action appeals, and speech conclusions, 287–288
Action step, and persuasive speech 360–361
Adaptor, 70, 73
Affect display, 70, 73
Allness statement, 56, 58, 61
Analogies, in speeches, 255–256
   sources of, 258
Analysis, audience, 230–236
   attitudinal, 231–232
   demographic, 231
   environmental, 232–233
   methods of, 233–236
Anxiety, 331
Appearance. *See* Personal appearance
Aristotle, and persuasion, 352–354
Attending, and listening, 125, 126
Attention step, and persuasive speech, 359, 361
Attitude, 52, 53
   impact of words on, 55
Attitudinal analysis, 231–232, 233
Attraction, interpersonal, 103–104, 105
Audience, 226
   adapting persuasive speech to, 346–352
   analysis of, 230–236, 325, 346
   apathetic, 348–349, 350
   friendly, 347–348, 350

neutral, 349–350
and speech organization, 269, 270
Audio aids, use of in speeches, 308
Audio resources, 258, 259
Audiovisual aids, 309
Authoritarian leader, 209, 210, 211
Average, 252
Avoiding, 112

Baker Model, 100–102
Barriers. *See* Words
Behavior
   impact of words on, 55
   of group leaders, 209
Belief, 51–52, 53
Biases, of interviewers, 162
*Body Language,* 69
Body posture, and public speaking, 303
Bonding, 110
Brainstorming, 204
   and speech preparation, 230
Broadcast media, 262
Bryan, William Jennings, 287
Bush, George, 286
Bypassing, 55–56, 58, 61

Campaign interview, 151
Causal reasoning, 355–356
Cause–effect pattern, of speech organization, 277–278

Chalkboards, use of, in speeches, 307
Channel, 9
Chronological pattern, of speech organization, 274
Circumscribing, 111
Classes, as resource for speeches, 262
Closed questions, 154–155
Closure principle, 48, 49
Clothing, 80
Cognitive dissonance, 343
Cognitive function, of eye contact, 72, 75
Cohesiveness, 178
College or university libraries, 260
Color, as environmental factor, 79
Communication
   complexity of, 7–8
   components of, 11
   content and relationship aspects of, 6–7
   defensive and supportive, 112–116
   effective, 4
   as group characteristic, 184–185
   nonverbal, 66–91
   oral vs. written, 228
   and self-concept, 8, 34–35
   small group, 171–196
   *See also* Speech communication
Communication competence, 99
Communication process, components of, 8–11
Competence, 98
   and credibility, 241

**387**